GRAPHIC NOVEL

CERES™
Celestial Legend

VOL. 5: MIKAGE

CERES™
Celestial Legend
VOL. 5: Mikage
Shôjo Edition

This volume contains the CERES: CELESTIAL LEGEND installments from
Part 5, issue 1 in addition to material previously unreleased in English.

STORY & ART BY Yuu WATASE

Editor's Note: At the author's request, the spelling of Ms. Watase's first name has
been changed from "Yû," as it has appeared on previous VIZ publications, to "Yuu."

English Adaptation/Gary Leach
Translaton/Lillian Olsen
Touch-Up Art & Lettering/Bill Schuch
Cover Design/Hidemi Sahara
Graphic Design/Carolina Ugalde
Editor/Andy Nakatani

Managing Editor/Annette Roman
Director of Production/Noboru Watanabe
Vice Precident of Publishing/Alvin Lu
Sr. Director of Acquisitions/Rika Inouye
Vice President of Sales & Marketing/Liza Coppola
Publisher/Hyoe Narita

Printed in Canada

Published by VIZ Media, LLC
P.O. Box 77010 • San Francisco, CA 94107

Shôjo Edition
10 9 8 7 6 5 4 3 2
First printing, October 2003
Second printing, May 2005

store.viz.com

www.animerica-mag.com

VIZ GRAPHIC NOVEL

Ceres™
Celestial Legend
VOL. 5: MIKAGE

Story and Art by
Yuu Watase

Note: You may have noticed some unfamiliar people and things mentioned in Ceres. VIZ left these Japanese pop-culture references as they originally appeared in Japanese manga series. Here's an explanation for those who may not be as J-Pop savvy as others.

page 13 panel 3:	Puffy – Power-pop girl duo.
page 13 panel 5:	GeSang – Fictitious (to the world of CERES) boy band duo.
Page 14 panel 5:	Glay – "Visual" pop band featuring a pretty-boy front man.
page 14 panel 5:	Denki Groove (or "Den Guru") – Practitioners of the techno-pop arts.
page 14 panel 6:	SPEED – Four young girls singing and dancing to teenie-bopper pop. One of their biggest hits was the song, GO GO HEAVEN. (page 15 panel 2)
page 15 panel 2:	MAX – Four girl pop idol unit, singing, dancing, and mostly looking pop idol cute.

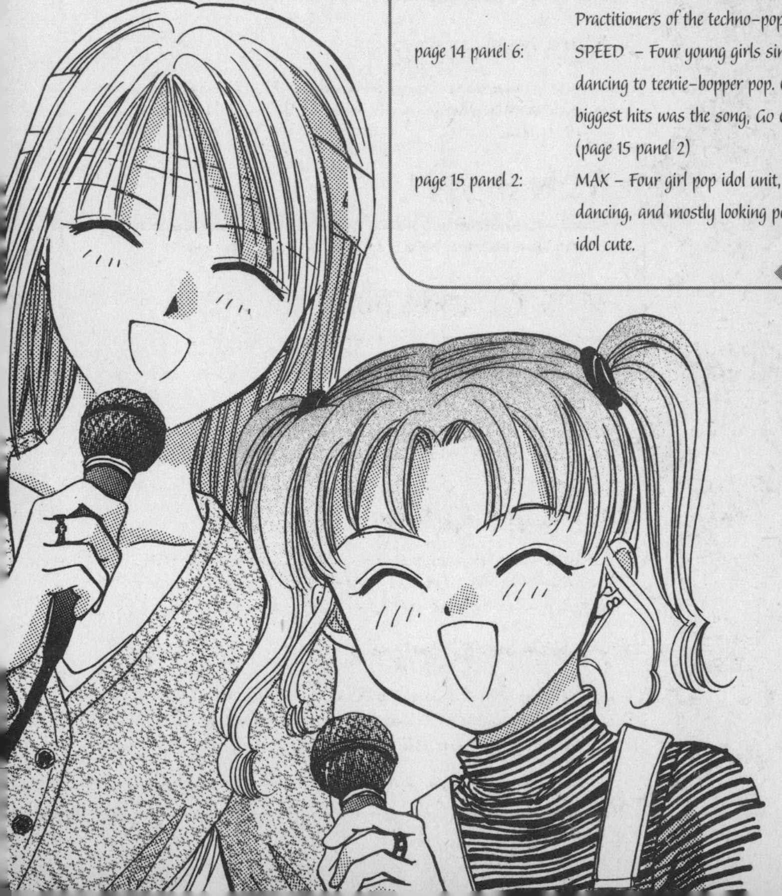

Ceres

Long long ago a tennyo (celestial maiden) named Ceres descended to earth. A mortal man stole her hagoromo (feathered robe) without which she could not return to the heavens. The man forced Ceres to bear his children, beginning the Mikage family line. Awakened after aeons of waiting, Ceres wants her hagoromo back and vows to use all her celestial powers to get revenge against the descendents of the man who wronged her ages ago.

Aya Mikage

Ceres is taking over 16-year-old Aya Mikage's mind and body. To prevent Ceres from destroying the Mikage clan, Aya's own family is trying to kill her. Despite all the turmoil, Aya finds herself falling in love with Tôya—a man hired by Kagami to keep an eye on her.

Aki Mikage

Aya's twin brother. While the consciousness of Ceres is taking over Aya, Aki is showing signs of bearing the consciousness of the founder of the Mikage family line. He has been put under confinement by the Mikage family to keep him separated from Aya.

Suzumi Aogiri

An instructor of traditional Japanese dance and a descendent of a tennyo. Suzumi has welcomed Aya into her household and provides Aya with all the protection, assistance, and support that she can.

Yûhi Aogiri

Suzumi's sixteen-year-old brother-in-law. Yûhi is an aspiring chef and a proficient martial artist. Suzumi has ordered Yûhi to be Aya's watchful protector and guardian.

Mrs. Q. (oda kyu)

Bizarre but faithful servant of Suzumi's household.

Tôya

A mysterious man who has come to Aya's aid on numerous occasions. Tôya has lost his memory and he works for Mikage International in exchange for their help in getting his memory back.

Kagami Mikage

Although the Mikage family wants to kill off Ceres through Aya, Kagami, the head of Mikage International's research and development department, has enacted C-Project, a plan to gather descendants of tennyo and use their power to further his own agenda.

Chidori Kuruma

In the last volume, young Chidori Kuruma awakened to her celestial powers when her brother Shôta was put in mortal danger. Tôya had a chance to capture Chidori but instead decided to defy Kagami's orders and let her go. Chidori has subsequently decided to help Aya in the search for the hagoromo.

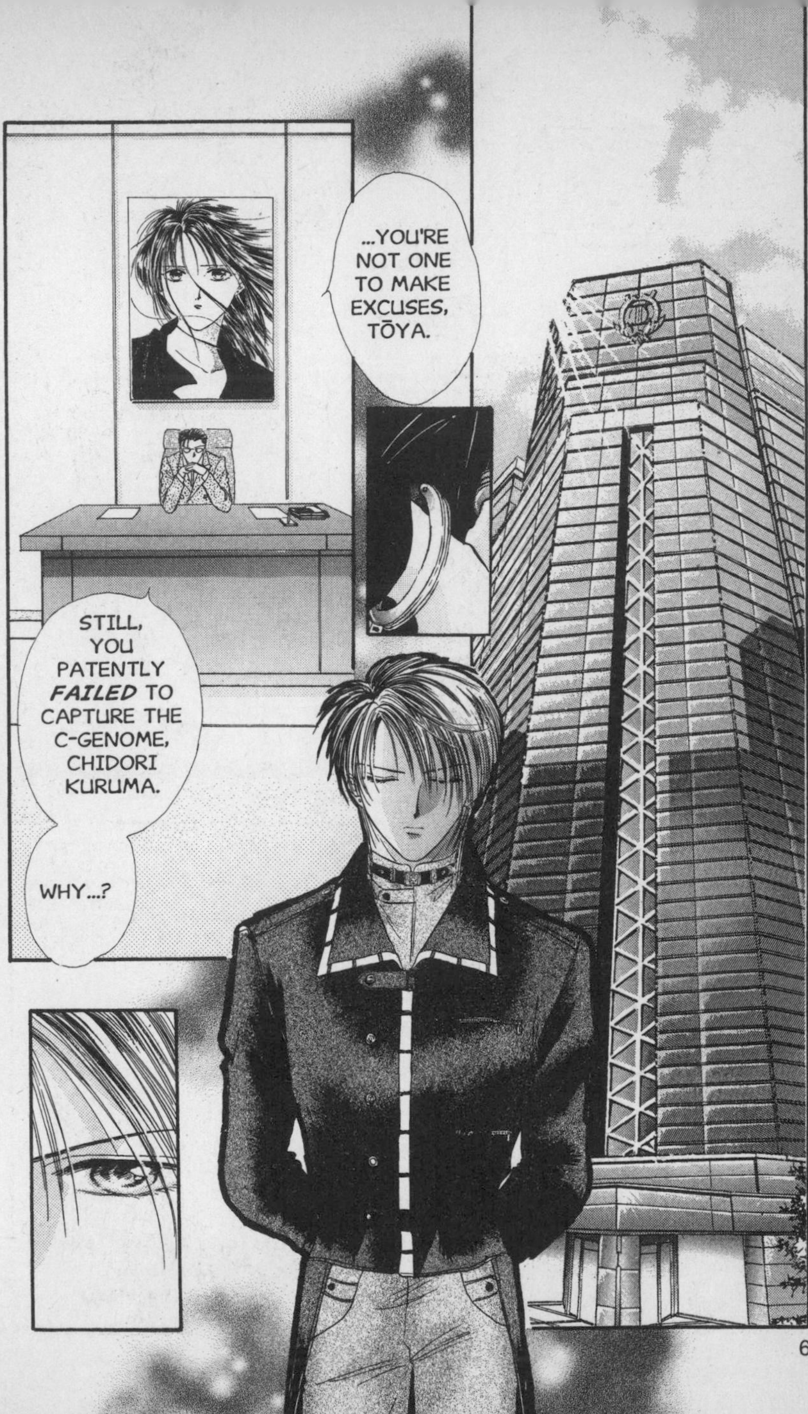
...YOU'RE NOT ONE TO MAKE EXCUSES, TŌYA.
STILL, YOU PATENTLY *FAILED* TO CAPTURE THE C-GENOME, CHIDORI KURUMA.
WHY...?

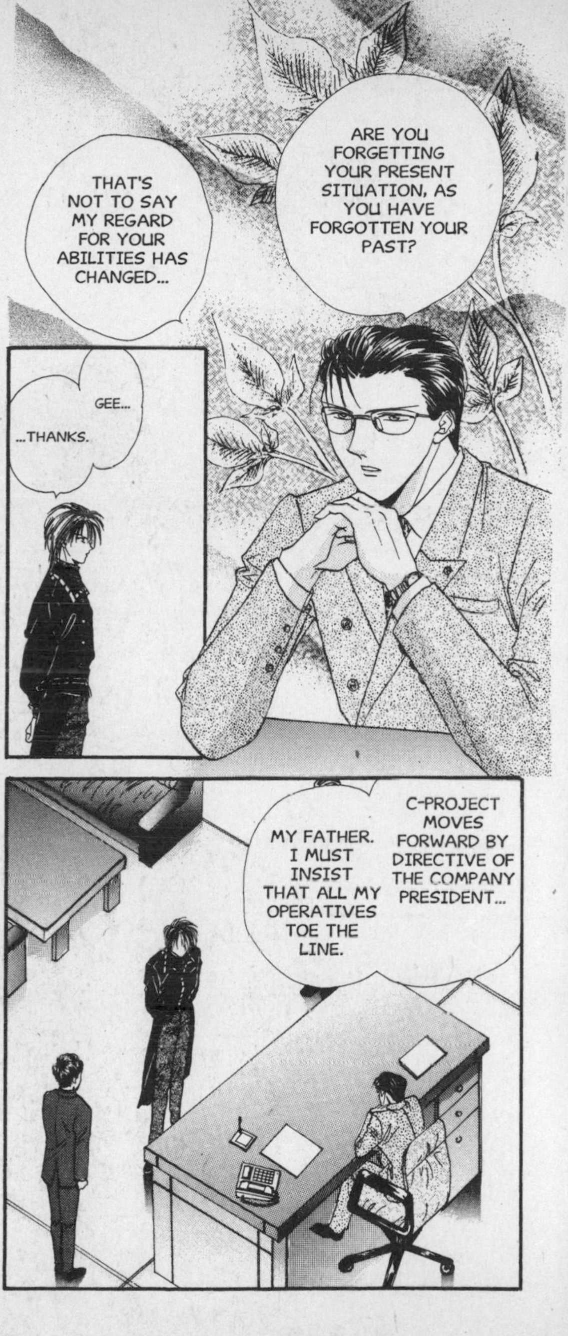
ARE YOU FORGETTING YOUR PRESENT SITUATION, AS YOU HAVE FORGOTTEN YOUR PAST?
THAT'S NOT TO SAY MY REGARD FOR YOUR ABILITIES HAS CHANGED...
GEE...
...THANKS.
C-PROJECT MOVES FORWARD BY DIRECTIVE OF THE COMPANY PRESIDENT...
MY FATHER. I MUST INSIST THAT ALL MY OPERATIVES TOE THE LINE.

Ceres: 5

It's me, Watase! Woohoo! Yippee! Huh? Why am I in such a good mood, you ask? I'm not, really! ◡̈ But the pizza bun snack I had was delicious! Well...we're already up to volume five! I was pretty excited while I was working on a lot of these episodes, so I couldn't help being meticulous when I was going over them for the graphic novels. And so I ended up doing more revisions and retouch than usual.

It was a lot of work... But you won't be able to tell what's different unless you saw its original run in Sho-Comi, and you still have the issues around for comparison. (I couldn't change much in vol.4.) I try to fix things up for the graphic novels as much as I can, so it's actually a rare case when the GNs turn out exactly the same as when they were first serialized. I guess that just means I'm not satisfied with my finished work that much. ...Sniff.

In any case, handwriting is difficult for me. I noticed recently that the way I hold a pen is a bit unusual. My grip is suited towards drawing manga, but it's actually difficult to write with it. Hey! That must be why I have bad handwriting! And that's why my handwriting is different than it was before I became pro. But it doesn't matter. It's an ultimate(?) grip that's efficient and doesn't cause calluses (I've never had one). I tried to teach the grip to my assistants, but it seems hard to pick up. What's it look like, you ask? I'm not telling. ◡̈ It's weird and it's kind of hard to do.

Now then. Last time, I wrote about my trip to Florida. The biggest surprise was that it doesn't get dark until around 9 p.m. It would be past nine o'clock and the sun would just be beginning to set. Well, it makes sense if you think about it, but it's still weird for me, because I'm used to the way things are in Japan.

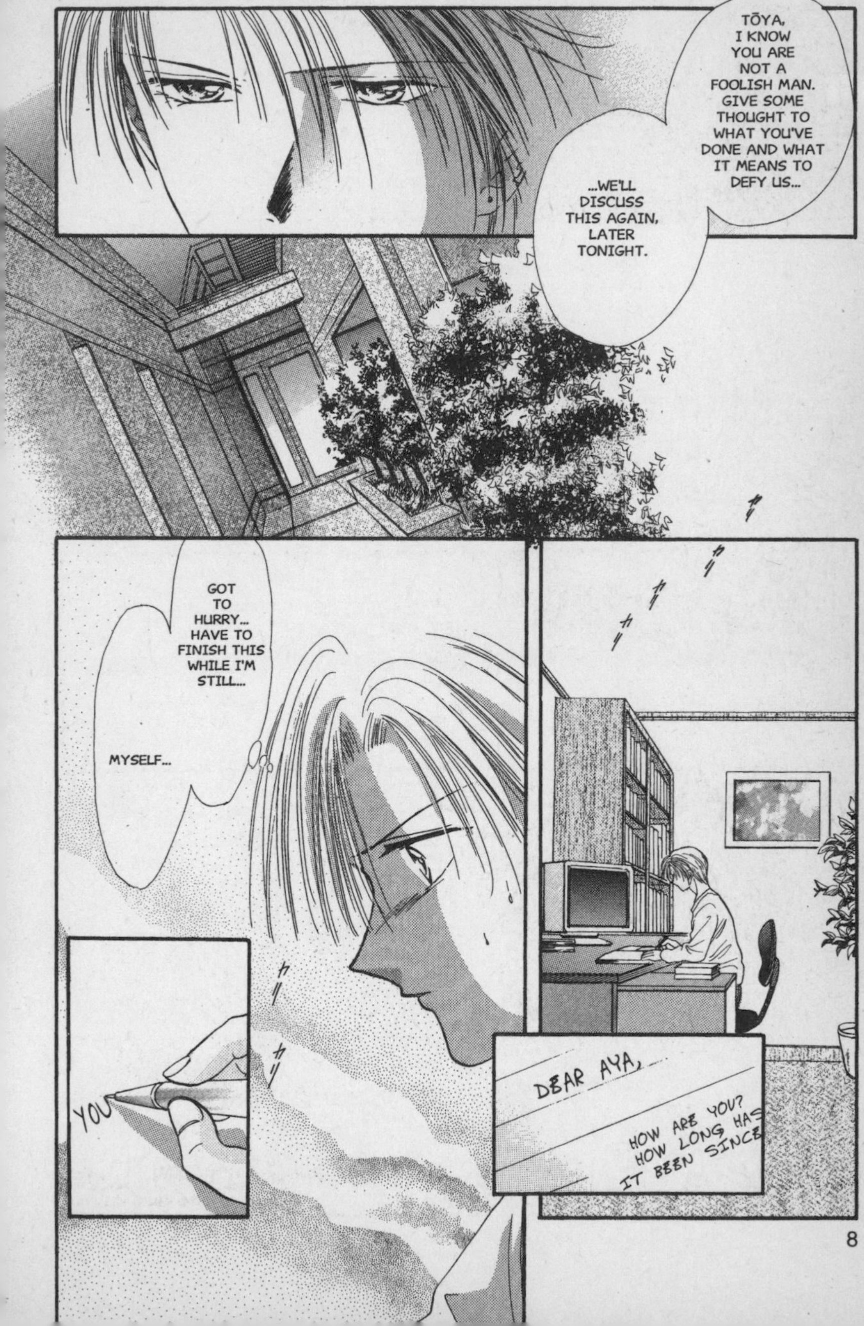
TŌYA, I KNOW YOU ARE NOT A FOOLISH MAN. GIVE SOME THOUGHT TO WHAT YOU'VE DONE AND WHAT IT MEANS TO DEFY US...
...WE'LL DISCUSS THIS AGAIN, LATER TONIGHT.
DEAR AYA,
HOW ARE YOU? HOW LONG HAS IT BEEN SINCE
GOT TO HURRY... HAVE TO FINISH THIS WHILE I'M STILL...
MYSELF...
YOU

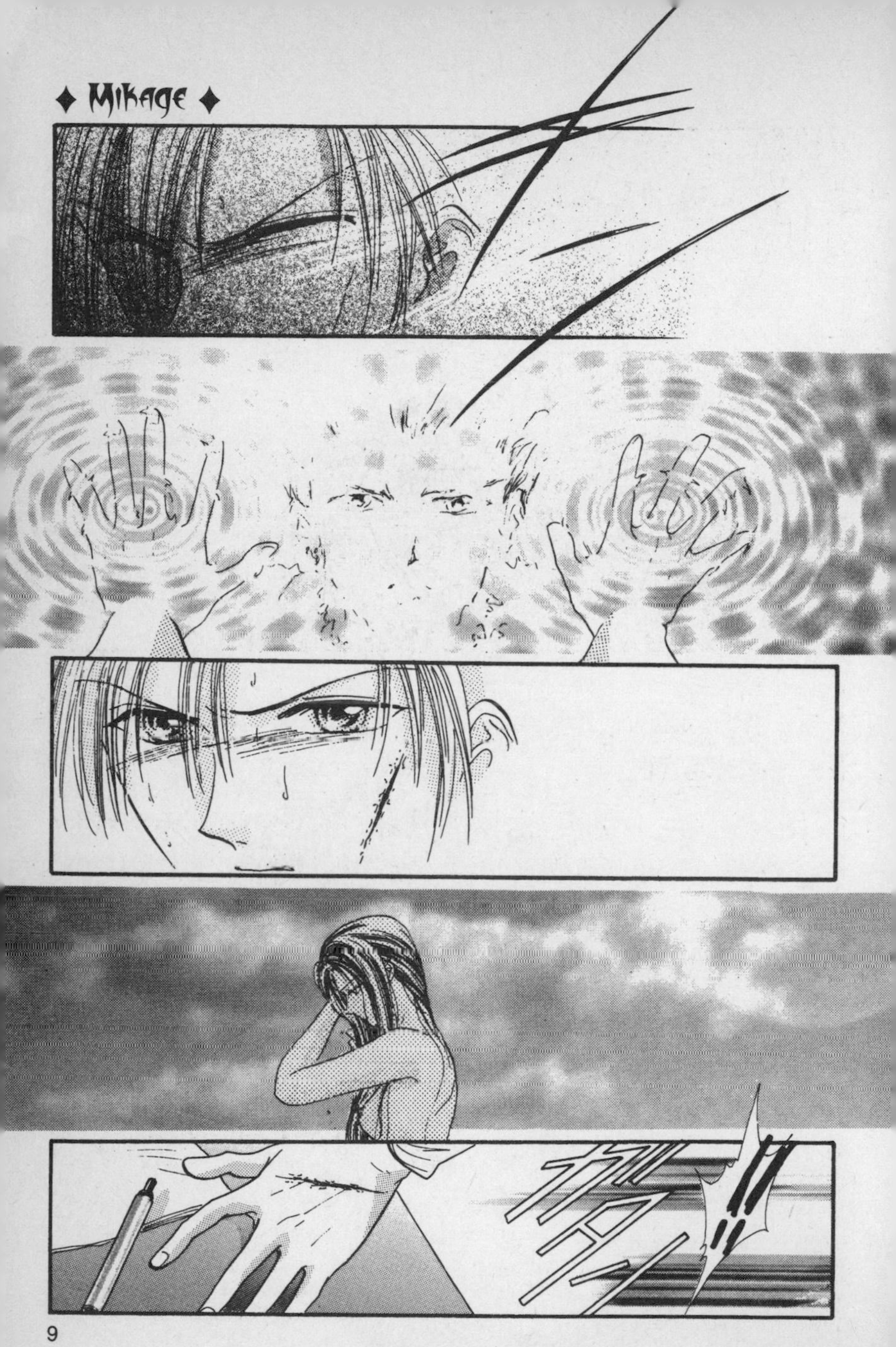

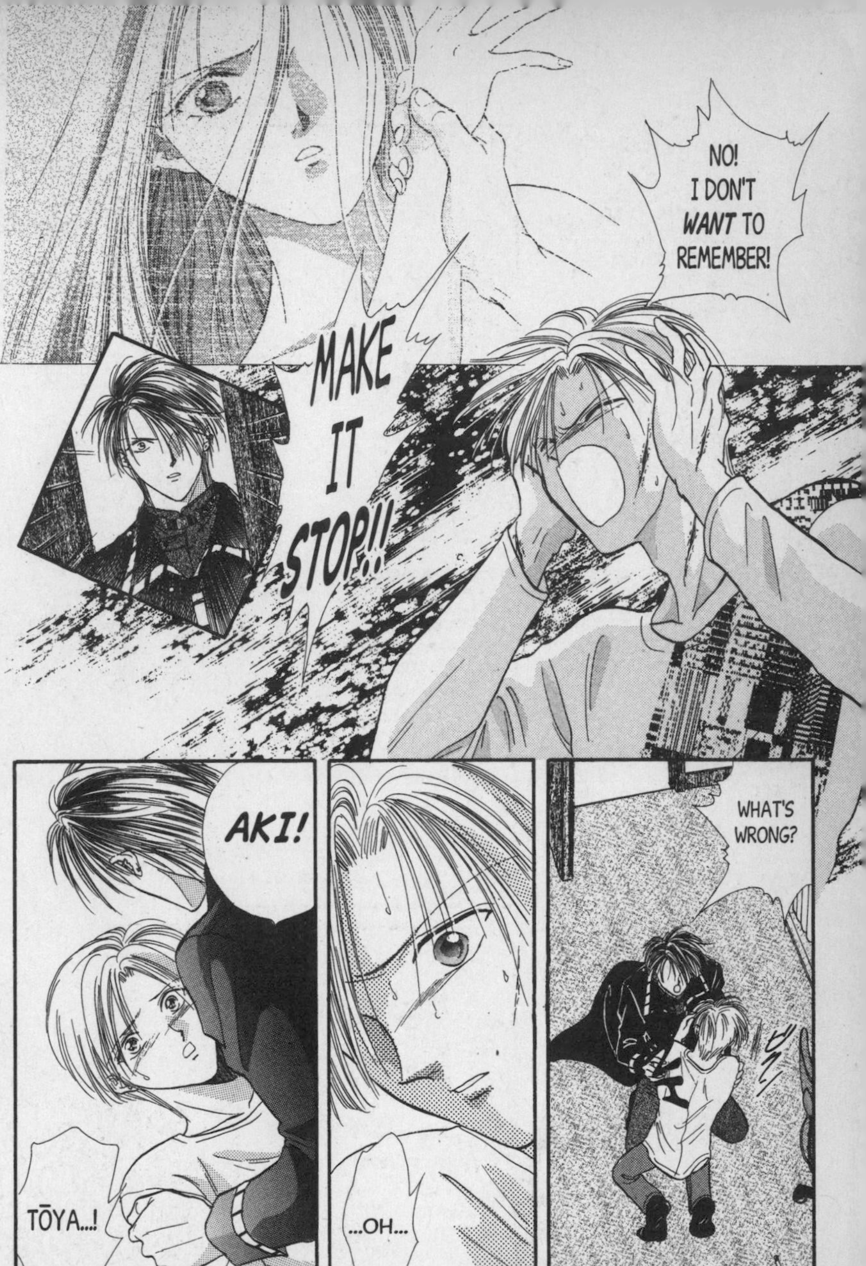
NO! I DON'T *WANT* TO REMEMBER!
MAKE IT STOP!!
WHAT'S WRONG?
...OH...
AKI!
TŌYA...!

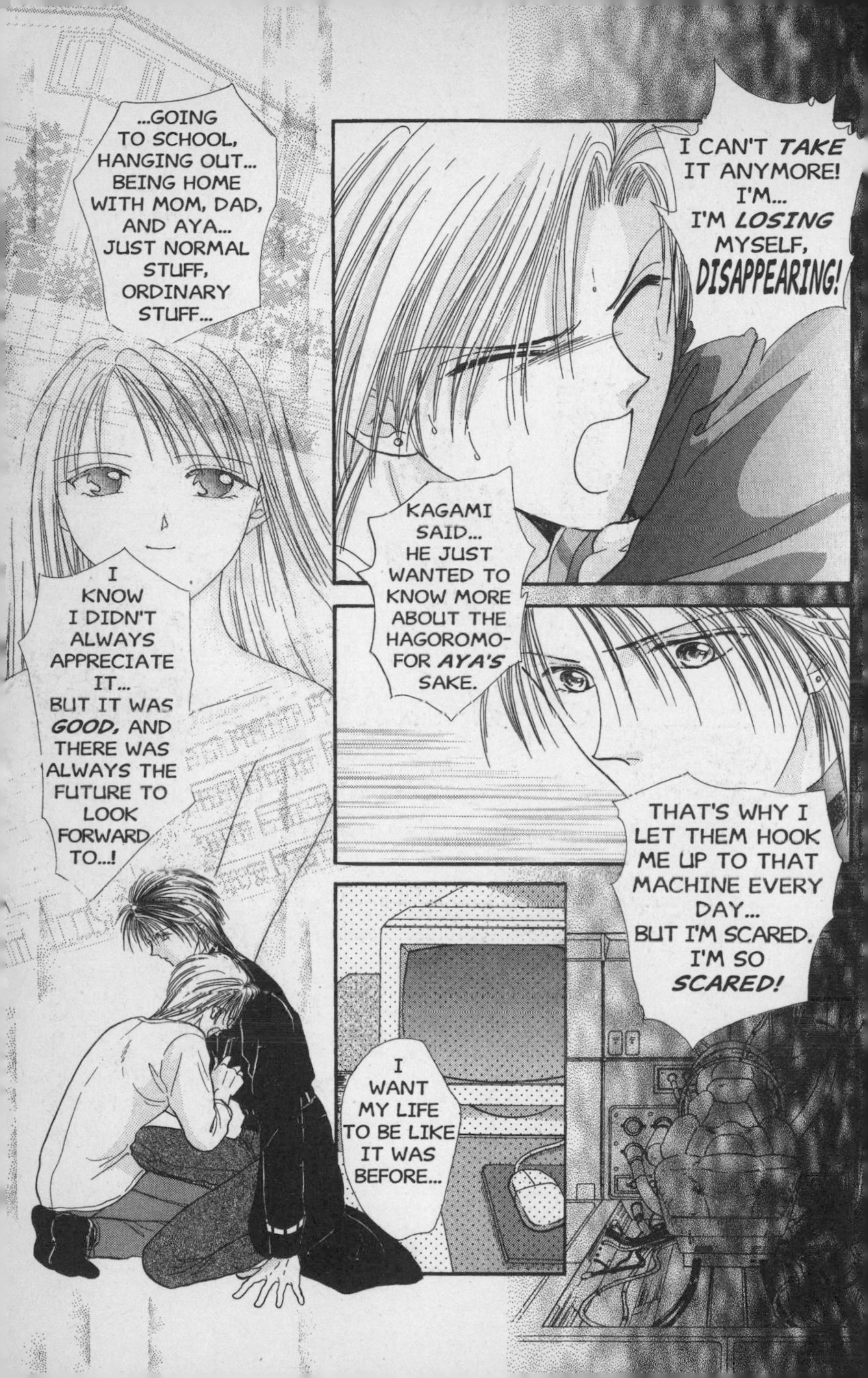
I CAN'T TAKE IT ANYMORE! I'M... I'M LOSING MYSELF, DISAPPEARING!
KAGAMI SAID... HE JUST WANTED TO KNOW MORE ABOUT THE HAGOROMO- FOR AYA'S SAKE.
THAT'S WHY I LET THEM HOOK ME UP TO THAT MACHINE EVERY DAY... BUT I'M SCARED. I'M SO SCARED!
I WANT MY LIFE TO BE LIKE IT WAS BEFORE...
...GOING TO SCHOOL, HANGING OUT... BEING HOME WITH MOM, DAD, AND AYA... JUST NORMAL STUFF, ORDINARY STUFF...
I KNOW I DIDN'T ALWAYS APPRECIATE IT... BUT IT WAS GOOD, AND THERE WAS ALWAYS THE FUTURE TO LOOK FORWARD TO...!

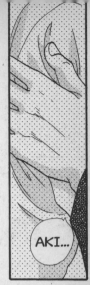

LET'S LEAVE THIS PLACE...

AKI...

THE TWO OF US, WE'LL ESCAPE FROM HERE TOGETHER...

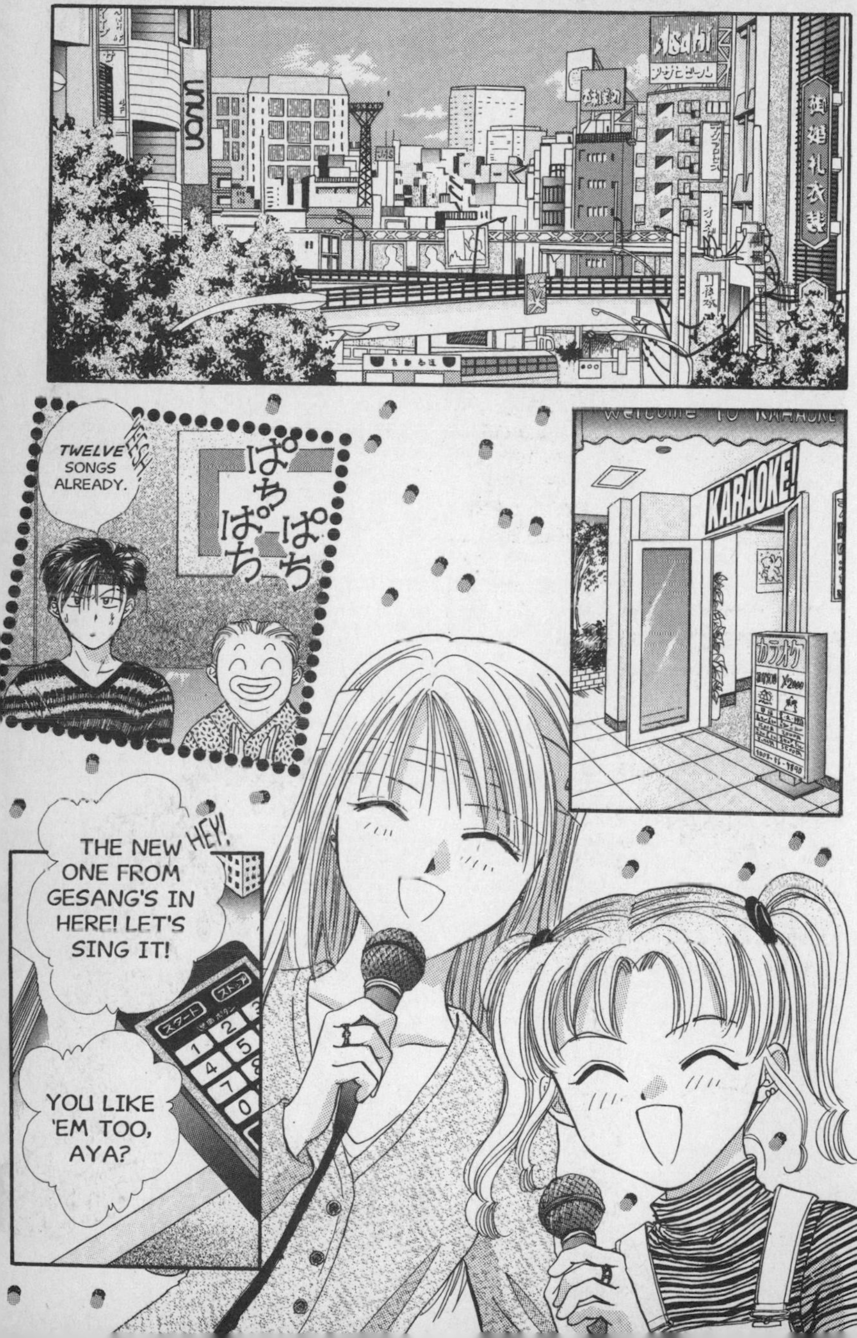
KARAOKE!
カラオケ
YEESH
TWELVE SONGS ALREADY.
ぱちぱちぱちぱち
THE NEW ONE FROM GESANG'S IN HERE! LET'S SING IT!
HEY!
YOU LIKE 'EM TOO, AYA?

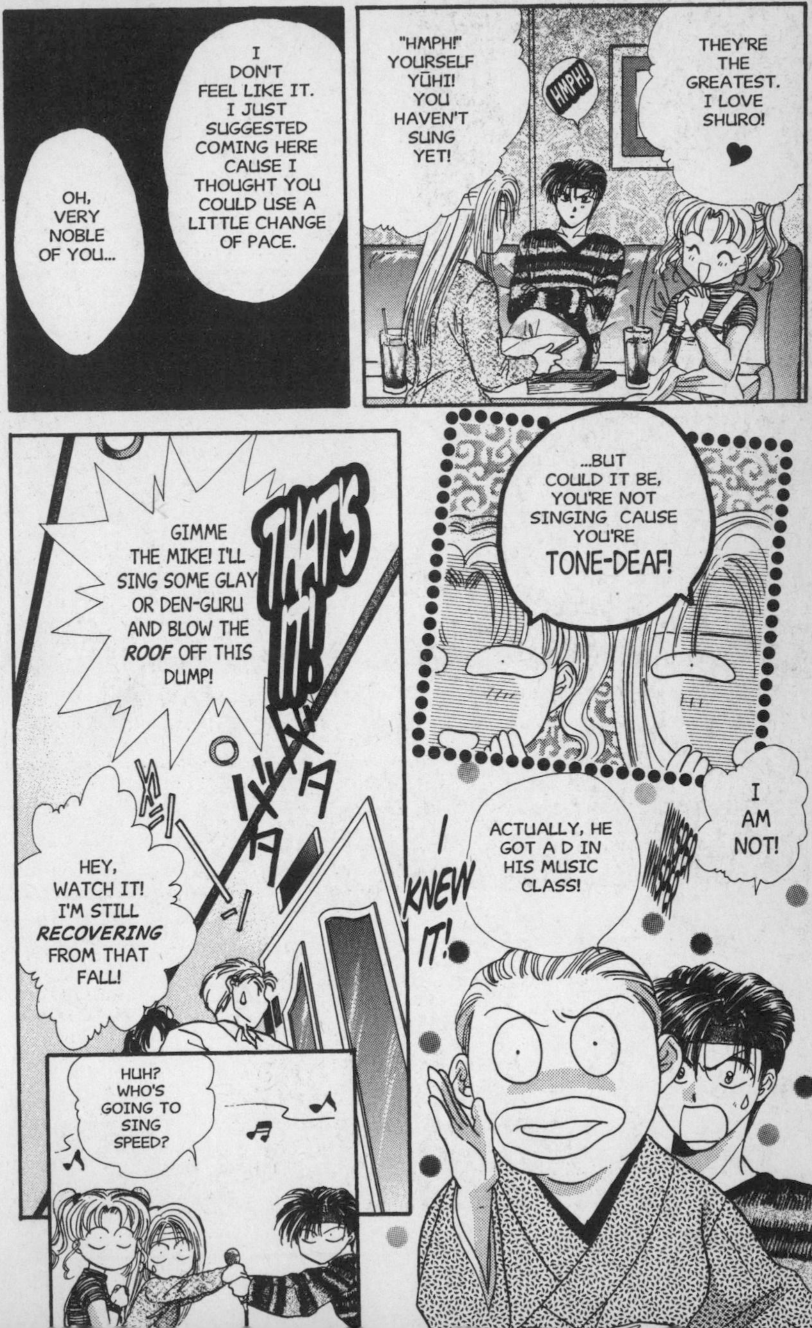
THEY'RE THE GREATEST. I LOVE SHURO! ♥
HMPH!
"HMPH!" YOURSELF YŪHI! YOU HAVEN'T SUNG YET!
I DON'T FEEL LIKE IT. I JUST SUGGESTED COMING HERE CAUSE I THOUGHT YOU COULD USE A LITTLE CHANGE OF PACE.
OH, VERY NOBLE OF YOU...
...BUT COULD IT BE, YOU'RE NOT SINGING CAUSE YOU'RE TONE-DEAF!
I AM NOT!
ACTUALLY, HE GOT A D IN HIS MUSIC CLASS!
I KNEW IT!
THAT'S IT!
GIMME THE MIKE! I'LL SING SOME GLAY OR DEN-GURU AND BLOW THE *ROOF* OFF THIS DUMP!
HEY, WATCH IT! I'M STILL *RECOVERING* FROM THAT FALL!
HUH? WHO'S GOING TO SING SPEED?

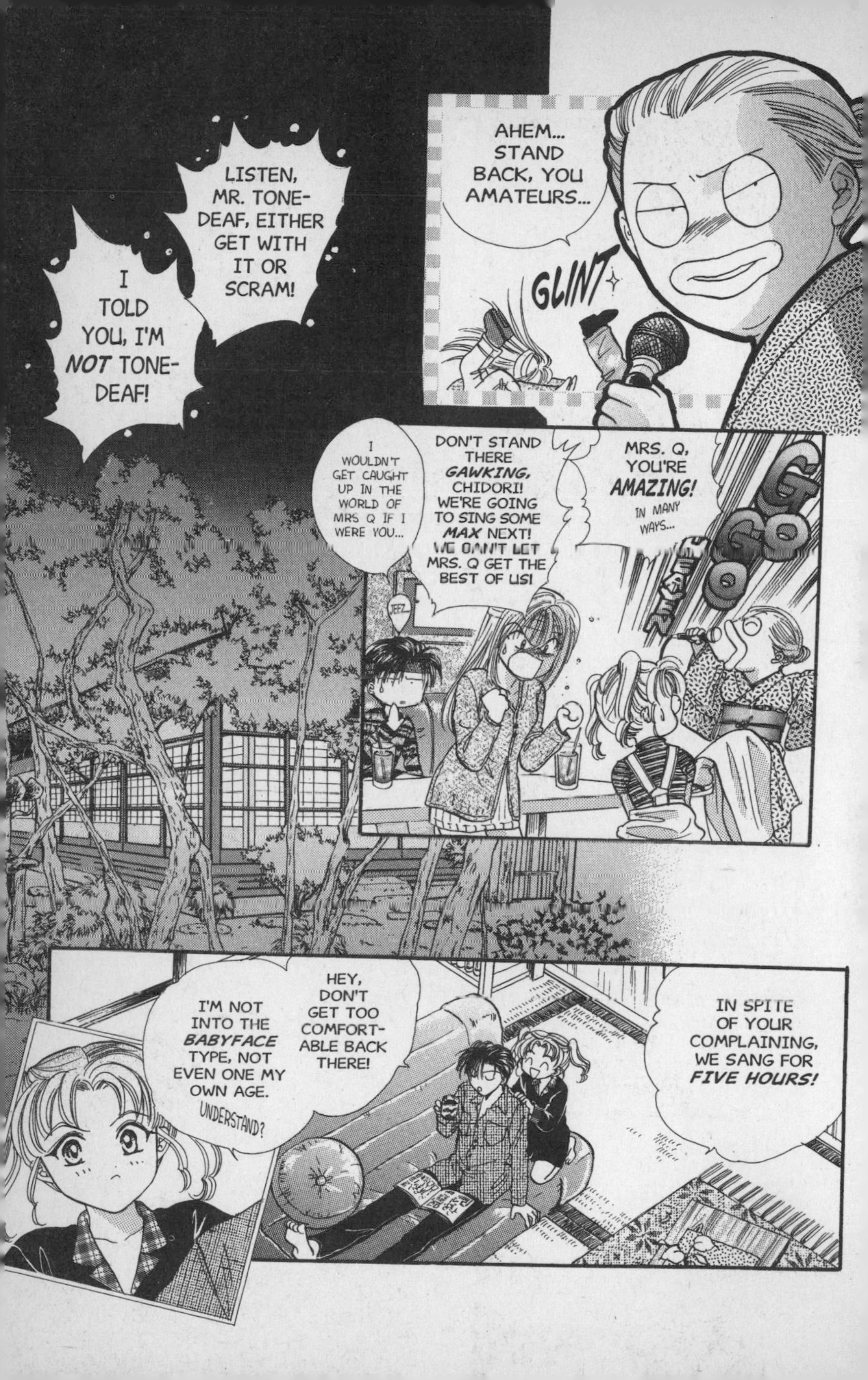
AHEM... STAND BACK, YOU AMATEURS...
GLINT
LISTEN, MR. TONE-DEAF, EITHER GET WITH IT OR SCRAM!
I TOLD YOU, I'M *NOT* TONE-DEAF!
MRS. Q, YOU'RE *AMAZING!*
IN MANY WAYS...
DON'T STAND THERE *GAWKING,* CHIDORI! WE'RE GOING TO SING SOME *MAX* NEXT! WE CAN'T LET MRS. Q GET THE BEST OF US!
I WOULDN'T GET CAUGHT UP IN THE WORLD OF MRS Q IF I WERE YOU...
JEEZ
IN SPITE OF YOUR COMPLAINING, WE SANG FOR *FIVE HOURS!*
HEY, DON'T GET TOO COMFORT-ABLE BACK THERE!
I'M NOT INTO THE *BABYFACE* TYPE, NOT EVEN ONE MY OWN AGE.
UNDERSTAND?

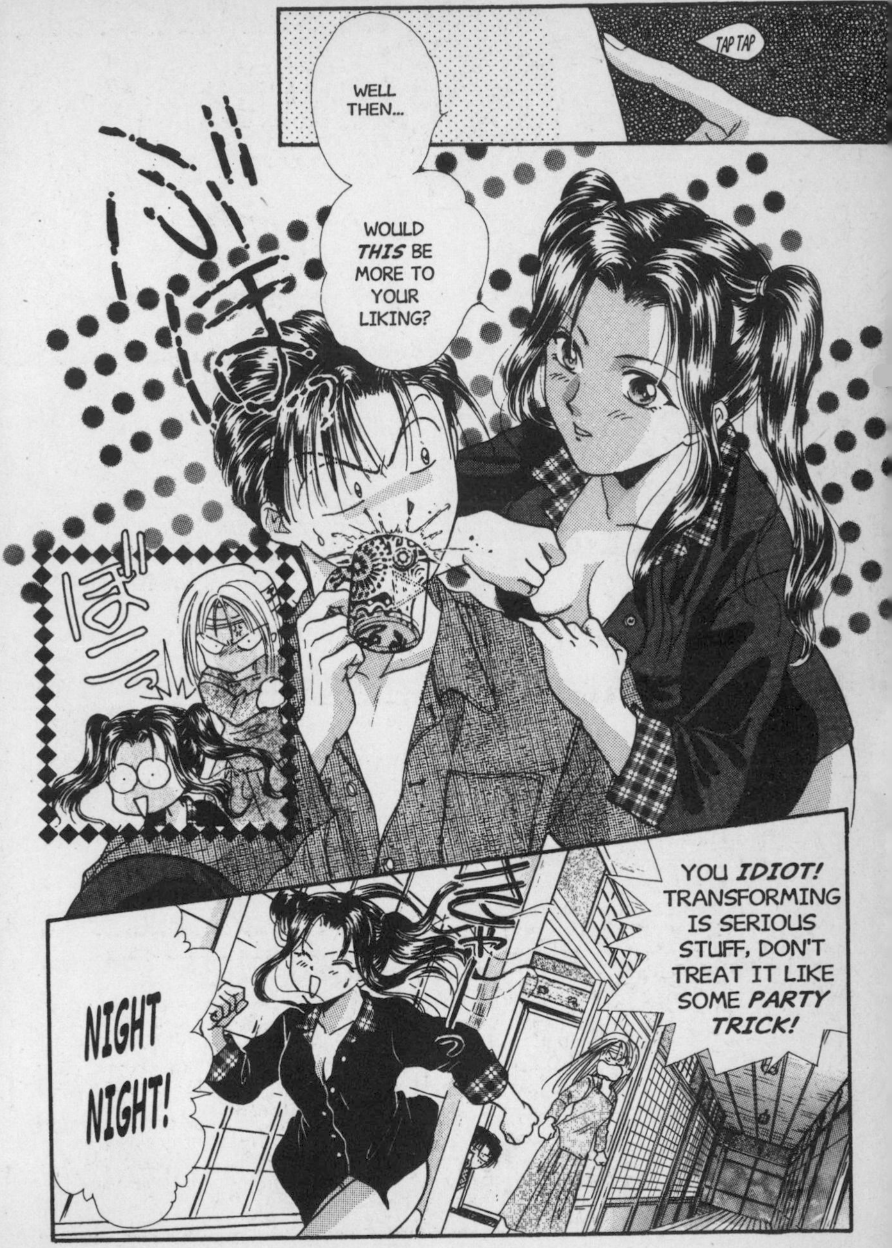
TAP TAP
WELL THEN...
WOULD *THIS* BE MORE TO YOUR LIKING?
YOU *IDIOT!* TRANSFORMING IS SERIOUS STUFF, DON'T TREAT IT LIKE SOME *PARTY TRICK!*
NIGHT NIGHT!

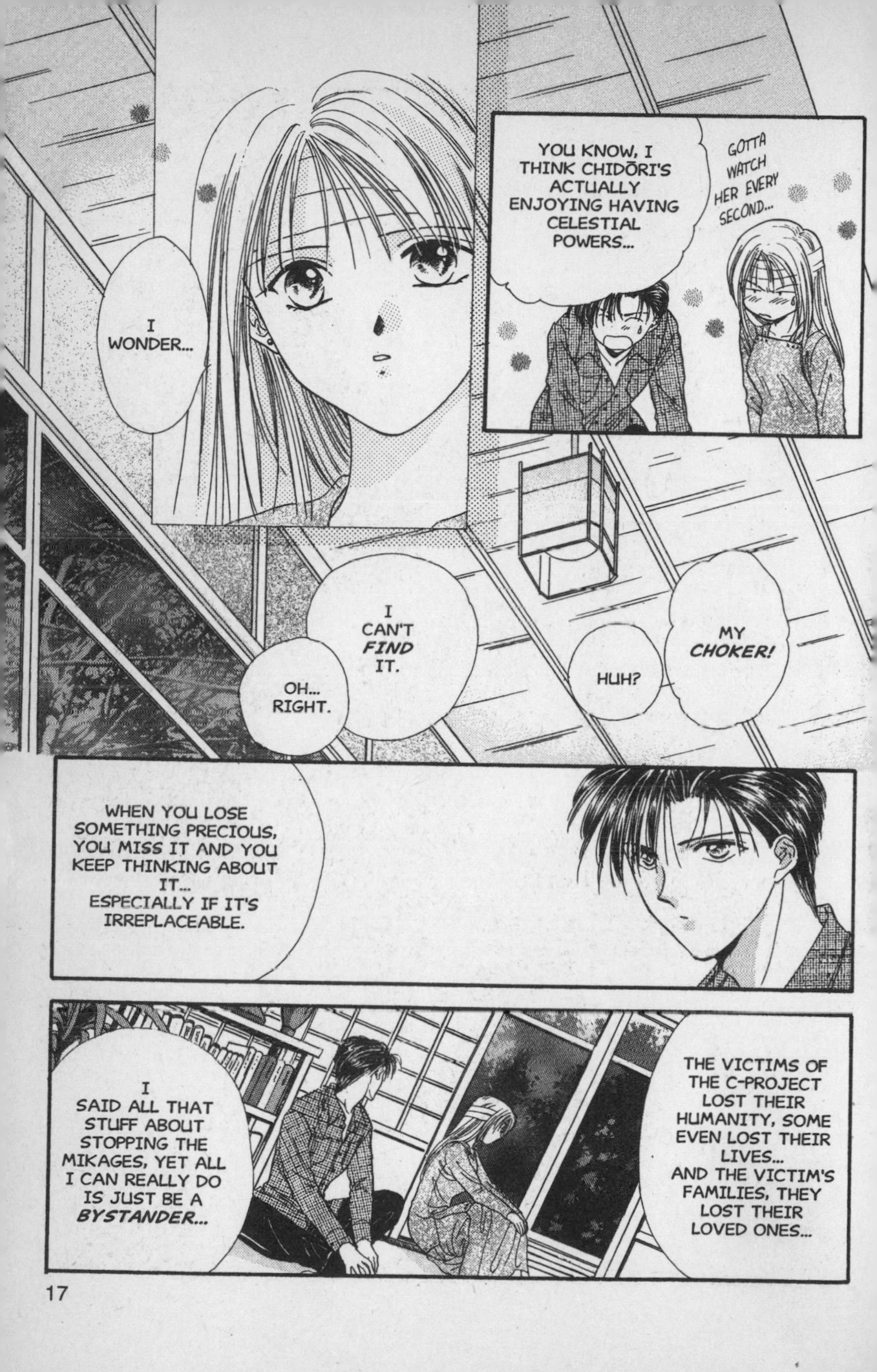
GOTTA WATCH HER EVERY SECOND...
YOU KNOW, I THINK CHIDŌRI'S ACTUALLY ENJOYING HAVING CELESTIAL POWERS...
I WONDER...
MY *CHOKER!*
HUH?
I CAN'T *FIND* IT.
OH... RIGHT.
WHEN YOU LOSE SOMETHING PRECIOUS, YOU MISS IT AND YOU KEEP THINKING ABOUT IT... ESPECIALLY IF IT'S IRREPLACEABLE.
THE VICTIMS OF THE C-PROJECT LOST THEIR HUMANITY, SOME EVEN LOST THEIR LIVES... AND THE VICTIM'S FAMILIES, THEY LOST THEIR LOVED ONES...
I SAID ALL THAT STUFF ABOUT STOPPING THE MIKAGES, YET ALL I CAN REALLY DO IS JUST BE A *BYSTANDER...*

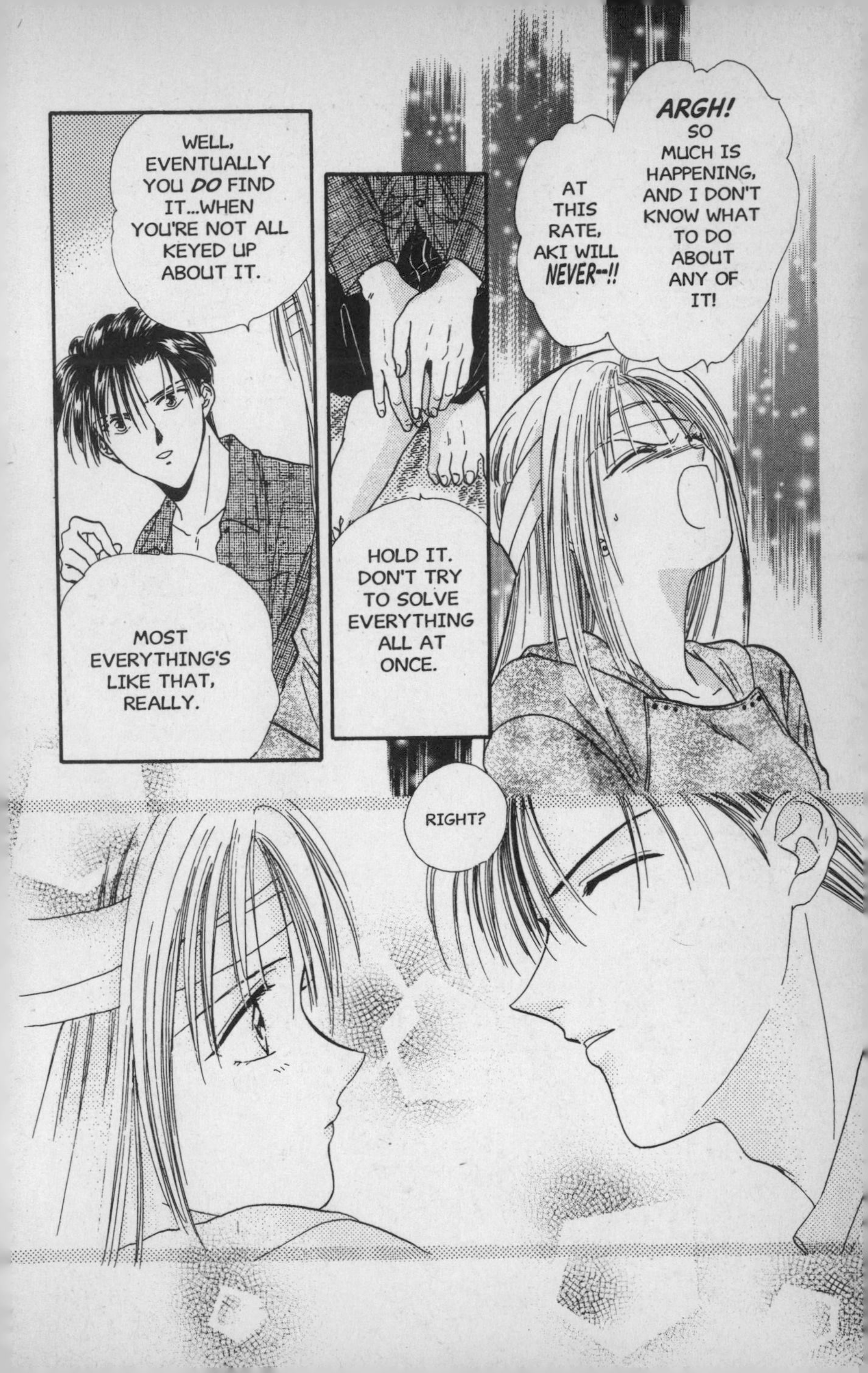
ARGH! SO MUCH IS HAPPENING, AND I DON'T KNOW WHAT TO DO ABOUT ANY OF IT!
AT THIS RATE, AKI WILL NEVER--!!
HOLD IT. DON'T TRY TO SOLVE EVERYTHING ALL AT ONCE.
WELL, EVENTUALLY YOU DO FIND IT...WHEN YOU'RE NOT ALL KEYED UP ABOUT IT.
MOST EVERYTHING'S LIKE THAT, REALLY.
RIGHT?

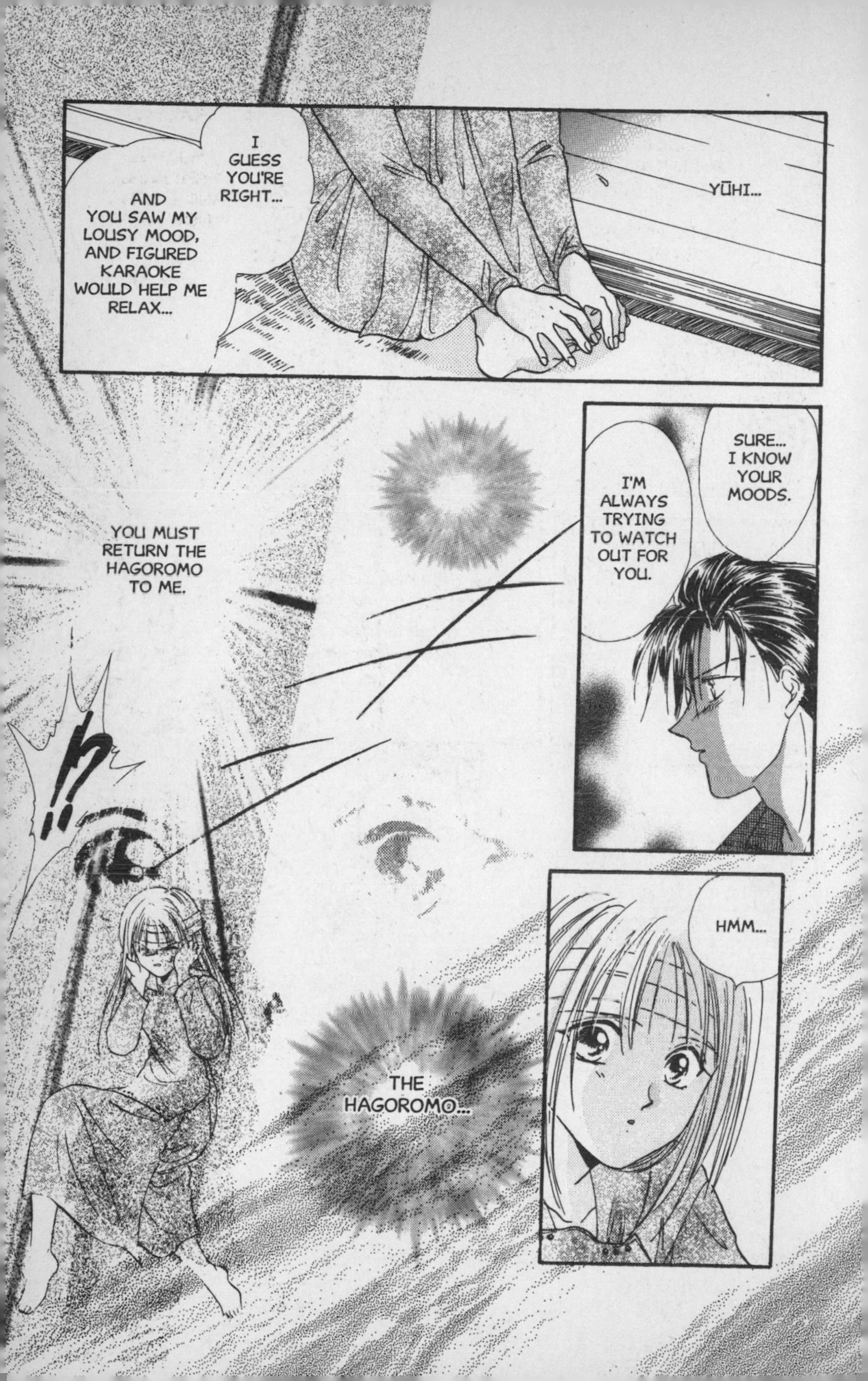
YŪHI...
I GUESS YOU'RE RIGHT...
AND YOU SAW MY LOUSY MOOD, AND FIGURED KARAOKE WOULD HELP ME RELAX...
SURE... I KNOW YOUR MOODS.
I'M ALWAYS TRYING TO WATCH OUT FOR YOU.
HMM...
YOU MUST RETURN THE HAGOROMO TO ME.
!!
THE HAGOROMO...

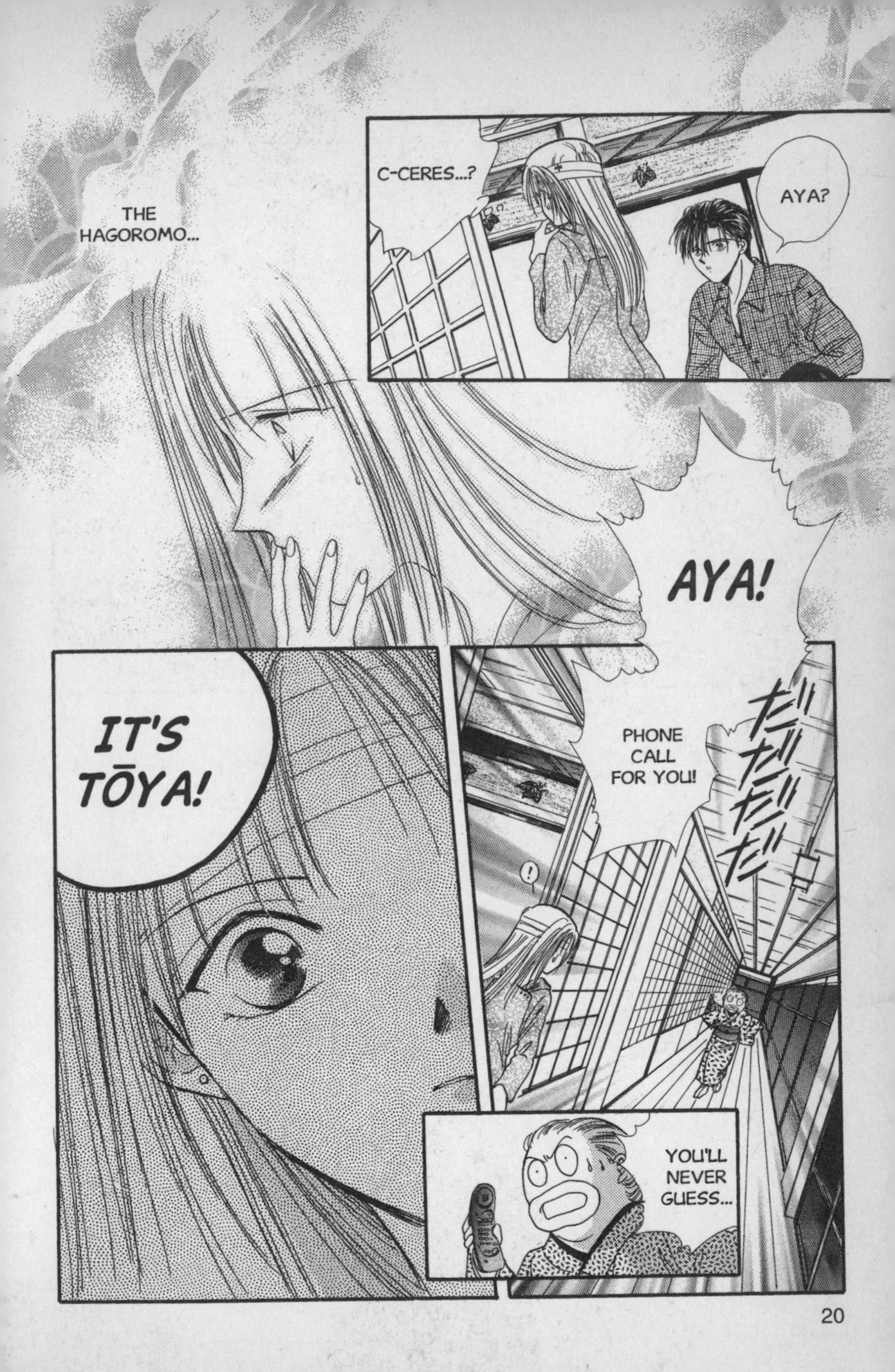
AYA?
C-CERES...?
THE HAGOROMO...
AYA!
PHONE CALL FOR YOU!
!
YOU'LL NEVER GUESS...
IT'S TŌYA!

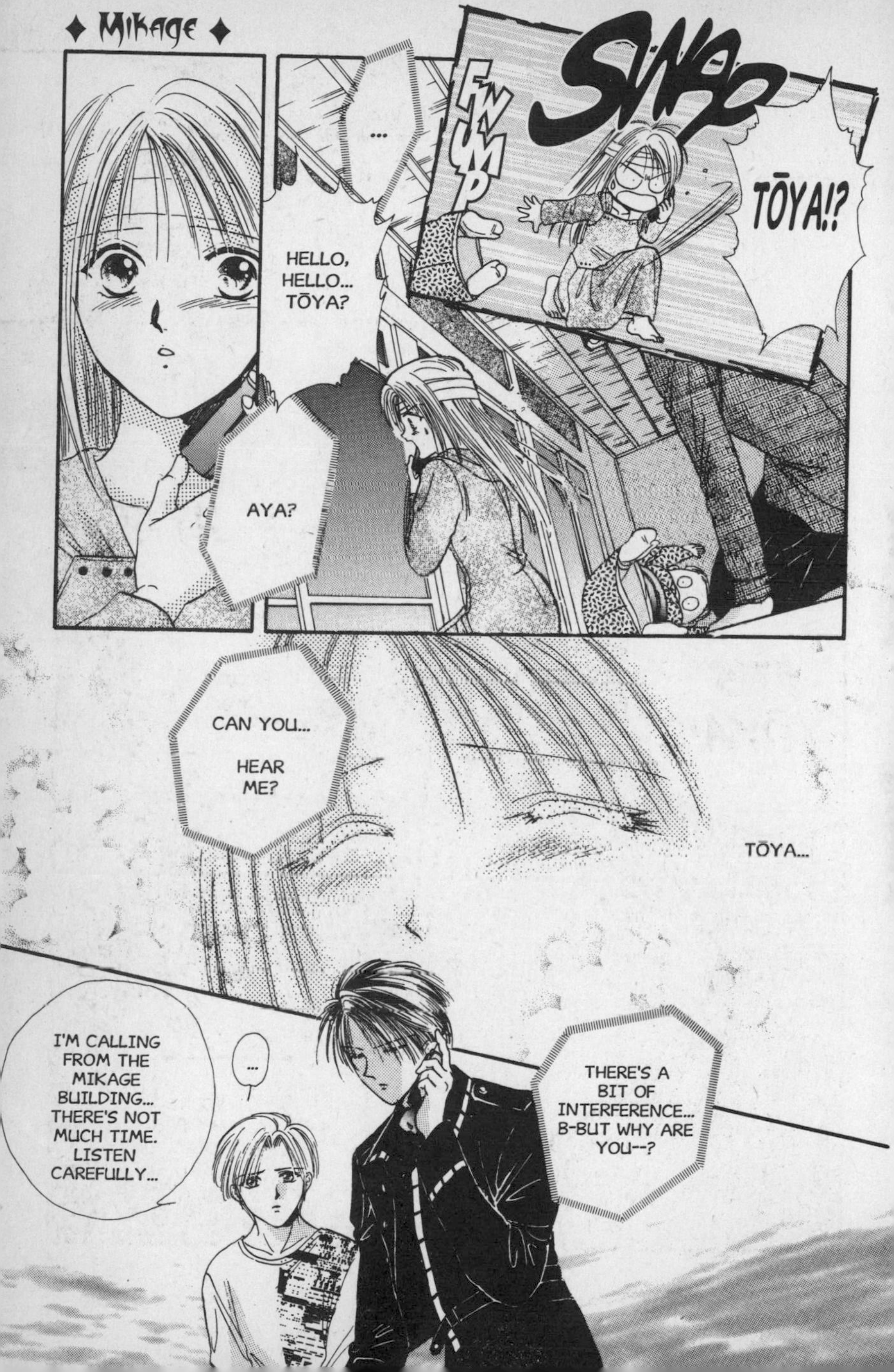
FWUMP
TŌYA!?
...
HELLO, HELLO... TŌYA?
AYA?
TŌYA...
CAN YOU... HEAR ME?
THERE'S A BIT OF INTERFERENCE... B-BUT WHY ARE YOU--?
...
I'M CALLING FROM THE MIKAGE BUILDING... THERE'S NOT MUCH TIME. LISTEN CAREFULLY...

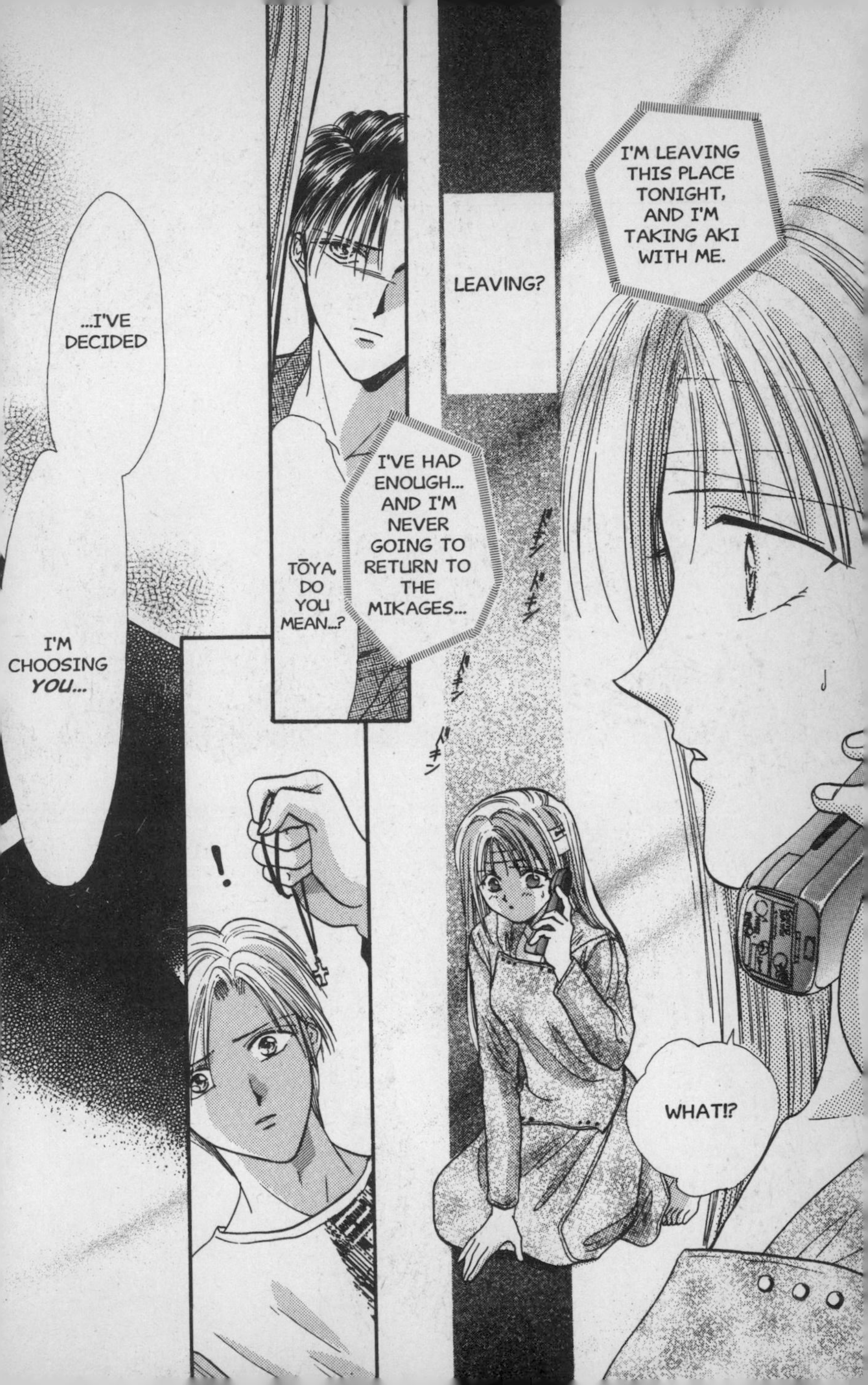
I'M LEAVING THIS PLACE TONIGHT, AND I'M TAKING AKI WITH ME.
WHAT!?
LEAVING?
I'VE HAD ENOUGH... AND I'M NEVER GOING TO RETURN TO THE MIKAGES...
TŌYA, DO YOU MEAN...?
...I'VE DECIDED
I'M CHOOSING *YOU*...

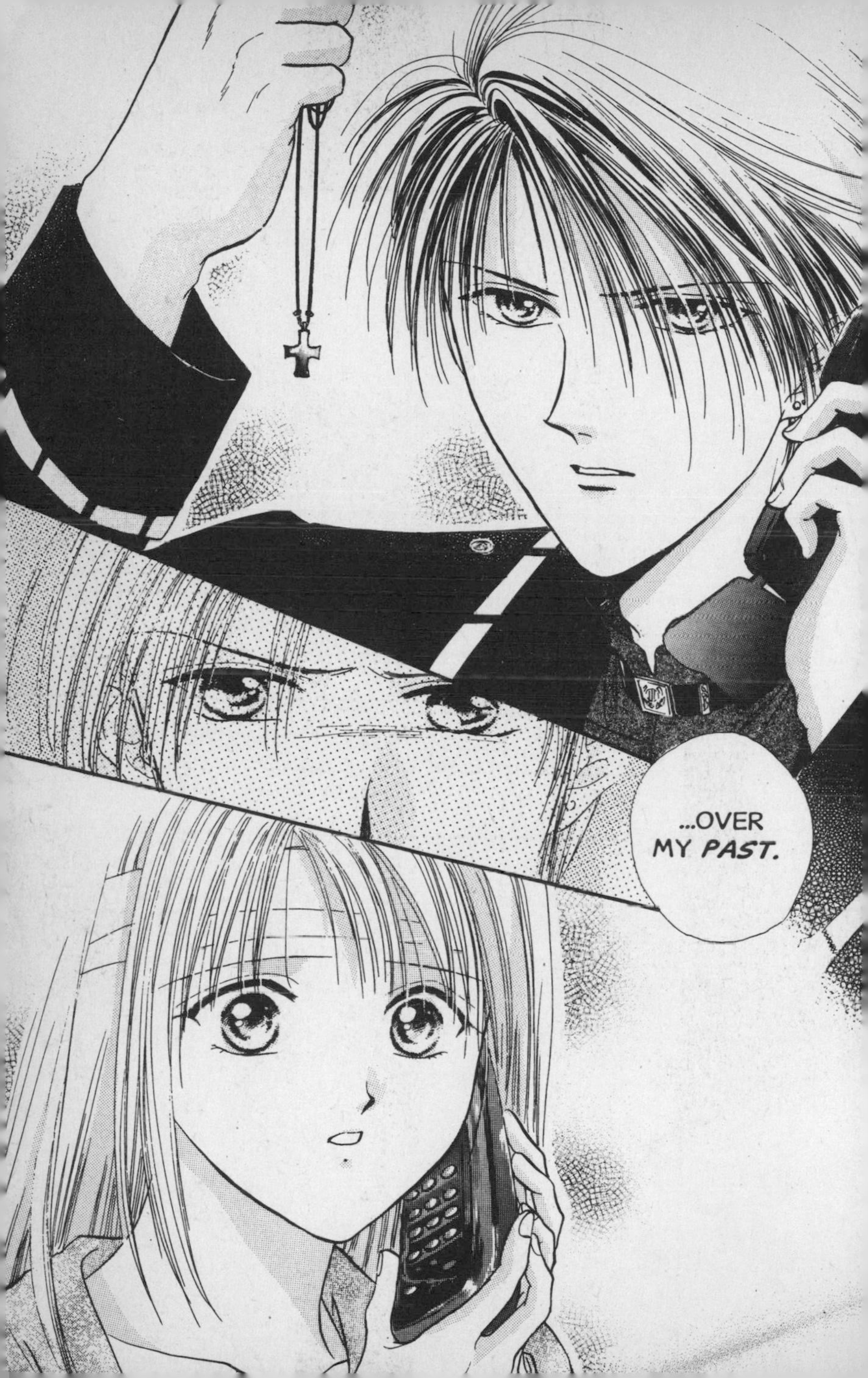
...OVER MY PAST.

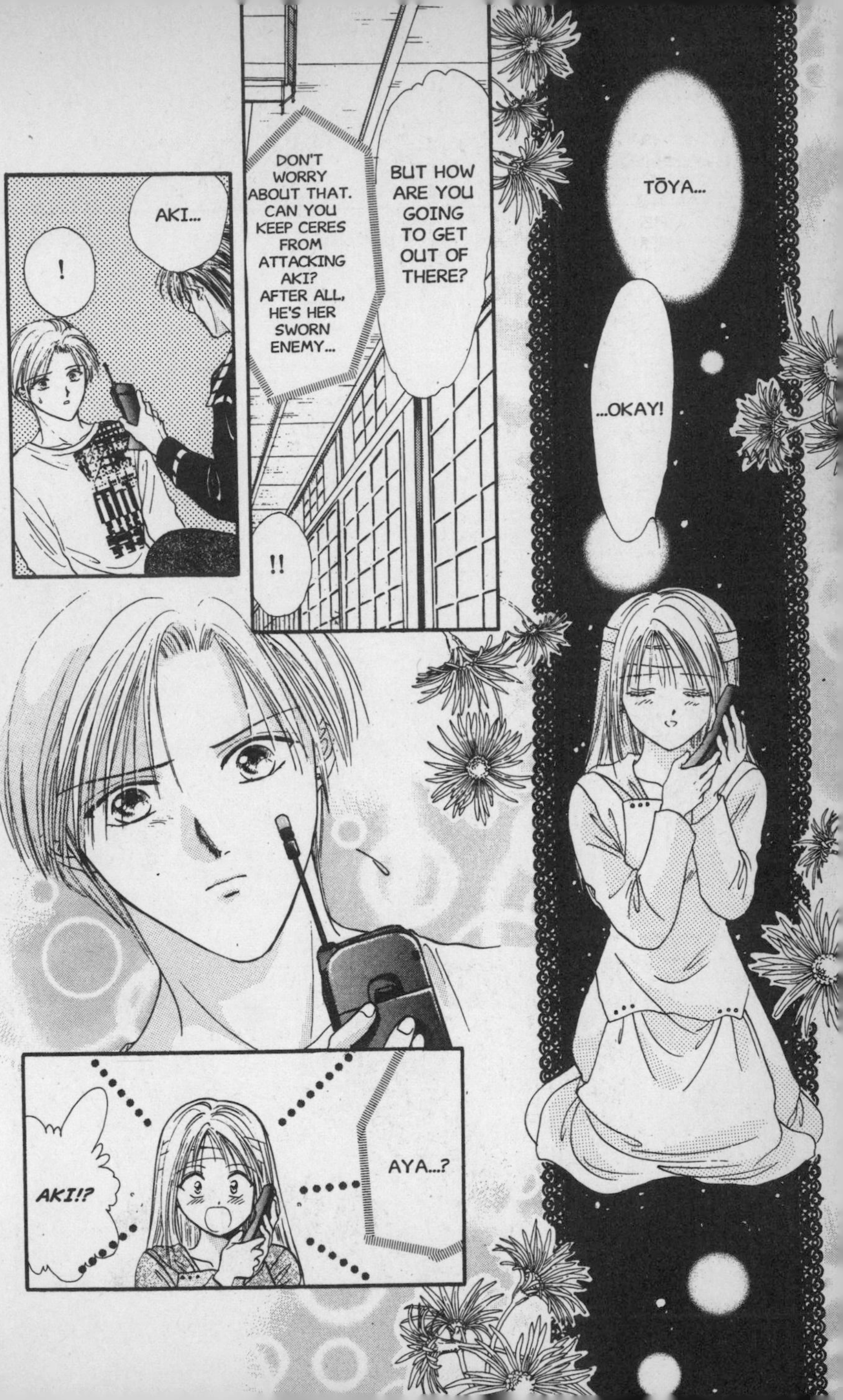
TŌYA...
...OKAY!
BUT HOW ARE YOU GOING TO GET OUT OF THERE?
DON'T WORRY ABOUT THAT. CAN YOU KEEP CERES FROM ATTACKING AKI? AFTER ALL, HE'S HER SWORN ENEMY...
!!
AKI...
!
AYA...?
AKI!?

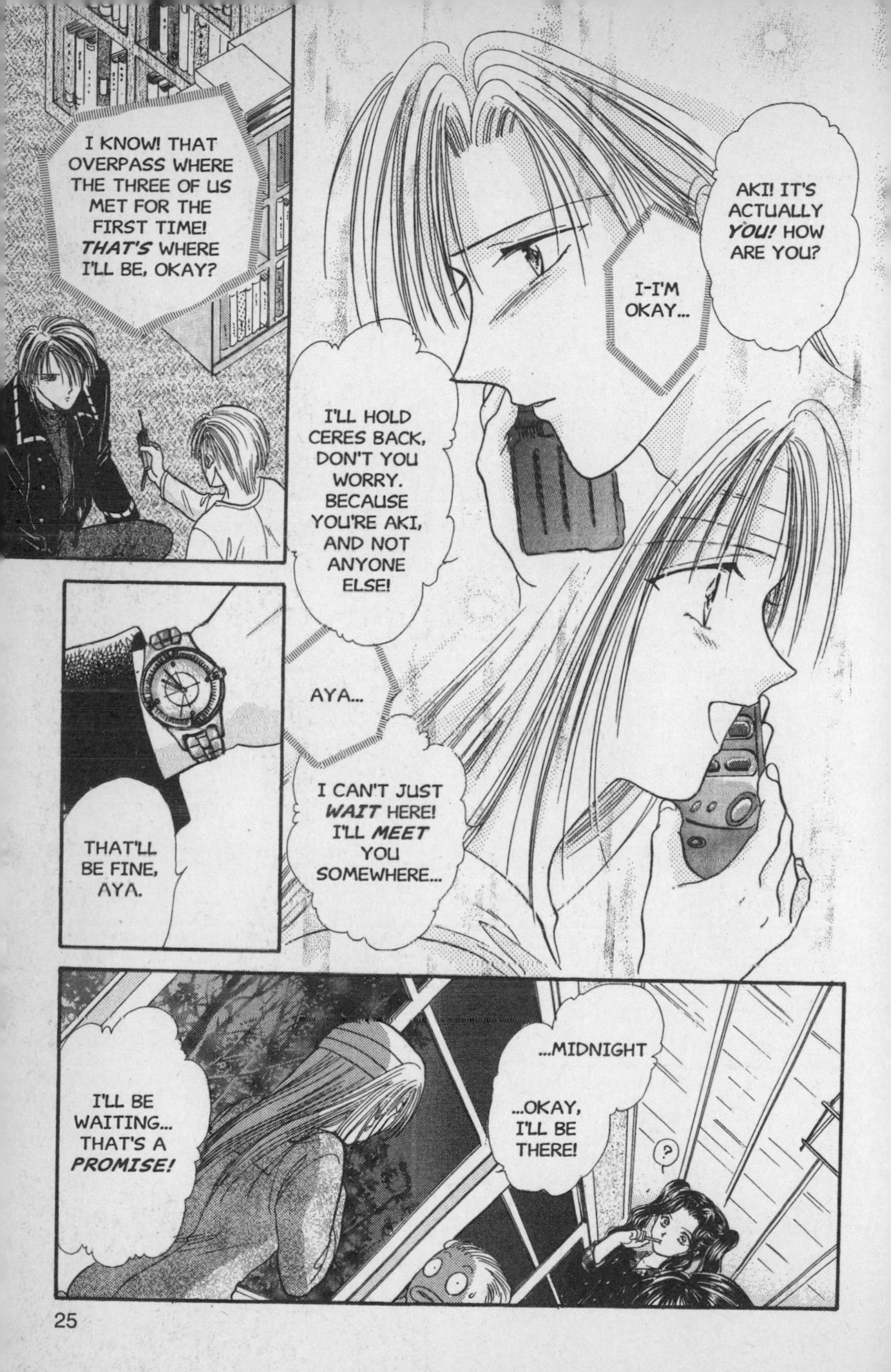
AKI! IT'S ACTUALLY *YOU!* HOW ARE YOU?
I-I'M OKAY...
I'LL HOLD CERES BACK, DON'T YOU WORRY. BECAUSE YOU'RE AKI, AND NOT ANYONE ELSE!
AYA...
I CAN'T JUST *WAIT* HERE! I'LL *MEET* YOU SOMEWHERE...
I KNOW! THAT OVERPASS WHERE THE THREE OF US MET FOR THE FIRST TIME! *THAT'S* WHERE I'LL BE, OKAY?
THAT'LL BE FINE, AYA.
...MIDNIGHT
...OKAY, I'LL BE THERE!
?
I'LL BE WAITING... THAT'S A *PROMISE!*

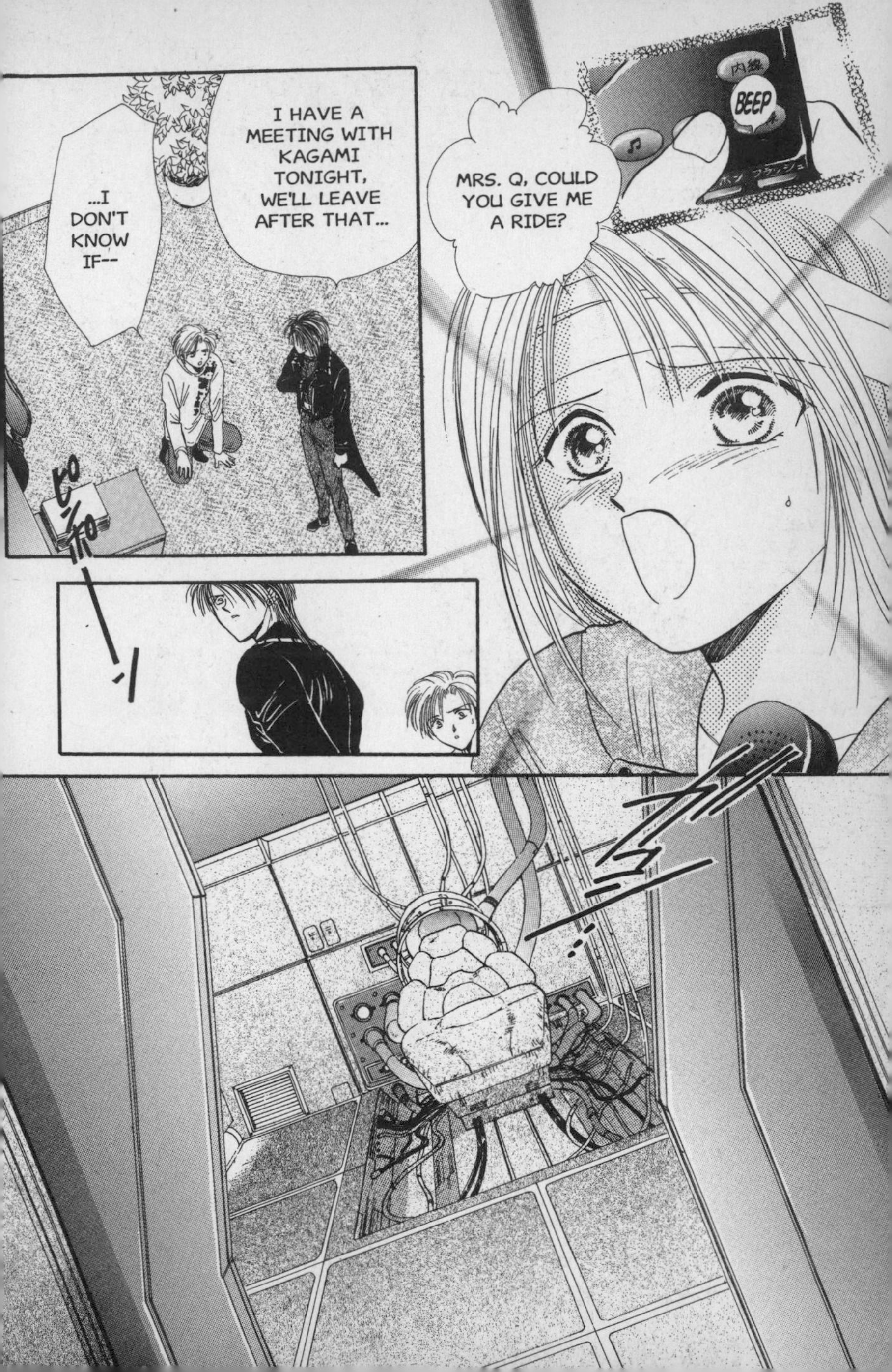
BEEP
MRS. Q, COULD YOU GIVE ME A RIDE?
I HAVE A MEETING WITH KAGAMI TONIGHT, WE'LL LEAVE AFTER THAT...
...I DON'T KNOW IF--

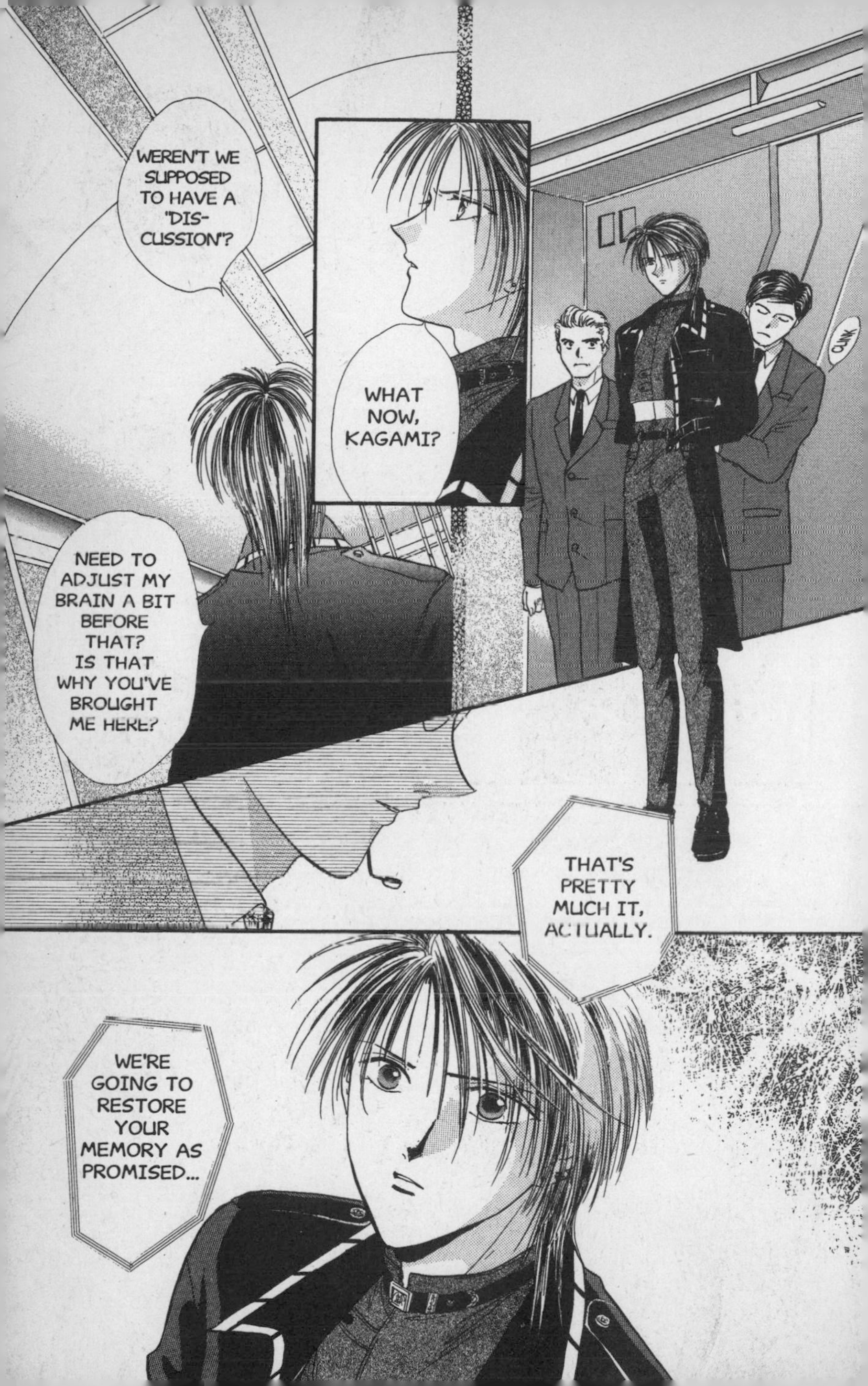
CLINK
WHAT NOW, KAGAMI?
WEREN'T WE SUPPOSED TO HAVE A "DIS-CUSSION"?
NEED TO ADJUST MY BRAIN A BIT BEFORE THAT? IS THAT WHY YOU'VE BROUGHT ME HERE?
THAT'S PRETTY MUCH IT, ACTUALLY.
WE'RE GOING TO RESTORE YOUR MEMORY AS PROMISED...

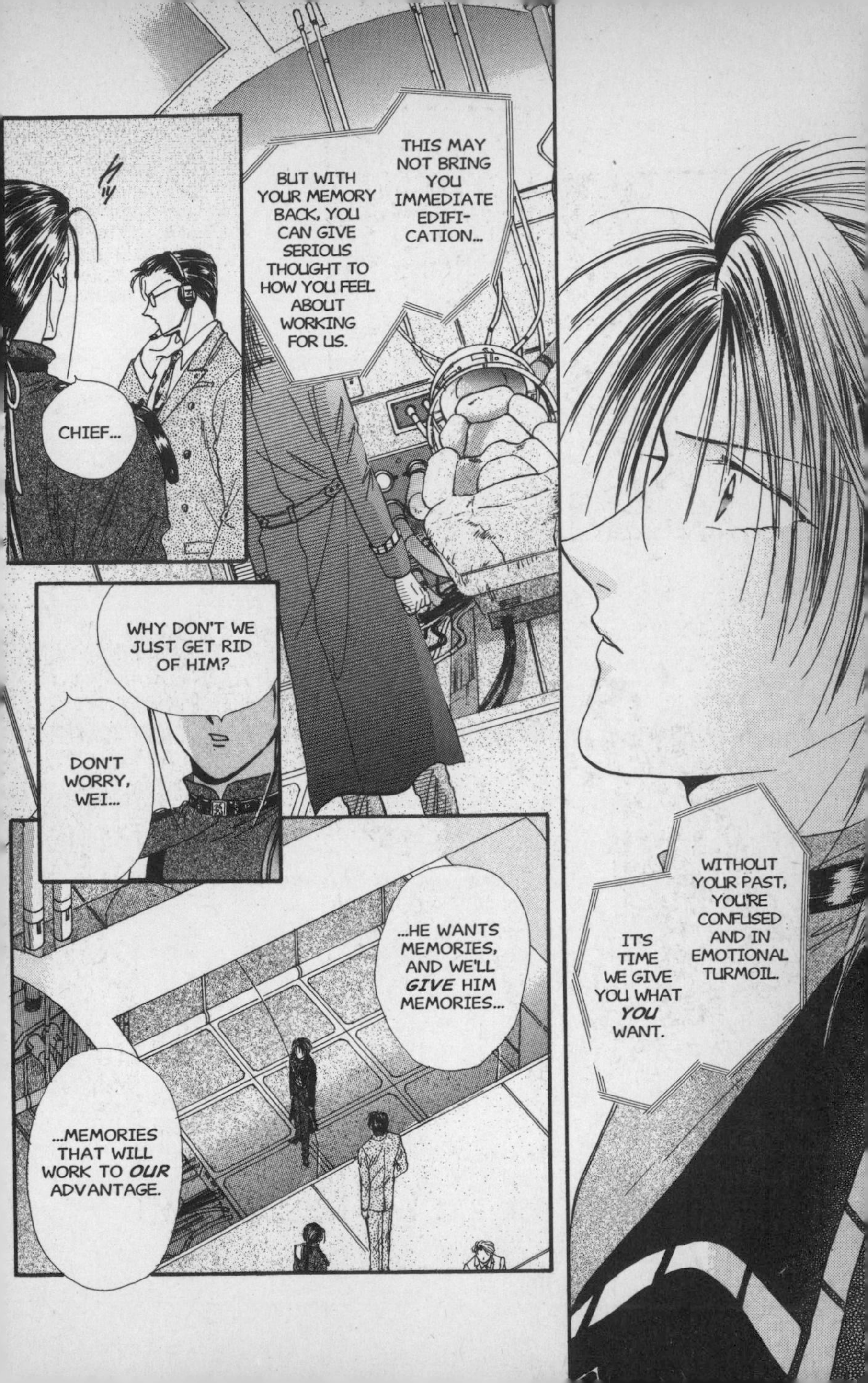
WITHOUT YOUR PAST, YOU'RE CONFUSED AND IN EMOTIONAL TURMOIL.
IT'S TIME WE GIVE YOU WHAT *YOU* WANT.
THIS MAY NOT BRING YOU IMMEDIATE EDIFI-CATION...
BUT WITH YOUR MEMORY BACK, YOU CAN GIVE SERIOUS THOUGHT TO HOW YOU FEEL ABOUT WORKING FOR US.
CHIEF...
WHY DON'T WE JUST GET RID OF HIM?
DON'T WORRY, WEI...
...HE WANTS MEMORIES, AND WE'LL *GIVE* HIM MEMORIES...
...MEMORIES THAT WILL WORK TO *OUR* ADVANTAGE.

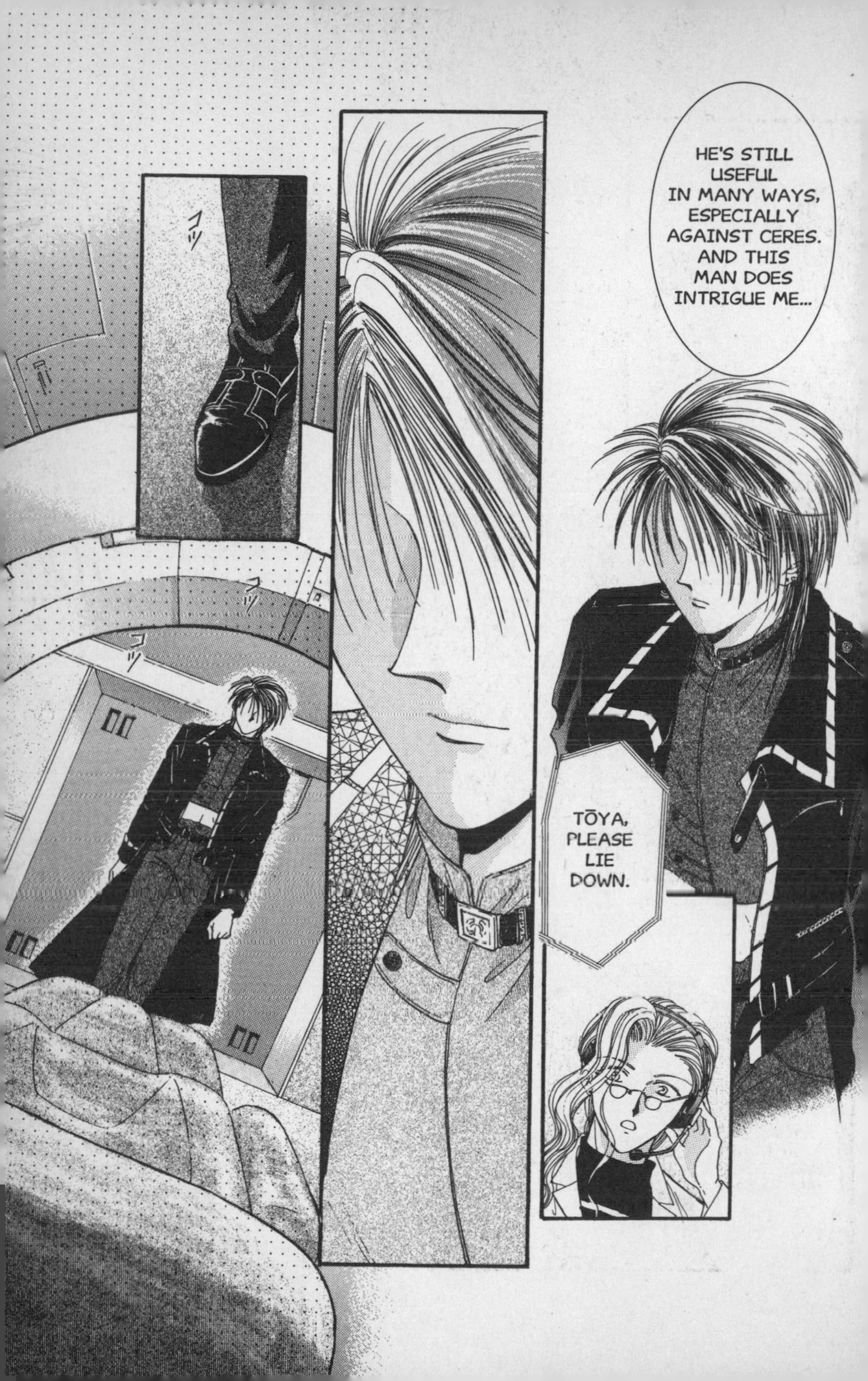
HE'S STILL USEFUL IN MANY WAYS, ESPECIALLY AGAINST CERES. AND THIS MAN DOES INTRIGUE ME...
TŌYA, PLEASE LIE DOWN.
コツ
コツ
コツ

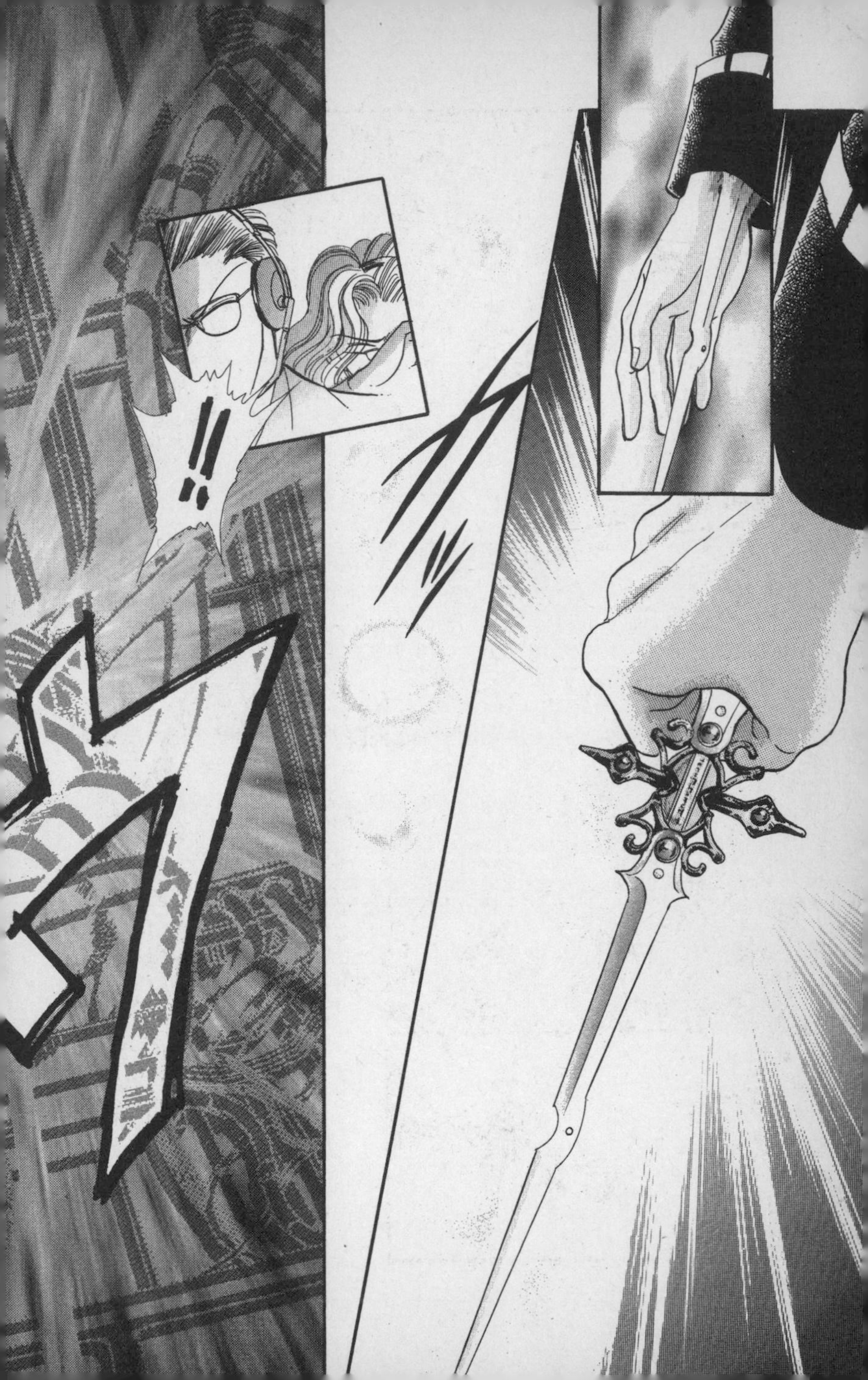
!!

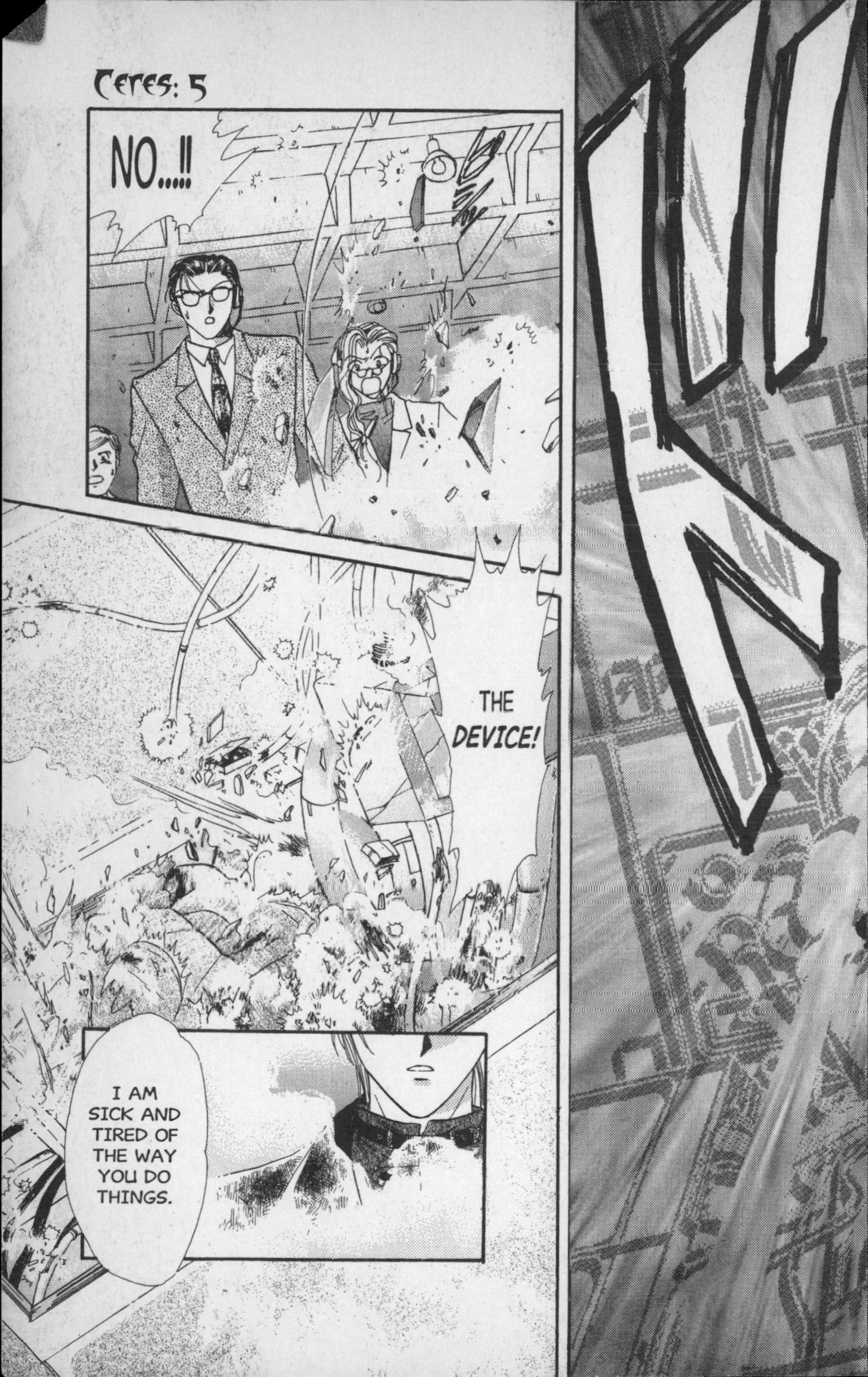
NO...!!
THE DEVICE!
I AM SICK AND TIRED OF THE WAY YOU DO THINGS.

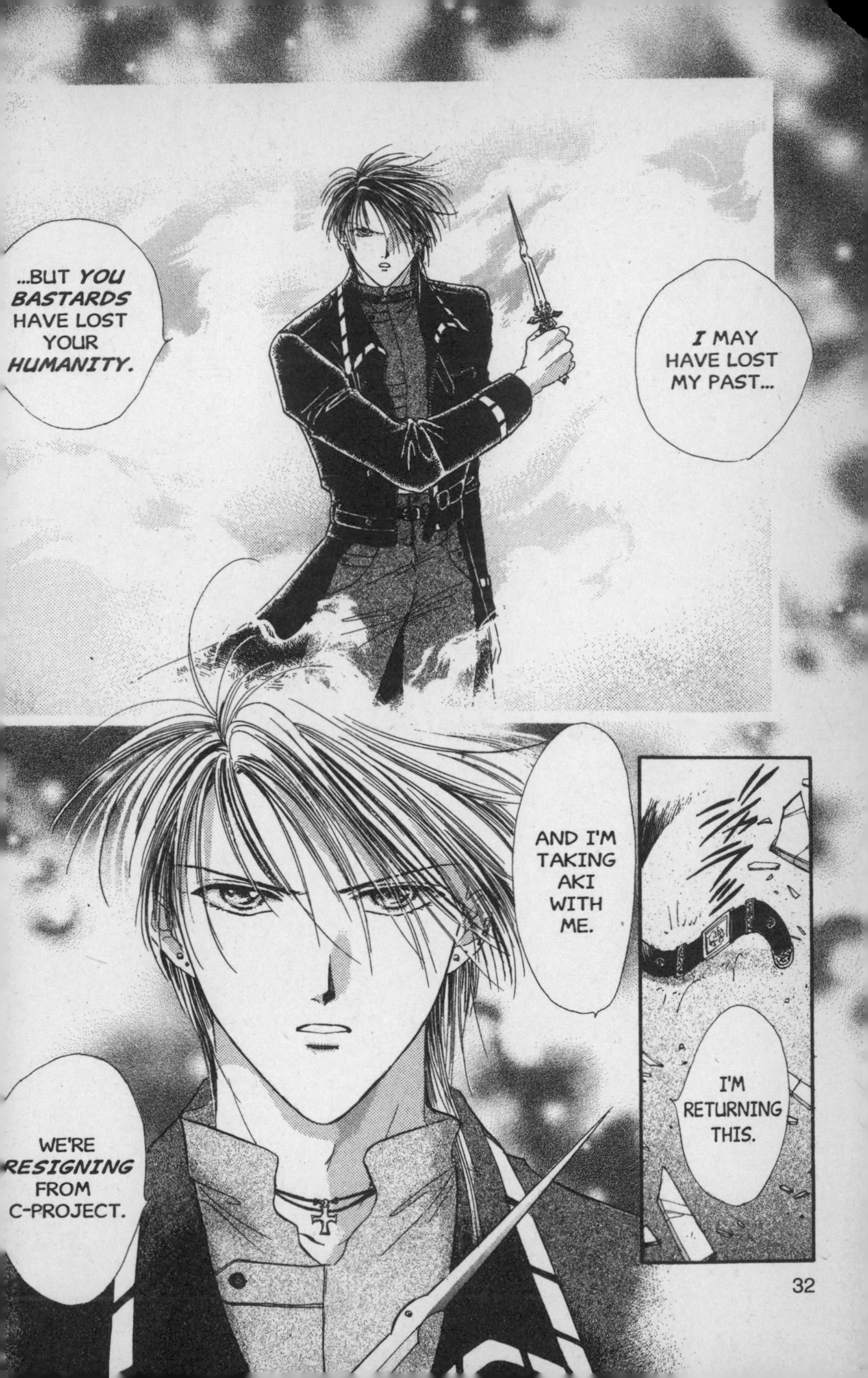
I MAY HAVE LOST MY PAST...
...BUT *YOU BASTARDS* HAVE LOST YOUR *HUMANITY.*
I'M RETURNING THIS.
AND I'M TAKING AKI WITH ME.
WE'RE *RESIGNING* FROM C-PROJECT.

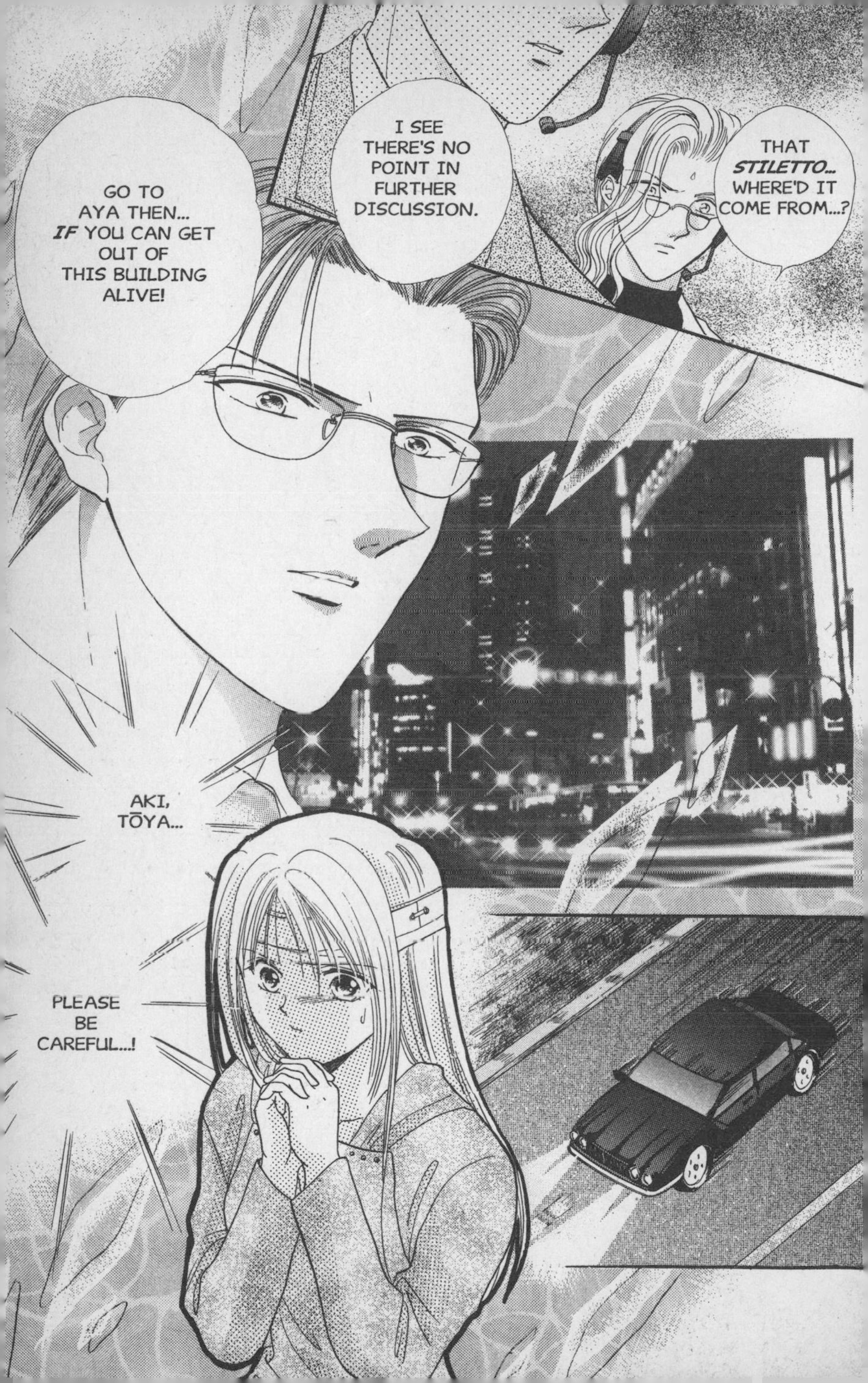
THAT *STILETTO...* WHERE'D IT COME FROM...?
I SEE THERE'S NO POINT IN FURTHER DISCUSSION.
GO TO AYA THEN... *IF* YOU CAN GET OUT OF THIS BUILDING ALIVE!
AKI, TŌYA...
PLEASE BE CAREFUL...!

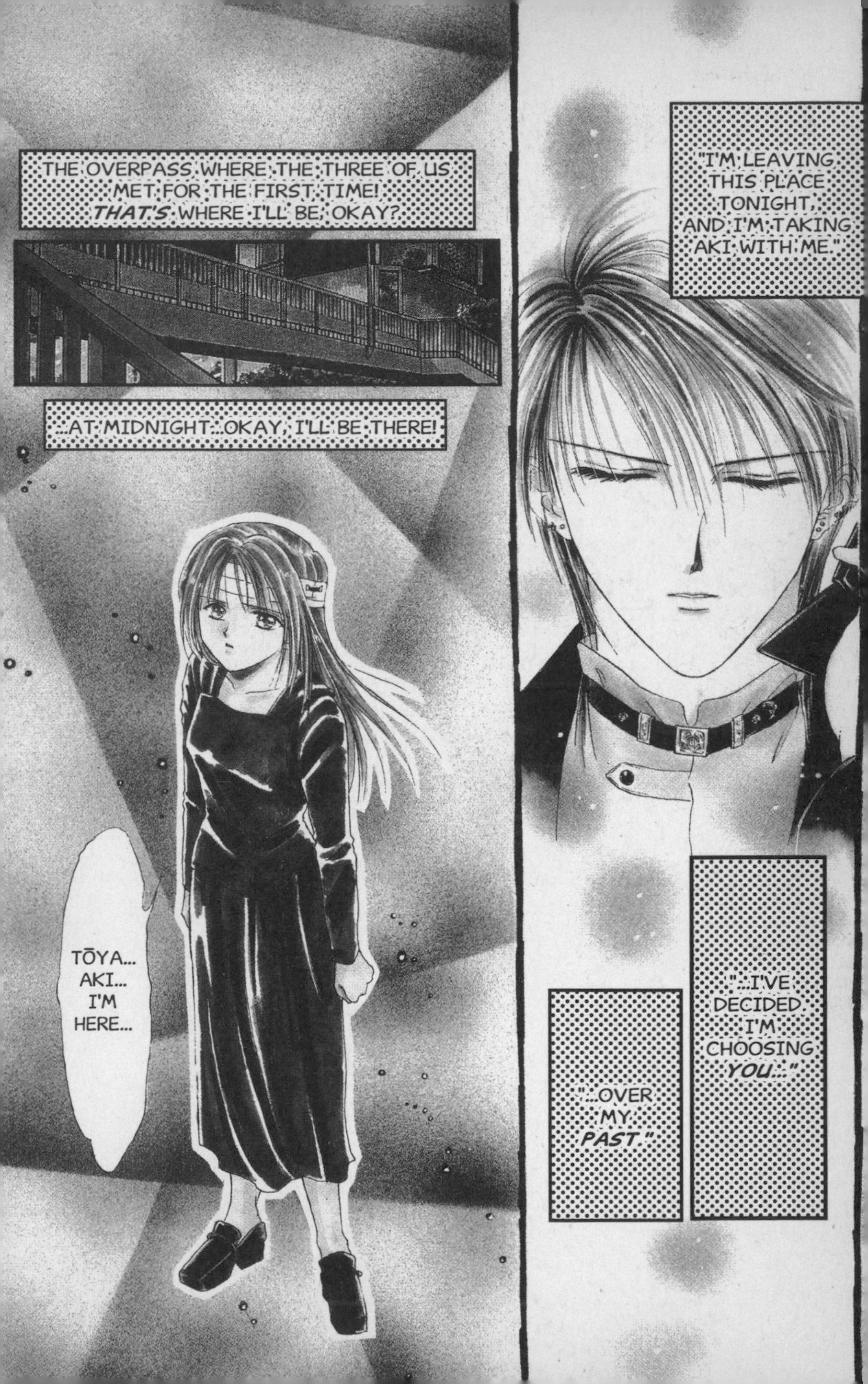
"I'M LEAVING THIS PLACE TONIGHT, AND I'M TAKING AKI WITH ME."
"...I'VE DECIDED I'M CHOOSING *YOU*..."
"...OVER MY *PAST*."
THE OVERPASS WHERE THE THREE OF US MET FOR THE FIRST TIME! *THAT'S* WHERE I'LL BE, OKAY?
...AT MIDNIGHT...OKAY, I'LL BE THERE!
TŌYA... AKI... I'M HERE...

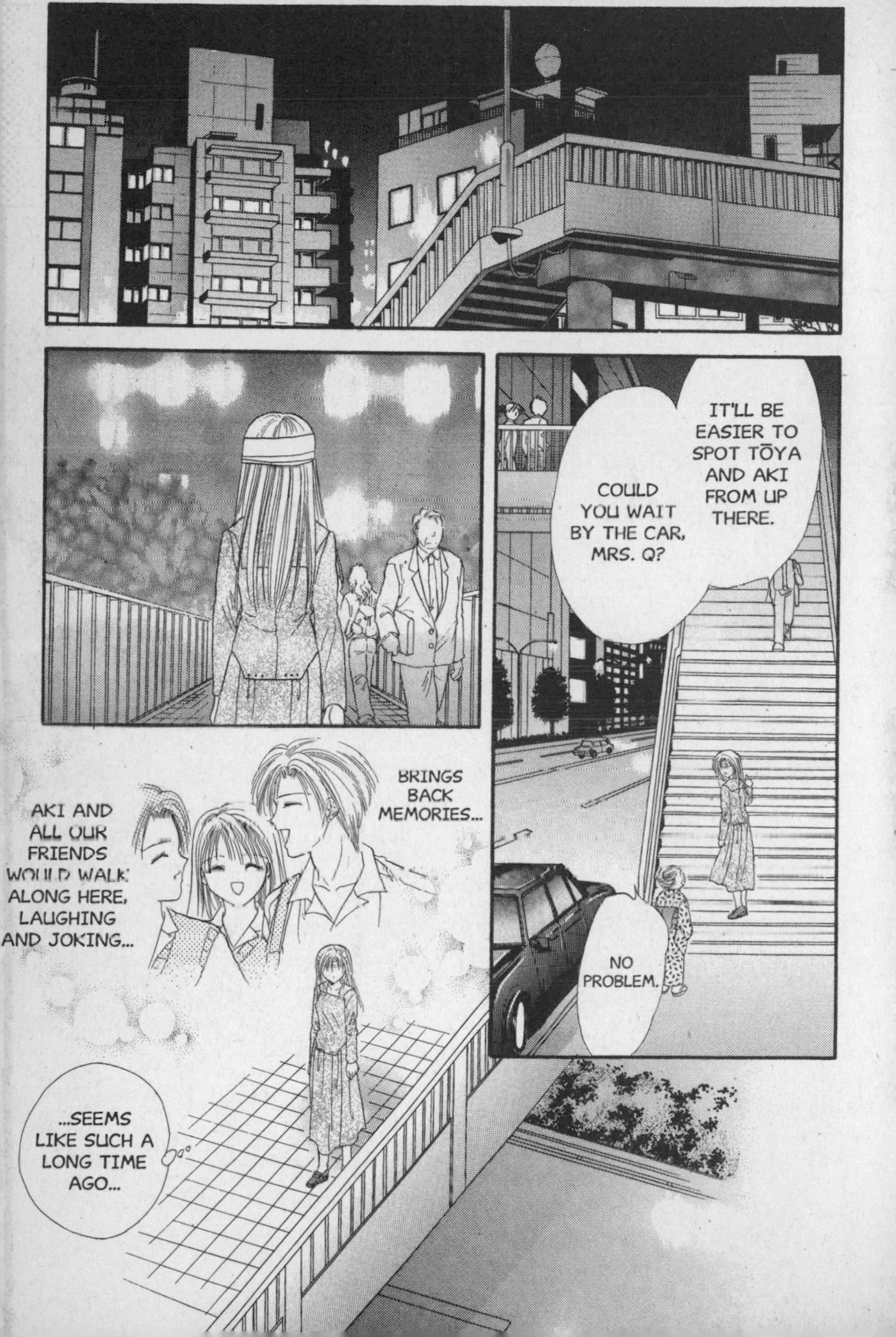
IT'LL BE EASIER TO SPOT TŌYA AND AKI FROM UP THERE.
COULD YOU WAIT BY THE CAR, MRS. Q?
NO PROBLEM.
BRINGS BACK MEMORIES...
AKI AND ALL OUR FRIENDS WOULD WALK ALONG HERE, LAUGHING AND JOKING...
...SEEMS LIKE SUCH A LONG TIME AGO...

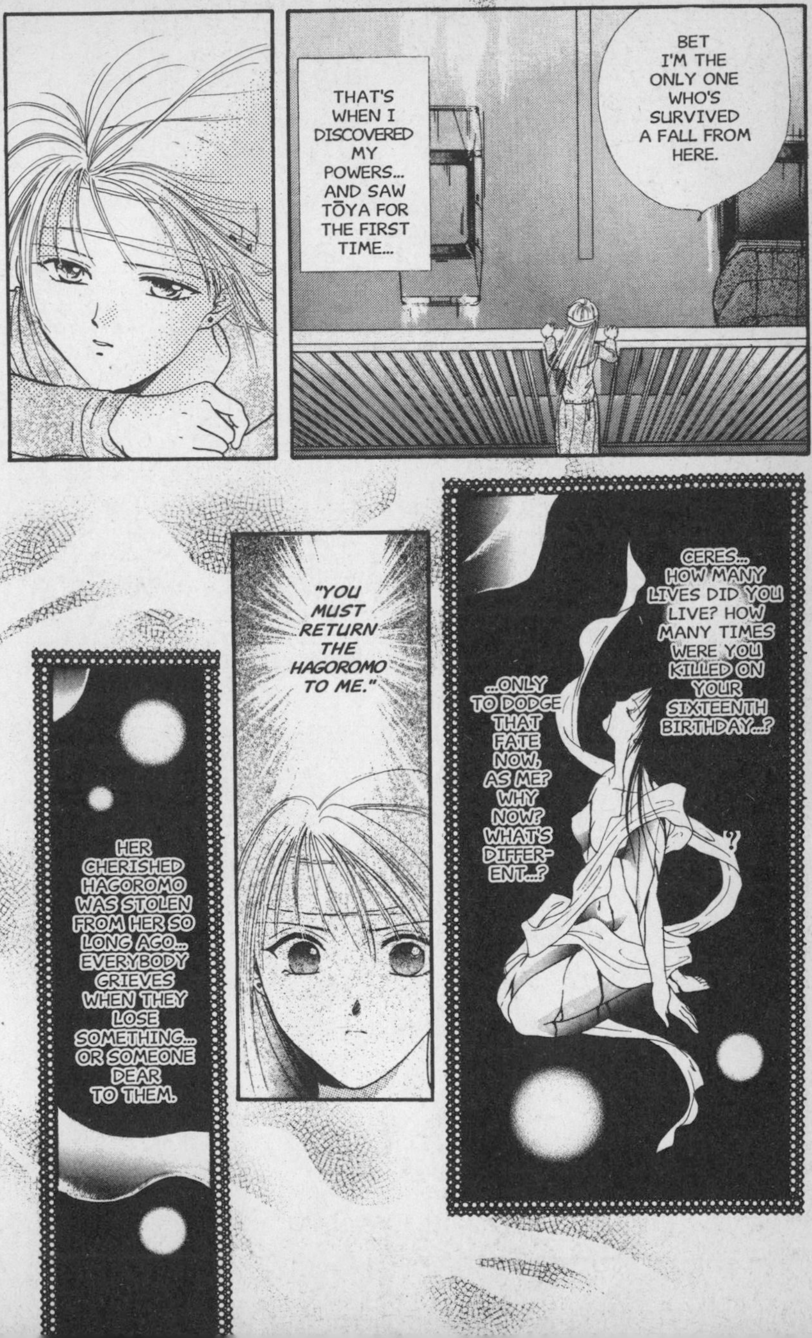
BET I'M THE ONLY ONE WHO'S SURVIVED A FALL FROM HERE.
THAT'S WHEN I DISCOVERED MY POWERS... AND SAW TŌYA FOR THE FIRST TIME...
CERES... HOW MANY LIVES DID YOU LIVE? HOW MANY TIMES WERE YOU KILLED ON YOUR SIXTEENTH BIRTHDAY...?
...ONLY TO DODGE THAT FATE NOW, AS ME? WHY NOW? WHAT'S DIFFER-ENT...?
"YOU MUST RETURN THE HAGOROMO TO ME."
HER CHERISHED HAGOROMO WAS STOLEN FROM HER SO LONG AGO... EVERYBODY GRIEVES WHEN THEY LOSE SOMETHING... OR SOMEONE DEAR TO THEM.

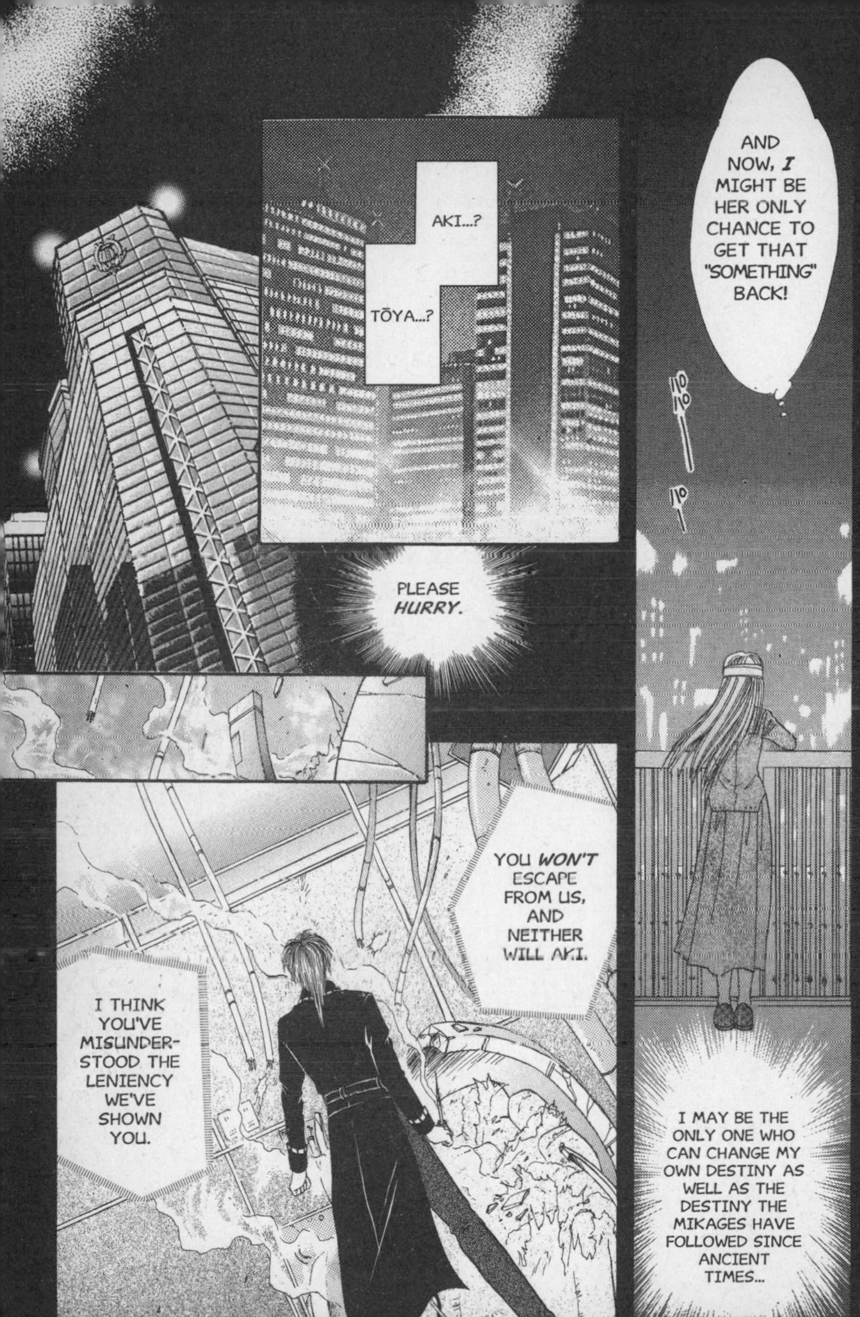
AND NOW, I MIGHT BE HER ONLY CHANCE TO GET THAT "SOMETHING" BACK!
I MAY BE THE ONLY ONE WHO CAN CHANGE MY OWN DESTINY AS WELL AS THE DESTINY THE MIKAGES HAVE FOLLOWED SINCE ANCIENT TIMES...
AKI...?
TŌYA...?
PLEASE HURRY.
YOU WON'T ESCAPE FROM US, AND NEITHER WILL AKI.
I THINK YOU'VE MISUNDER-STOOD THE LENIENCY WE'VE SHOWN YOU.

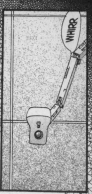

WHIRR

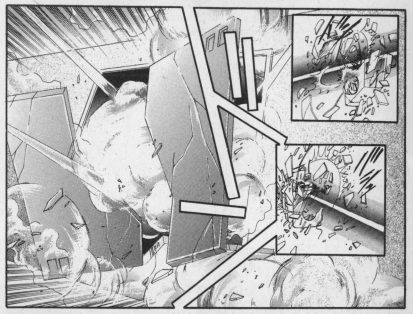

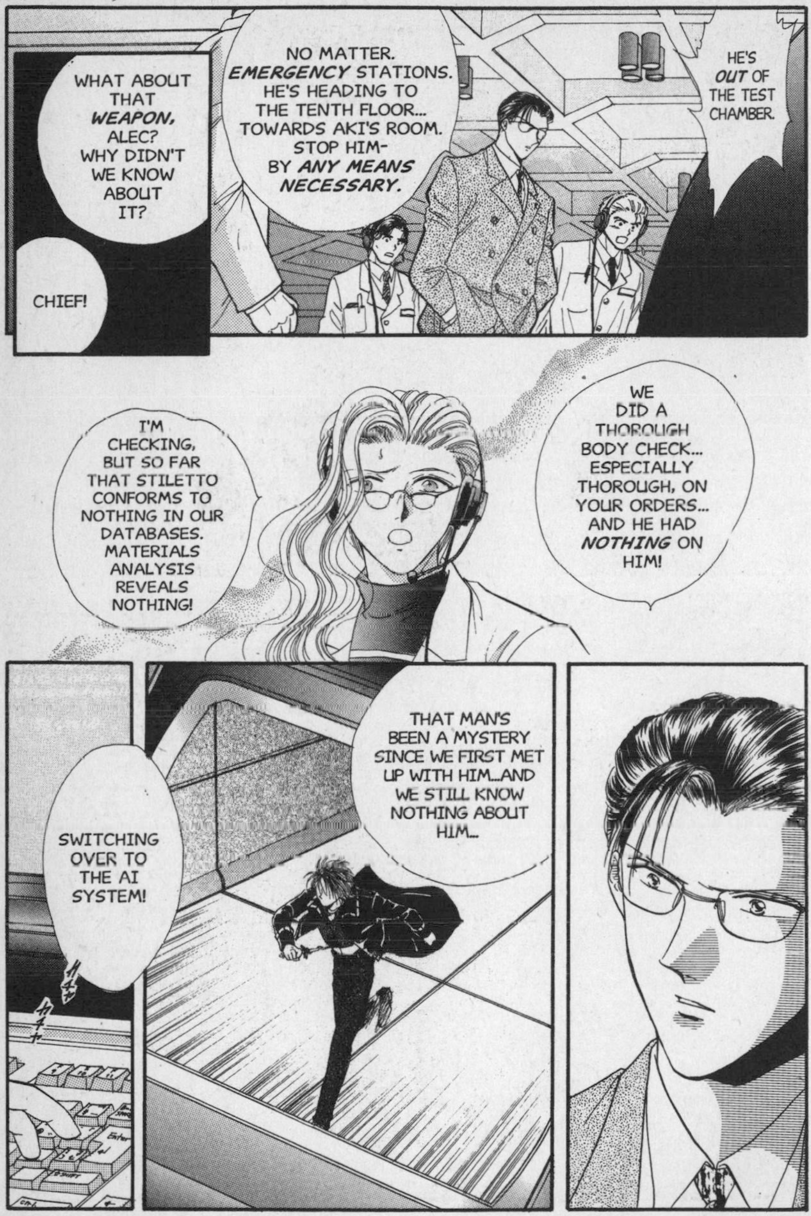
HE'S OUT OF THE TEST CHAMBER.
NO MATTER. EMERGENCY STATIONS. HE'S HEADING TO THE TENTH FLOOR... TOWARDS AKI'S ROOM. STOP HIM- BY ANY MEANS NECESSARY.
WHAT ABOUT THAT WEAPON, ALEC? WHY DIDN'T WE KNOW ABOUT IT?
CHIEF!
WE DID A THOROUGH BODY CHECK... ESPECIALLY THOROUGH, ON YOUR ORDERS... AND HE HAD NOTHING ON HIM!
I'M CHECKING, BUT SO FAR THAT STILETTO CONFORMS TO NOTHING IN OUR DATABASES. MATERIALS ANALYSIS REVEALS NOTHING!
THAT MAN'S BEEN A MYSTERY SINCE WE FIRST MET UP WITH HIM...AND WE STILL KNOW NOTHING ABOUT HIM...
SWITCHING OVER TO THE AI SYSTEM!

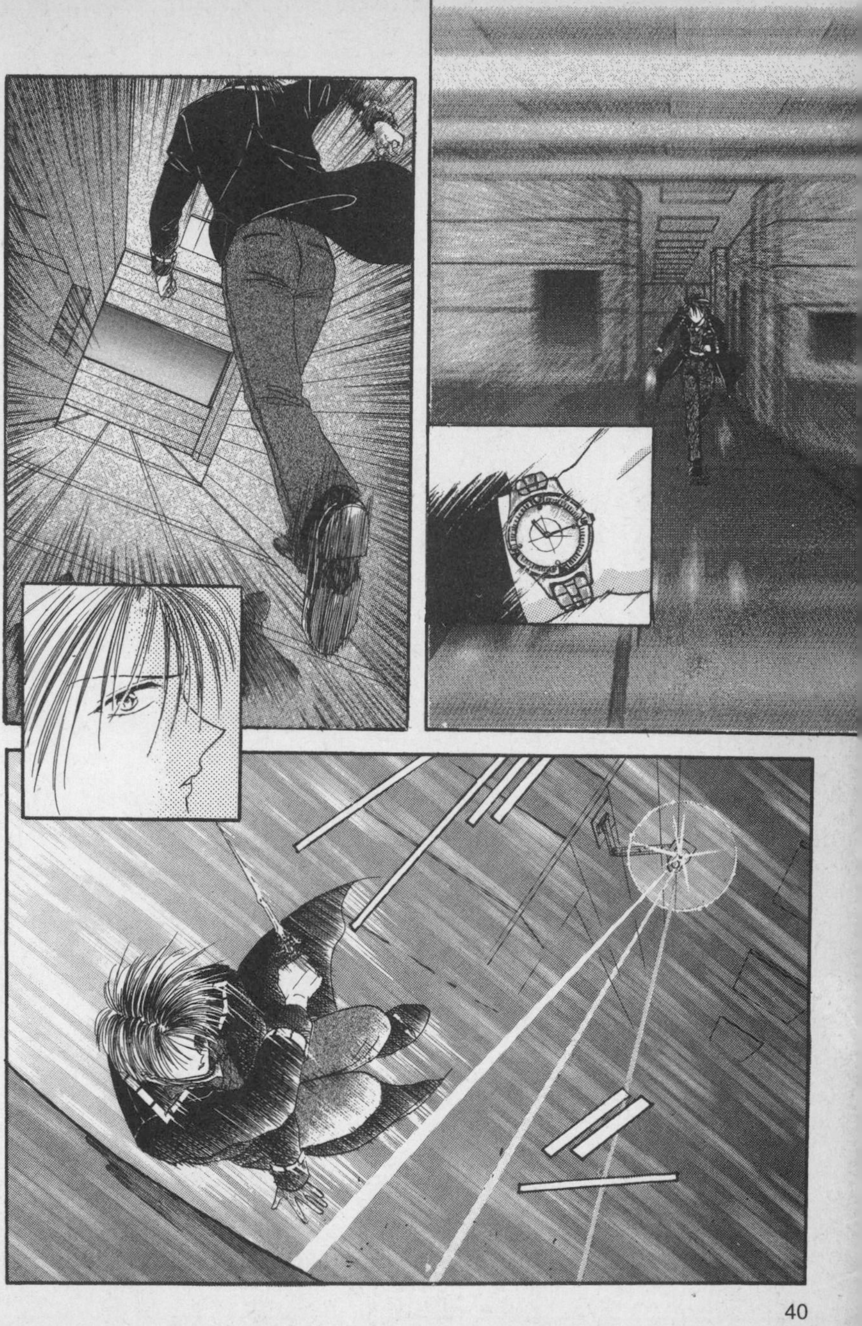

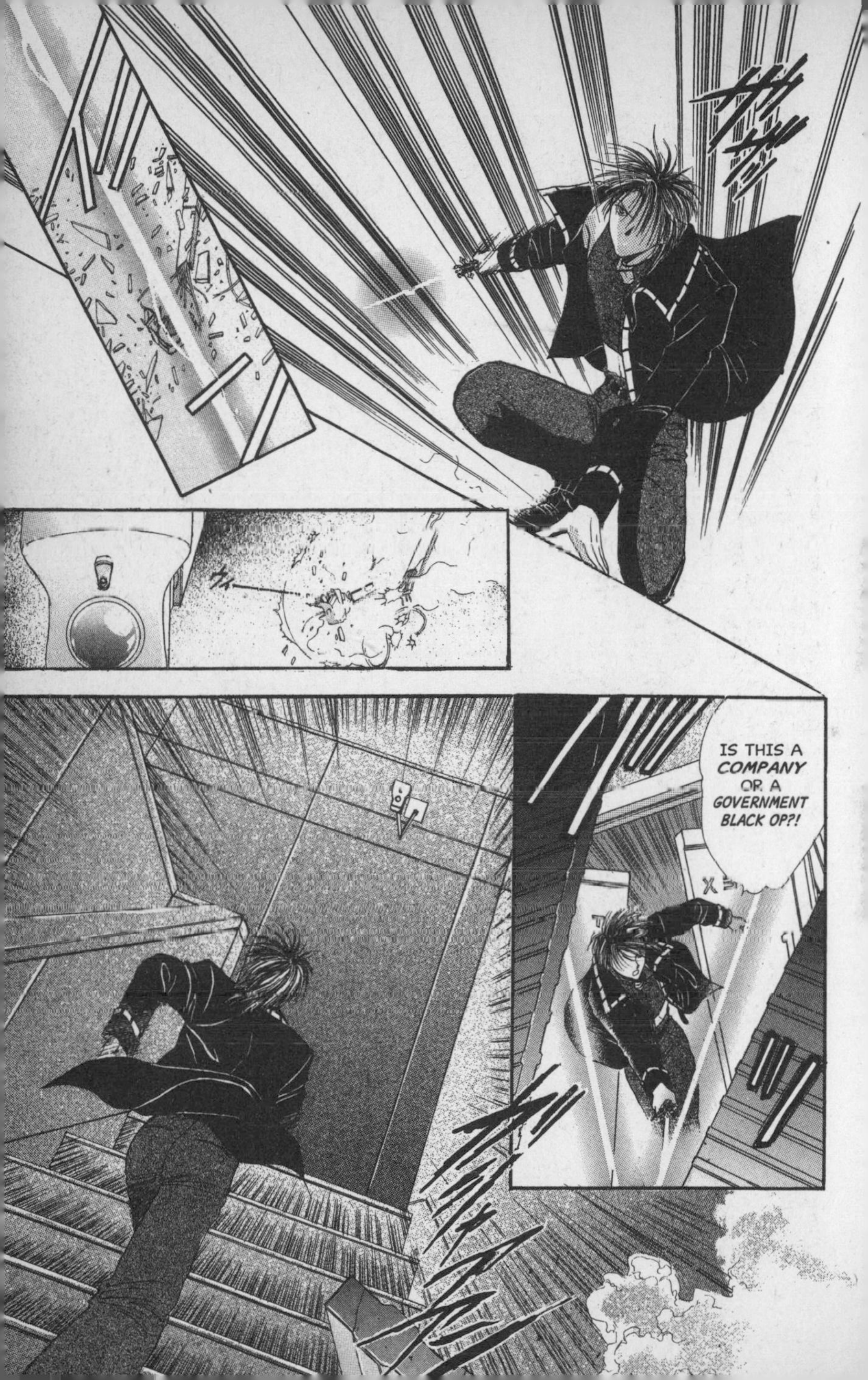
IS THIS A *COMPANY* OR A *GOVERNMENT BLACK OP?!*

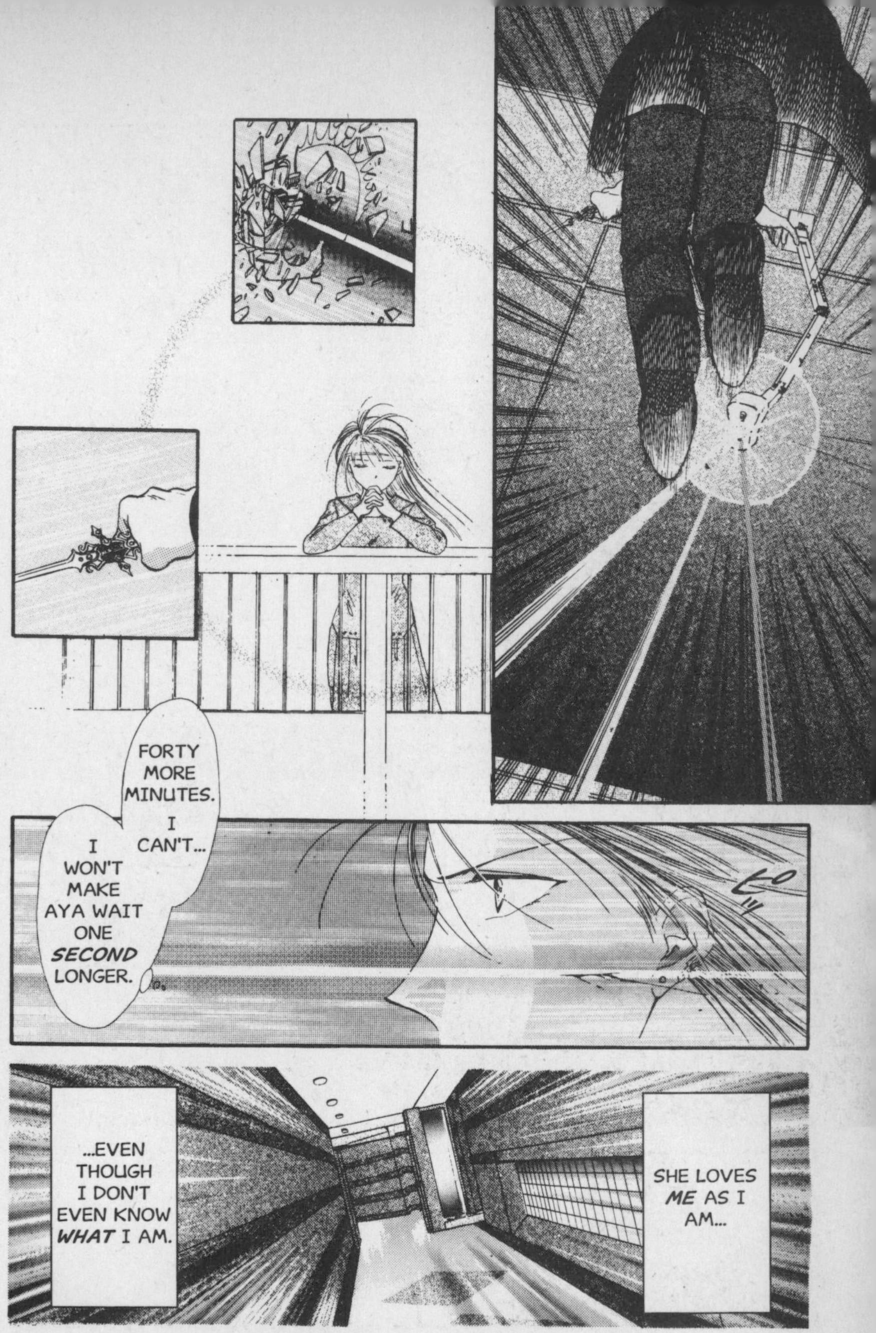
FORTY MORE MINUTES.
I CAN'T... I WON'T MAKE AYA WAIT ONE *SECOND* LONGER.
SHE LOVES *ME* AS I AM...
...EVEN THOUGH I DON'T EVEN KNOW *WHAT* I AM.

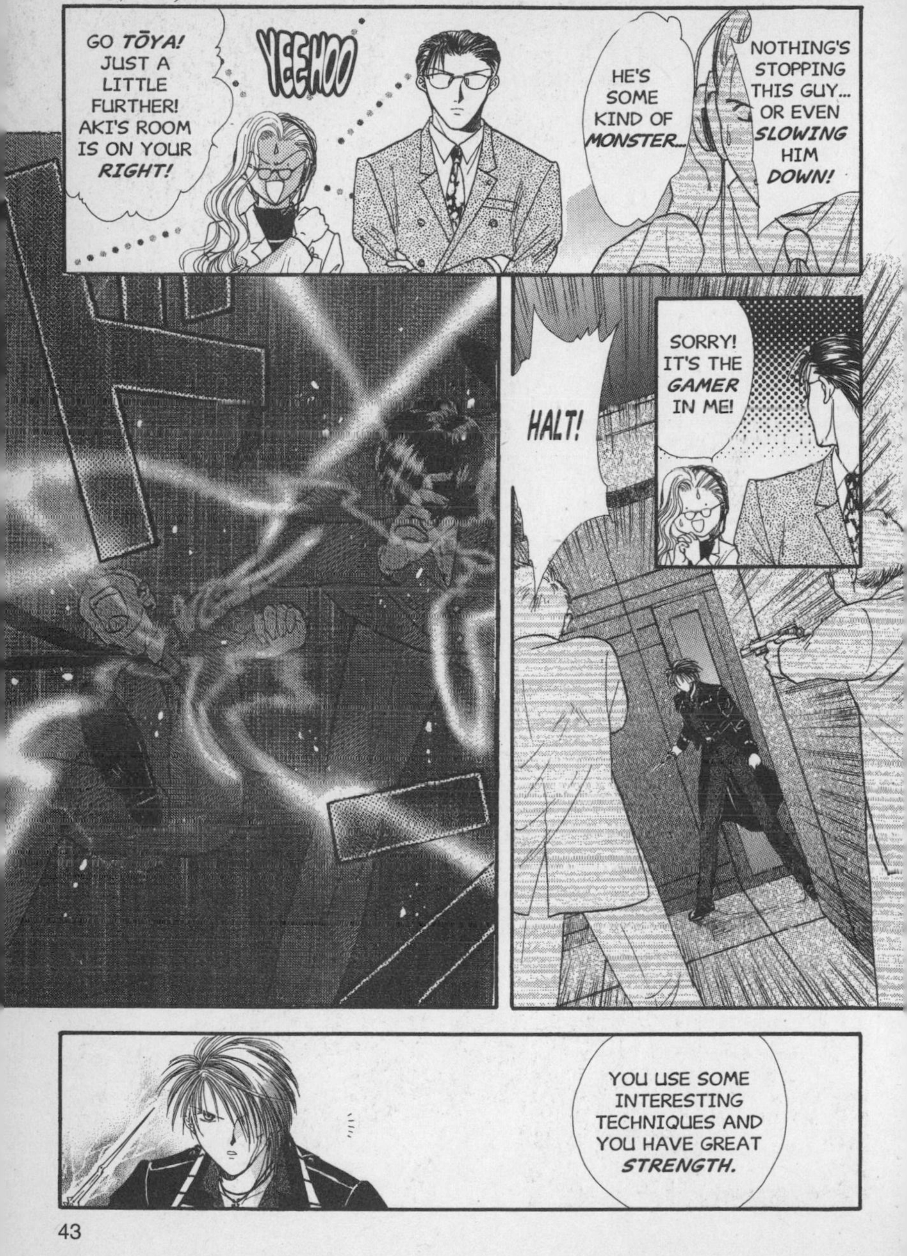
NOTHING'S STOPPING THIS GUY... OR EVEN SLOWING HIM DOWN!
HE'S SOME KIND OF MONSTER...
YEEHOO
GO TŌYA! JUST A LITTLE FURTHER! AKI'S ROOM IS ON YOUR RIGHT!
SORRY! IT'S THE GAMER IN ME!
HALT!
YOU USE SOME INTERESTING TECHNIQUES AND YOU HAVE GREAT STRENGTH.

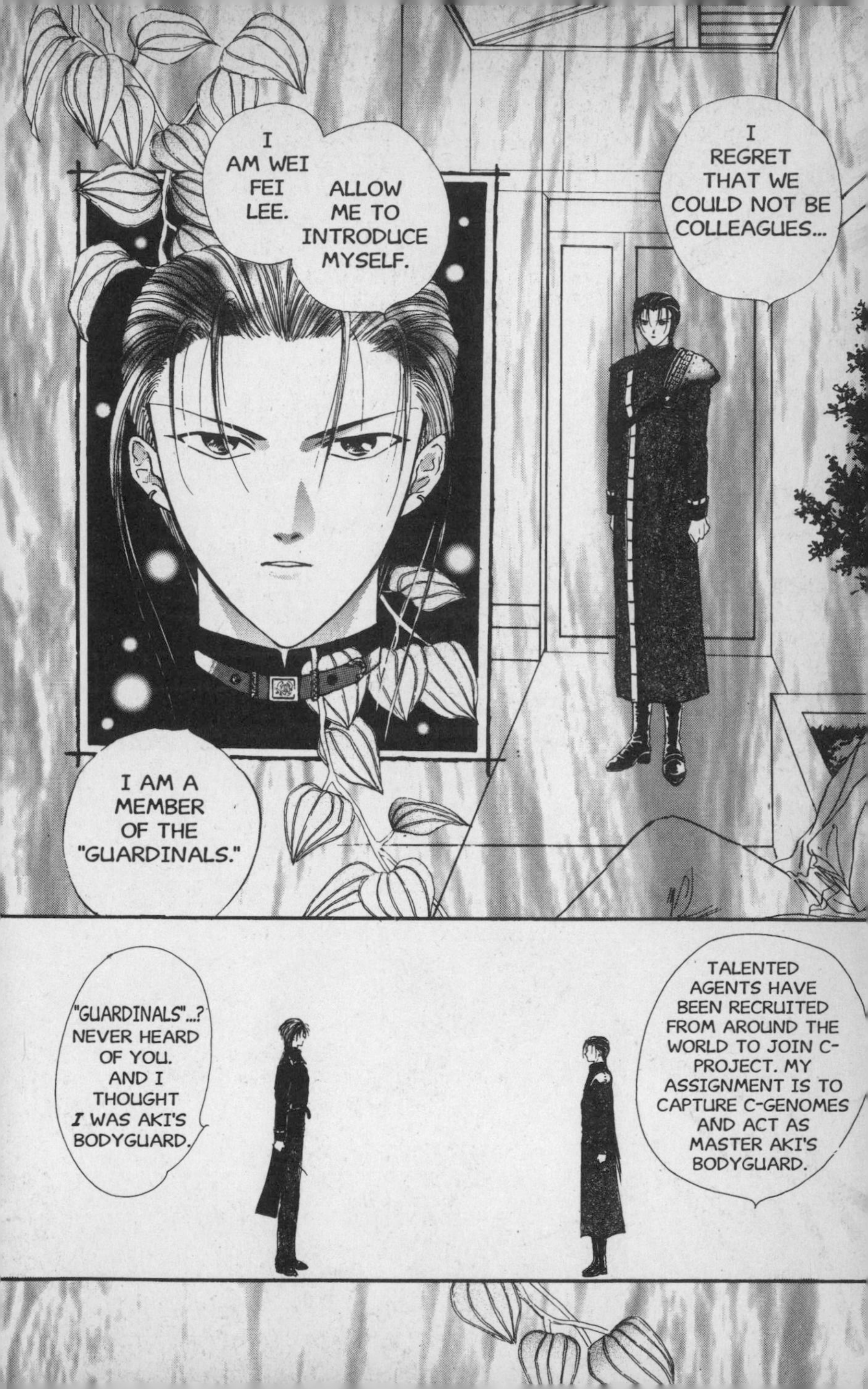
I REGRET THAT WE COULD NOT BE COLLEAGUES...
I AM WEI FEI LEE. ALLOW ME TO INTRODUCE MYSELF.
I AM A MEMBER OF THE "GUARDINALS."
TALENTED AGENTS HAVE BEEN RECRUITED FROM AROUND THE WORLD TO JOIN C-PROJECT. MY ASSIGNMENT IS TO CAPTURE C-GENOMES AND ACT AS MASTER AKI'S BODYGUARD.
"GUARDINALS"...? NEVER HEARD OF YOU. AND I THOUGHT *I* WAS AKI'S BODYGUARD.

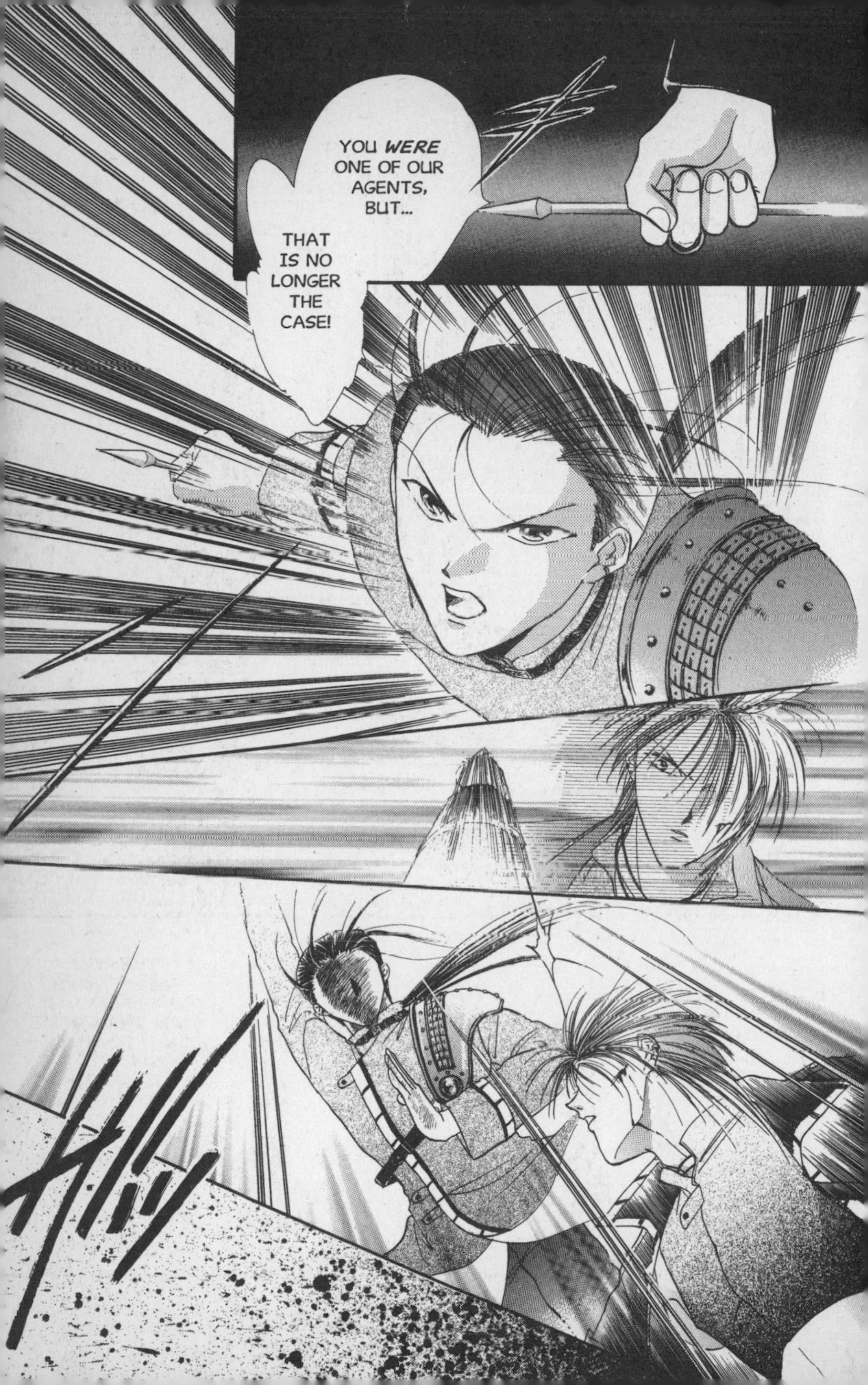
YOU WERE ONE OF OUR AGENTS, BUT...
THAT IS NO LONGER THE CASE!

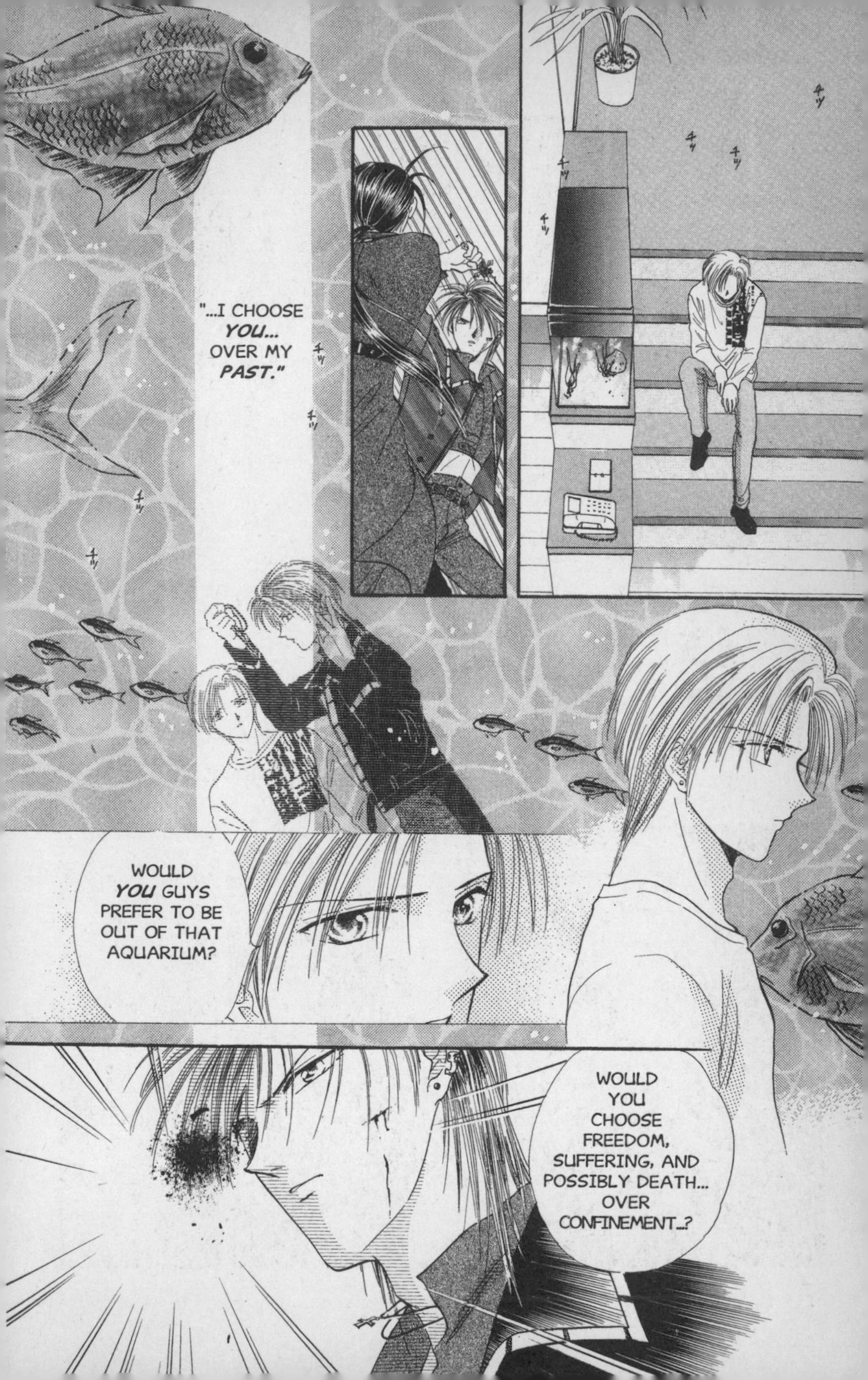
"...I CHOOSE *YOU*... OVER MY *PAST*."
WOULD *YOU* GUYS PREFER TO BE OUT OF THAT AQUARIUM?
WOULD YOU CHOOSE FREEDOM, SUFFERING, AND POSSIBLY DEATH... OVER CONFINEMENT...?

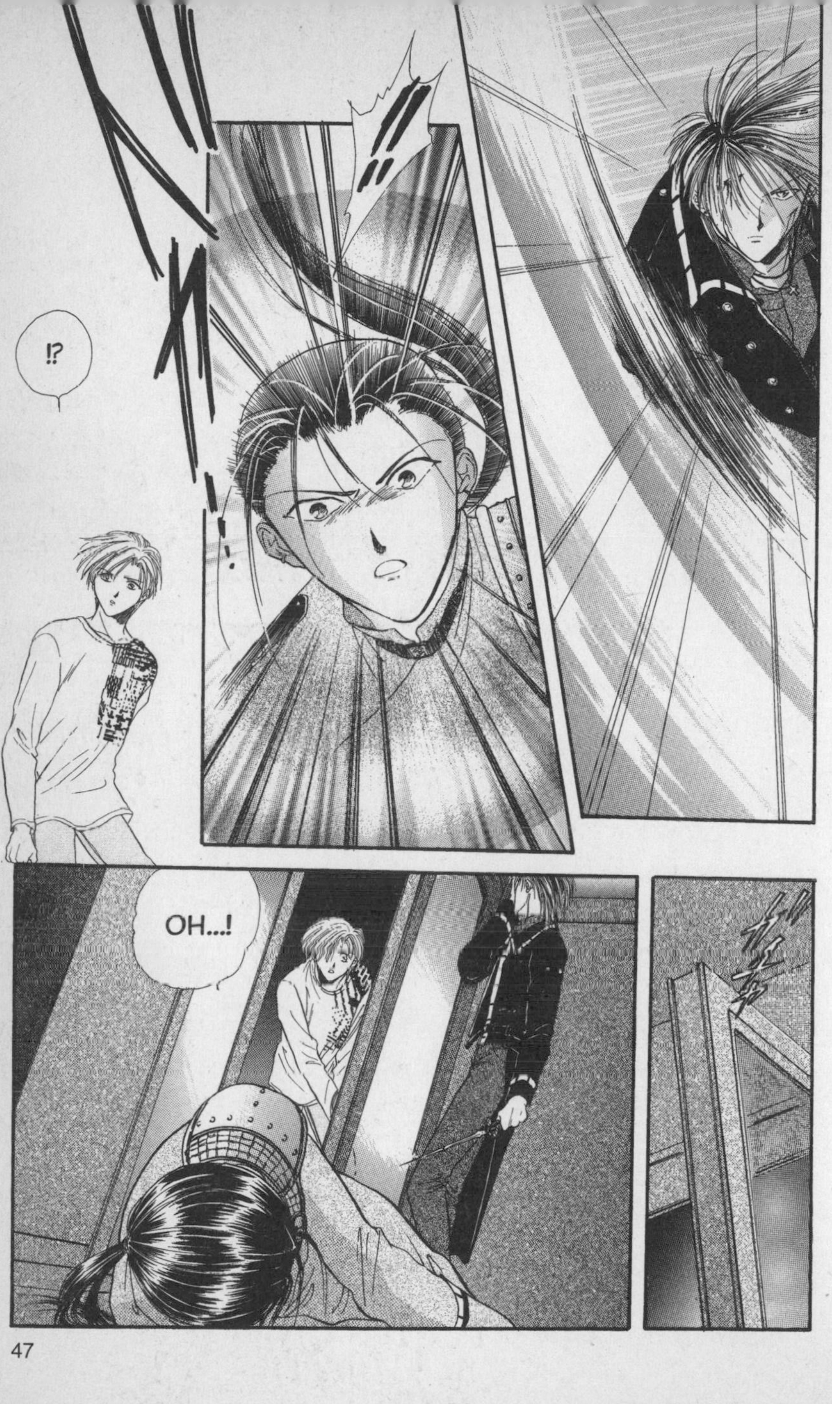
!?
OH...!

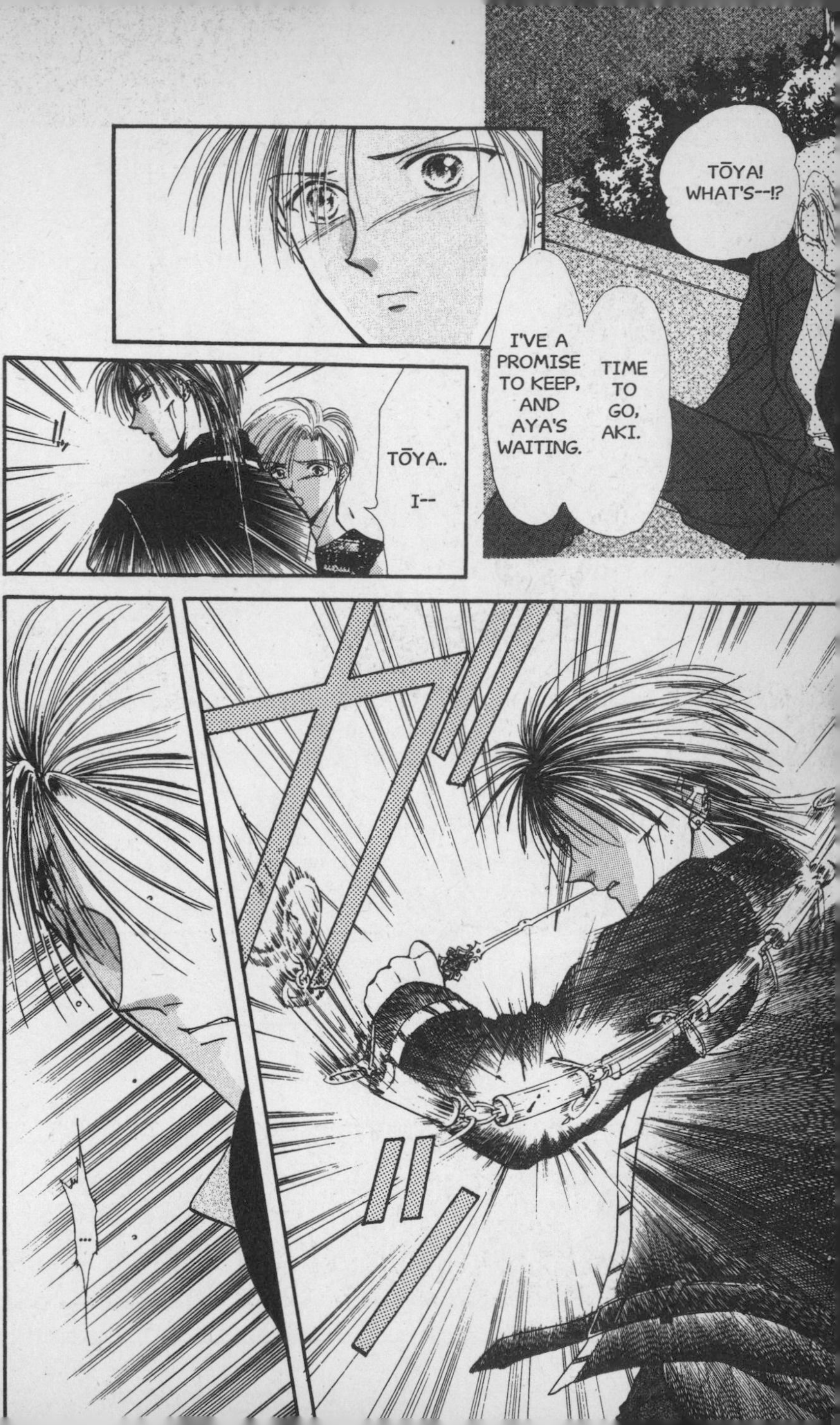
TŌYA! WHAT'S--!?
TIME TO GO, AKI.
I'VE A PROMISE TO KEEP, AND AYA'S WAITING.
TŌYA..
I--
...

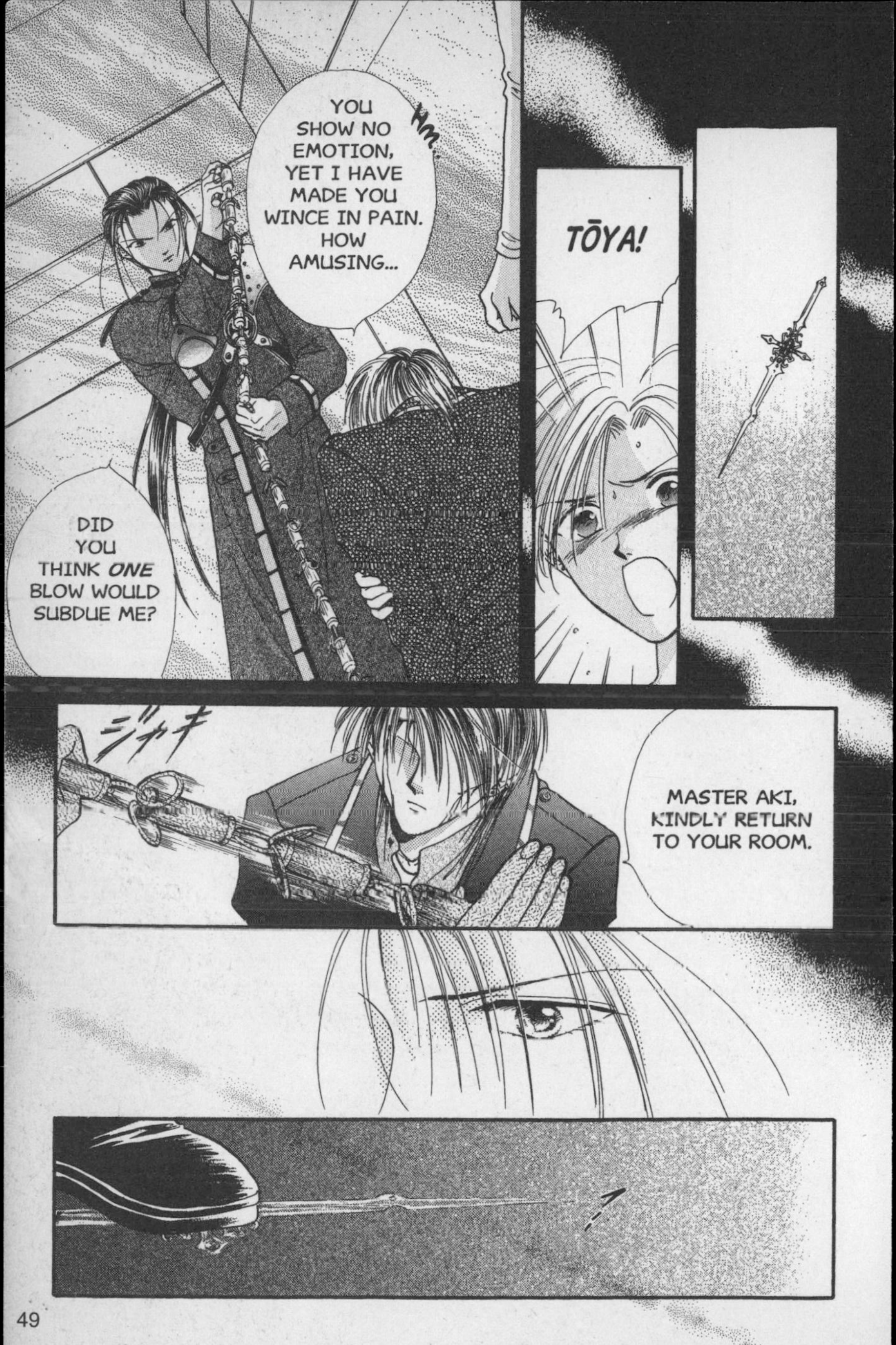
TŌYA!
YOU SHOW NO EMOTION, YET I HAVE MADE YOU WINCE IN PAIN. HOW AMUSING...
Hm
DID YOU THINK *ONE* BLOW WOULD SUBDUE ME?
MASTER AKI, KINDLY RETURN TO YOUR ROOM.
ジャキ

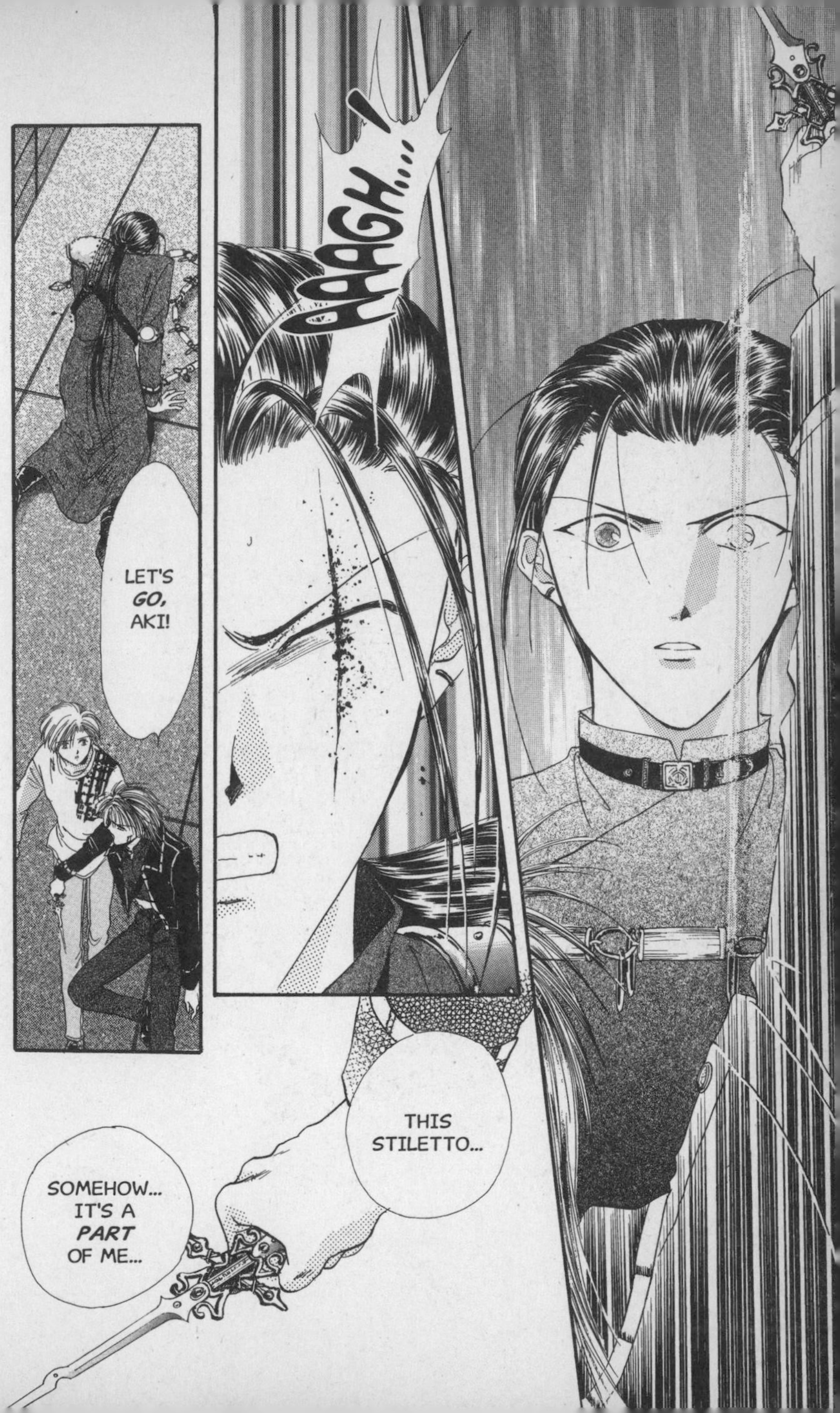
THIS STILETTO...
SOMEHOW... IT'S A *PART* OF ME...
AAAGH...!
LET'S *GO,* AKI!

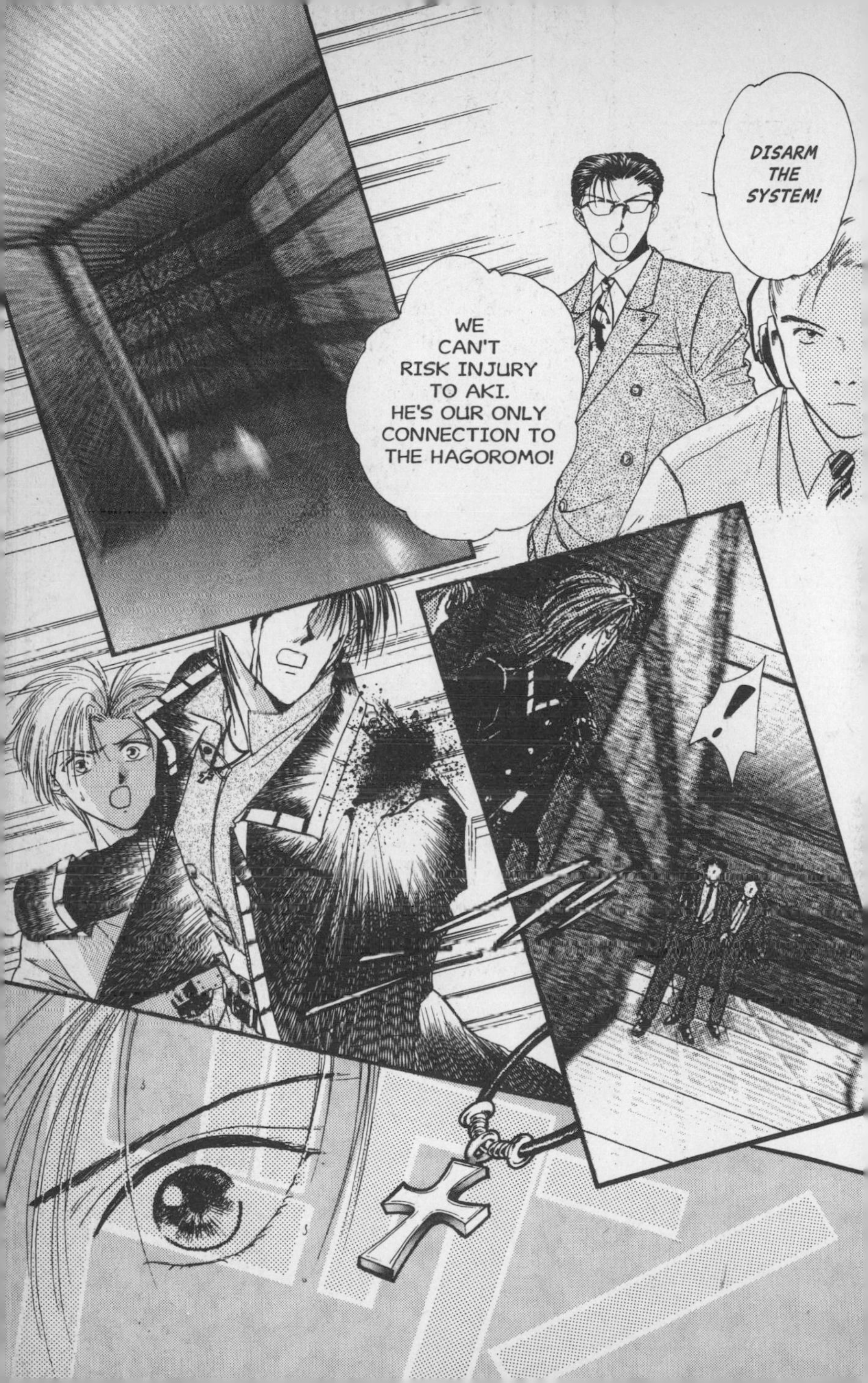
DISARM THE SYSTEM!
WE CAN'T RISK INJURY TO AKI. HE'S OUR ONLY CONNECTION TO THE HAGOROMO!
!

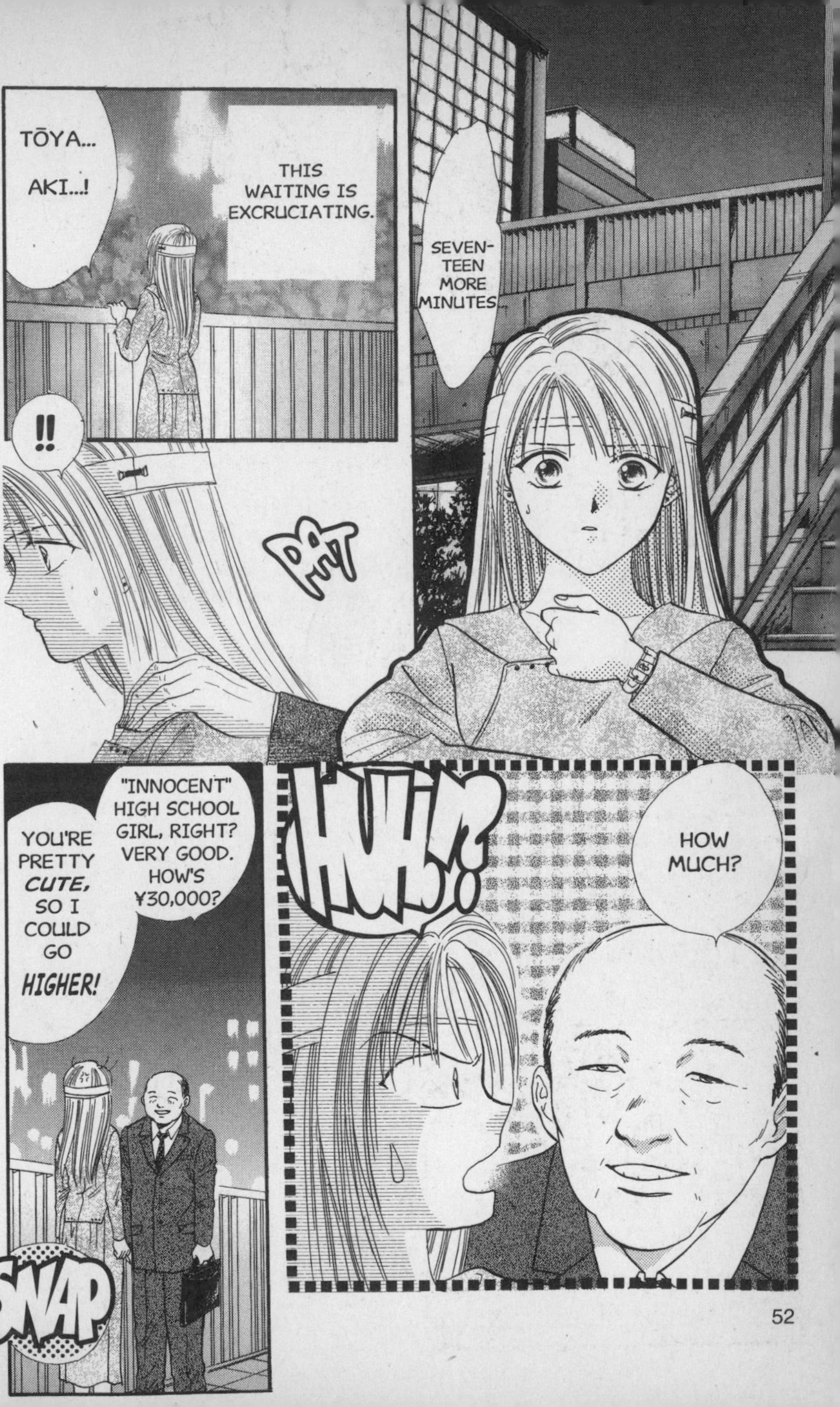
SEVEN-TEEN MORE MINUTES
THIS WAITING IS EXCRUCIATING.
TŌYA...
AKI...!
!!
HOW MUCH?
HUH!?
"INNOCENT" HIGH SCHOOL GIRL, RIGHT? VERY GOOD. HOW'S ¥30,000?
YOU'RE PRETTY *CUTE,* SO I COULD GO *HIGHER!*
SNAP

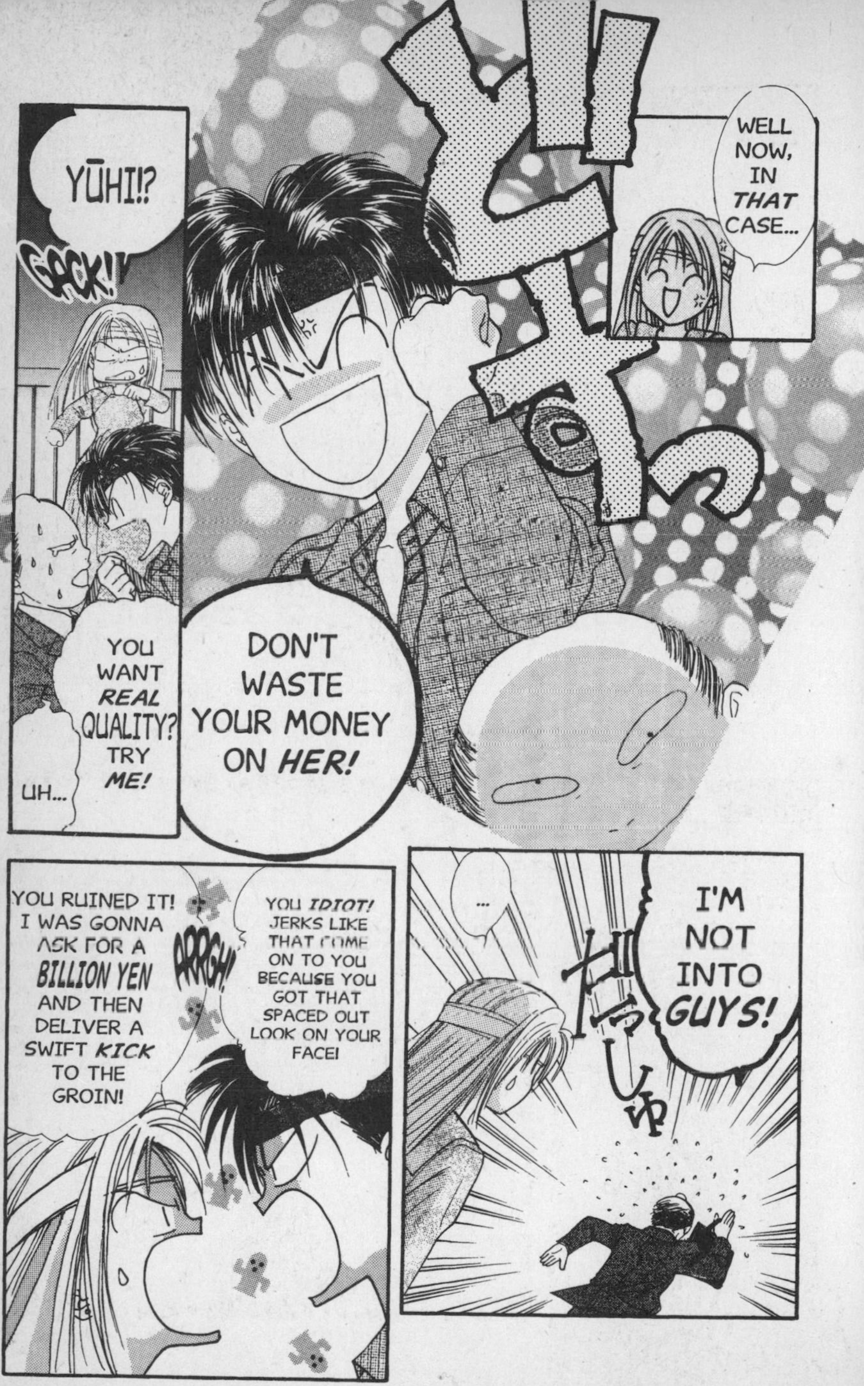

WELL NOW, IN *THAT* CASE...
DON'T WASTE YOUR MONEY ON *HER!*
YŪHI!?
GACK!
YOU WANT *REAL* QUALITY? TRY *ME!*
UH...
...
I'M NOT INTO *GUYS!*
YOU *IDIOT!* JERKS LIKE THAT COME ON TO YOU BECAUSE YOU GOT THAT SPACED OUT LOOK ON YOUR FACE!
YOU RUINED IT! I WAS GONNA ASK FOR A BILLION YEN AND THEN DELIVER A SWIFT *KICK* TO THE GROIN!
ARRGH!

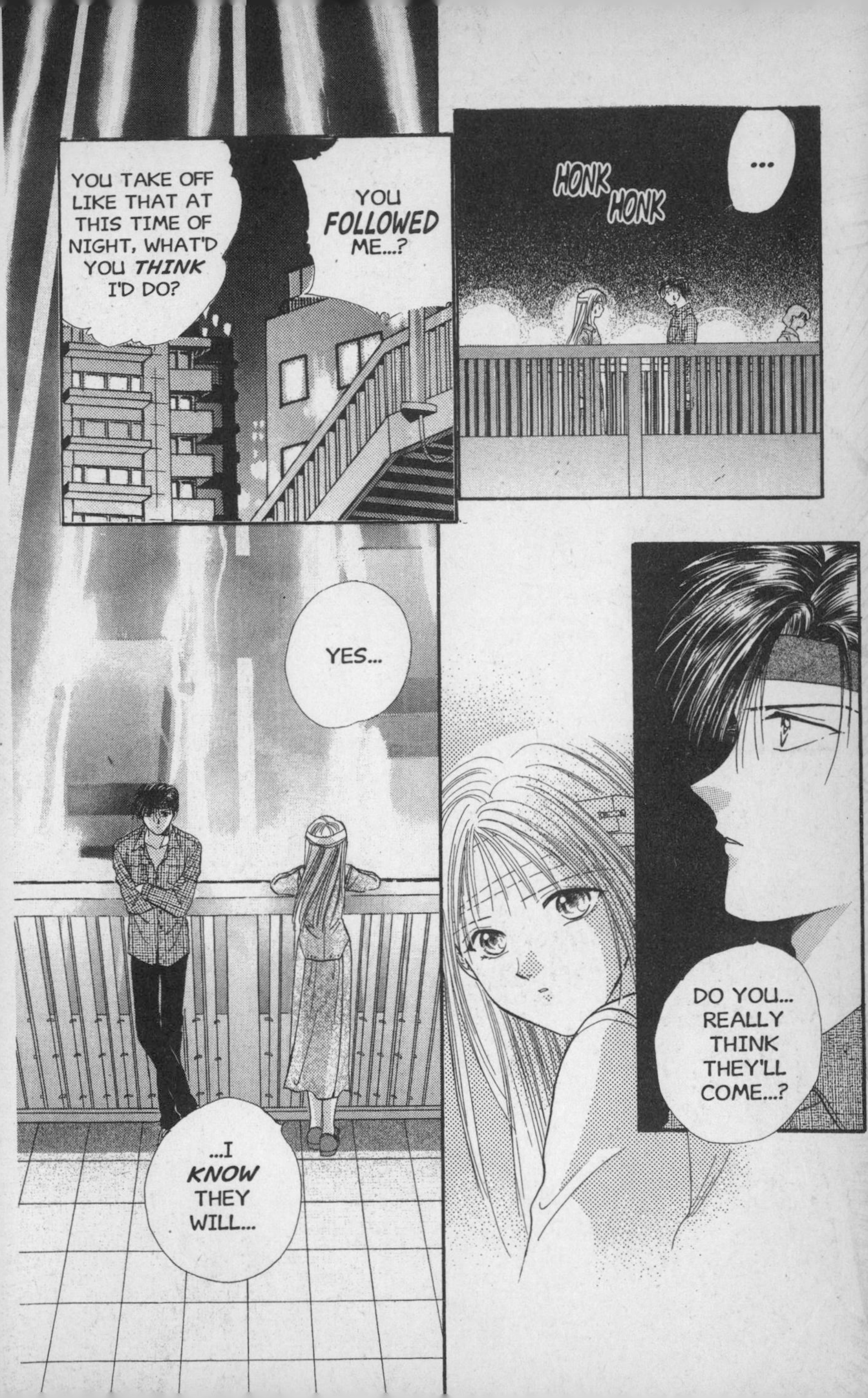
HONK HONK
...
YOU FOLLOWED ME...?
YOU TAKE OFF LIKE THAT AT THIS TIME OF NIGHT, WHAT'D YOU THINK I'D DO?
DO YOU... REALLY THINK THEY'LL COME...?
YES...
...I KNOW THEY WILL...

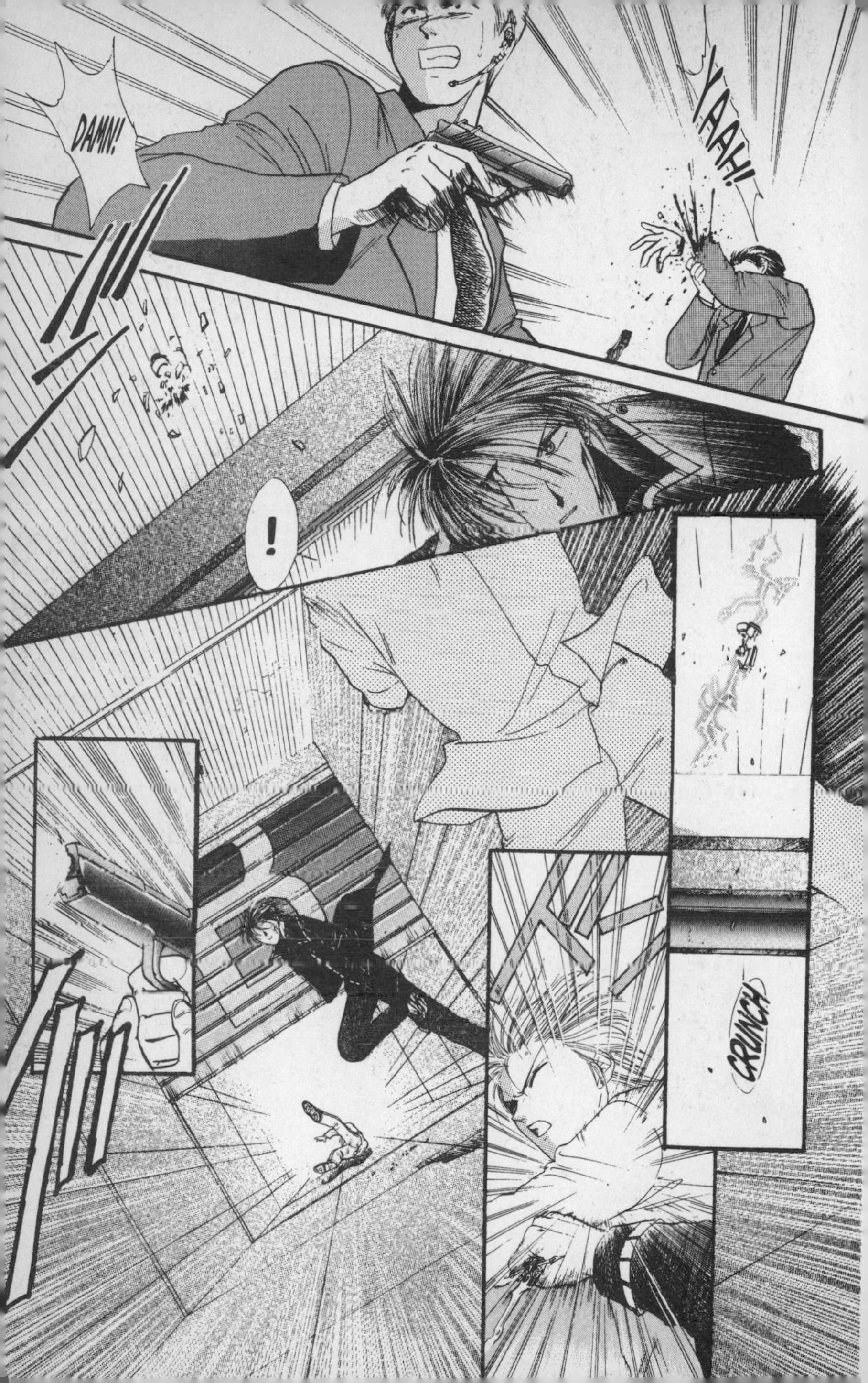
YAAAH!
DAMN!
!
CRUNCH

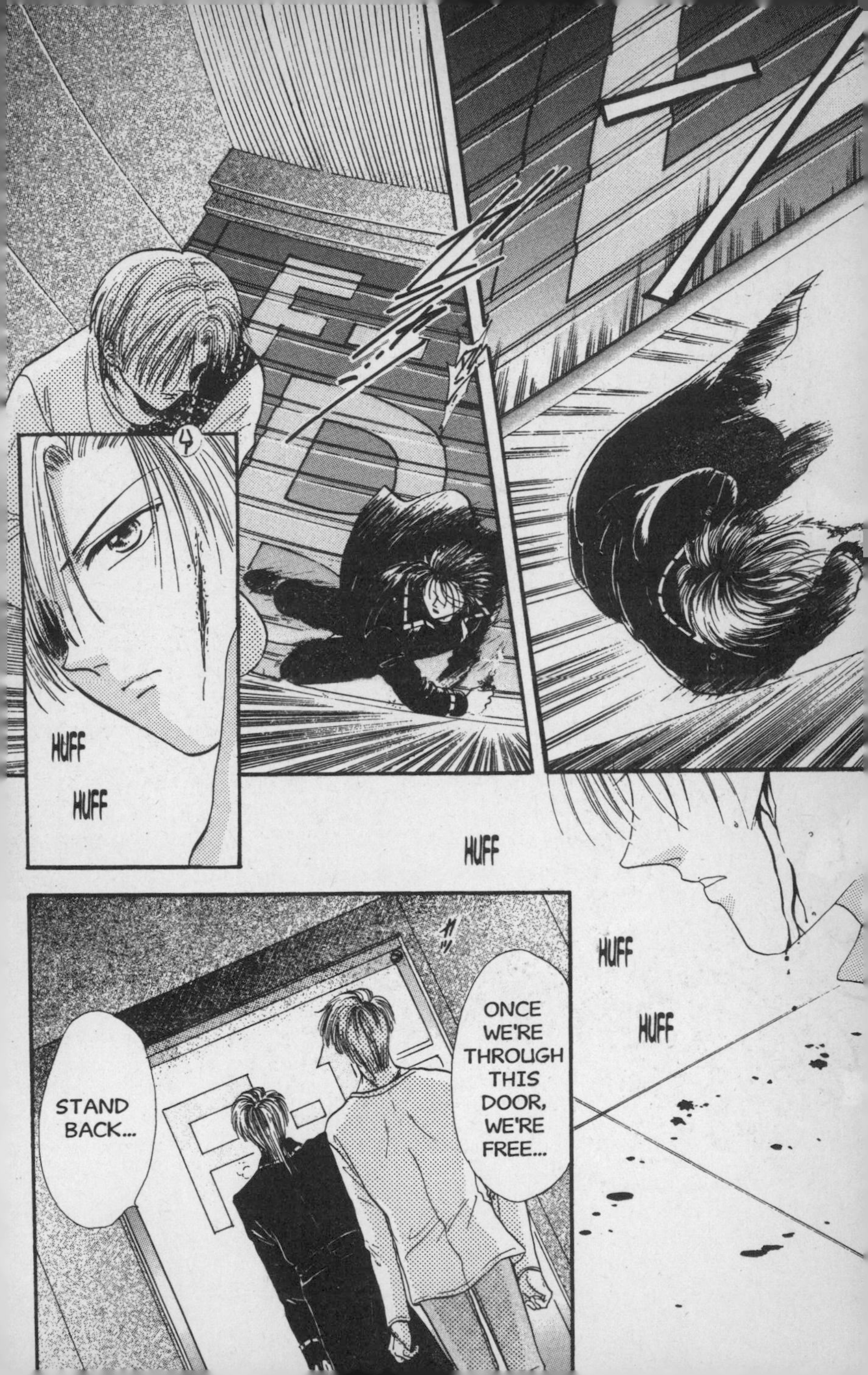
HUFF
HUFF
HUFF
HUFF
HUFF
ONCE WE'RE THROUGH THIS DOOR, WE'RE FREE...
STAND BACK...

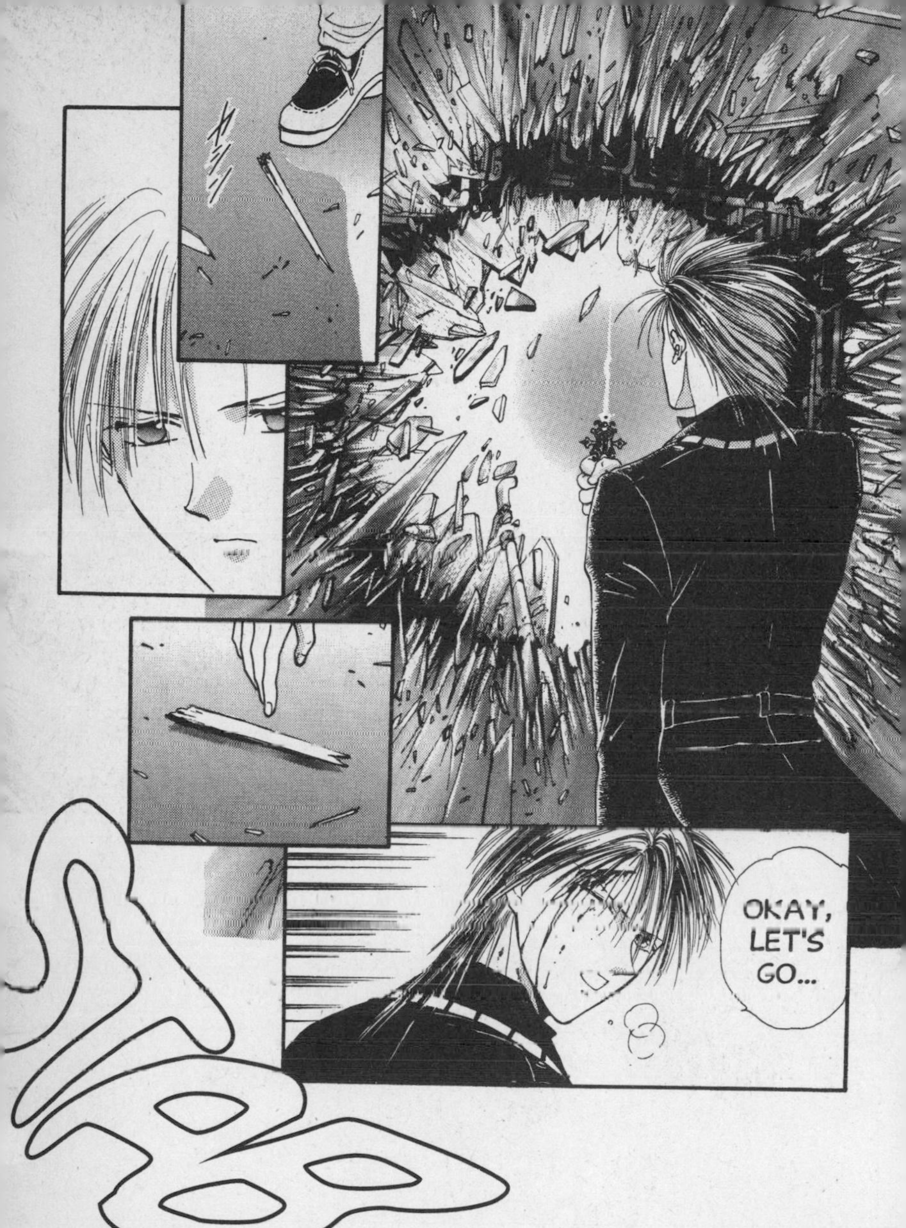
OKAY, LET'S GO...

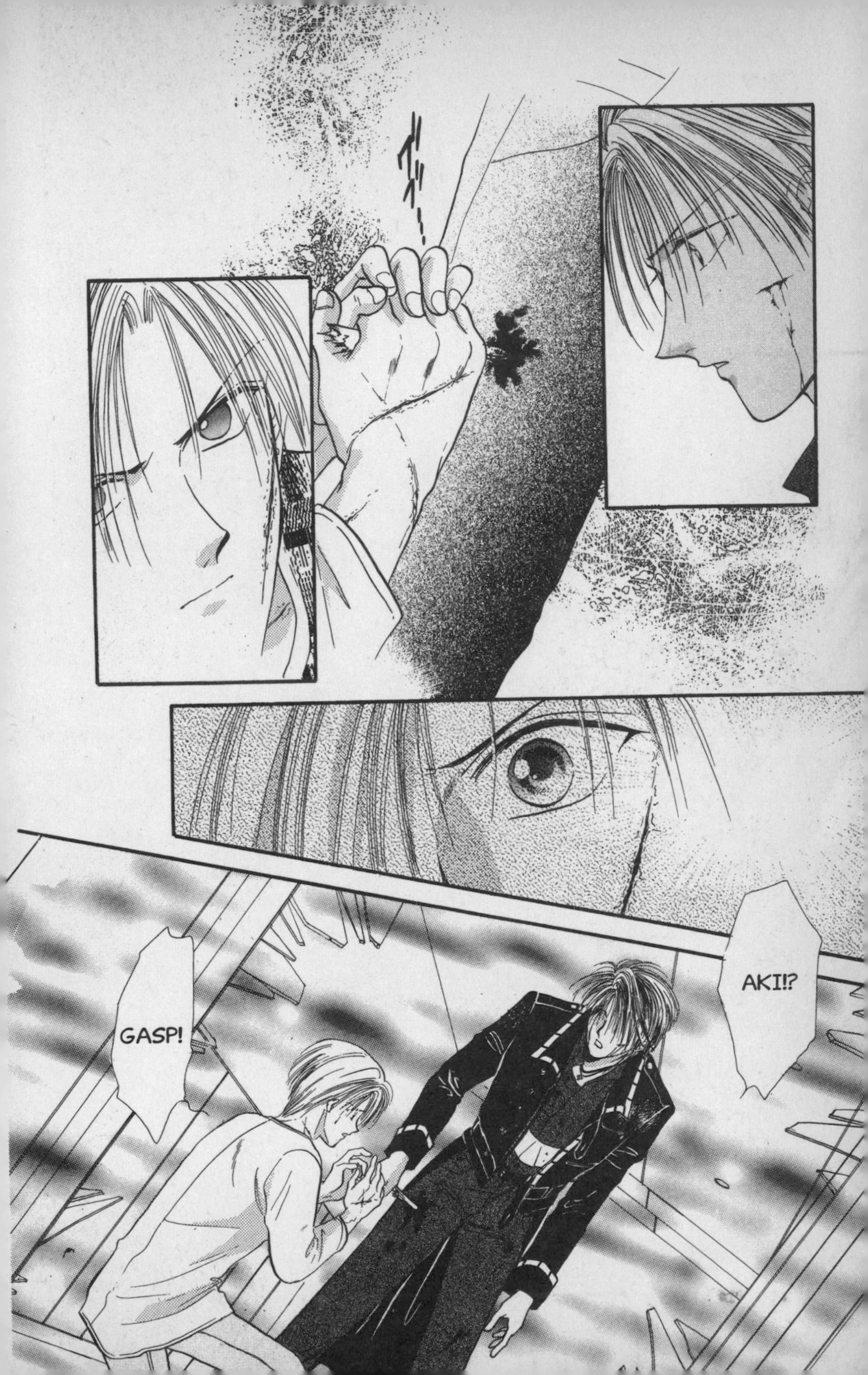
AKI!?
GASP!

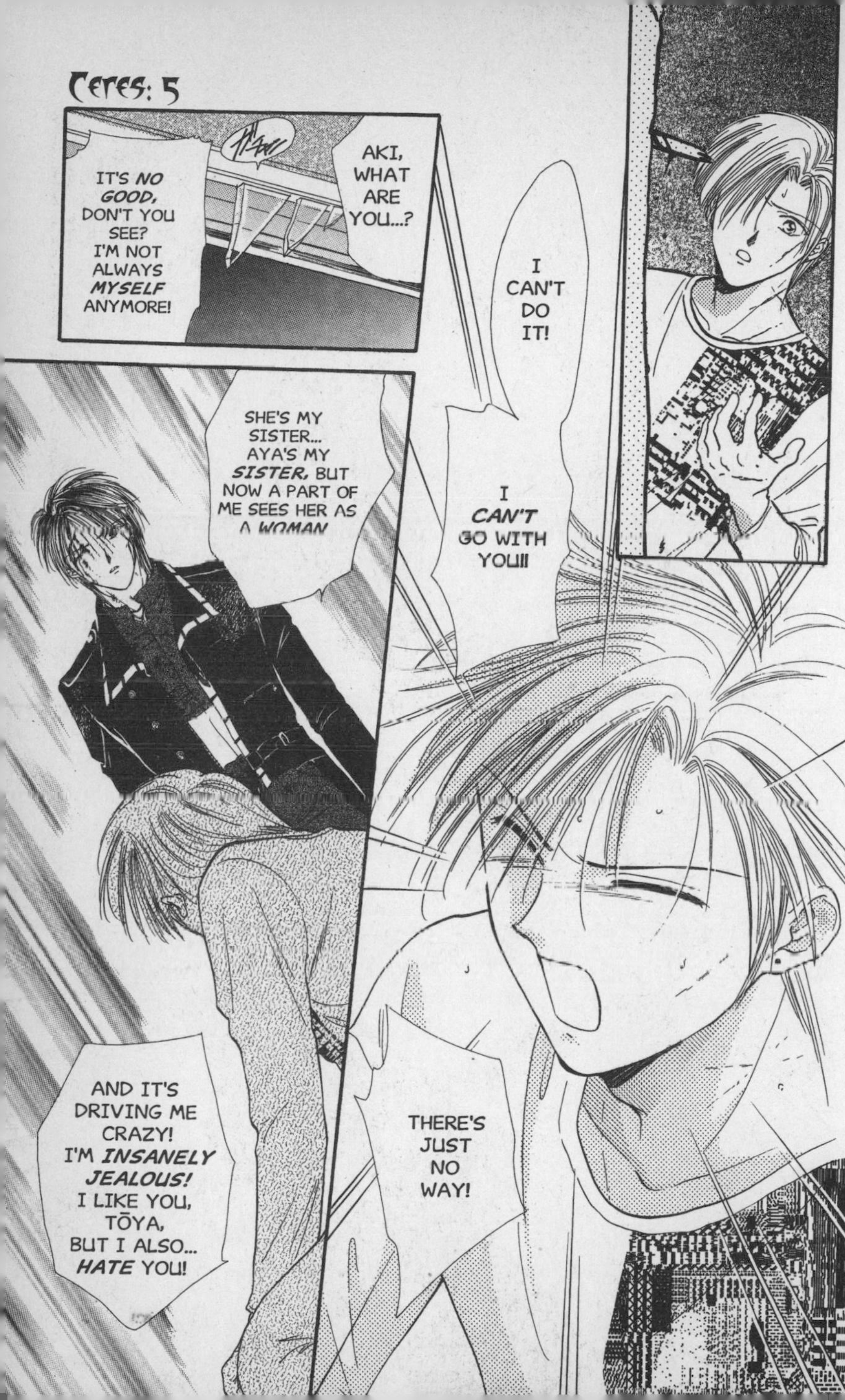
AKI, WHAT ARE YOU...?
IT'S NO GOOD, DON'T YOU SEE? I'M NOT ALWAYS MYSELF ANYMORE!
I CAN'T DO IT!
I CAN'T GO WITH YOU!!
THERE'S JUST NO WAY!
SHE'S MY SISTER... AYA'S MY SISTER, BUT NOW A PART OF ME SEES HER AS A WOMAN.
AND IT'S DRIVING ME CRAZY! I'M INSANELY JEALOUS! I LIKE YOU, TŌYA, BUT I ALSO... HATE YOU!

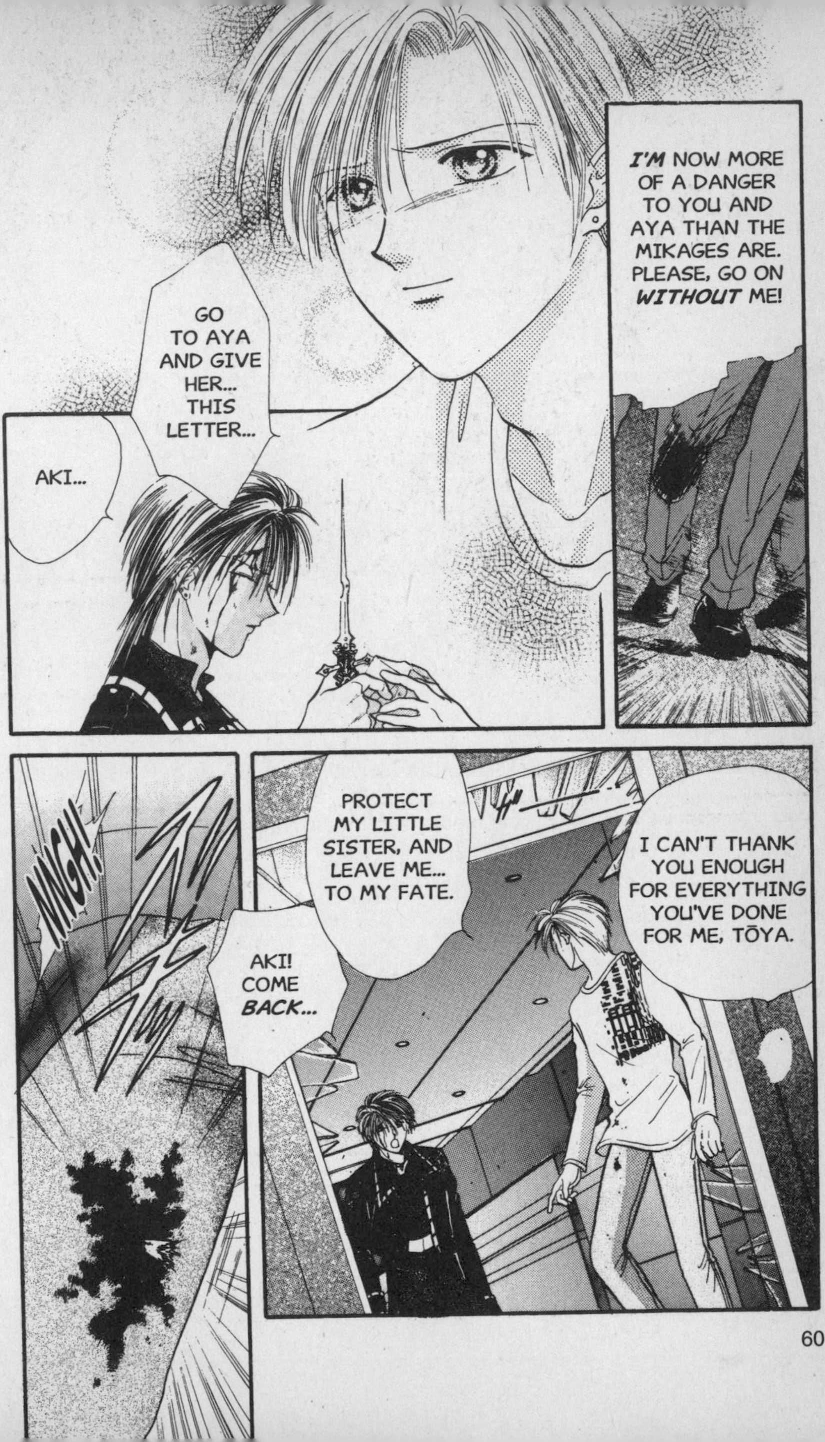
I'M NOW MORE OF A DANGER TO YOU AND AYA THAN THE MIKAGES ARE. PLEASE, GO ON *WITHOUT* ME!
GO TO AYA AND GIVE HER... THIS LETTER...
AKI...
I CAN'T THANK YOU ENOUGH FOR EVERYTHING YOU'VE DONE FOR ME, TŌYA.
PROTECT MY LITTLE SISTER, AND LEAVE ME... TO MY FATE.
AKI! COME *BACK*...
NNGH!

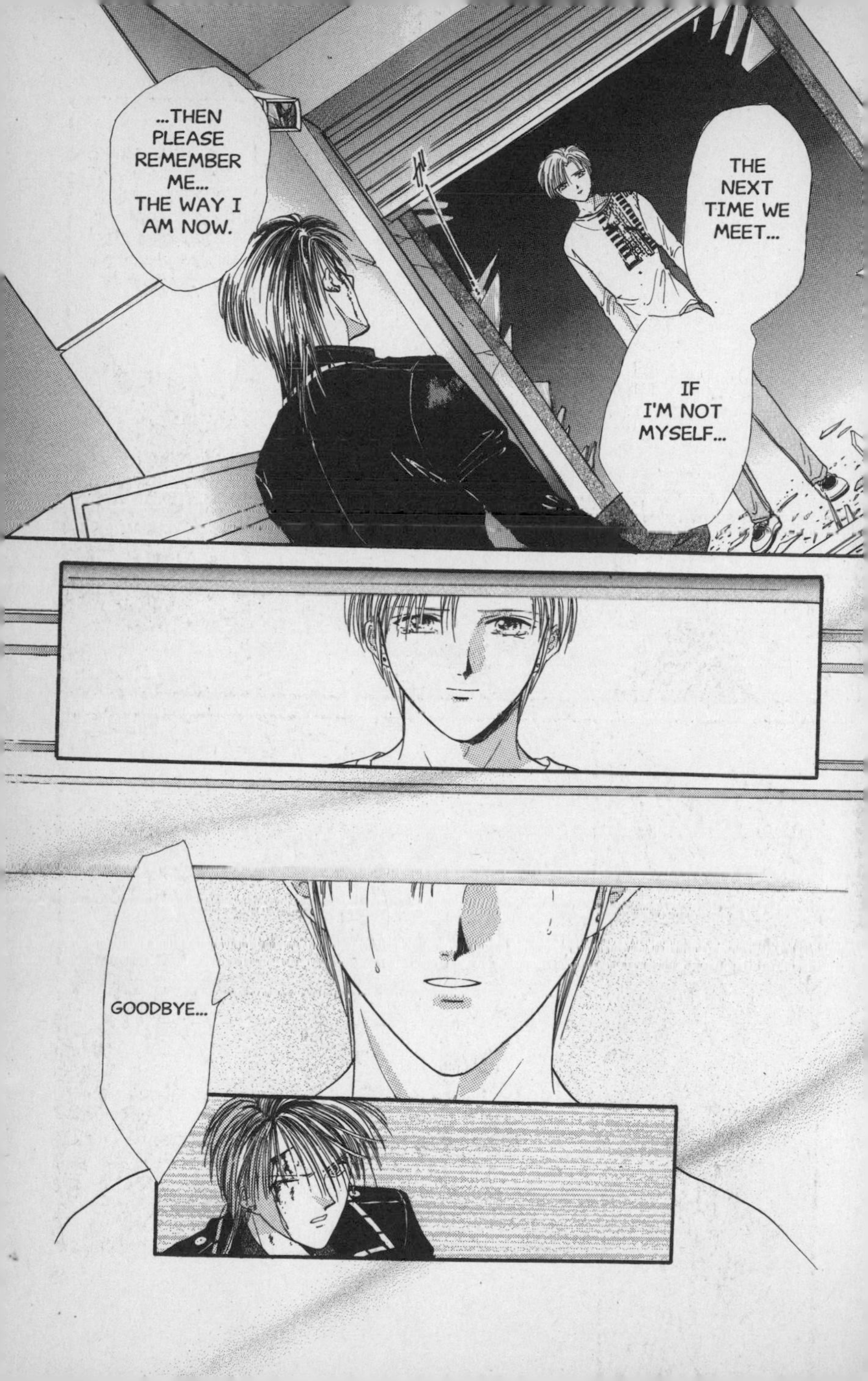
THE NEXT TIME WE MEET...
IF I'M NOT MYSELF...
...THEN PLEASE REMEMBER ME... THE WAY I AM NOW.
GOODBYE...

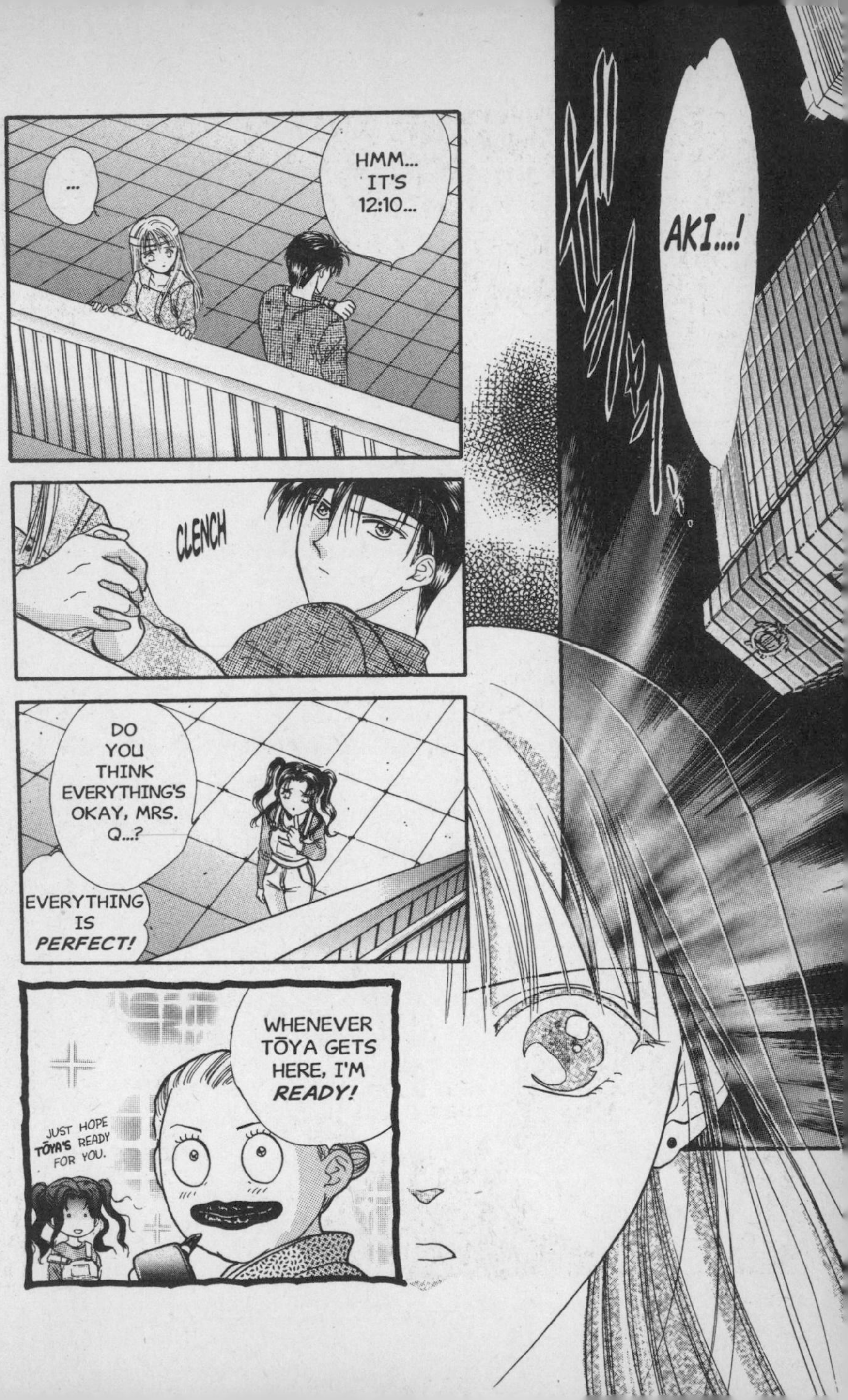
AKI...!
HMM... IT'S 12:10...
...
CLENCH
DO YOU THINK EVERYTHING'S OKAY, MRS. Q...?
EVERYTHING IS *PERFECT!*
WHENEVER TŌYA GETS HERE, I'M *READY!*
JUST HOPE TŌYA'S READY FOR YOU.

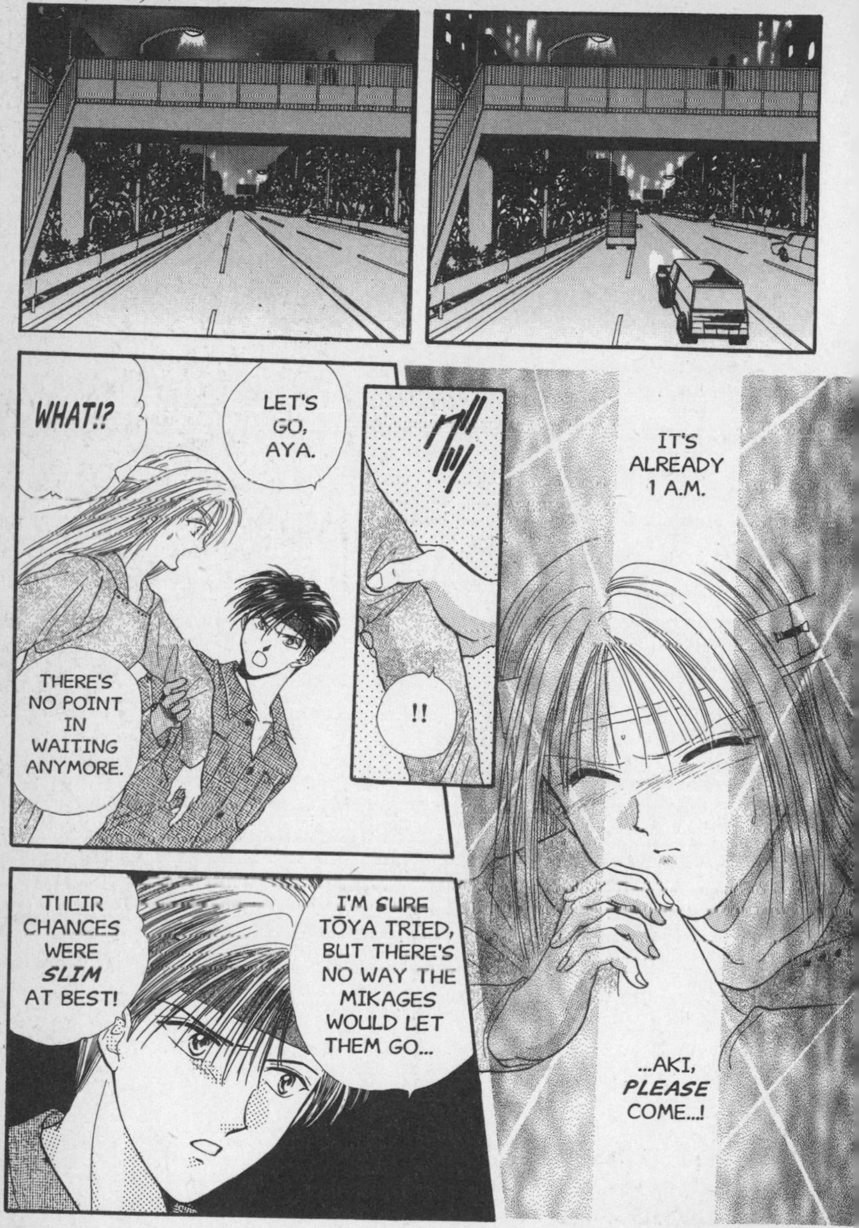
IT'S ALREADY 1 A.M.
...AKI, *PLEASE* COME...!
!!
LET'S GO, AYA.
WHAT!?
THERE'S NO POINT IN WAITING ANYMORE.
I'M SURE TŌYA TRIED, BUT THERE'S NO WAY THE MIKAGES WOULD LET THEM GO...
THEIR CHANCES WERE *SLIM* AT BEST!

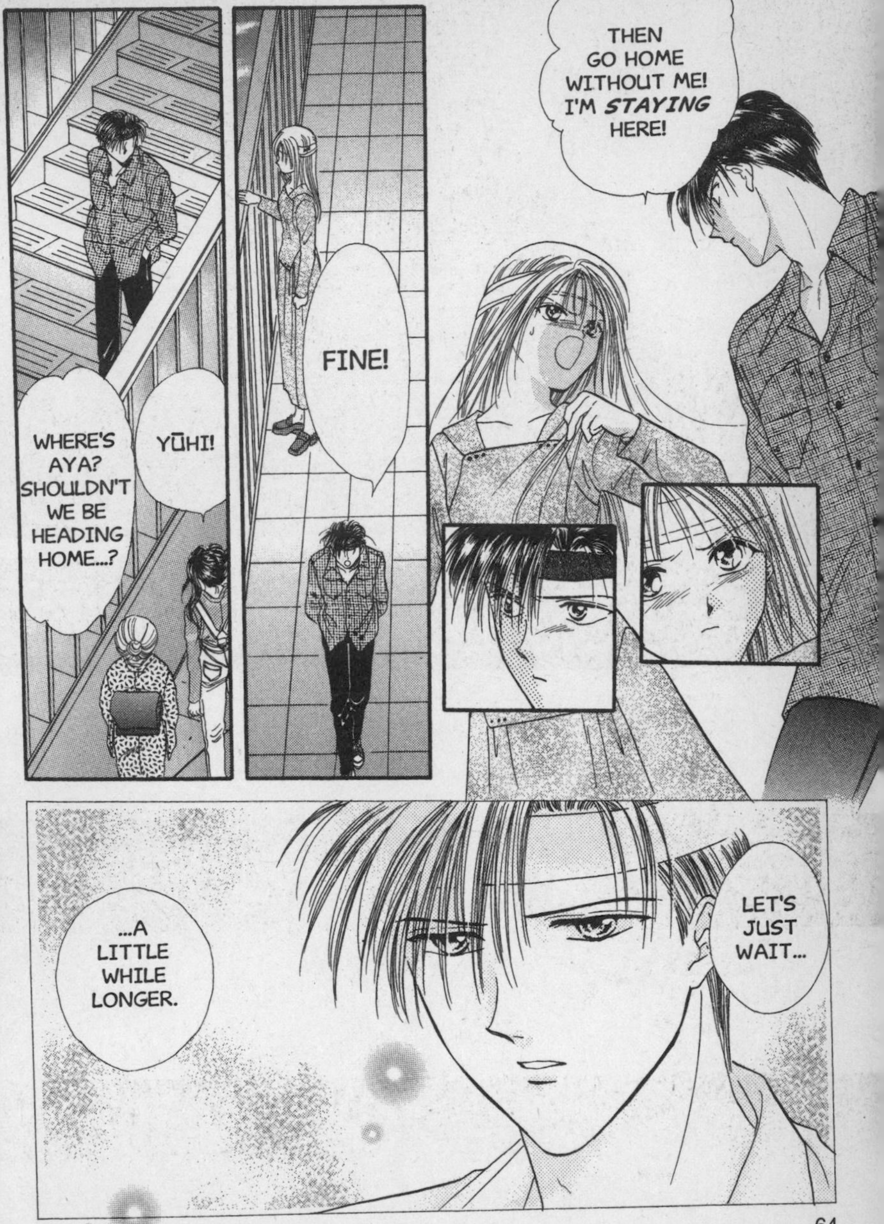
THEN GO HOME WITHOUT ME! I'M *STAYING* HERE!
FINE!
YŪHI!
WHERE'S AYA? SHOULDN'T WE BE HEADING HOME...?
LET'S JUST WAIT...
...A LITTLE WHILE LONGER.

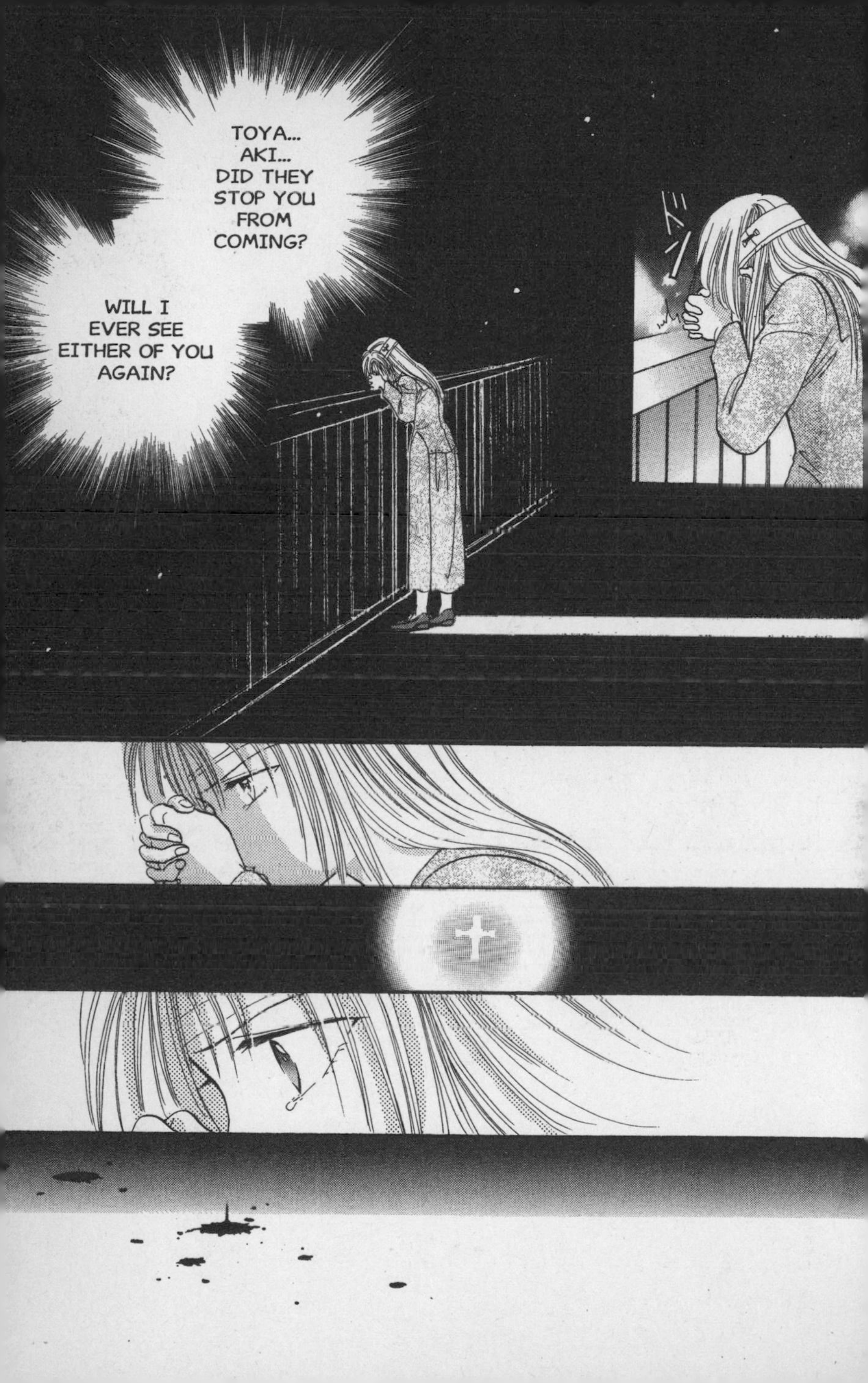
TOYA... AKI... DID THEY STOP YOU FROM COMING?
WILL I EVER SEE EITHER OF YOU AGAIN?

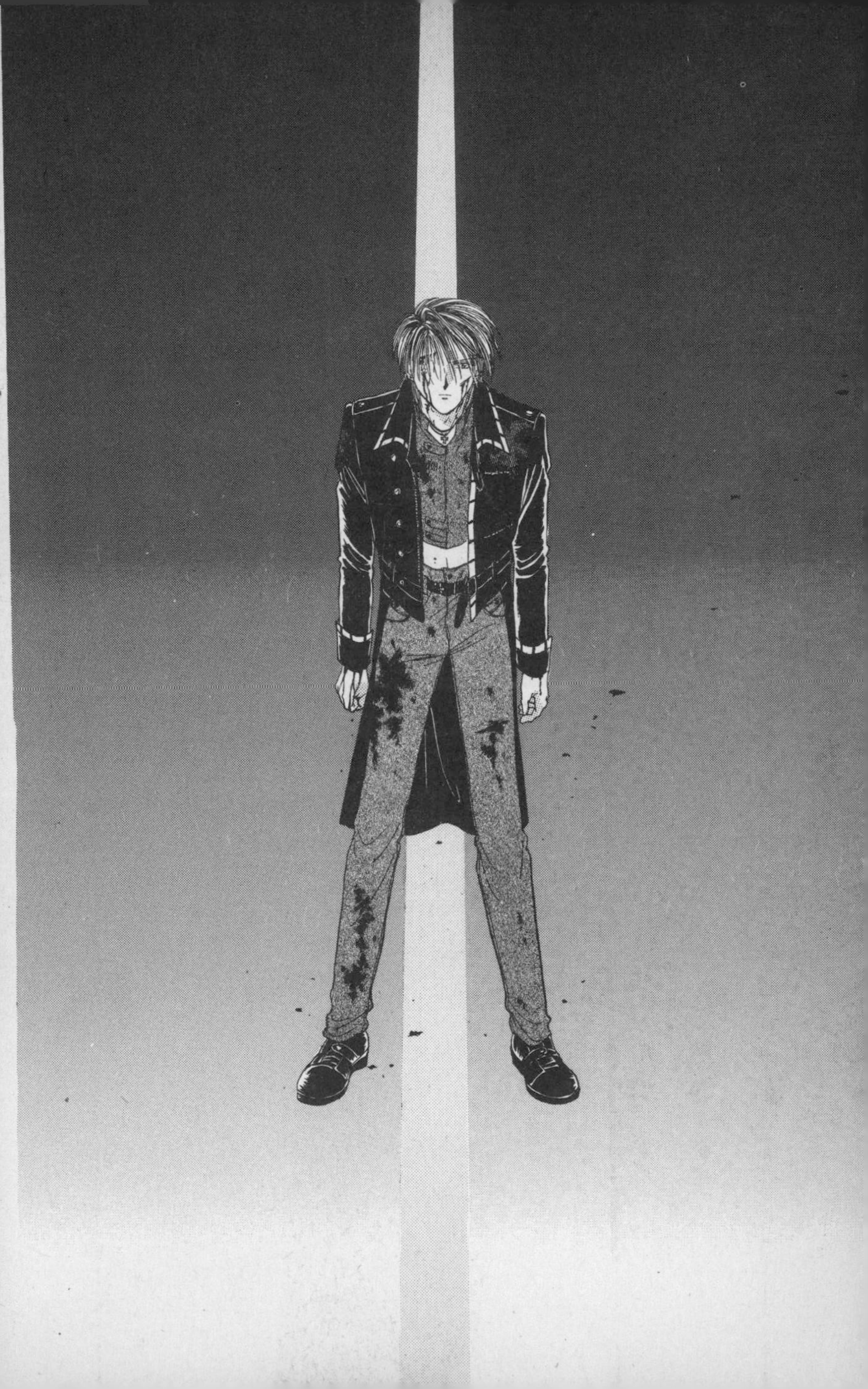

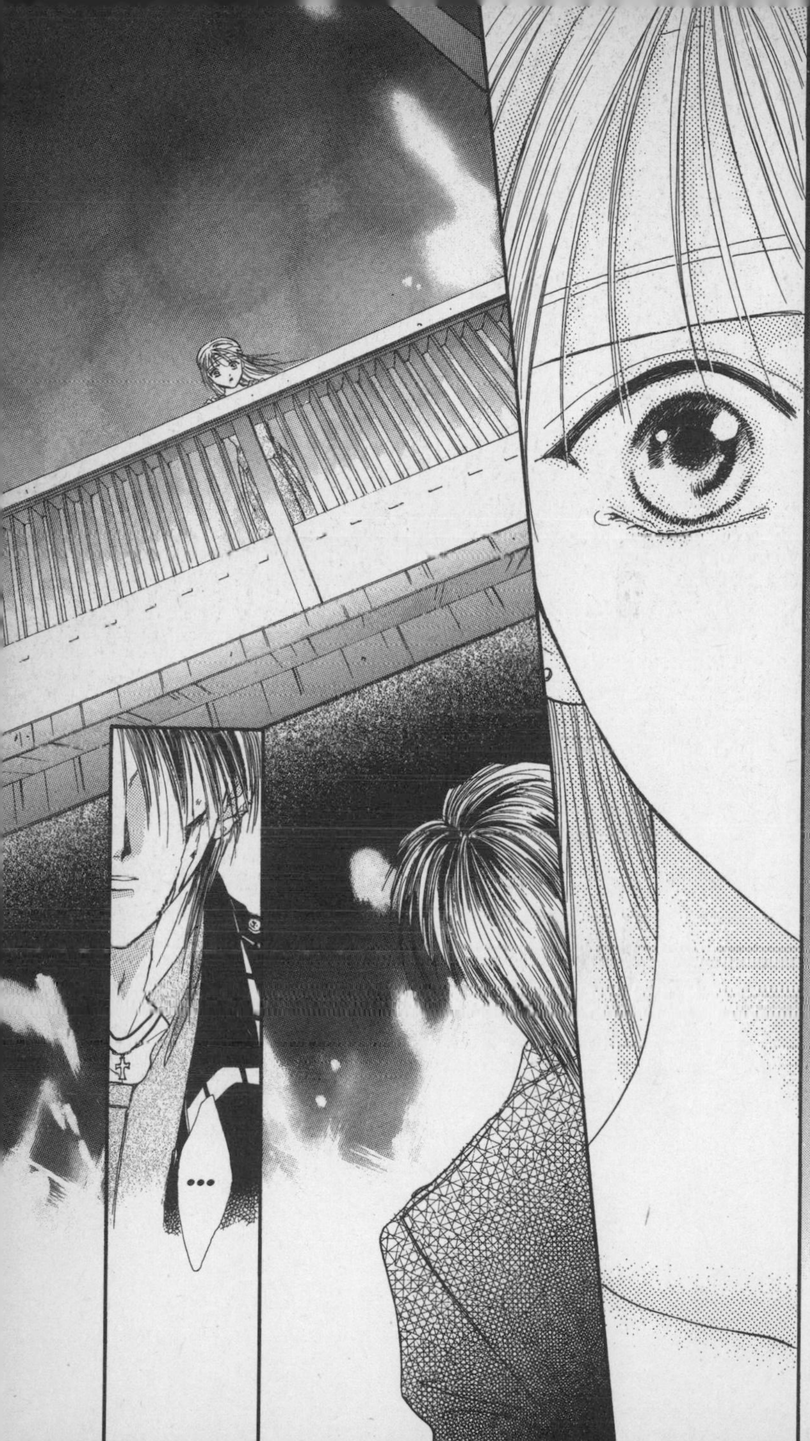
...

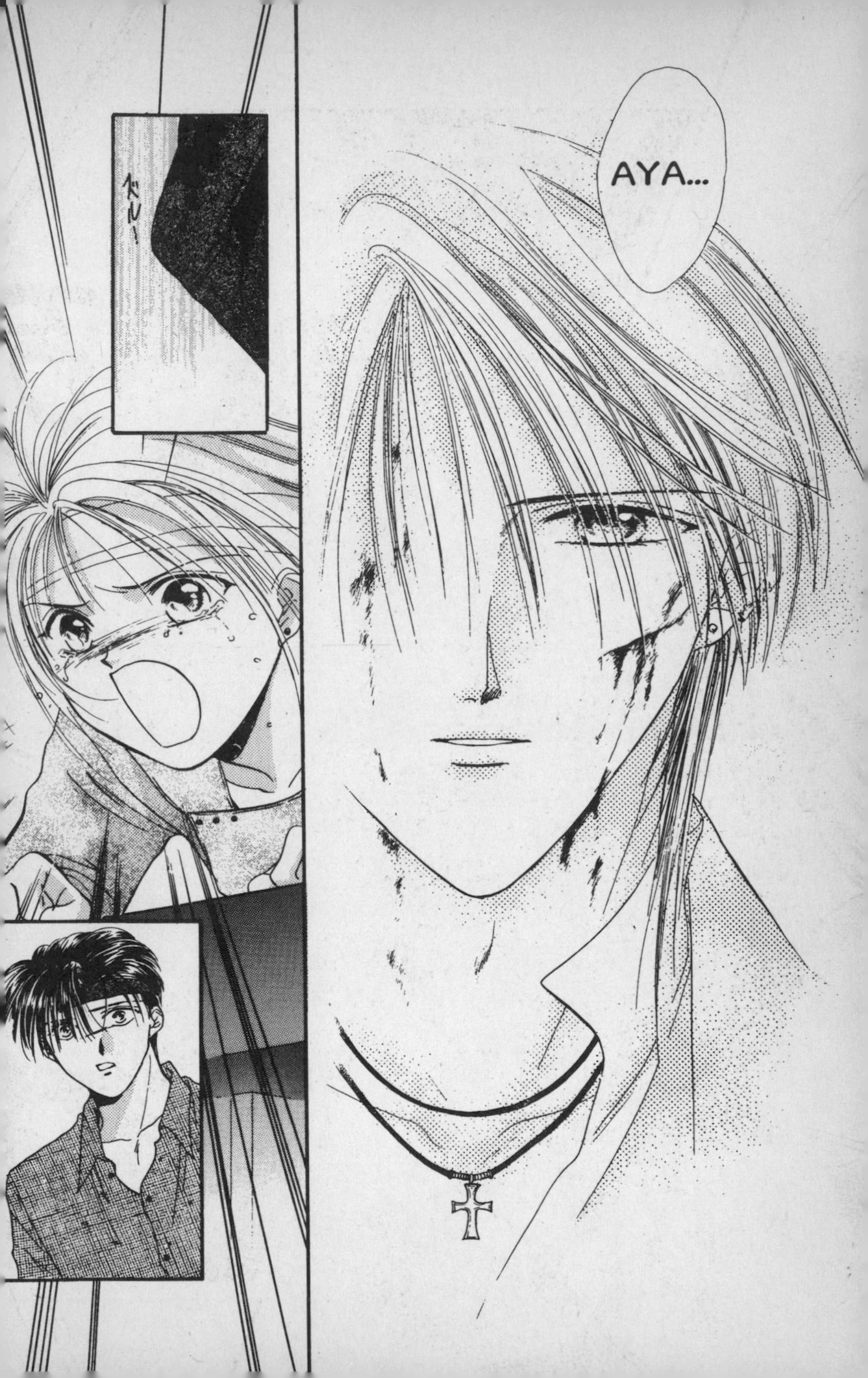
AYA...
べルー

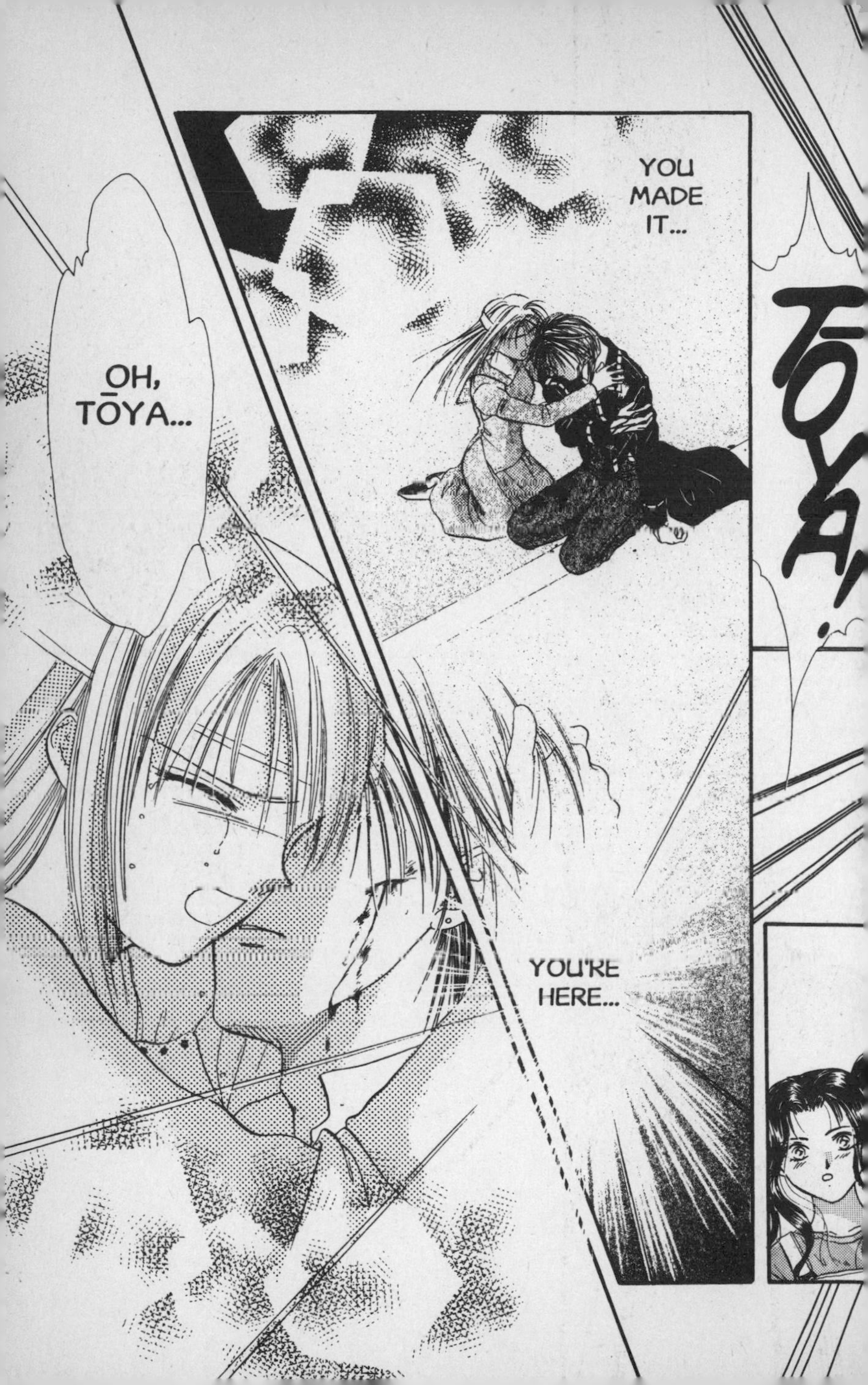
TŌYA!
YOU MADE IT...
YOU'RE HERE...
OH, TŌYA...

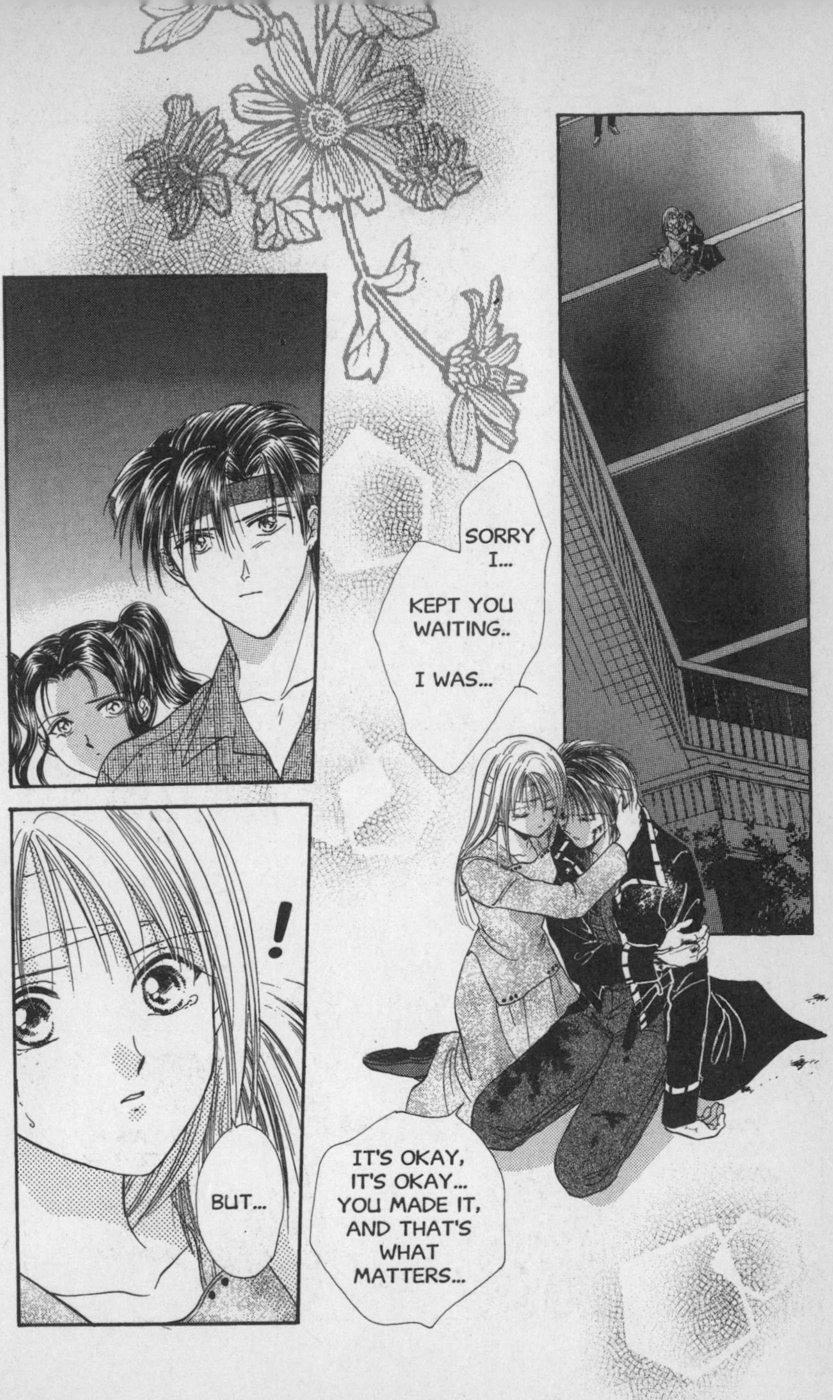
SORRY I... KEPT YOU WAITING.. I WAS...
IT'S OKAY, IT'S OKAY... YOU MADE IT, AND THAT'S WHAT MATTERS...
!
BUT...

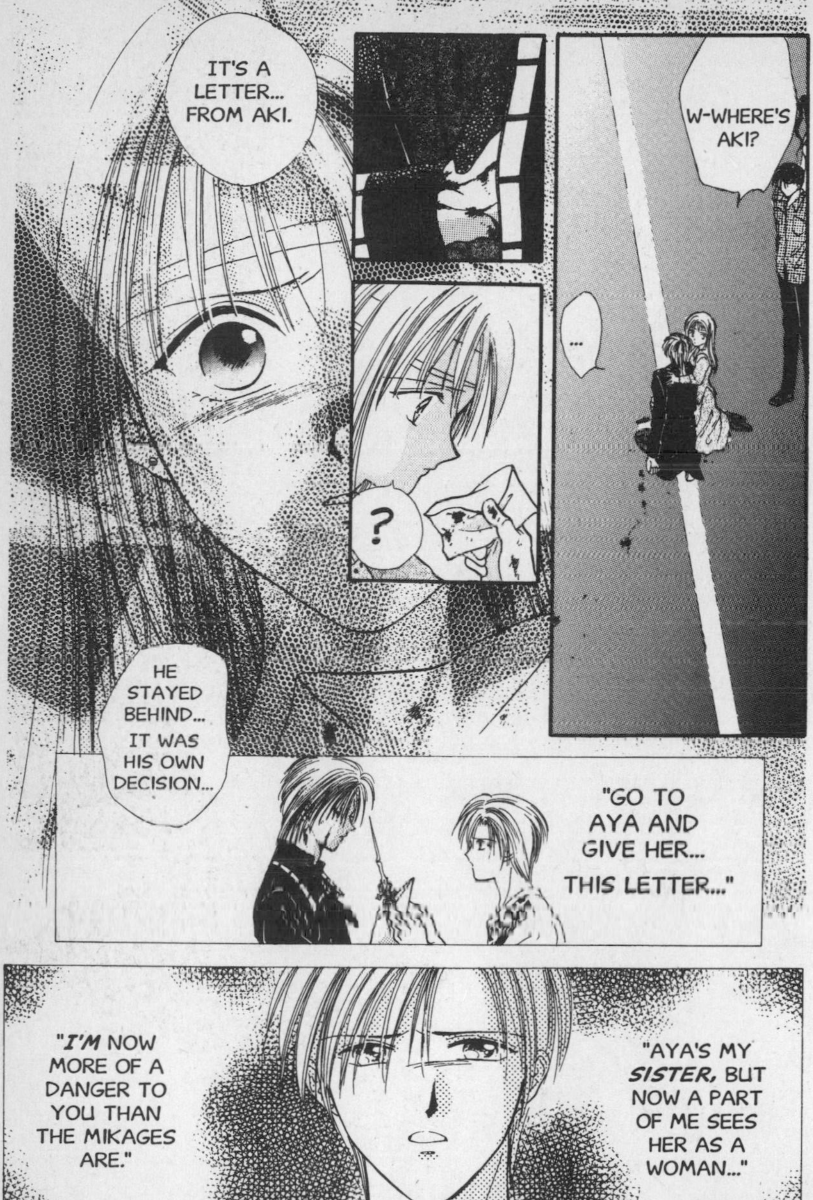
W-WHERE'S AKI?
...
?
IT'S A LETTER... FROM AKI.
HE STAYED BEHIND... IT WAS HIS OWN DECISION...
"GO TO AYA AND GIVE HER... THIS LETTER..."
"AYA'S MY *SISTER,* BUT NOW A PART OF ME SEES HER AS A WOMAN..."
"*I'M* NOW MORE OF A DANGER TO YOU THAN THE MIKAGES ARE."

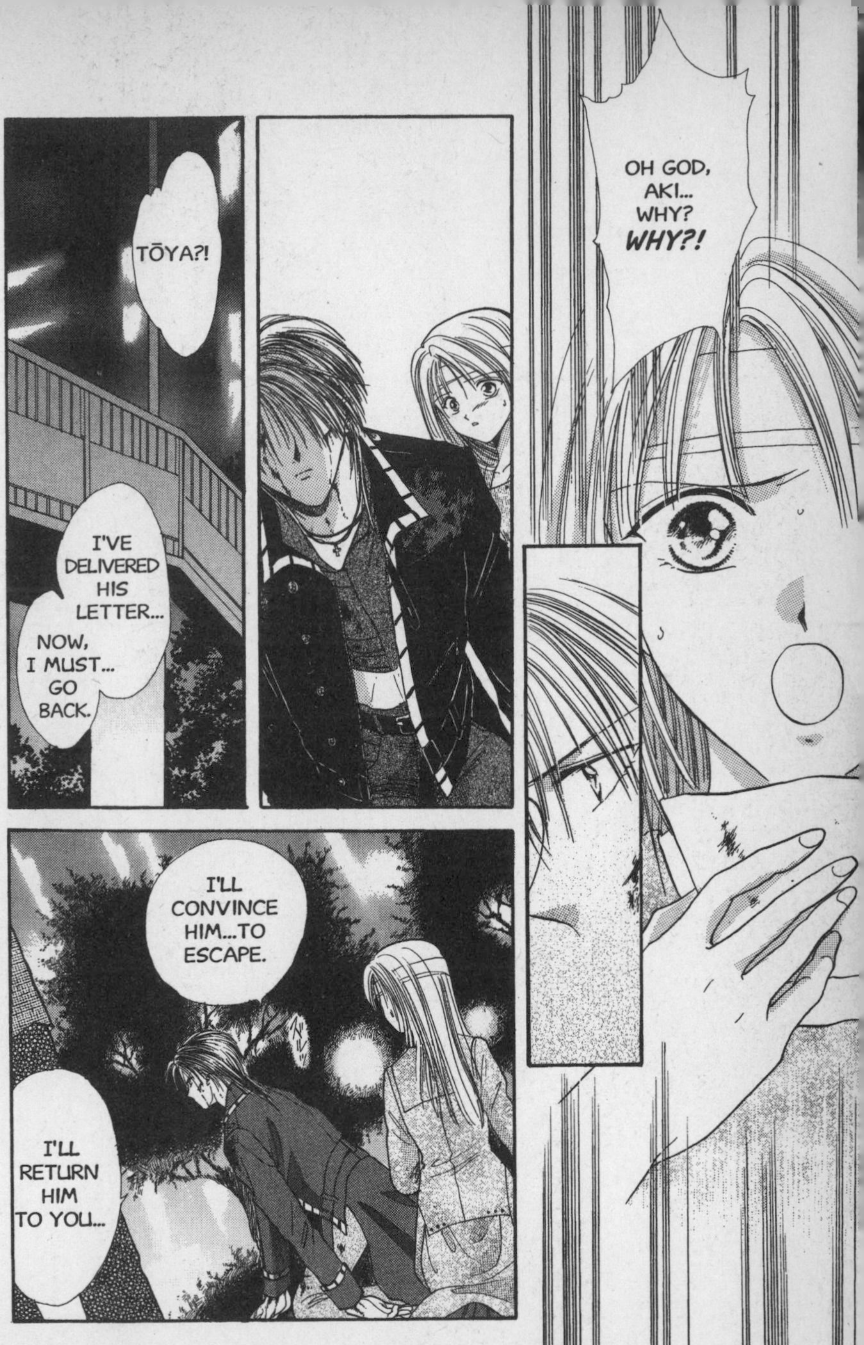
OH GOD, AKI... WHY? WHY?!
TŌYA?!
I'VE DELIVERED HIS LETTER...
NOW, I MUST... GO BACK.
I'LL CONVINCE HIM...TO ESCAPE.
I'LL RETURN HIM TO YOU...

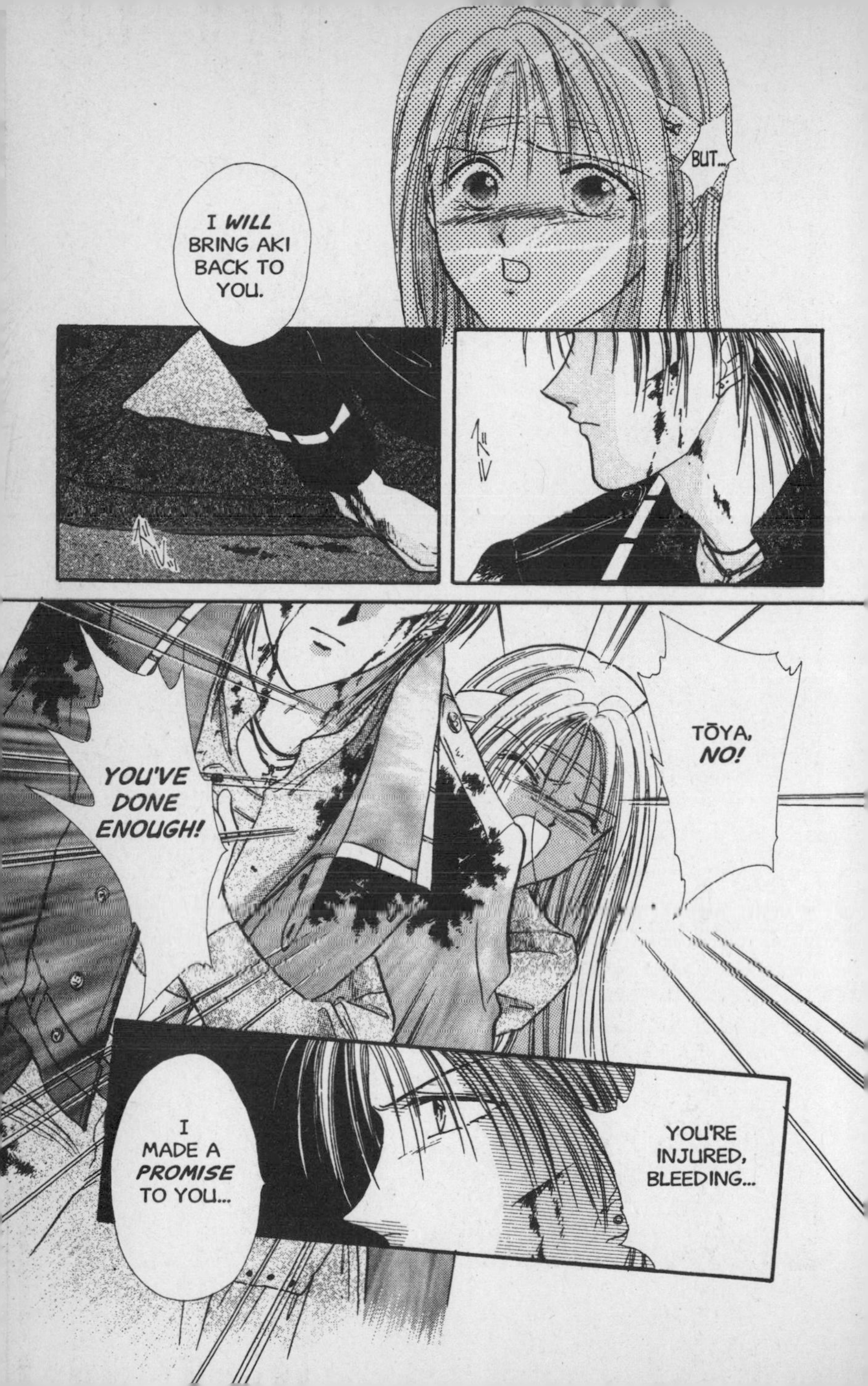
BUT...
I *WILL* BRING AKI BACK TO YOU.
TŌYA, *NO!*
YOU'VE DONE ENOUGH!
YOU'RE INJURED, BLEEDING...
I MADE A *PROMISE* TO YOU...

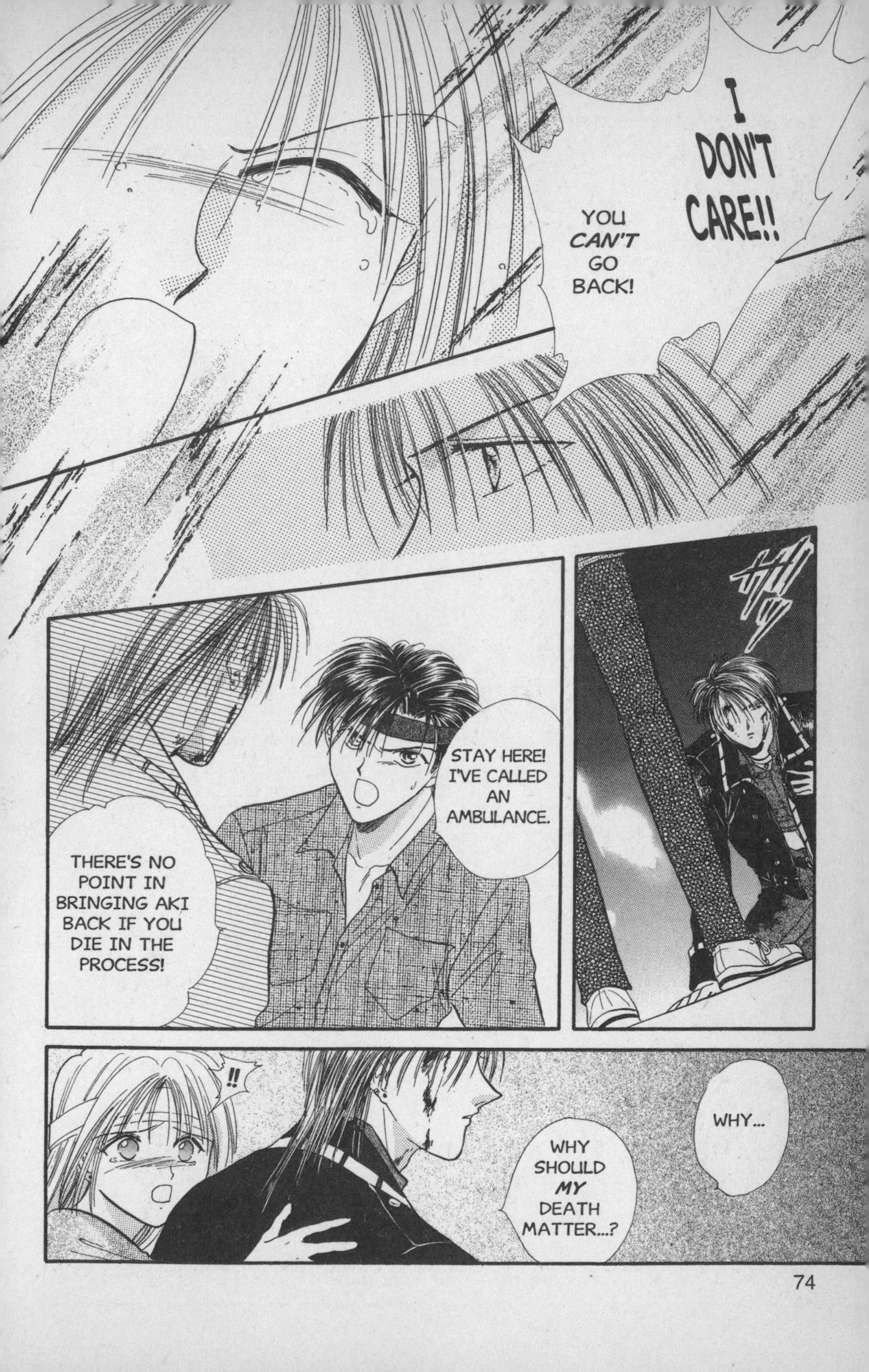
I DON'T CARE!!
YOU *CAN'T* GO BACK!
STAY HERE! I'VE CALLED AN AMBULANCE.
THERE'S NO POINT IN BRINGING AKI BACK IF YOU DIE IN THE PROCESS!
WHY...
WHY SHOULD *MY* DEATH MATTER...?
!!

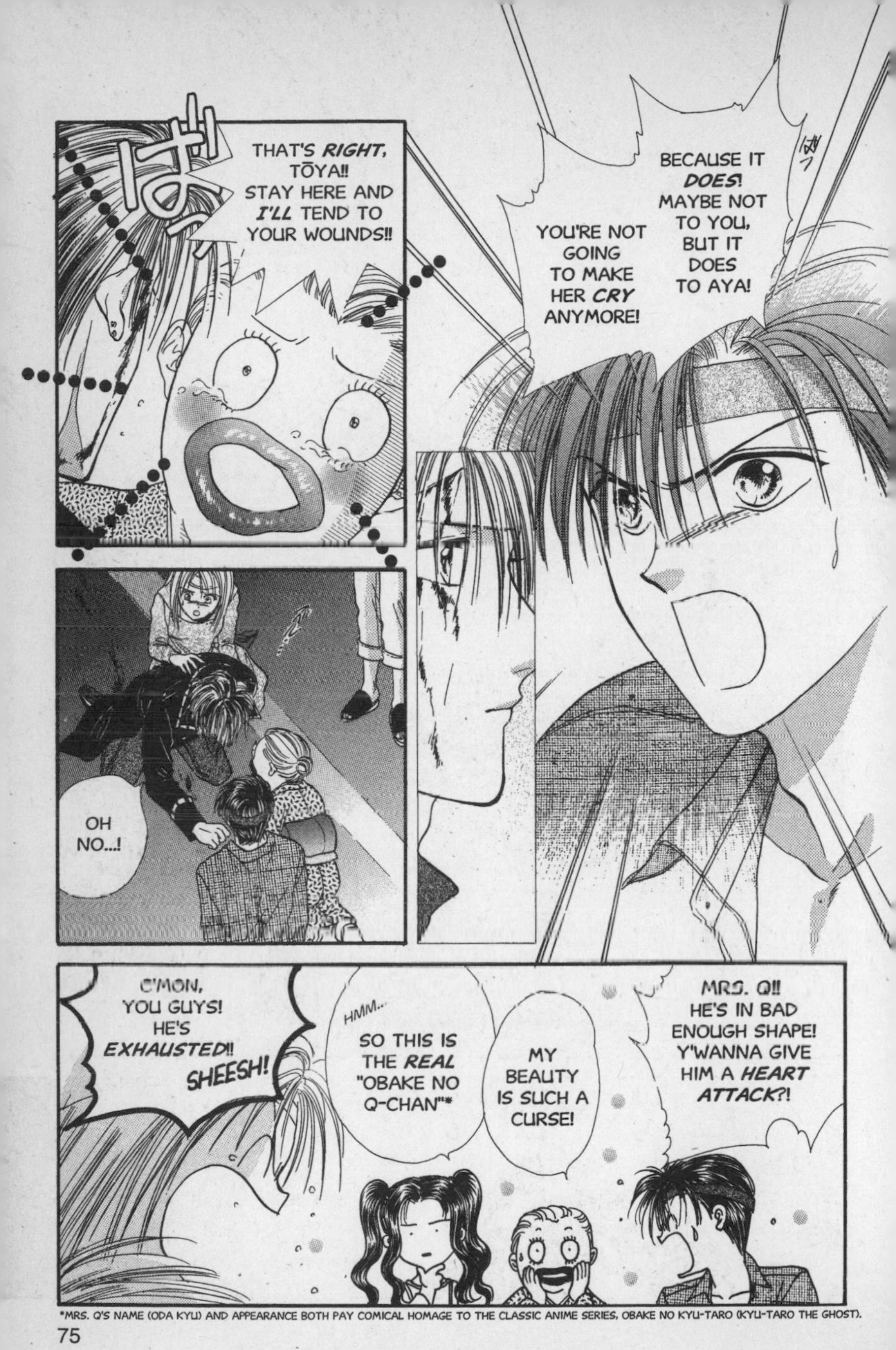
BECAUSE IT DOES! MAYBE NOT TO YOU, BUT IT DOES TO AYA!
YOU'RE NOT GOING TO MAKE HER CRY ANYMORE!
ぱっ
THAT'S RIGHT, TŌYA!! STAY HERE AND I'LL TEND TO YOUR WOUNDS!!
OH NO...!
MRS. Q!! HE'S IN BAD ENOUGH SHAPE! Y'WANNA GIVE HIM A HEART ATTACK?!
MY BEAUTY IS SUCH A CURSE!
HMM... SO THIS IS THE REAL "OBAKE NO Q-CHAN"*
C'MON, YOU GUYS! HE'S EXHAUSTED!! SHEESH!

*MRS. Q'S NAME (ODA KYU) AND APPEARANCE BOTH PAY COMICAL HOMAGE TO THE CLASSIC ANIME SERIES, OBAKE NO KYU-TARO (KYU-TARO THE GHOST).

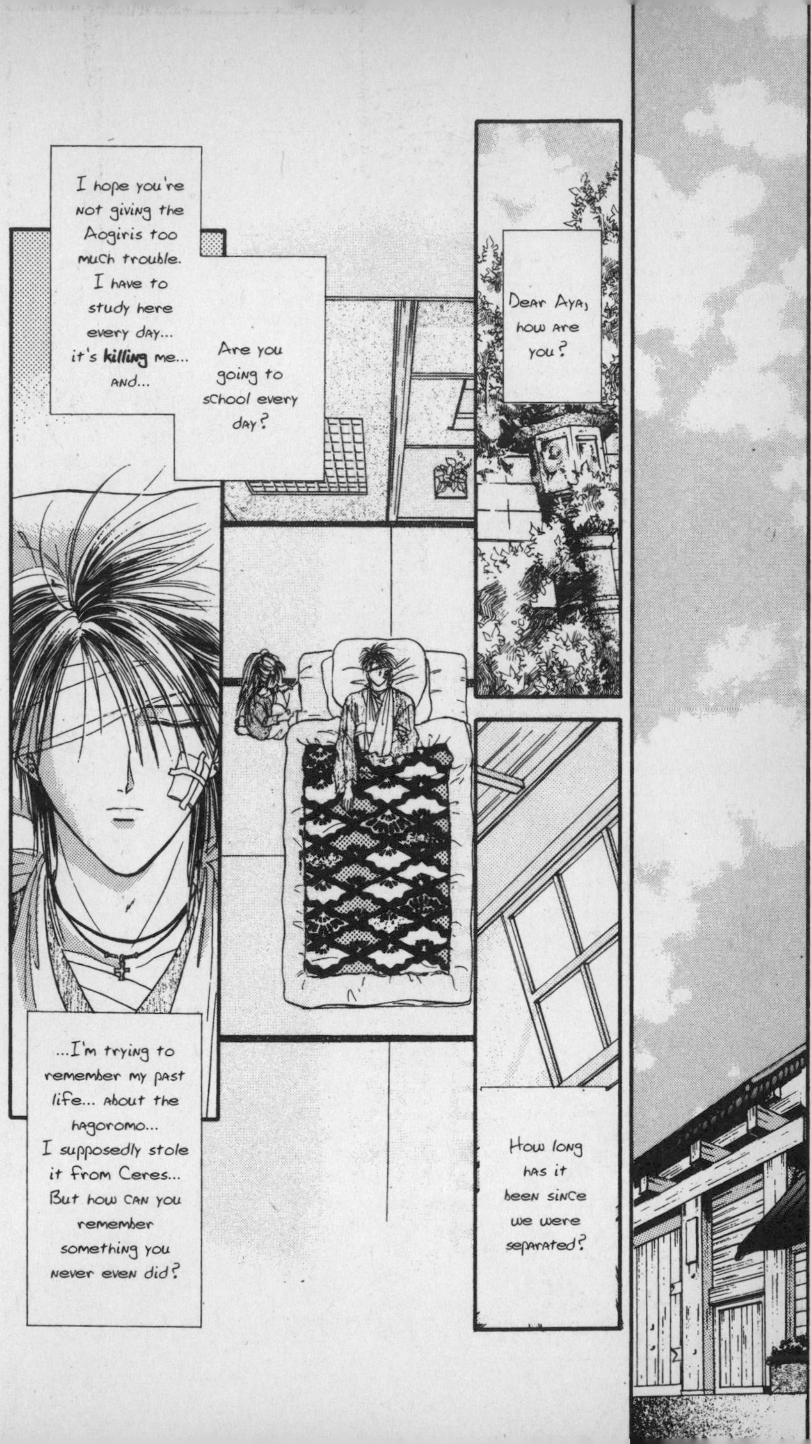
Dear Aya, how are you?
How long has it been since we were separated?
Are you going to school every day?
I hope you're not giving the Aogiris too much trouble. I have to study here every day... it's **killing** me... and...
...I'm trying to remember my past life... about the hagoromo... I supposedly stole it from Ceres... But how can you remember something you never even did?

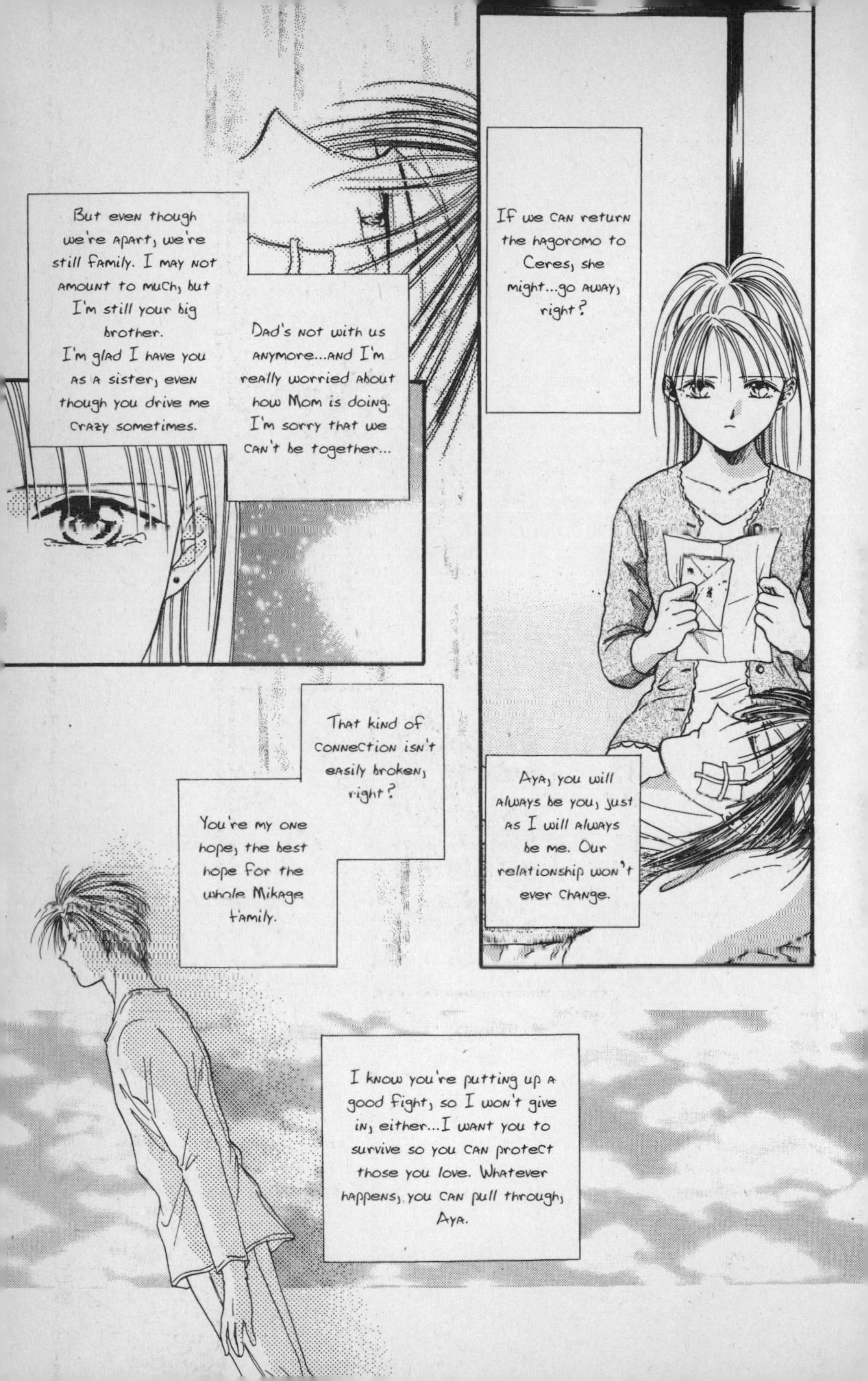
If we can return the hagoromo to Ceres, she might...go away, right?
Aya, you will always be you, just as I will always be me. Our relationship won't ever change.
Dad's not with us anymore...and I'm really worried about how Mom is doing. I'm sorry that we can't be together...
But even though we're apart, we're still family. I may not amount to much, but I'm still your big brother. I'm glad I have you as a sister, even though you drive me crazy sometimes.
That kind of connection isn't easily broken, right?
You're my one hope, the best hope for the whole Mikage family.
I know you're putting up a good fight, so I won't give in, either...I want you to survive so you can protect those you love. Whatever happens, you can pull through, Aya.

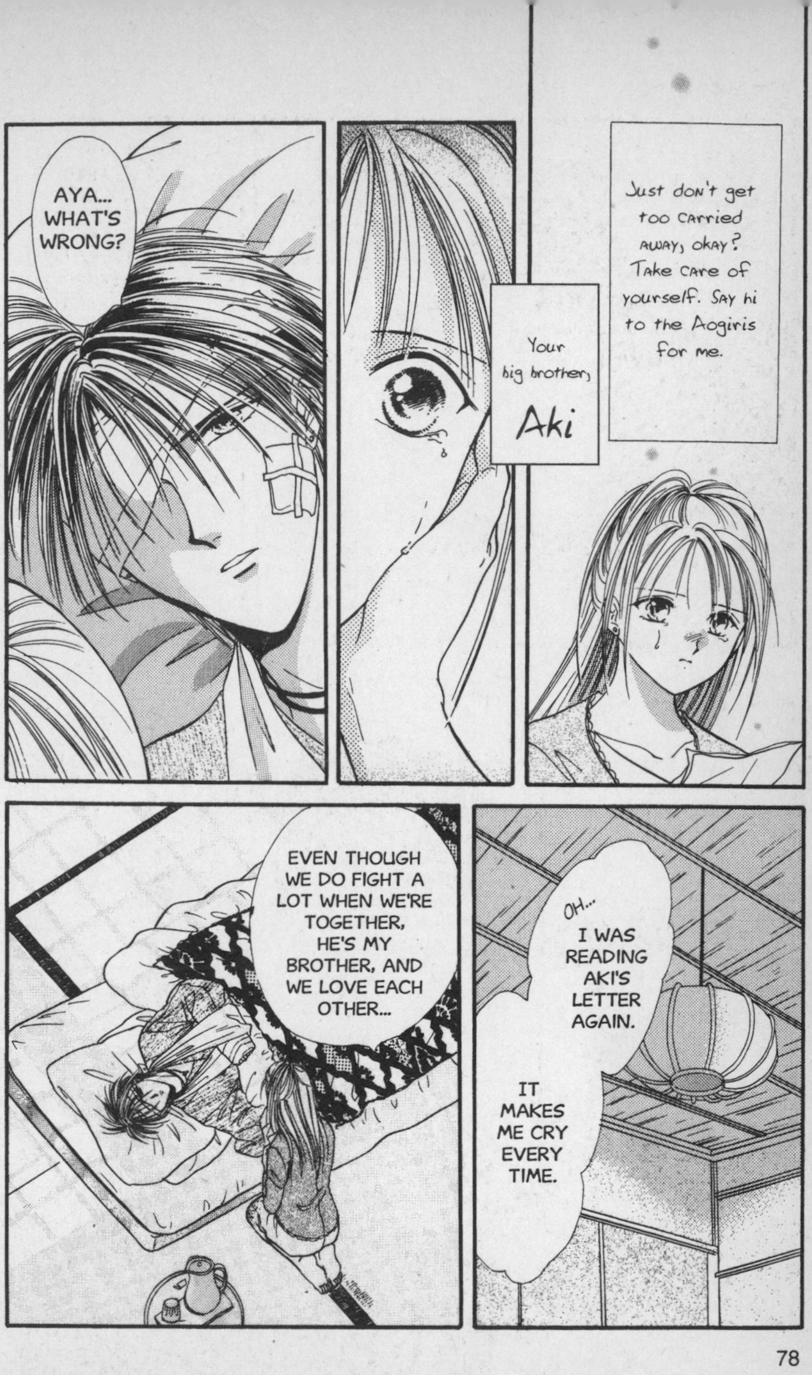
Just don't get too carried away, okay? Take care of yourself. Say hi to the Aogiris for me.
Your big brother,
Aki
AYA... WHAT'S WRONG?
OH... I WAS READING AKI'S LETTER AGAIN.
IT MAKES ME CRY EVERY TIME.
EVEN THOUGH WE DO FIGHT A LOT WHEN WE'RE TOGETHER, HE'S MY BROTHER, AND WE LOVE EACH OTHER...

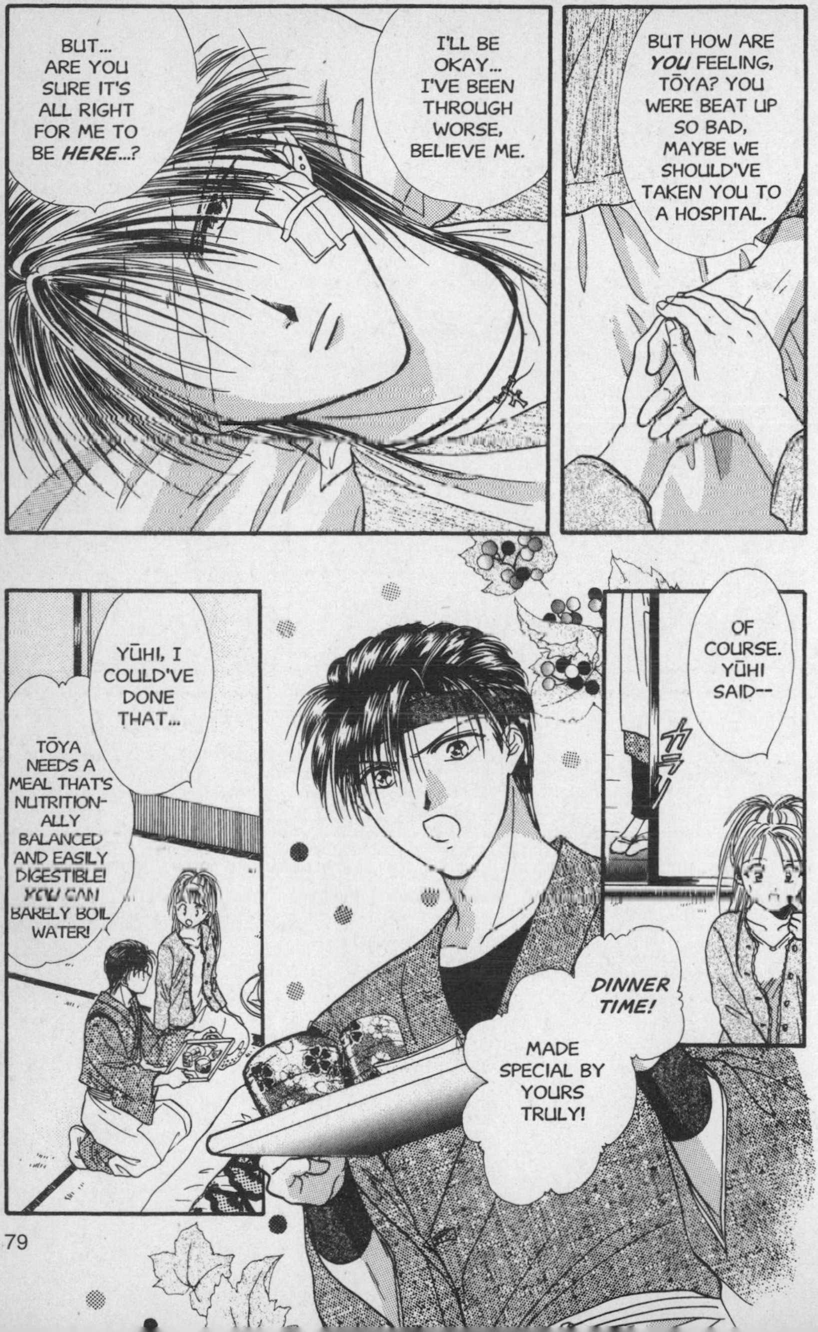
BUT HOW ARE *YOU* FEELING, TŌYA? YOU WERE BEAT UP SO BAD, MAYBE WE SHOULD'VE TAKEN YOU TO A HOSPITAL.
I'LL BE OKAY... I'VE BEEN THROUGH WORSE, BELIEVE ME.
BUT... ARE YOU SURE IT'S ALL RIGHT FOR ME TO BE *HERE*...?
OF COURSE. YŪHI SAID--
DINNER TIME!
MADE SPECIAL BY YOURS TRULY!
YŪHI, I COULD'VE DONE THAT...
TŌYA NEEDS A MEAL THAT'S NUTRITION-ALLY BALANCED AND EASILY DIGESTIBLE! YOU CAN BARELY BOIL WATER!

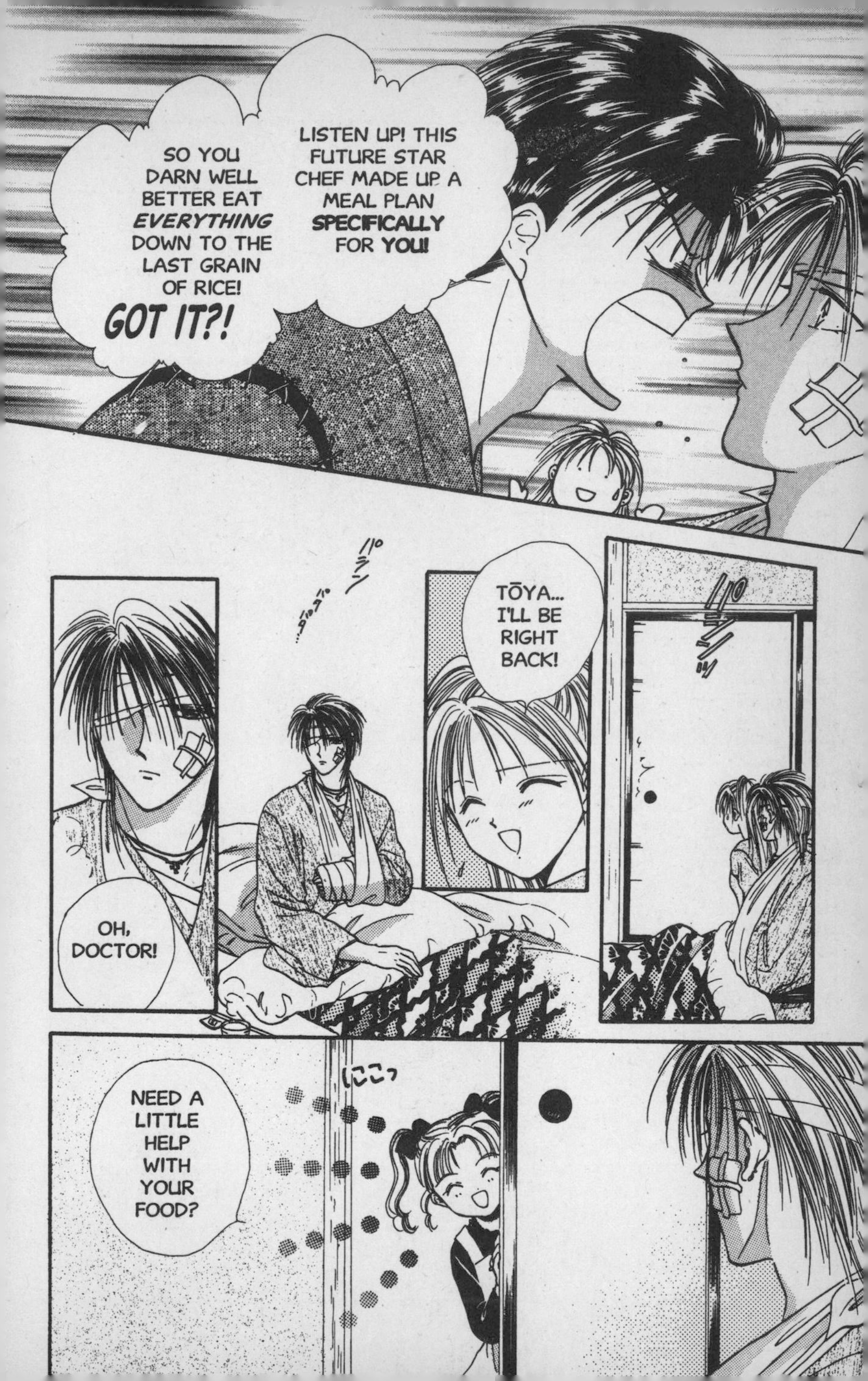
LISTEN UP! THIS FUTURE STAR CHEF MADE UP A MEAL PLAN SPECIFICALLY FOR YOU!
SO YOU DARN WELL BETTER EAT EVERYTHING DOWN TO THE LAST GRAIN OF RICE!
GOT IT?!
TŌYA... I'LL BE RIGHT BACK!
OH, DOCTOR!
にこっ
NEED A LITTLE HELP WITH YOUR FOOD?

♦ Mikage ♦

So it I was great to go on a trip with my friend. I went with a group of four people. And although I met two of them for the first time, we kept joking around in our Kansai dialects, and I was laughing my head off throughout the whole trip. In Disney World, we took a lot of pictures with Mickey and Minnie, (they came around to the tables while we had breakfast), as well as Winnie the Pooh, and characters from Toy Story. In any case, since they're Americans on the inside, they sure were touchy-feely. ☺ I felt like, "Hey, you're pettin' me too much!" "This is sexual harassment!" "Mickey, what do you think you're doing?!" And although I knew this before, the serving sizes were just too huge. They gave us sickening amounts of ice cream and soda. And we didn't even get double scoops or large size drinks! In general, had a tough time with the food. The tuna sandwiches were good (it was kind of like a hamburger), but we were having bread and meat everyday and it wasn't a very balanced diet. Thank goodness for Japanese food!

Well, it wasn't all fun - we did have some mishaps. ☺ My friend was more mad about it than I was. The main problem was that nobody would listen to what we were saying! Maybe I'll talk about the details later sometime but I suppose they just don't like to be bogged down by details... Cultural differences are interesting. Anyway, Disney World stays open until midnight over there, so we weren't getting much sleep. ☺ All the rides like Big Thunder seemed steeper and faster than the rides in Japan. The Haunted Mansion was really dark, and one look at Twilight Zone was enough for me to say, "nuh-uh." I can't handle that kind of thing. The elevator falls thirteen stories... No way! ☺

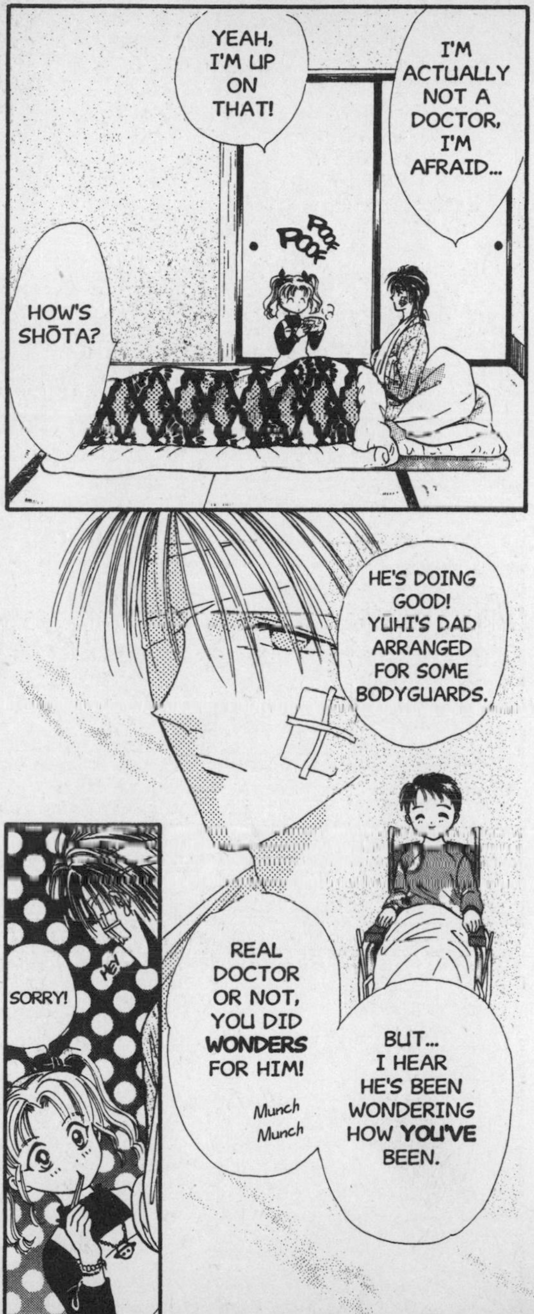
I'M ACTUALLY NOT A DOCTOR, I'M AFRAID...
YEAH, I'M UP ON THAT!
POOK POOK
HOW'S SHŌTA?
HE'S DOING GOOD! YUHI'S DAD ARRANGED FOR SOME BODYGUARDS.
BUT... I HEAR HE'S BEEN WONDERING HOW YOU'VE BEEN.
REAL DOCTOR OR NOT, YOU DID WONDERS FOR HIM!
Munch Munch
HEY
SORRY!

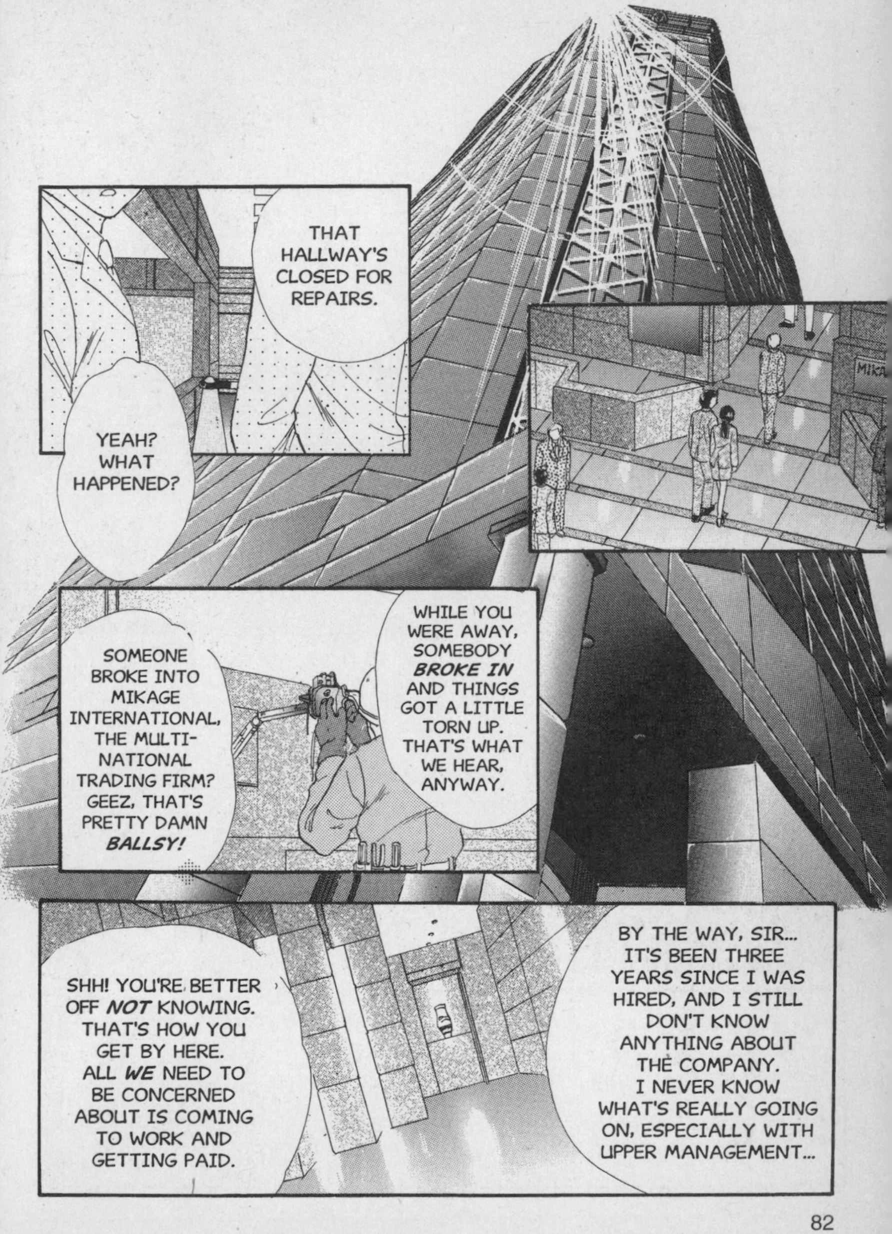
THAT HALLWAY'S CLOSED FOR REPAIRS.
YEAH? WHAT HAPPENED?
WHILE YOU WERE AWAY, SOMEBODY *BROKE IN* AND THINGS GOT A LITTLE TORN UP. THAT'S WHAT WE HEAR, ANYWAY.
SOMEONE BROKE INTO MIKAGE INTERNATIONAL, THE MULTI-NATIONAL TRADING FIRM? GEEZ, THAT'S PRETTY DAMN *BALLSY!*
BY THE WAY, SIR... IT'S BEEN THREE YEARS SINCE I WAS HIRED, AND I STILL DON'T KNOW ANYTHING ABOUT THE COMPANY. I NEVER KNOW WHAT'S REALLY GOING ON, ESPECIALLY WITH UPPER MANAGEMENT...
SHH! YOU'RE BETTER OFF *NOT* KNOWING. THAT'S HOW YOU GET BY HERE. ALL *WE* NEED TO BE CONCERNED ABOUT IS COMING TO WORK AND GETTING PAID.

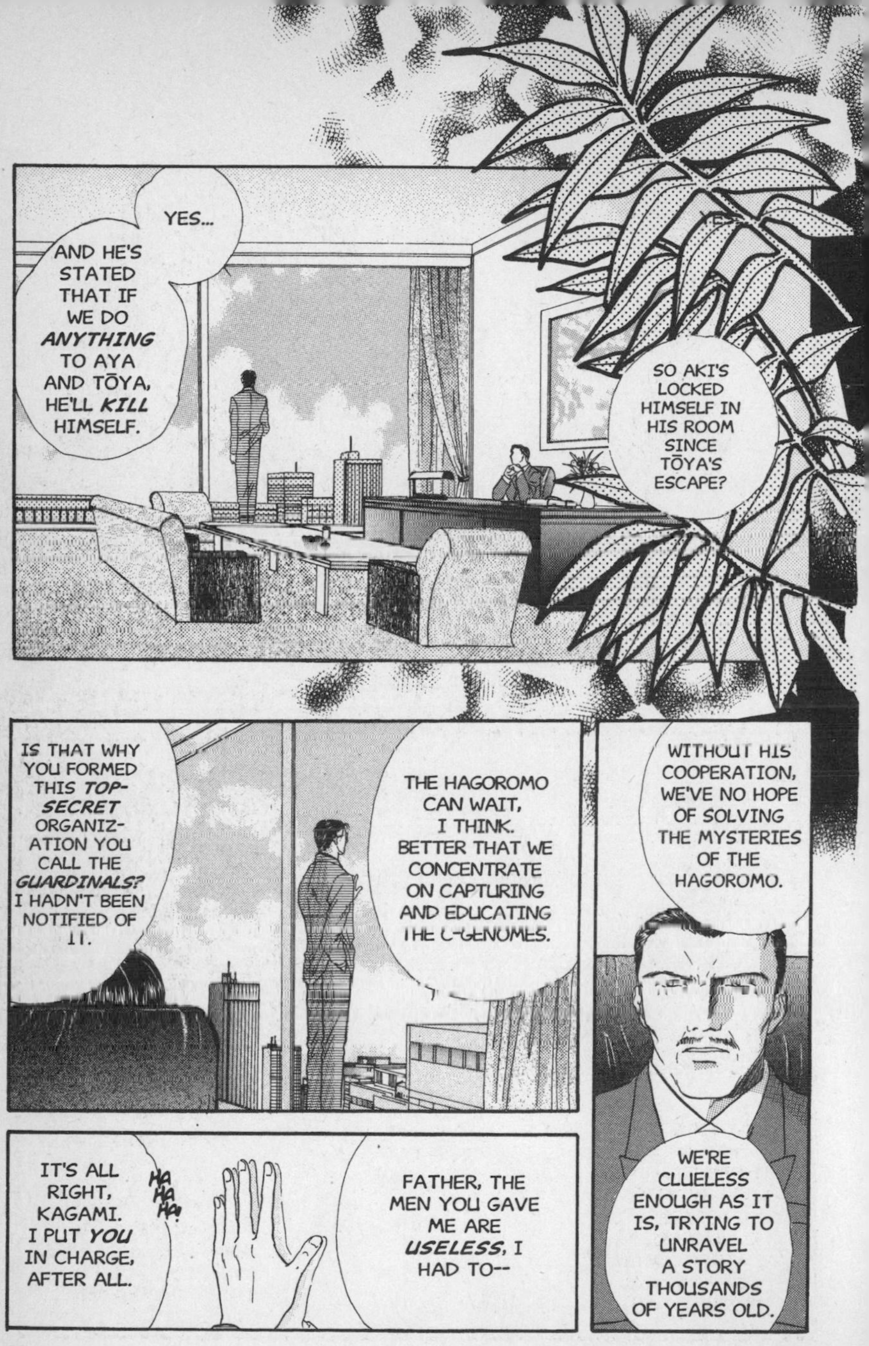
SO AKI'S LOCKED HIMSELF IN HIS ROOM SINCE TŌYA'S ESCAPE?
YES...
AND HE'S STATED THAT IF WE DO *ANYTHING* TO AYA AND TŌYA, HE'LL *KILL* HIMSELF.
WITHOUT HIS COOPERATION, WE'VE NO HOPE OF SOLVING THE MYSTERIES OF THE HAGOROMO.
WE'RE CLUELESS ENOUGH AS IT IS, TRYING TO UNRAVEL A STORY THOUSANDS OF YEARS OLD.
THE HAGOROMO CAN WAIT, I THINK. BETTER THAT WE CONCENTRATE ON CAPTURING AND EDUCATING THE C-GENOMES.
IS THAT WHY YOU FORMED THIS *TOP-SECRET* ORGANIZATION YOU CALL THE *GUARDINALS?* I HADN'T BEEN NOTIFIED OF IT.
FATHER, THE MEN YOU GAVE ME ARE *USELESS*, I HAD TO--
HA HA HA!
IT'S ALL RIGHT, KAGAMI. I PUT *YOU* IN CHARGE, AFTER ALL.

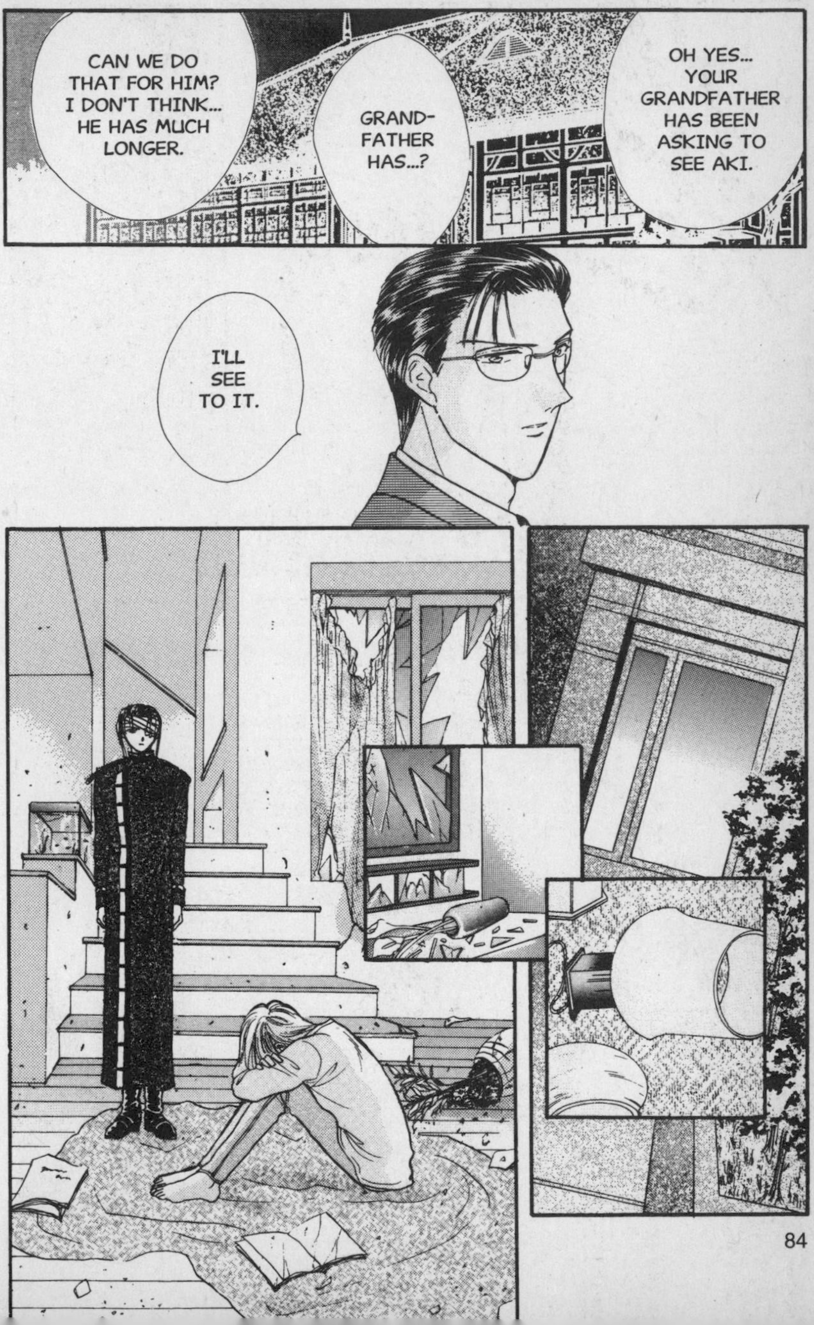
OH YES... YOUR GRANDFATHER HAS BEEN ASKING TO SEE AKI.
GRAND-FATHER HAS...?
CAN WE DO THAT FOR HIM? I DON'T THINK... HE HAS MUCH LONGER.
I'LL SEE TO IT.

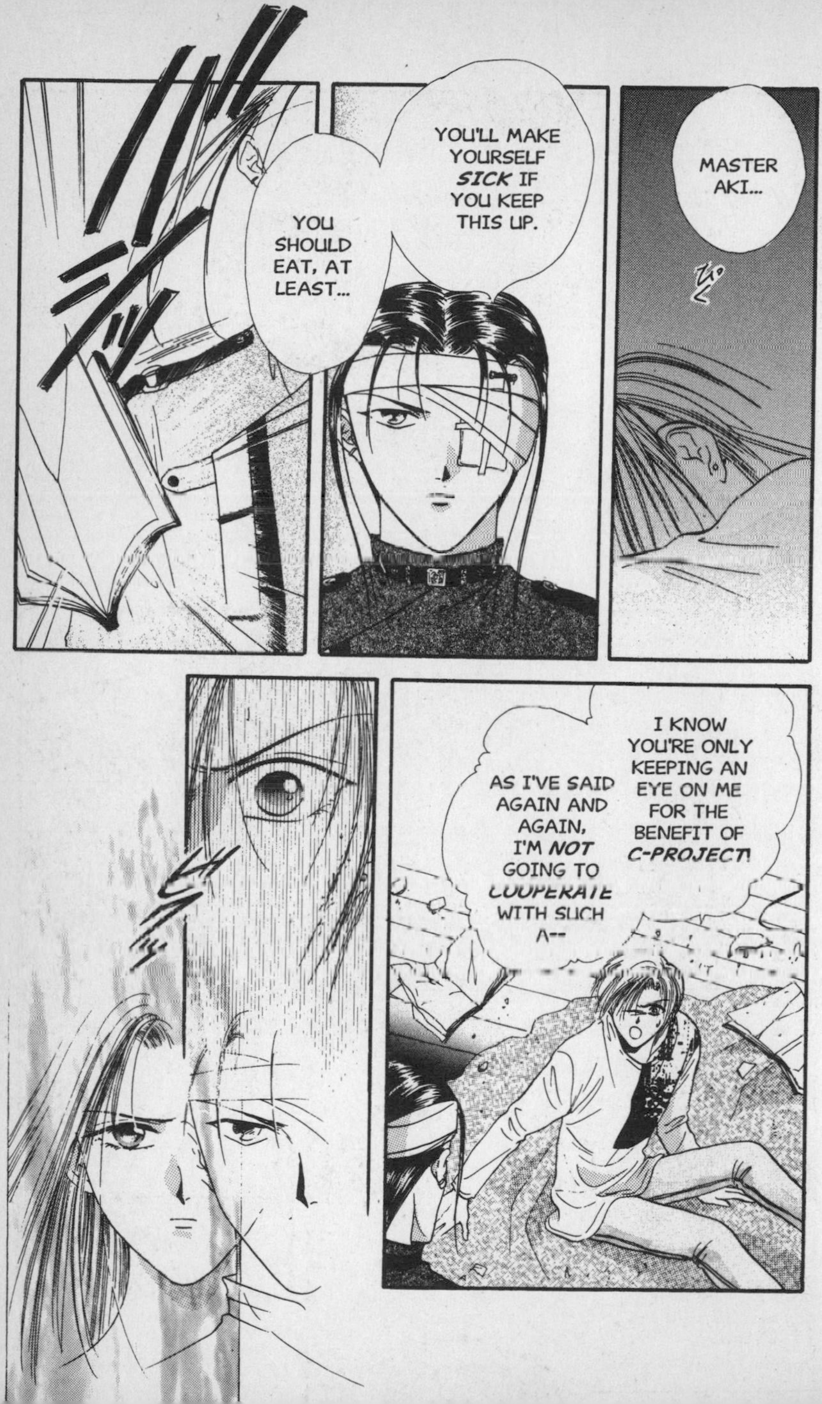
MASTER AKI...
ぴく
YOU'LL MAKE YOURSELF SICK IF YOU KEEP THIS UP.
YOU SHOULD EAT, AT LEAST...
I KNOW YOU'RE ONLY KEEPING AN EYE ON ME FOR THE BENEFIT OF C-PROJECT!
AS I'VE SAID AGAIN AND AGAIN, I'M NOT GOING TO COOPERATE WITH SUCH A--

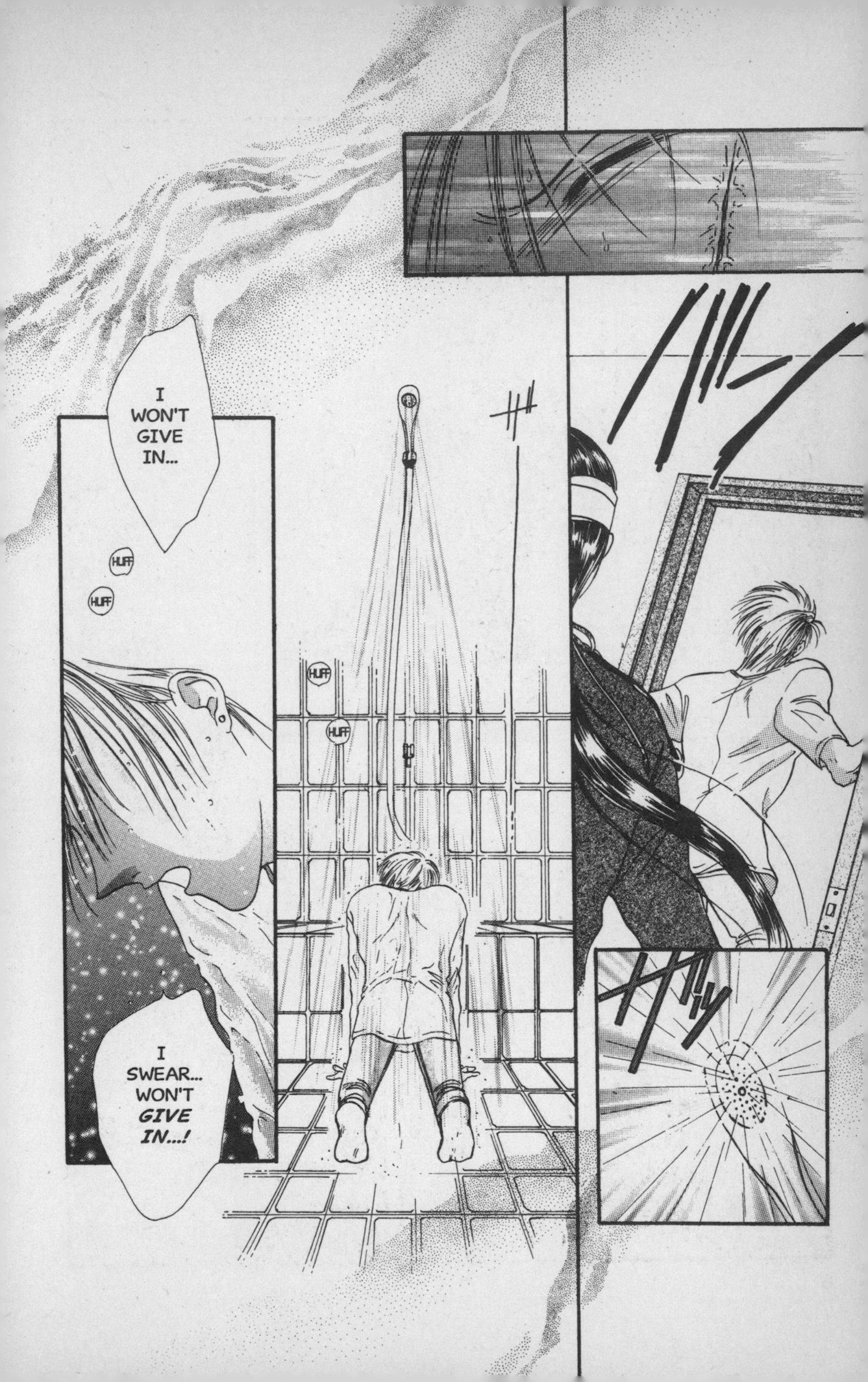
HUFF
HUFF
I WON'T GIVE IN...
HUFF
HUFF
I SWEAR... WON'T *GIVE IN...!*

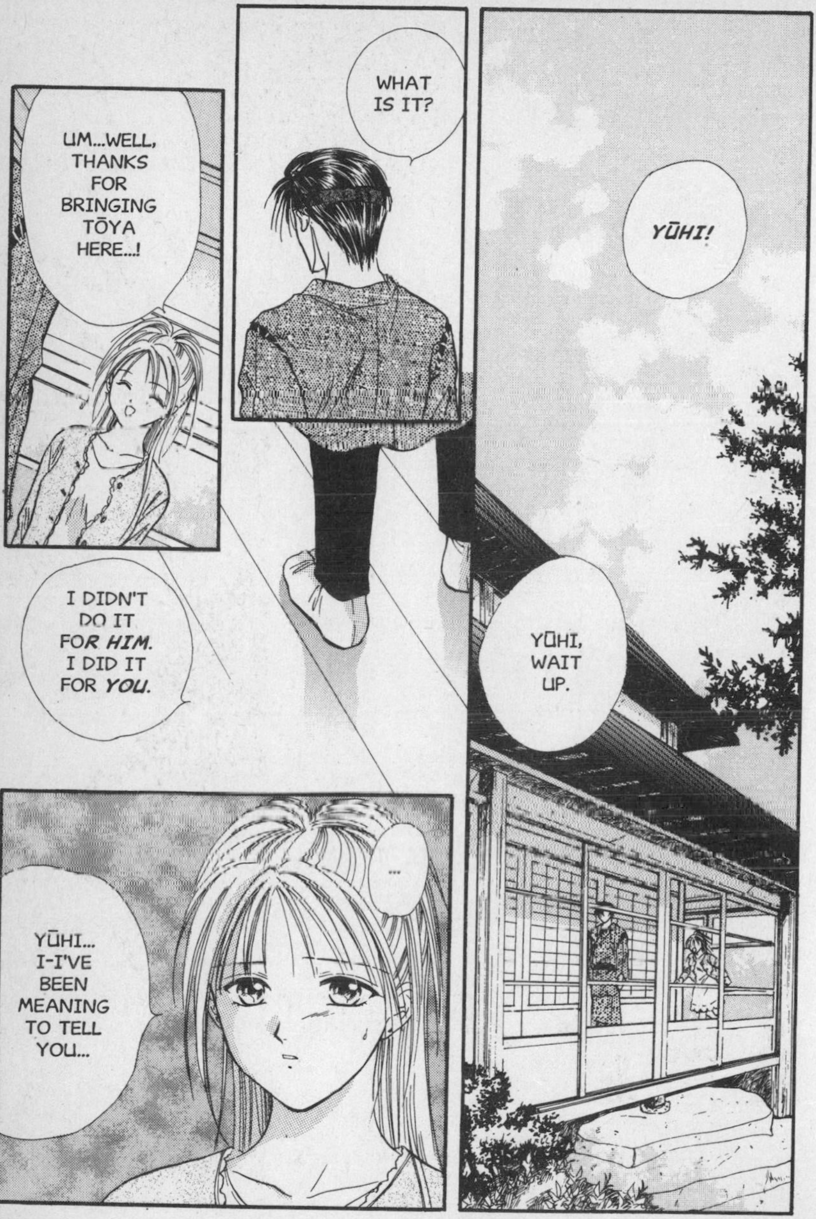
YŪHI!
YŪHI, WAIT UP.
WHAT IS IT?
UM...WELL, THANKS FOR BRINGING TŌYA HERE...!
I DIDN'T DO IT FOR HIM. I DID IT FOR YOU.
...
YŪHI... I-I'VE BEEN MEANING TO TELL YOU...

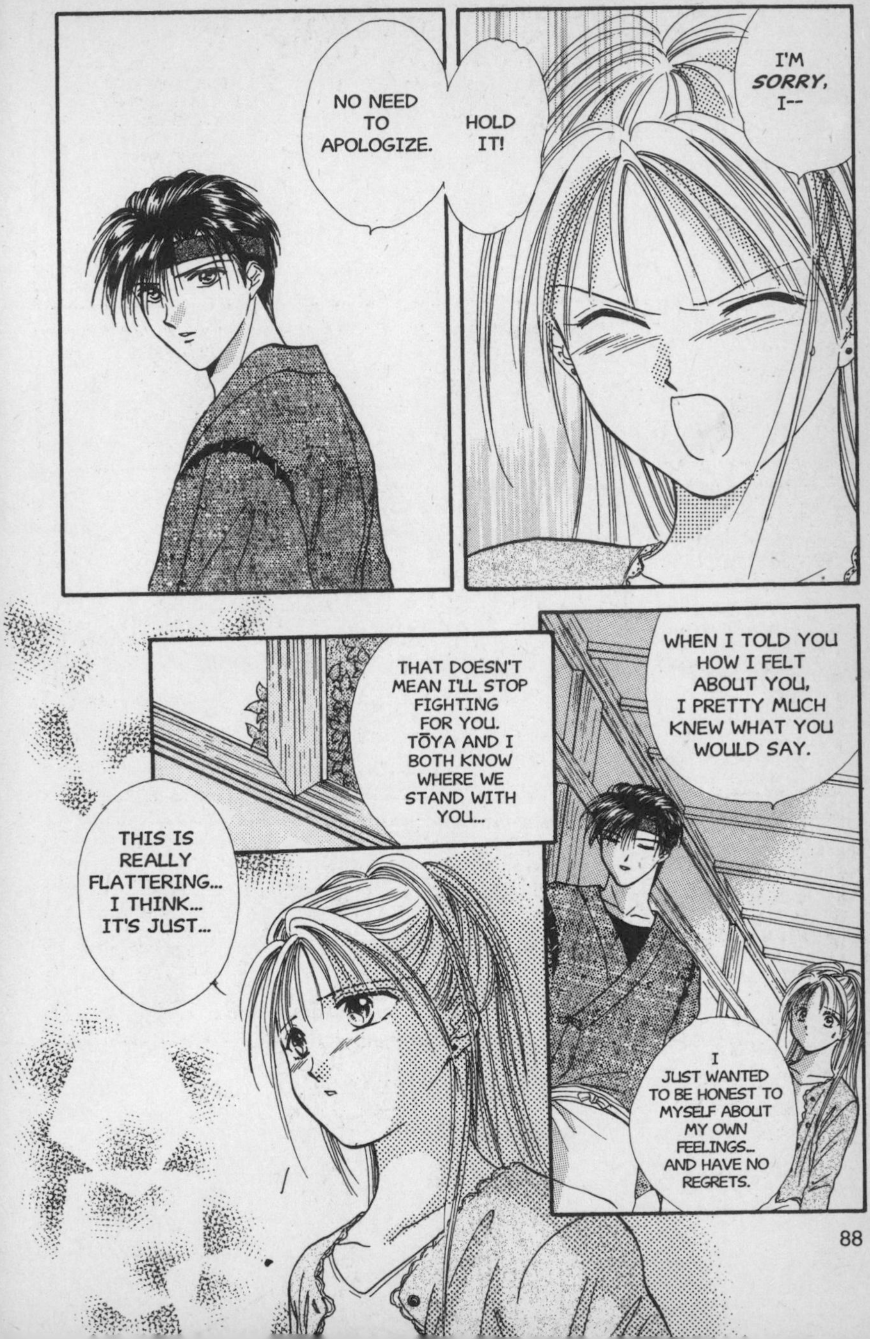
I'M SORRY, I--
HOLD IT!
NO NEED TO APOLOGIZE.
WHEN I TOLD YOU HOW I FELT ABOUT YOU, I PRETTY MUCH KNEW WHAT YOU WOULD SAY.
I JUST WANTED TO BE HONEST TO MYSELF ABOUT MY OWN FEELINGS... AND HAVE NO REGRETS.
THAT DOESN'T MEAN I'LL STOP FIGHTING FOR YOU. TŌYA AND I BOTH KNOW WHERE WE STAND WITH YOU...
THIS IS REALLY FLATTERING... I THINK... IT'S JUST...

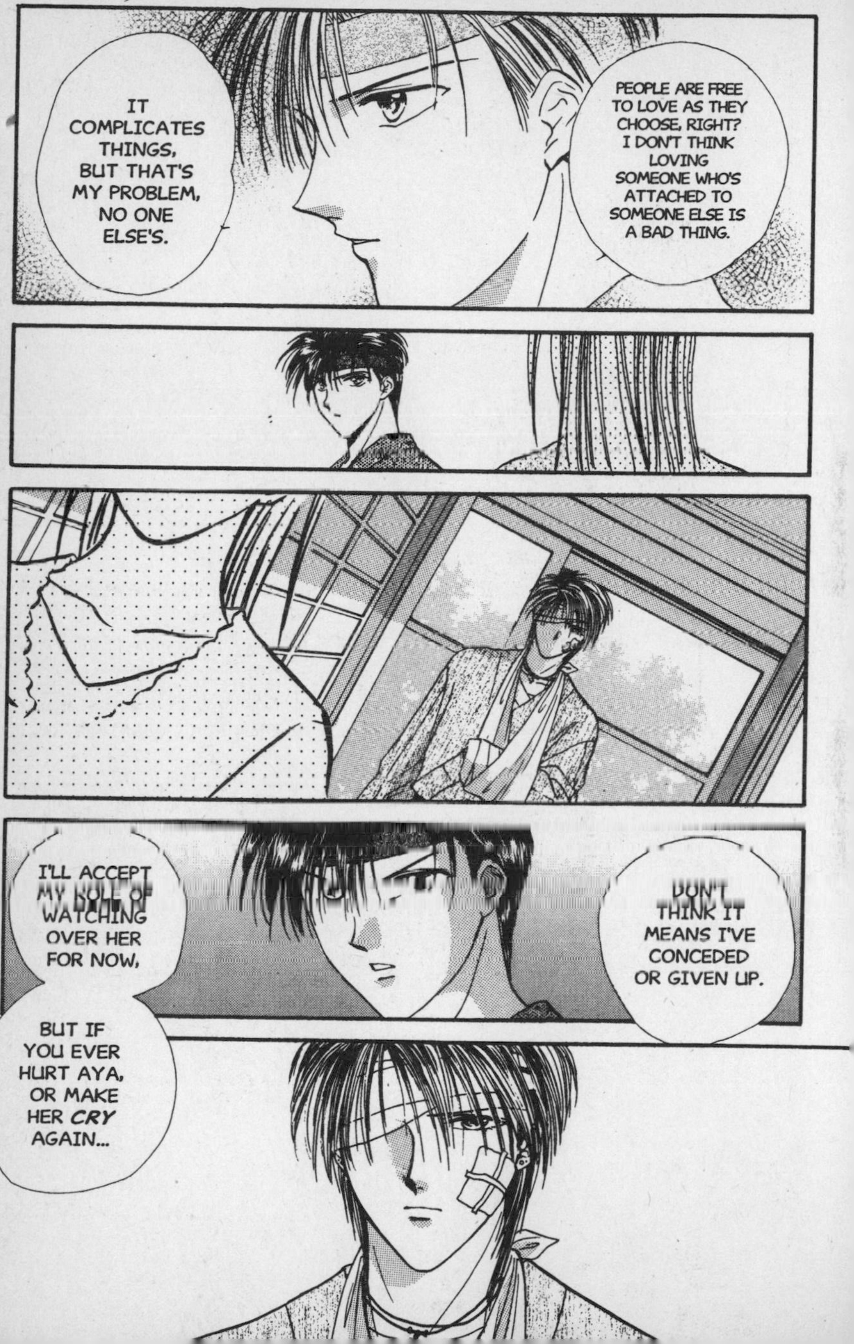
PEOPLE ARE FREE TO LOVE AS THEY CHOOSE, RIGHT? I DON'T THINK LOVING SOMEONE WHO'S ATTACHED TO SOMEONE ELSE IS A BAD THING.
IT COMPLICATES THINGS, BUT THAT'S MY PROBLEM, NO ONE ELSE'S.
DON'T THINK IT MEANS I'VE CONCEDED OR GIVEN UP.
I'LL ACCEPT MY ROLE OF WATCHING OVER HER FOR NOW,
BUT IF YOU EVER HURT AYA, OR MAKE HER *CRY* AGAIN...

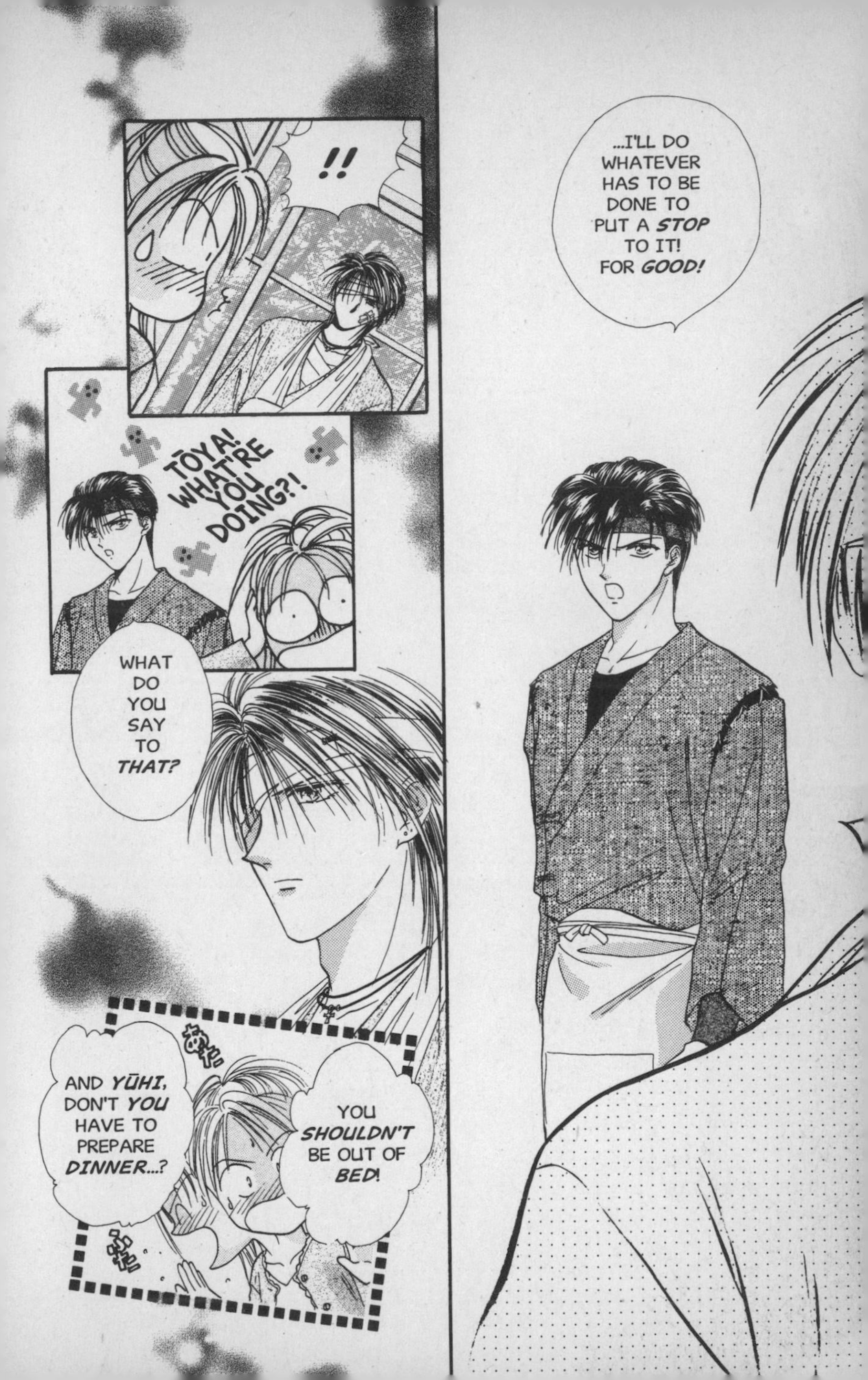
...I'LL DO WHATEVER HAS TO BE DONE TO PUT A *STOP* TO IT! FOR *GOOD!*
!!
TŌYA! WHAT'RE YOU DOING?!
WHAT DO YOU SAY TO *THAT?*
YOU *SHOULDN'T* BE OUT OF *BED*!
AND *YŪHI*, DON'T *YOU* HAVE TO PREPARE *DINNER*...?

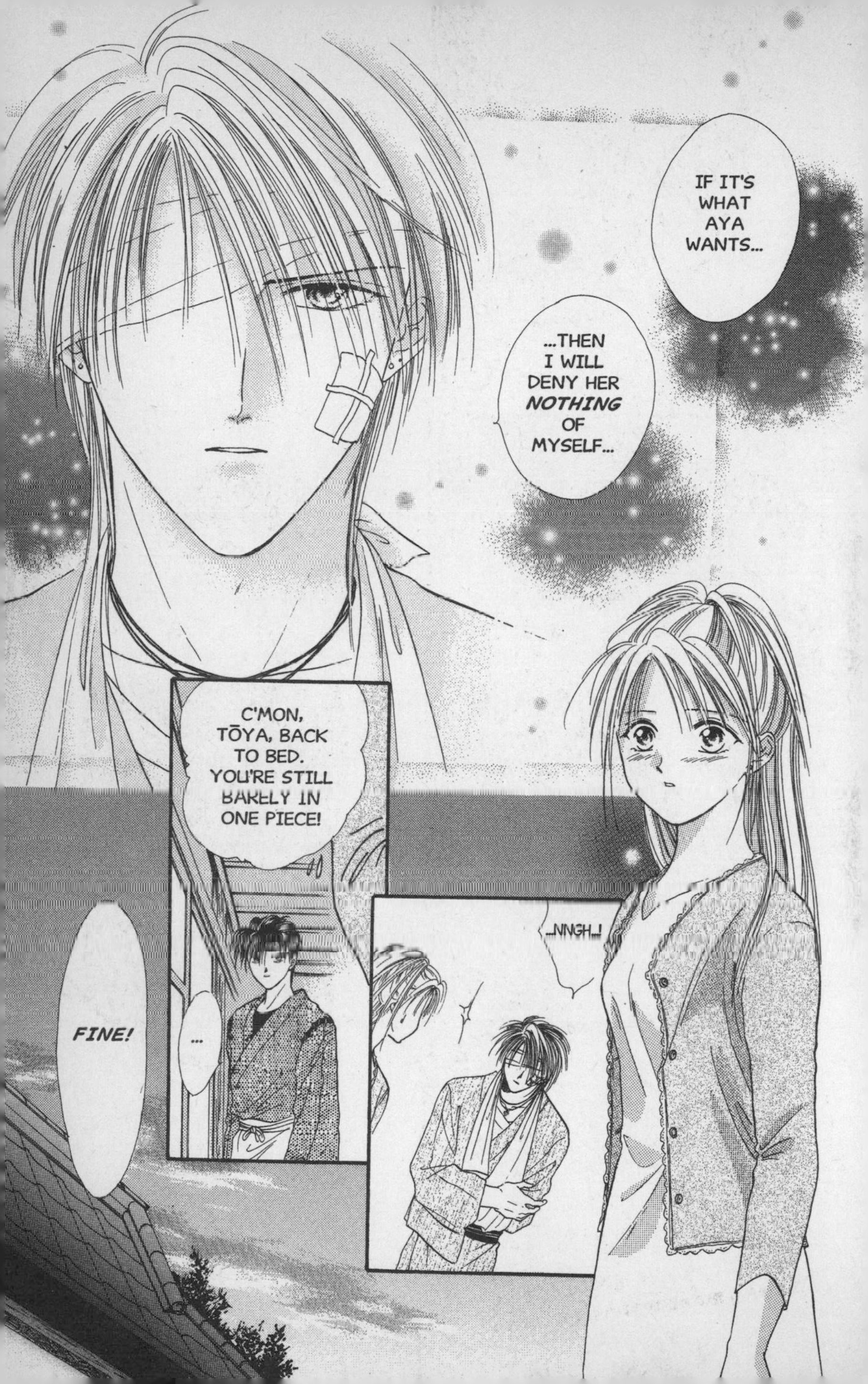
IF IT'S WHAT AYA WANTS...
...THEN I WILL DENY HER *NOTHING* OF MYSELF...
C'MON, TŌYA, BACK TO BED. YOU'RE STILL BARELY IN ONE PIECE!
...NNGH...!
...
FINE!

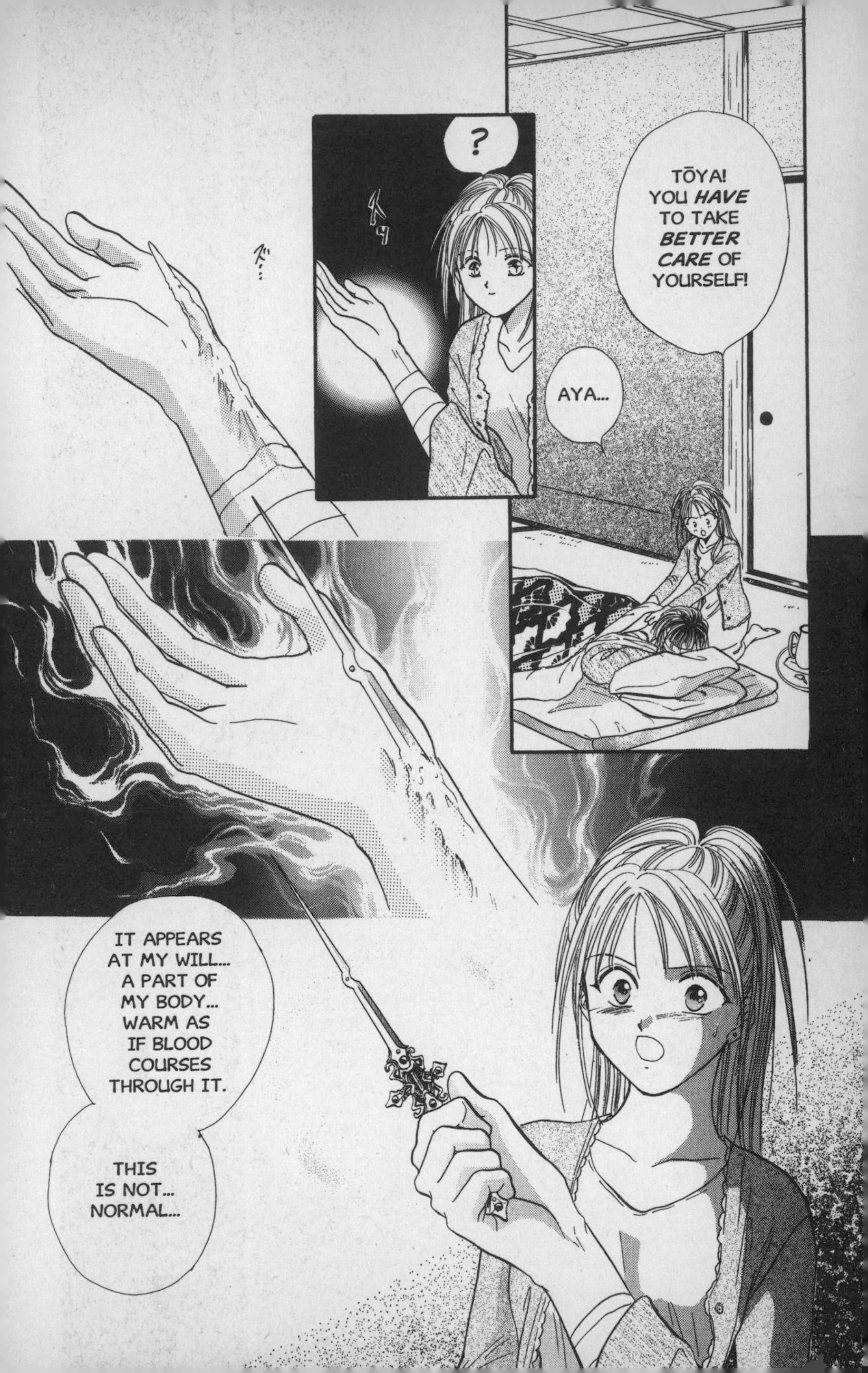
TŌYA! YOU HAVE TO TAKE BETTER CARE OF YOURSELF!
AYA...
?
IT APPEARS AT MY WILL... A PART OF MY BODY... WARM AS IF BLOOD COURSES THROUGH IT.
THIS IS NOT... NORMAL...

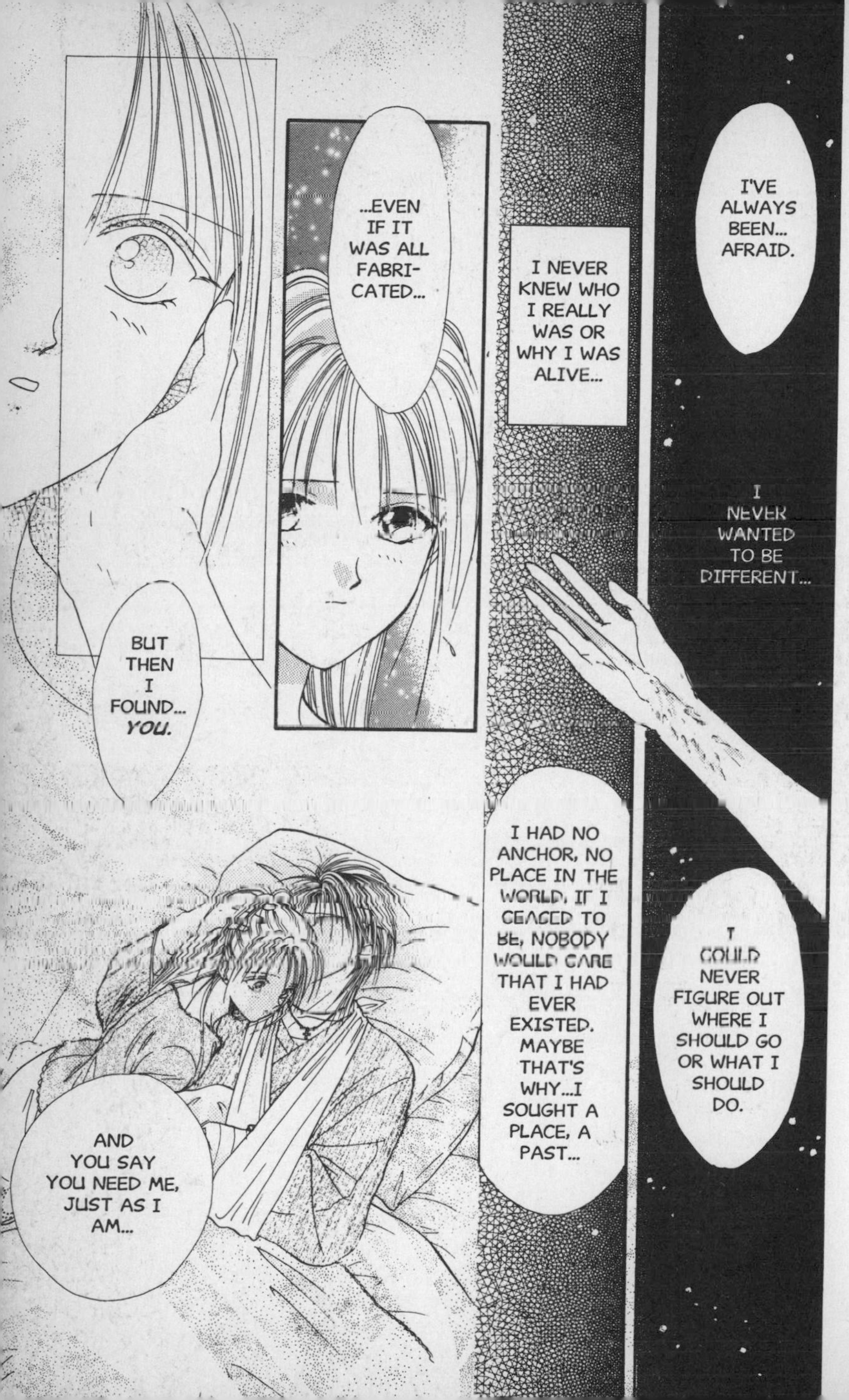
I'VE ALWAYS BEEN... AFRAID.
I NEVER WANTED TO BE DIFFERENT...
I COULD NEVER FIGURE OUT WHERE I SHOULD GO OR WHAT I SHOULD DO.
I NEVER KNEW WHO I REALLY WAS OR WHY I WAS ALIVE...
I HAD NO ANCHOR, NO PLACE IN THE WORLD. IF I CEASED TO BE, NOBODY WOULD CARE THAT I HAD EVER EXISTED. MAYBE THAT'S WHY...I SOUGHT A PLACE, A PAST...
...EVEN IF IT WAS ALL FABRICATED...
BUT THEN I FOUND... *YOU.*
AND YOU SAY YOU NEED ME, JUST AS I AM...

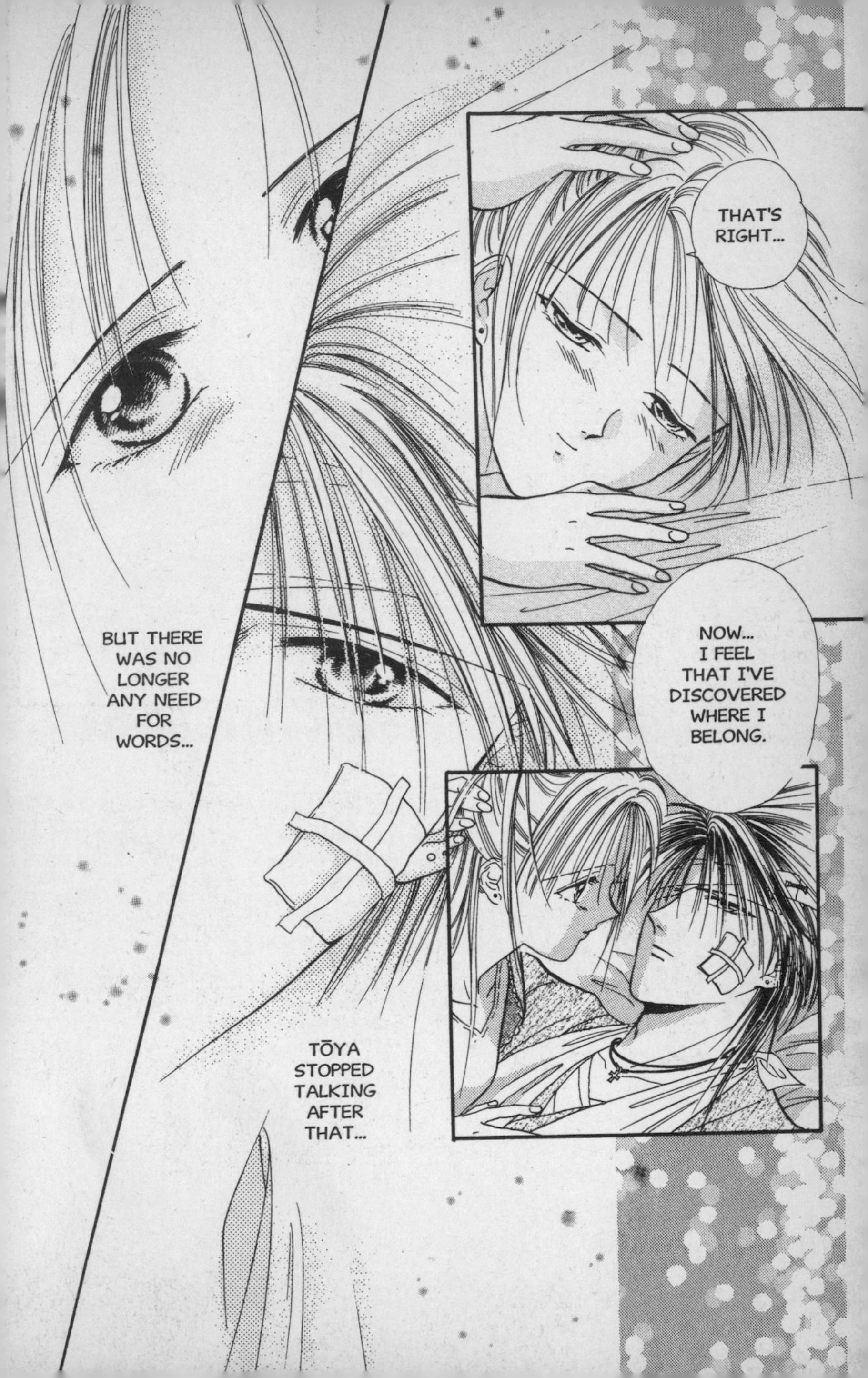
THAT'S RIGHT...
NOW... I FEEL THAT I'VE DISCOVERED WHERE I BELONG.
TŌYA STOPPED TALKING AFTER THAT...
BUT THERE WAS NO LONGER ANY NEED FOR WORDS...

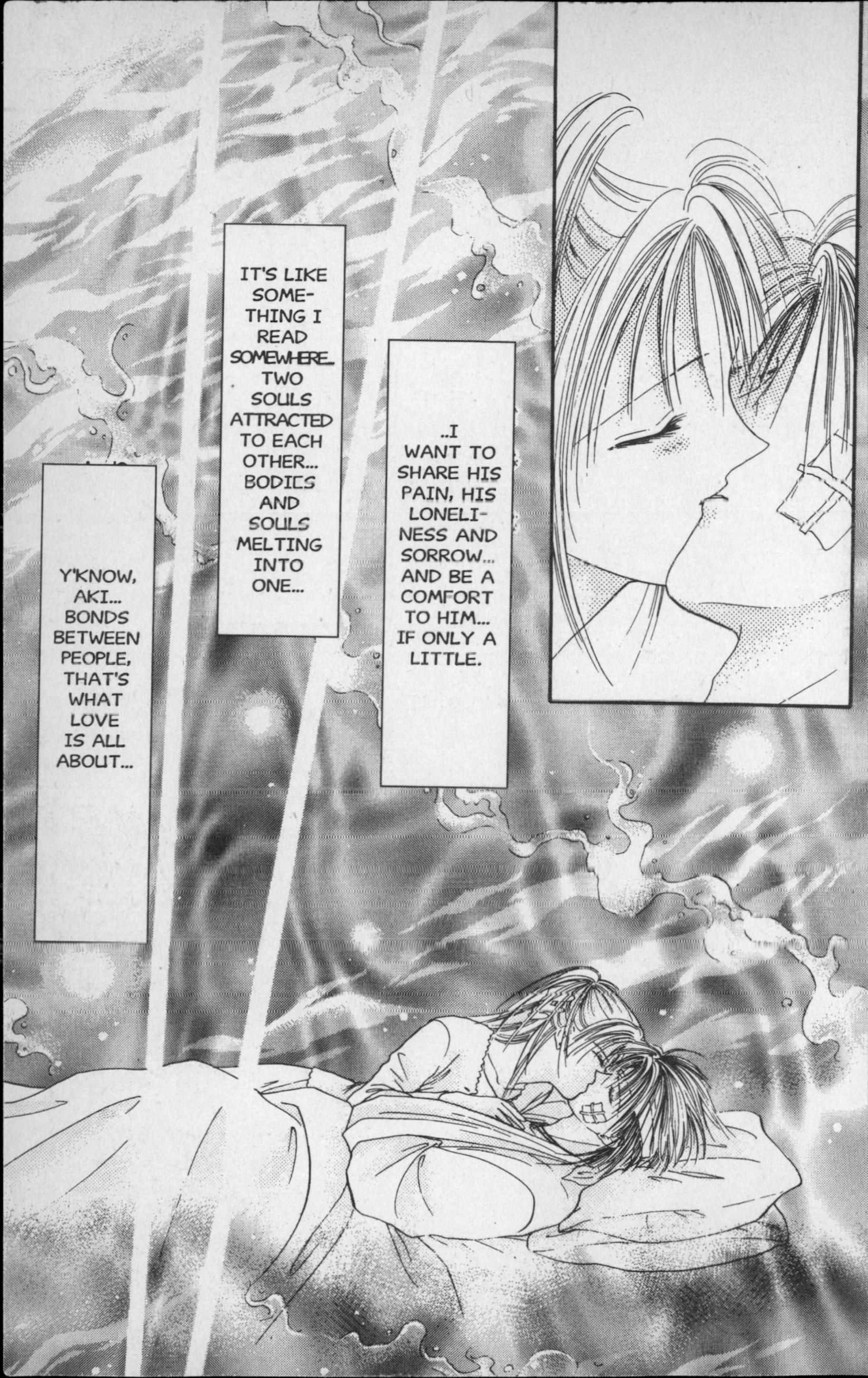
..I WANT TO SHARE HIS PAIN, HIS LONELI- NESS AND SORROW... AND BE A COMFORT TO HIM... IF ONLY A LITTLE.
IT'S LIKE SOME- THING I READ SOMEWHERE. TWO SOULS ATTRACTED TO EACH OTHER... BODIES AND SOULS MELTING INTO ONE...
Y'KNOW, AKI... BONDS BETWEEN PEOPLE, THAT'S WHAT LOVE IS ALL ABOUT...

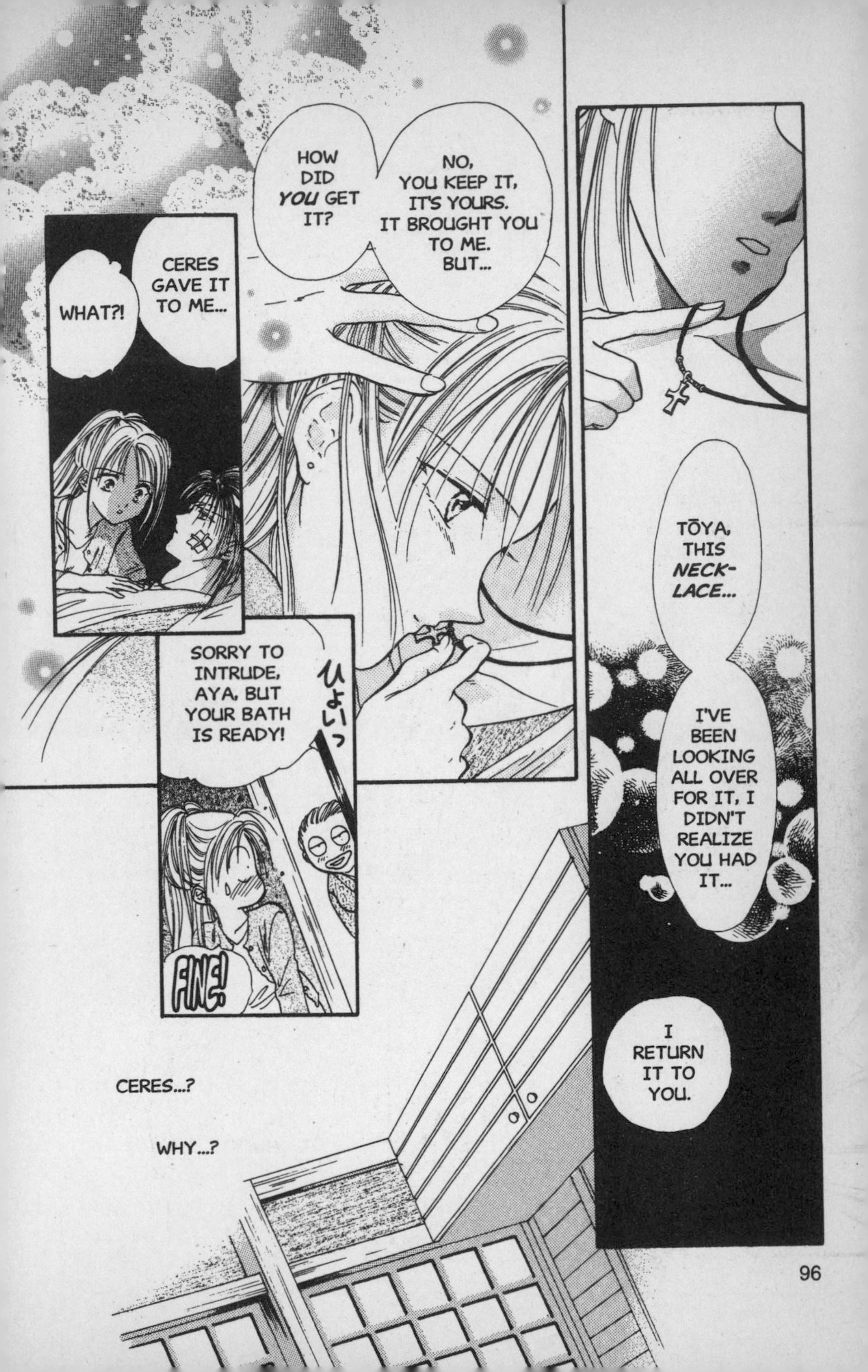

TŌYA, THIS NECKLACE...
I'VE BEEN LOOKING ALL OVER FOR IT, I DIDN'T REALIZE YOU HAD IT...
I RETURN IT TO YOU.
NO, YOU KEEP IT, IT'S YOURS. IT BROUGHT YOU TO ME. BUT...
HOW DID YOU GET IT?
CERES GAVE IT TO ME...
WHAT?!
ひょいっ
SORRY TO INTRUDE, AYA, BUT YOUR BATH IS READY!
FINE!
CERES...?
WHY...?

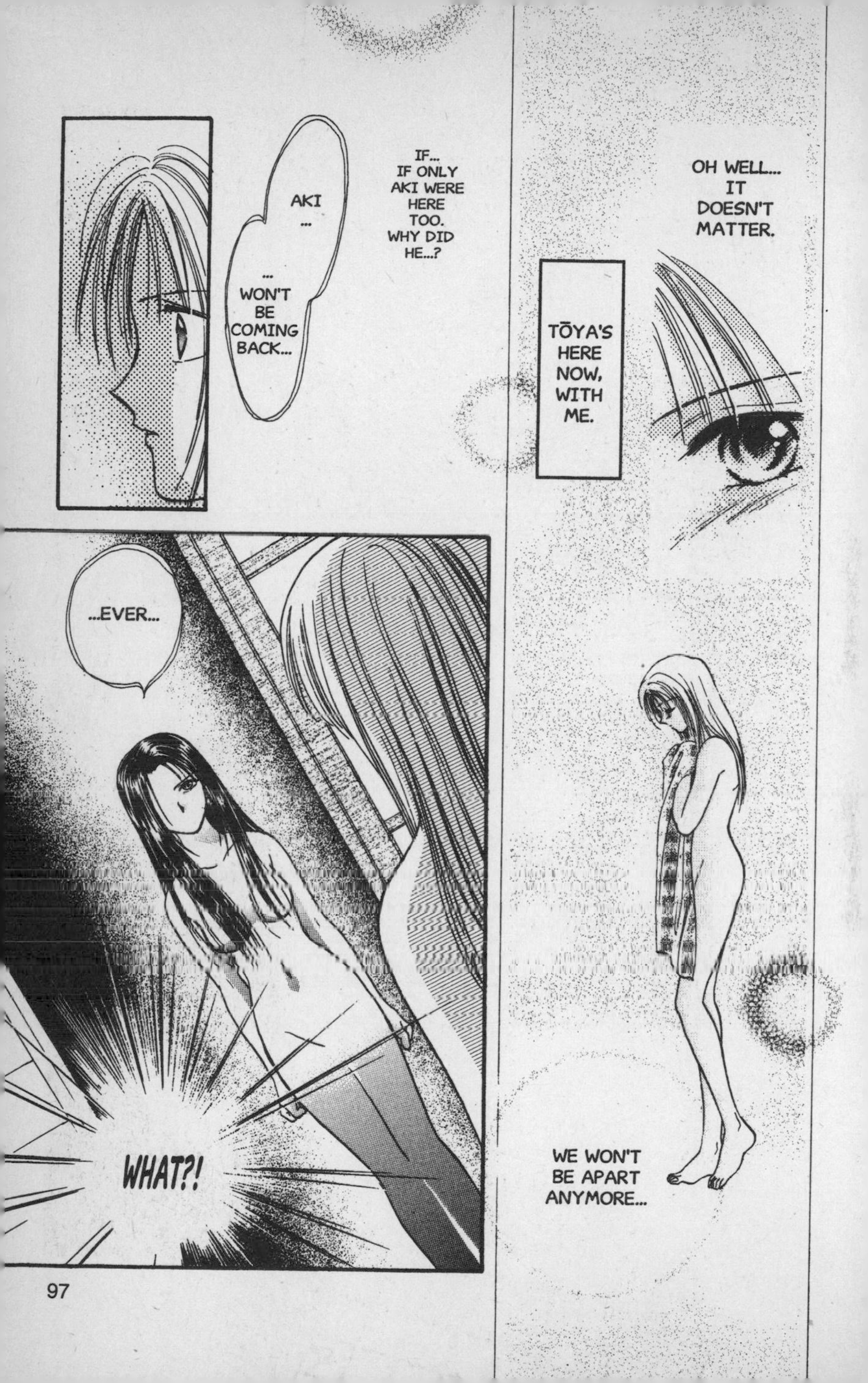
OH WELL... IT DOESN'T MATTER.
TŌYA'S HERE NOW, WITH ME.
WE WON'T BE APART ANYMORE...
IF... IF ONLY AKI WERE HERE TOO. WHY DID HE...?
AKI ...
... WON'T BE COMING BACK...
...EVER...
WHAT?!

BIRTHDAY: FEBRUARY 14. I'M 20 YEARS OLD ♡ (just kidding)

BLOOD TYPE: O (PROBABLY...)

HEIGHT: 4'11" BUST: 39" WAIST: 39" HIPS: 39"

HOBBIES: COLLECTING LOVELY KNICK KNACKS ♡

SPECIAL SKILLS: BEING A GROUPIE, DRIVING

...I'M ALSO A WONDERFUL MOTHER (TEE HEE ♡)

MRS. Q

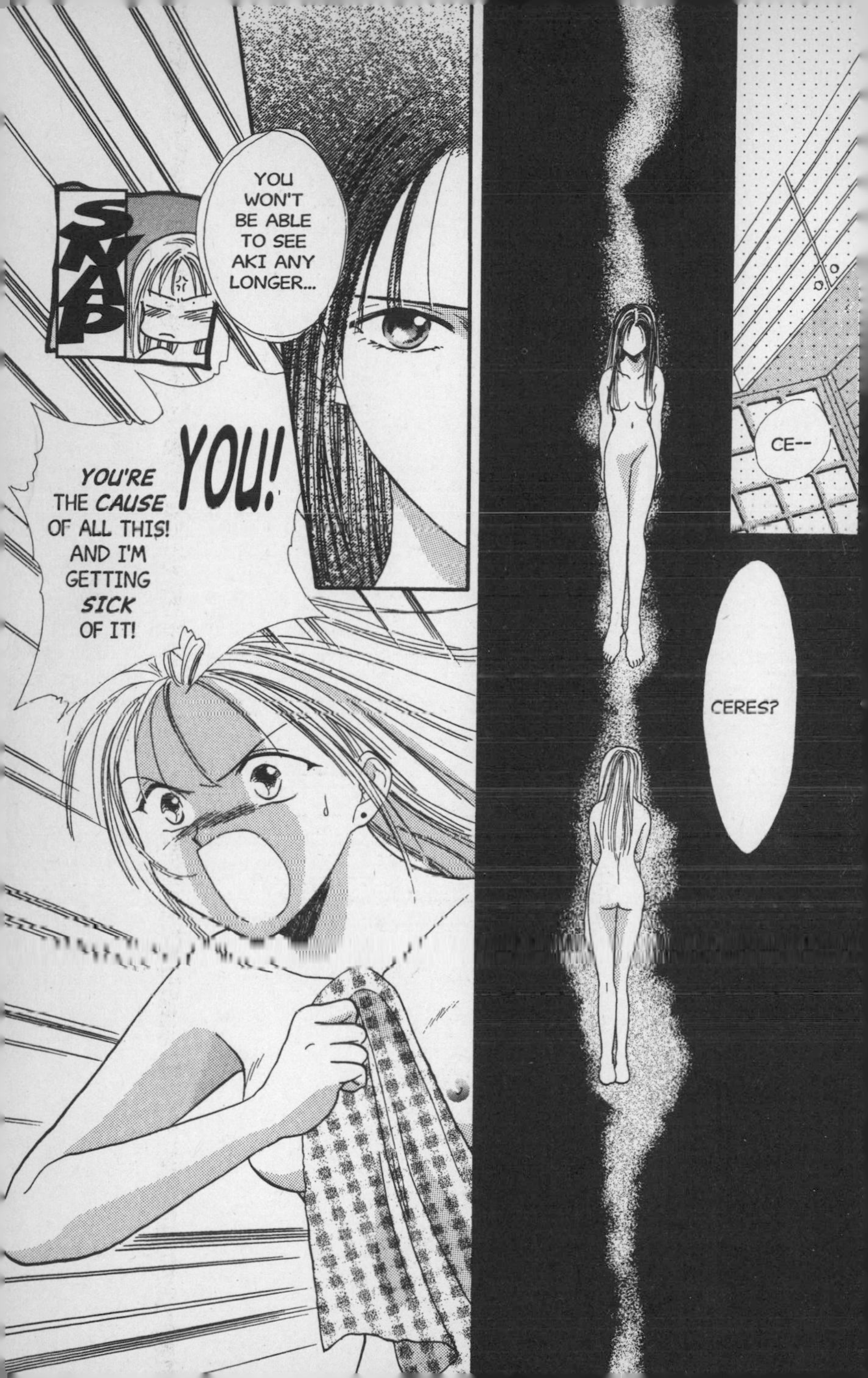
CE--
CERES?
YOU WON'T BE ABLE TO SEE AKI ANY LONGER...
SNAP
YOU!
YOU'RE THE CAUSE OF ALL THIS! AND I'M GETTING SICK OF IT!

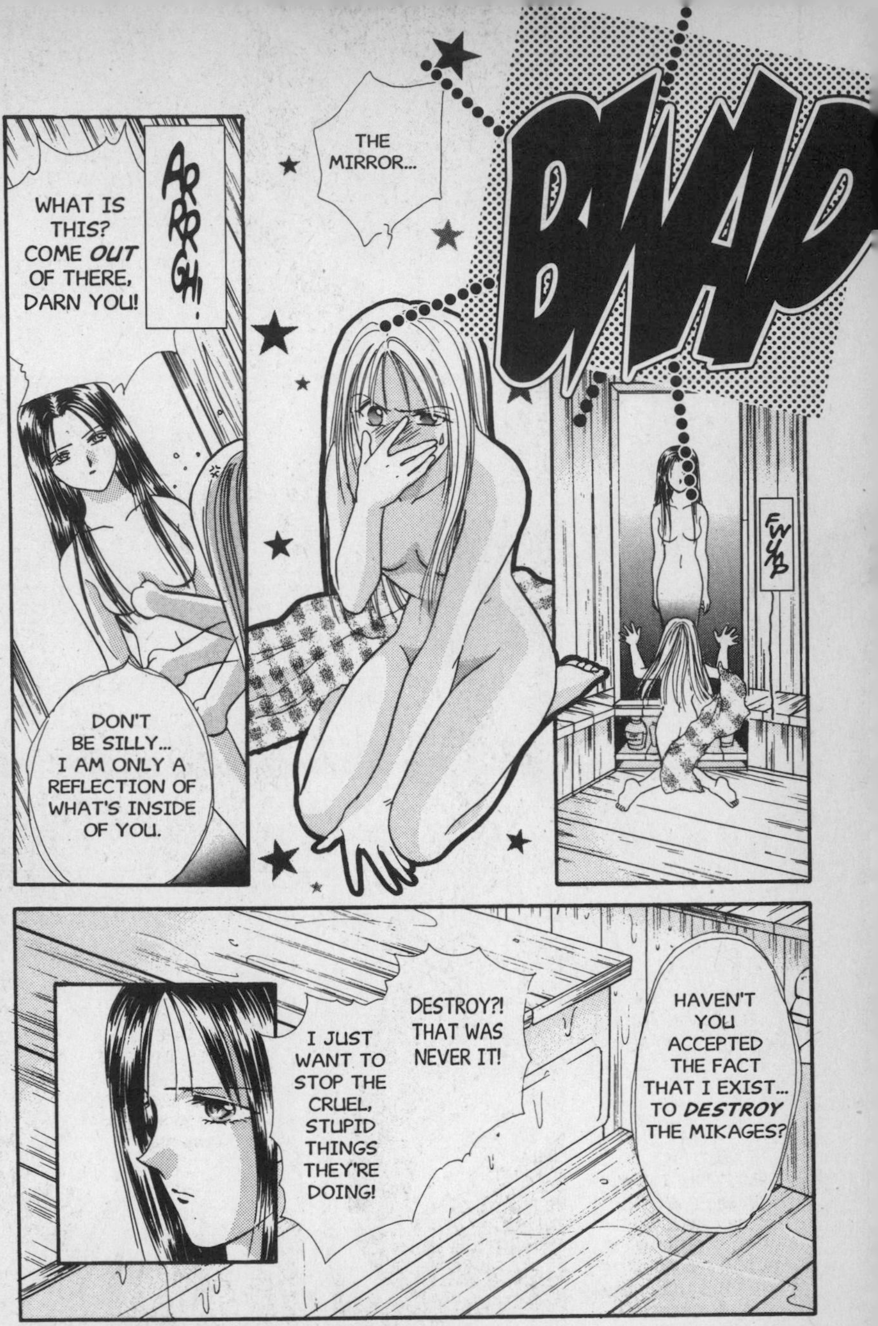
BWAP
FWUMP
THE MIRROR...
WHAT IS THIS? COME *OUT* OF THERE, DARN YOU!
ARRRGH!
DON'T BE SILLY... I AM ONLY A REFLECTION OF WHAT'S INSIDE OF YOU.
HAVEN'T YOU ACCEPTED THE FACT THAT I EXIST... TO *DESTROY* THE MIKAGES?
DESTROY?! THAT WAS NEVER IT!
I JUST WANT TO STOP THE CRUEL, STUPID THINGS THEY'RE DOING!

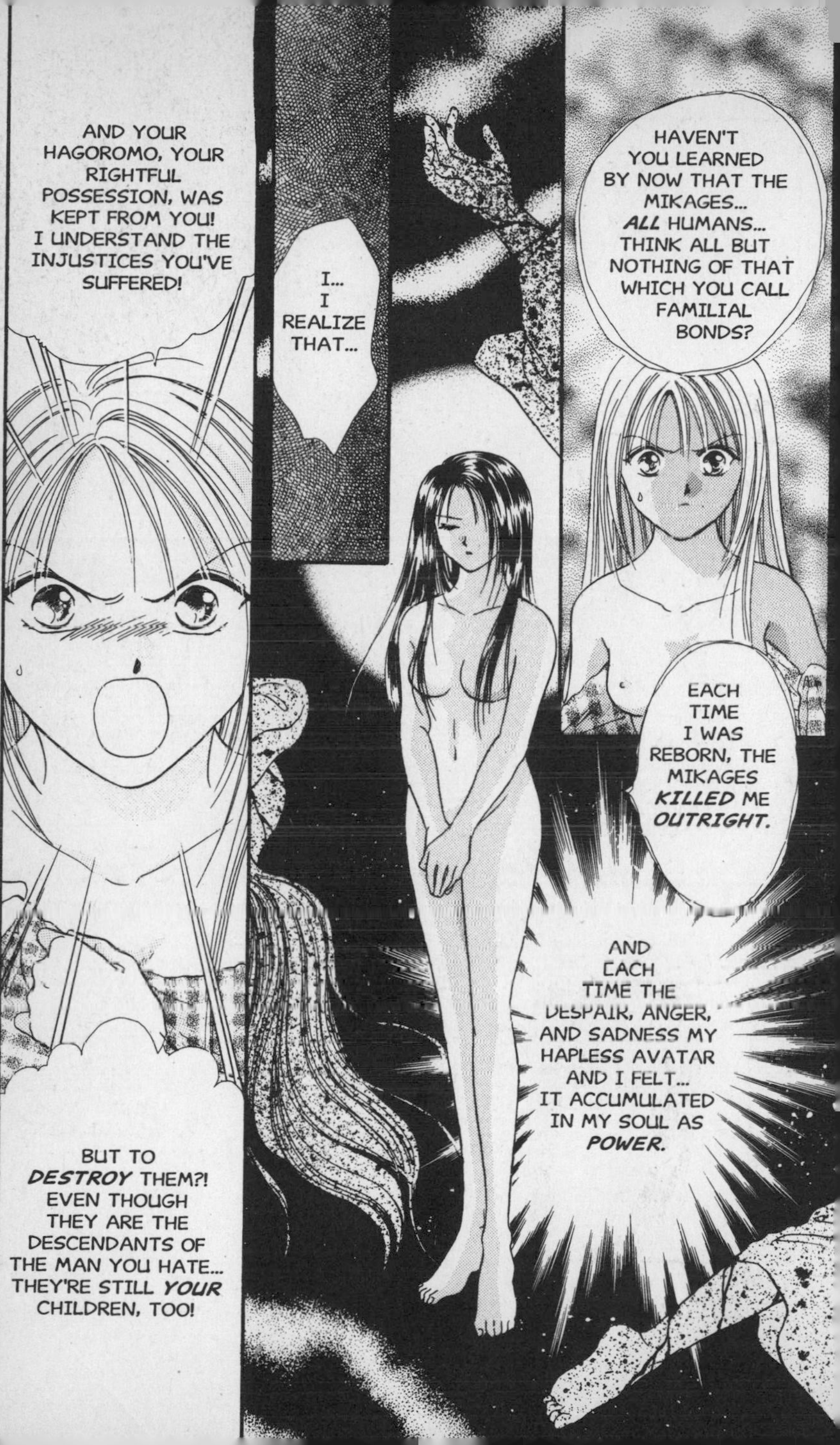
HAVEN'T YOU LEARNED BY NOW THAT THE MIKAGES... ***ALL*** HUMANS... THINK ALL BUT NOTHING OF THAT WHICH YOU CALL FAMILIAL BONDS?
I... I REALIZE THAT...
EACH TIME I WAS REBORN, THE MIKAGES ***KILLED*** ME ***OUTRIGHT.***
AND EACH TIME THE DESPAIR, ANGER, AND SADNESS MY HAPLESS AVATAR AND I FELT... IT ACCUMULATED IN MY SOUL AS ***POWER.***
AND YOUR HAGOROMO, YOUR RIGHTFUL POSSESSION, WAS KEPT FROM YOU! I UNDERSTAND THE INJUSTICES YOU'VE SUFFERED!
BUT TO ***DESTROY*** THEM?! EVEN THOUGH THEY ARE THE DESCENDANTS OF THE MAN YOU HATE... THEY'RE STILL ***YOUR*** CHILDREN, TOO!

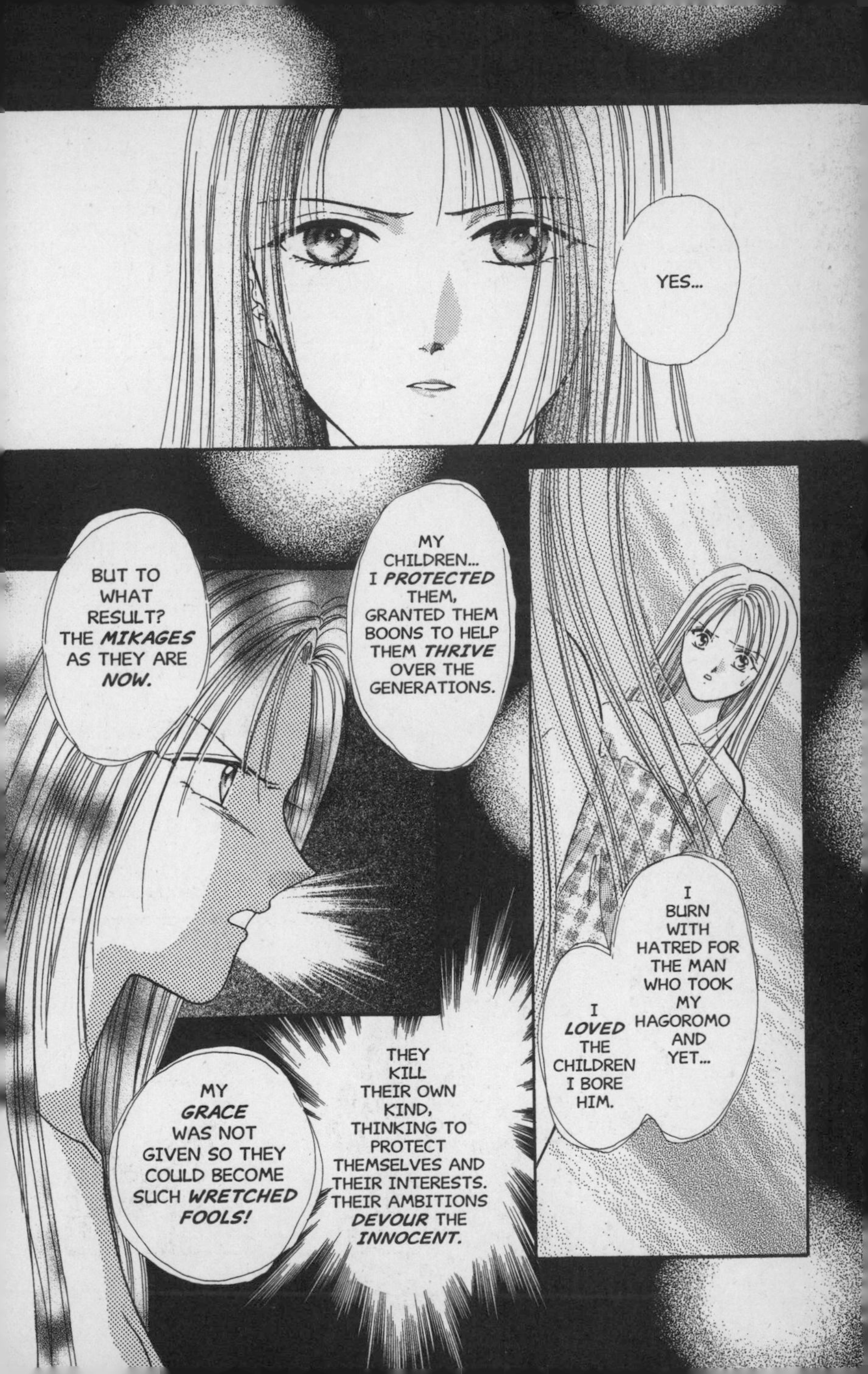
YES...
I BURN WITH HATRED FOR THE MAN WHO TOOK MY HAGOROMO AND YET...
I LOVED THE CHILDREN I BORE HIM.
MY CHILDREN... I PROTECTED THEM, GRANTED THEM BOONS TO HELP THEM THRIVE OVER THE GENERATIONS.
BUT TO WHAT RESULT? THE MIKAGES AS THEY ARE NOW.
THEY KILL THEIR OWN KIND, THINKING TO PROTECT THEMSELVES AND THEIR INTERESTS. THEIR AMBITIONS DEVOUR THE INNOCENT.
MY GRACE WAS NOT GIVEN SO THEY COULD BECOME SUCH WRETCHED FOOLS!

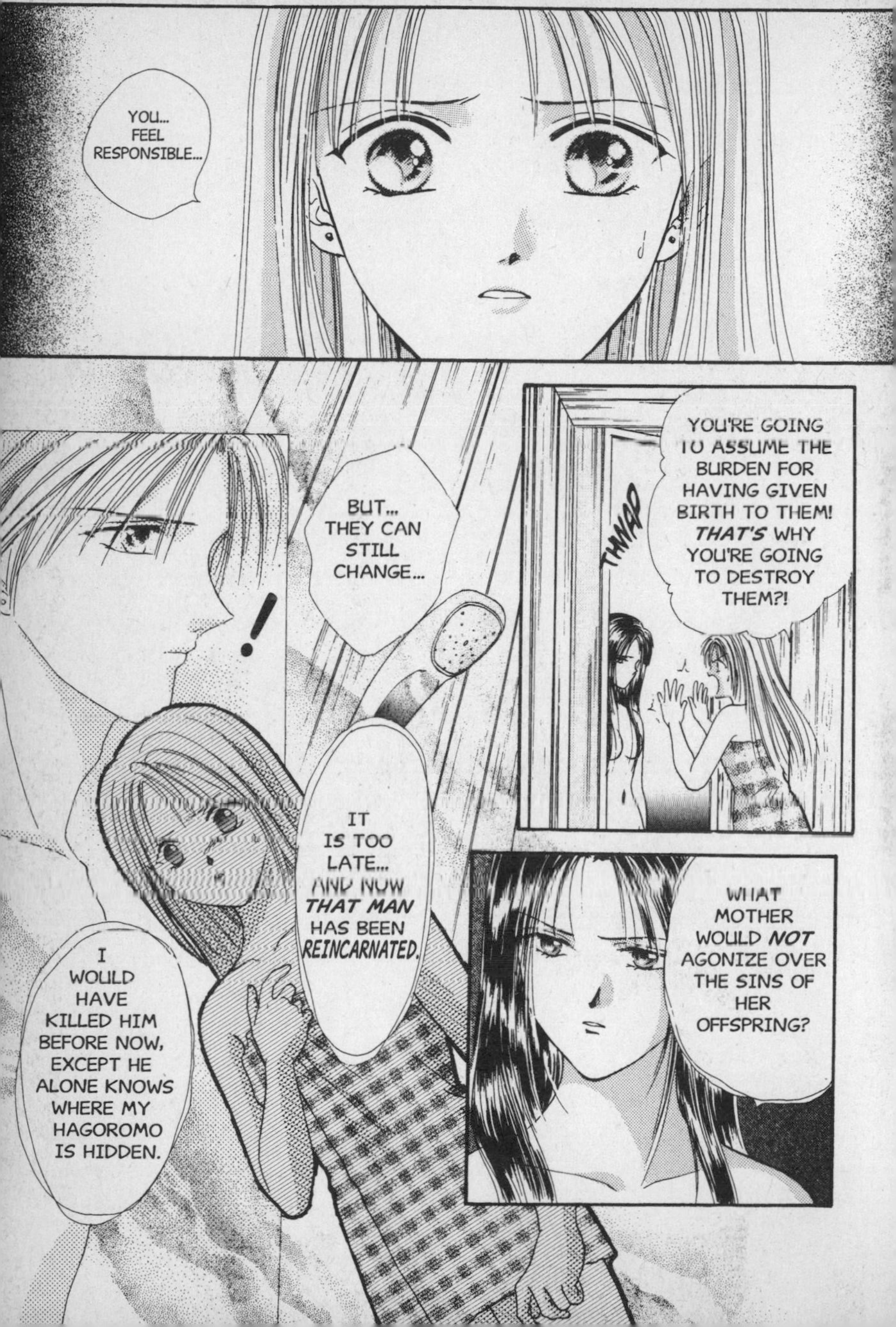
YOU... FEEL RESPONSIBLE...
YOU'RE GOING TO ASSUME THE BURDEN FOR HAVING GIVEN BIRTH TO THEM! *THAT'S* WHY YOU'RE GOING TO DESTROY THEM?!
THWAP
WHAT MOTHER WOULD *NOT* AGONIZE OVER THE SINS OF HER OFFSPRING?
BUT... THEY CAN STILL CHANGE...
!
IT IS TOO LATE... AND NOW *THAT MAN* HAS BEEN *REINCARNATED.*
I WOULD HAVE KILLED HIM BEFORE NOW, EXCEPT HE ALONE KNOWS WHERE MY HAGOROMO IS HIDDEN.

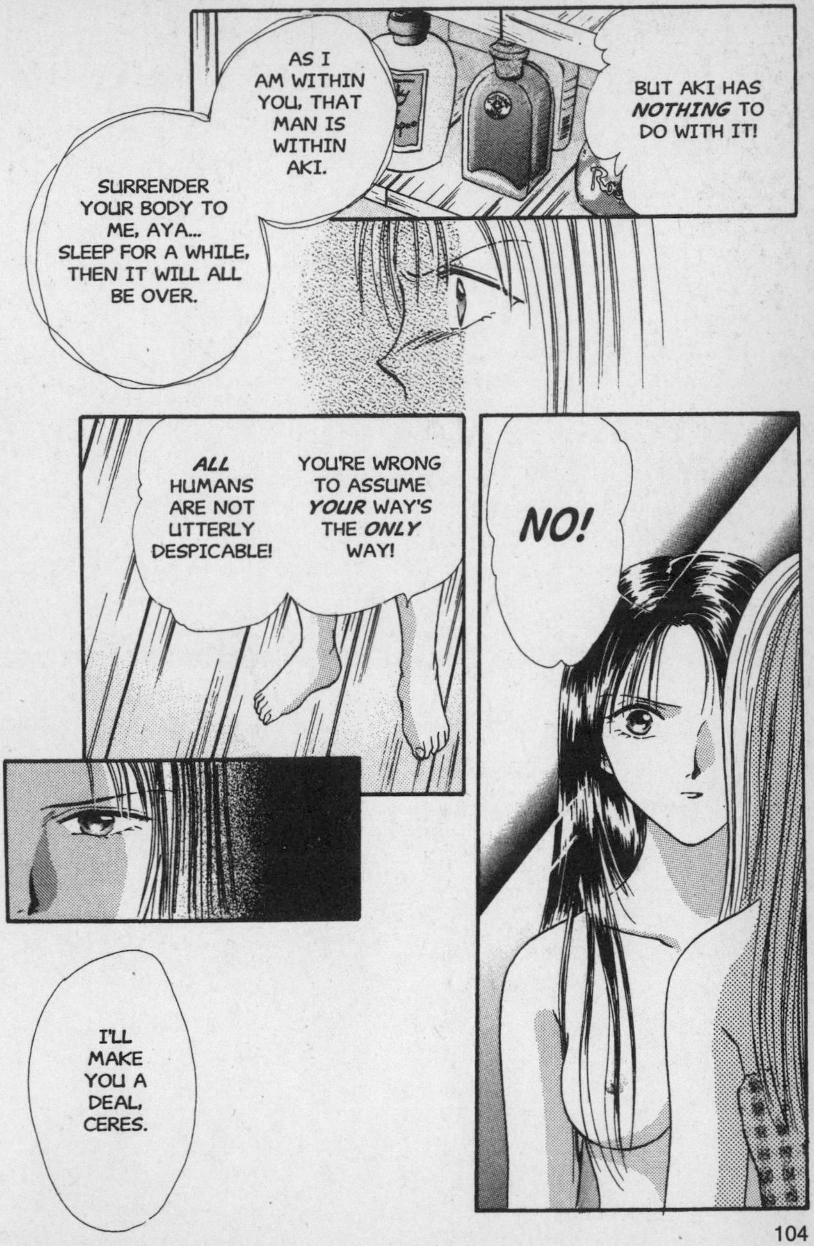
BUT AKI HAS *NOTHING* TO DO WITH IT!
AS I AM WITHIN YOU, THAT MAN IS WITHIN AKI.
SURRENDER YOUR BODY TO ME, AYA... SLEEP FOR A WHILE, THEN IT WILL ALL BE OVER.
NO!
YOU'RE WRONG TO ASSUME *YOUR* WAY'S THE *ONLY* WAY!
ALL HUMANS ARE NOT UTTERLY DESPICABLE!
I'LL MAKE YOU A DEAL, CERES.

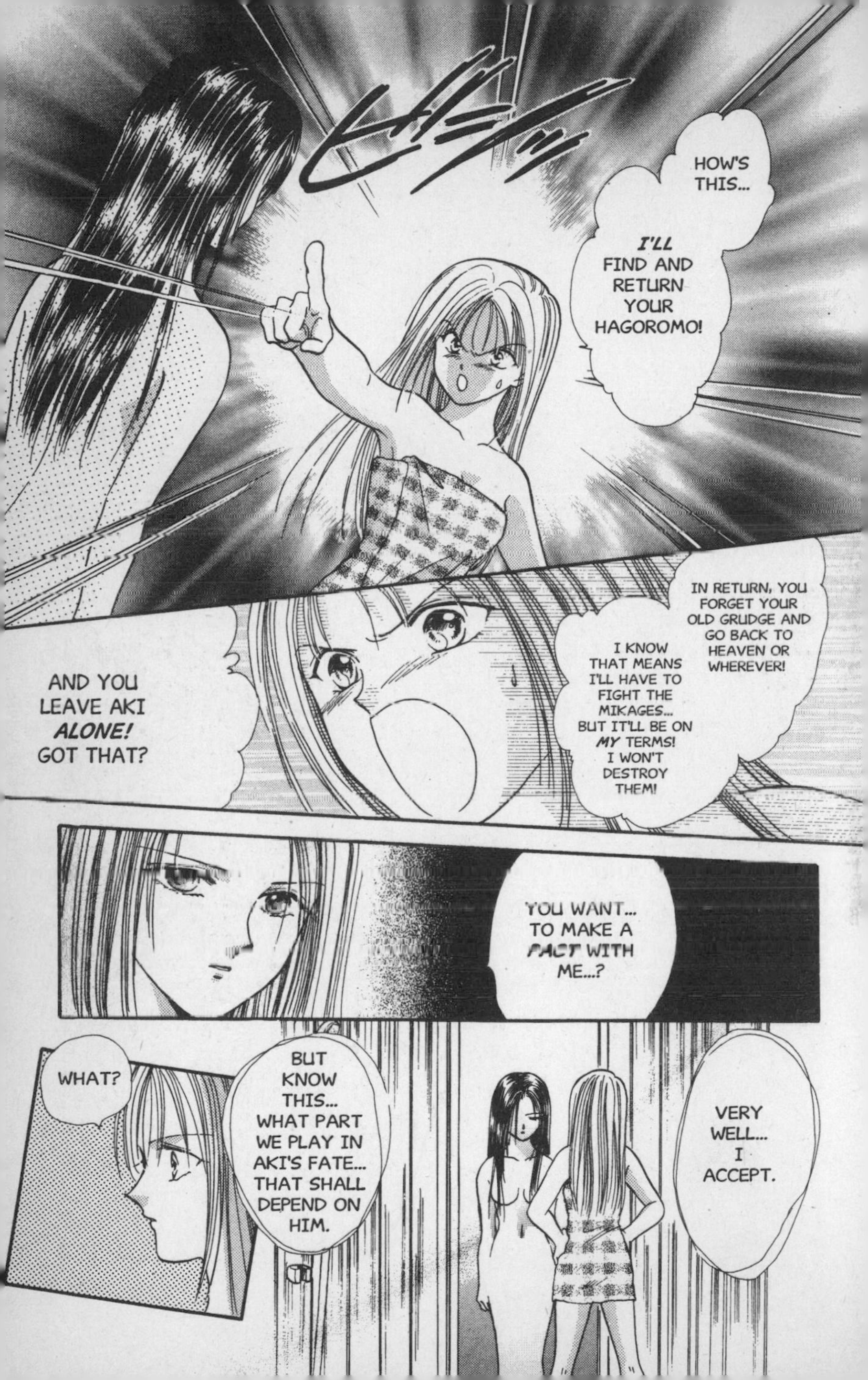
HOW'S THIS...
I'LL FIND AND RETURN YOUR HAGOROMO!
IN RETURN, YOU FORGET YOUR OLD GRUDGE AND GO BACK TO HEAVEN OR WHEREVER!
I KNOW THAT MEANS I'LL HAVE TO FIGHT THE MIKAGES... BUT IT'LL BE ON *MY* TERMS! I WON'T DESTROY THEM!
AND YOU LEAVE AKI *ALONE!* GOT THAT?
YOU WANT... TO MAKE A *PACT* WITH ME...?
VERY WELL... I ACCEPT.
BUT KNOW THIS... WHAT PART WE PLAY IN AKI'S FATE... THAT SHALL DEPEND ON HIM.
WHAT?

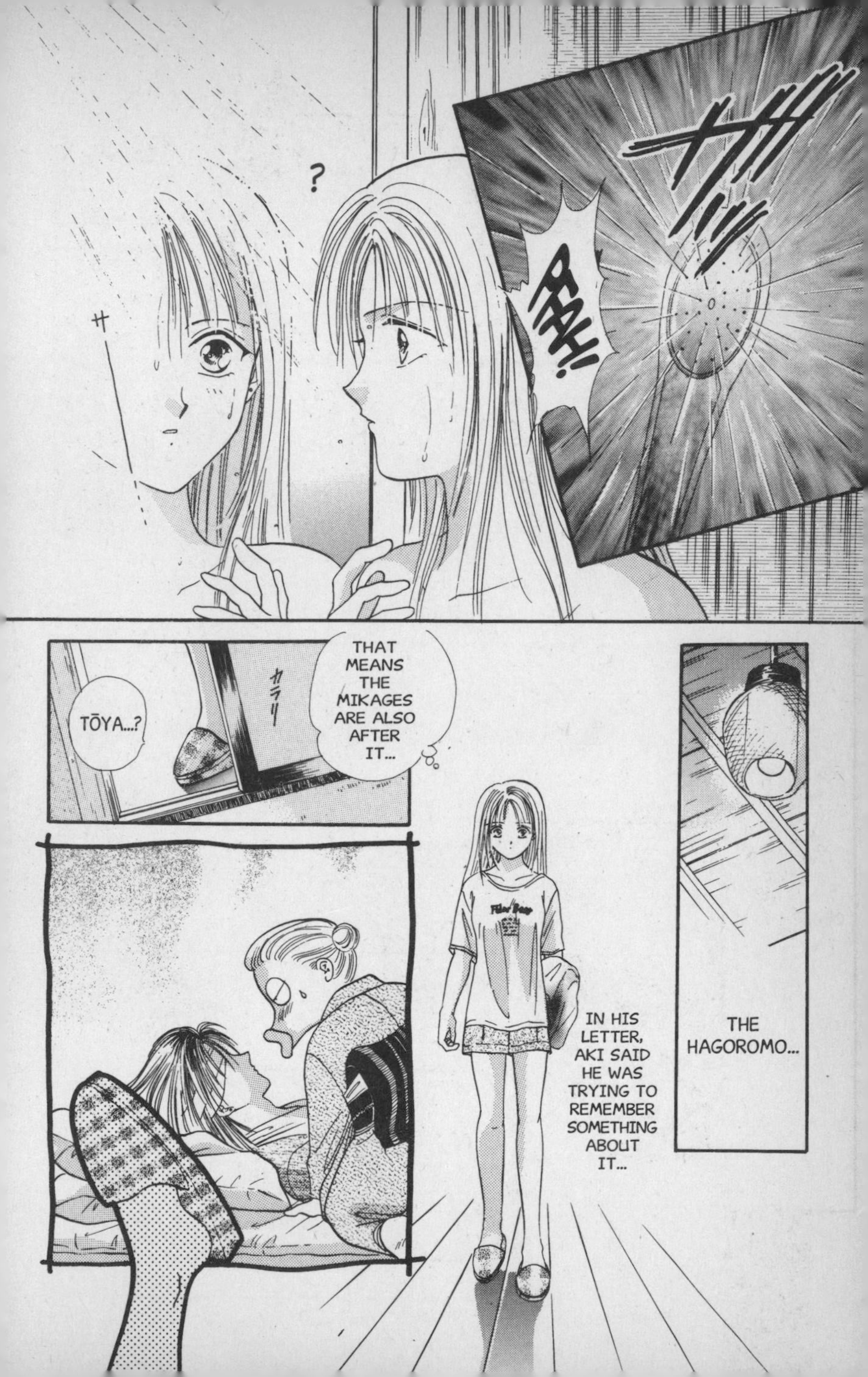
?
THE HAGOROMO...
IN HIS LETTER, AKI SAID HE WAS TRYING TO REMEMBER SOMETHING ABOUT IT...
THAT MEANS THE MIKAGES ARE ALSO AFTER IT...
カラリ
TŌYA...?

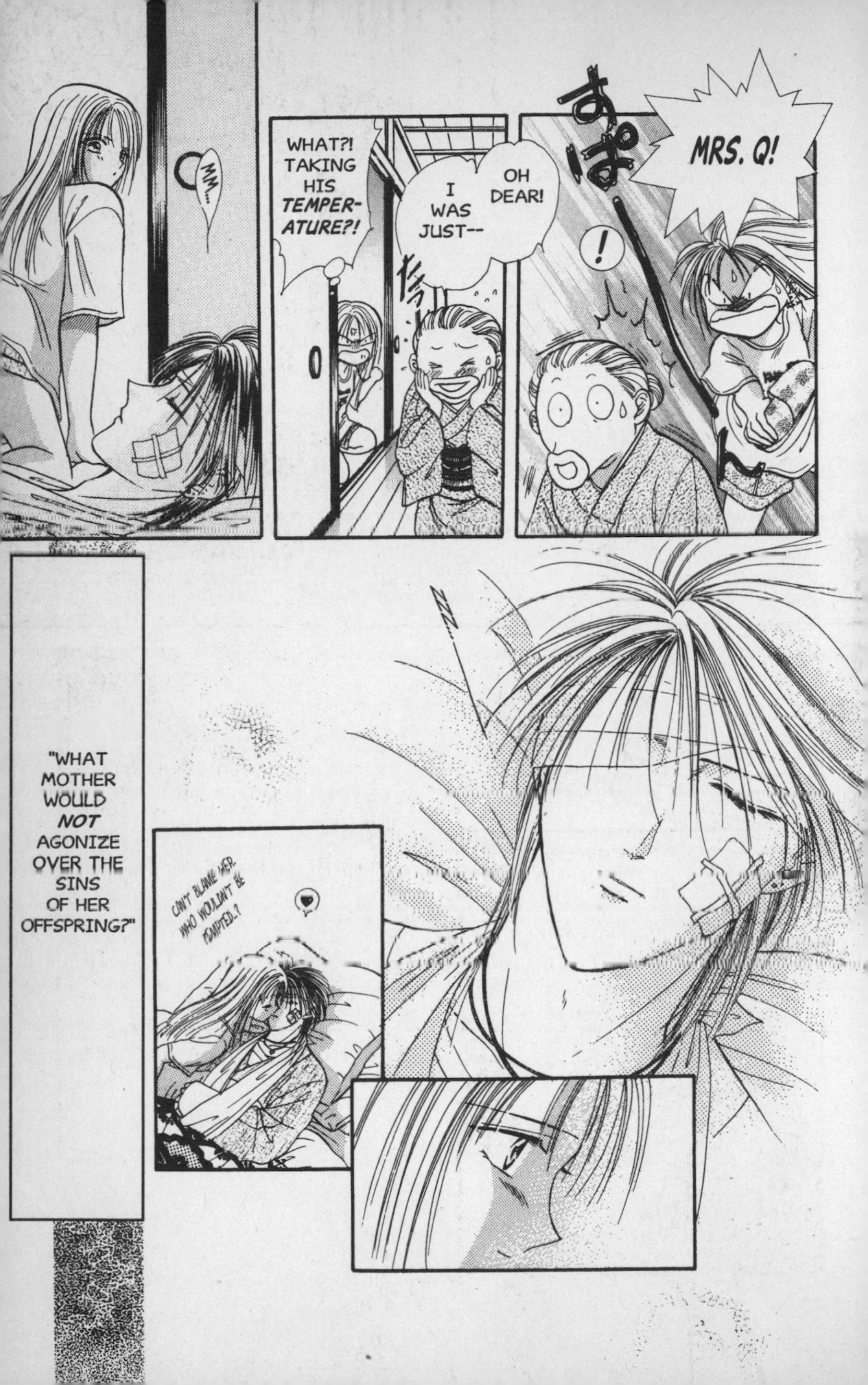
MRS. Q!
!
OH DEAR! I WAS JUST--
WHAT?! TAKING HIS TEMPERATURE?!
MM...
CAN'T BLAME HER. WHO WOULDN'T BE TEMPTED..?
"WHAT MOTHER WOULD NOT AGONIZE OVER THE SINS OF HER OFFSPRING?"

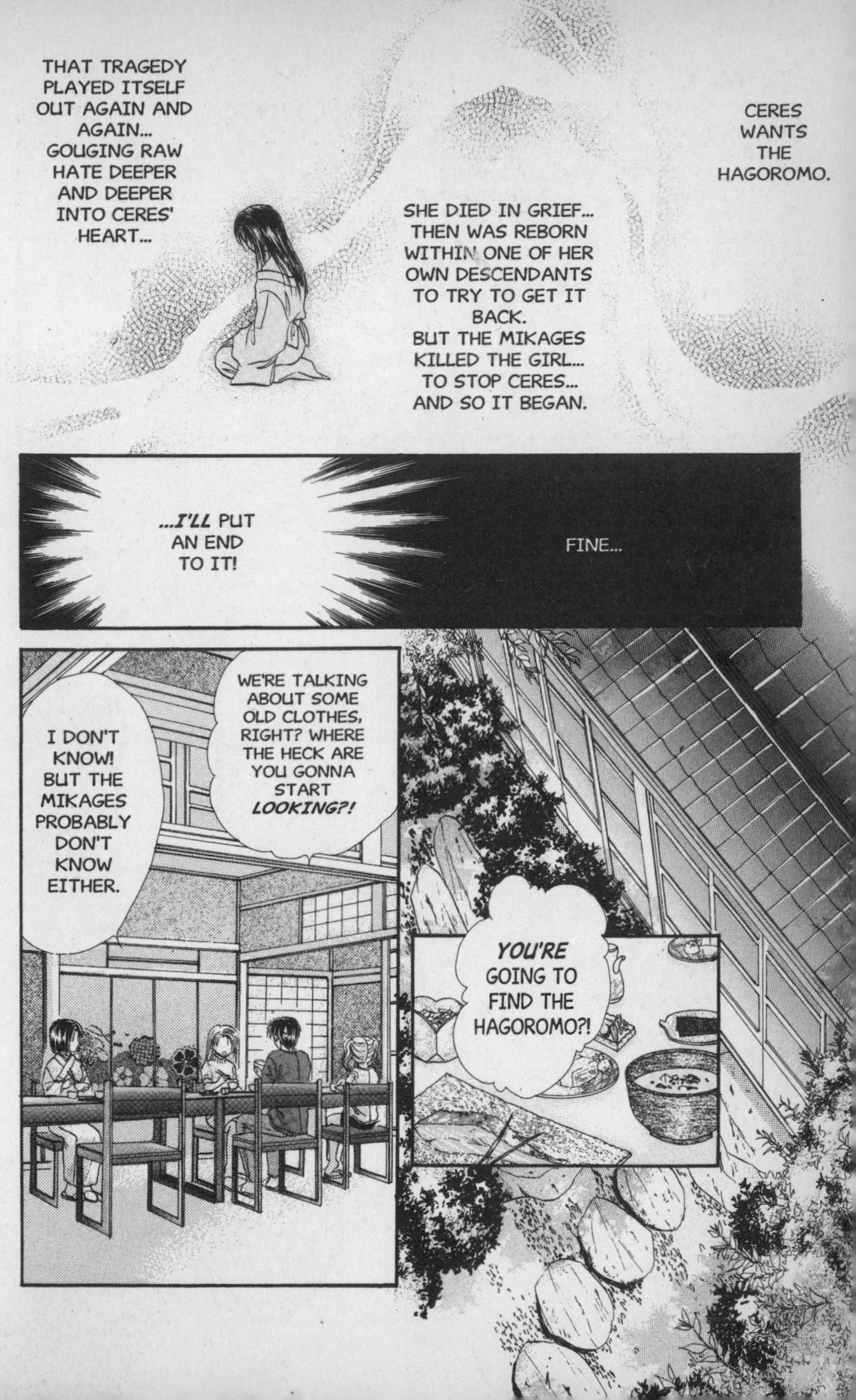
CERES WANTS THE HAGOROMO.
SHE DIED IN GRIEF... THEN WAS REBORN WITHIN ONE OF HER OWN DESCENDANTS TO TRY TO GET IT BACK. BUT THE MIKAGES KILLED THE GIRL... TO STOP CERES... AND SO IT BEGAN.
THAT TRAGEDY PLAYED ITSELF OUT AGAIN AND AGAIN... GOUGING RAW HATE DEEPER AND DEEPER INTO CERES' HEART...
FINE...
...*I'LL* PUT AN END TO IT!
YOU'RE GOING TO FIND THE HAGOROMO?!
WE'RE TALKING ABOUT SOME OLD CLOTHES, RIGHT? WHERE THE HECK ARE YOU GONNA START *LOOKING?!*
I DON'T KNOW! BUT THE MIKAGES PROBABLY DON'T KNOW EITHER.

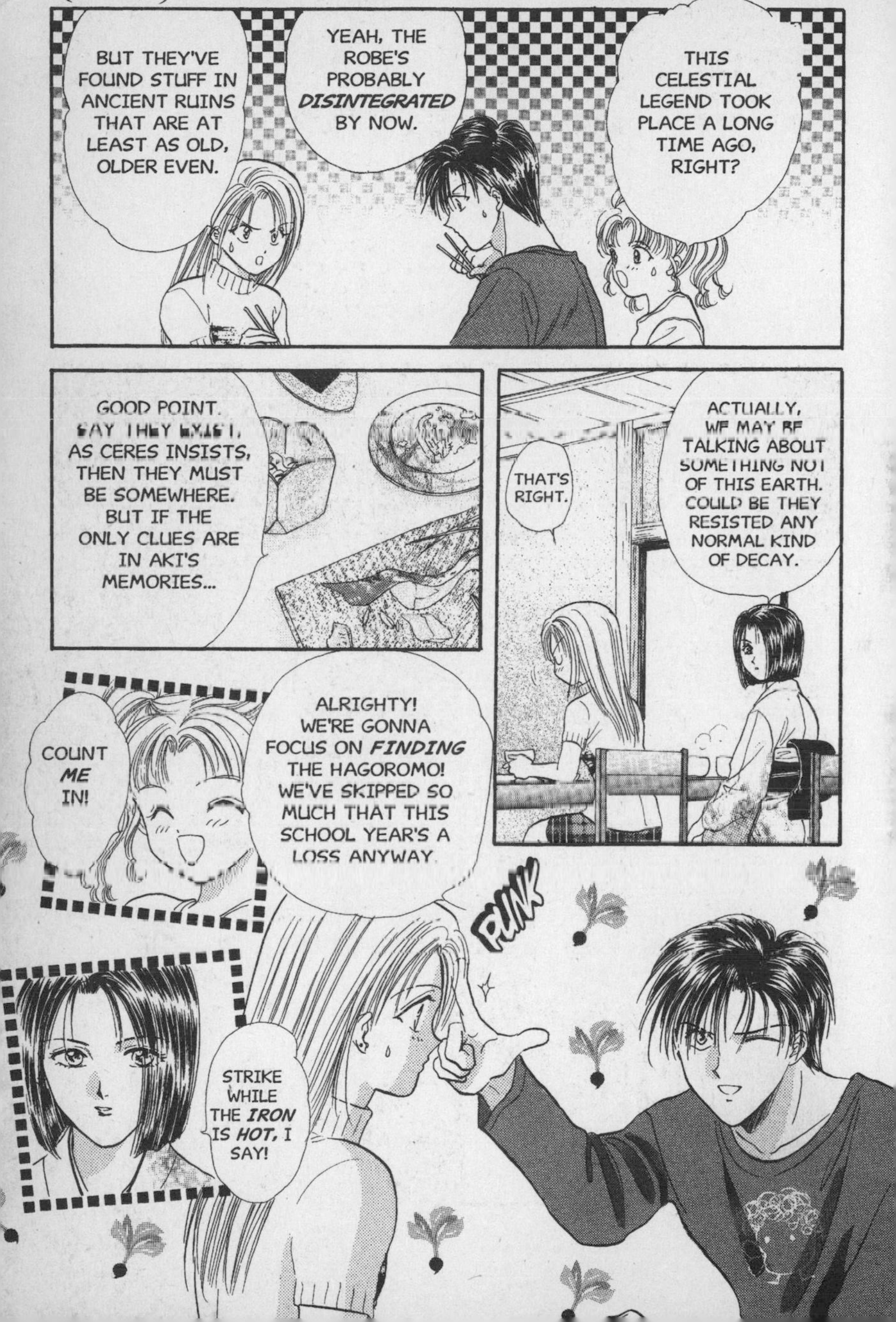
THIS CELESTIAL LEGEND TOOK PLACE A LONG TIME AGO, RIGHT?
YEAH, THE ROBE'S PROBABLY *DISINTEGRATED* BY NOW.
BUT THEY'VE FOUND STUFF IN ANCIENT RUINS THAT ARE AT LEAST AS OLD, OLDER EVEN.
ACTUALLY, WE MAY BE TALKING ABOUT SOMETHING NOT OF THIS EARTH. COULD BE THEY RESISTED ANY NORMAL KIND OF DECAY.
THAT'S RIGHT.
GOOD POINT. SAY THEY EXIST, AS CERES INSISTS, THEN THEY MUST BE SOMEWHERE. BUT IF THE ONLY CLUES ARE IN AKI'S MEMORIES...
ALRIGHTY! WE'RE GONNA FOCUS ON *FINDING* THE HAGOROMO! WE'VE SKIPPED SO MUCH THAT THIS SCHOOL YEAR'S A LOSS ANYWAY.
COUNT *ME* IN!
PUNK
STRIKE WHILE THE *IRON* IS *HOT*, I SAY!

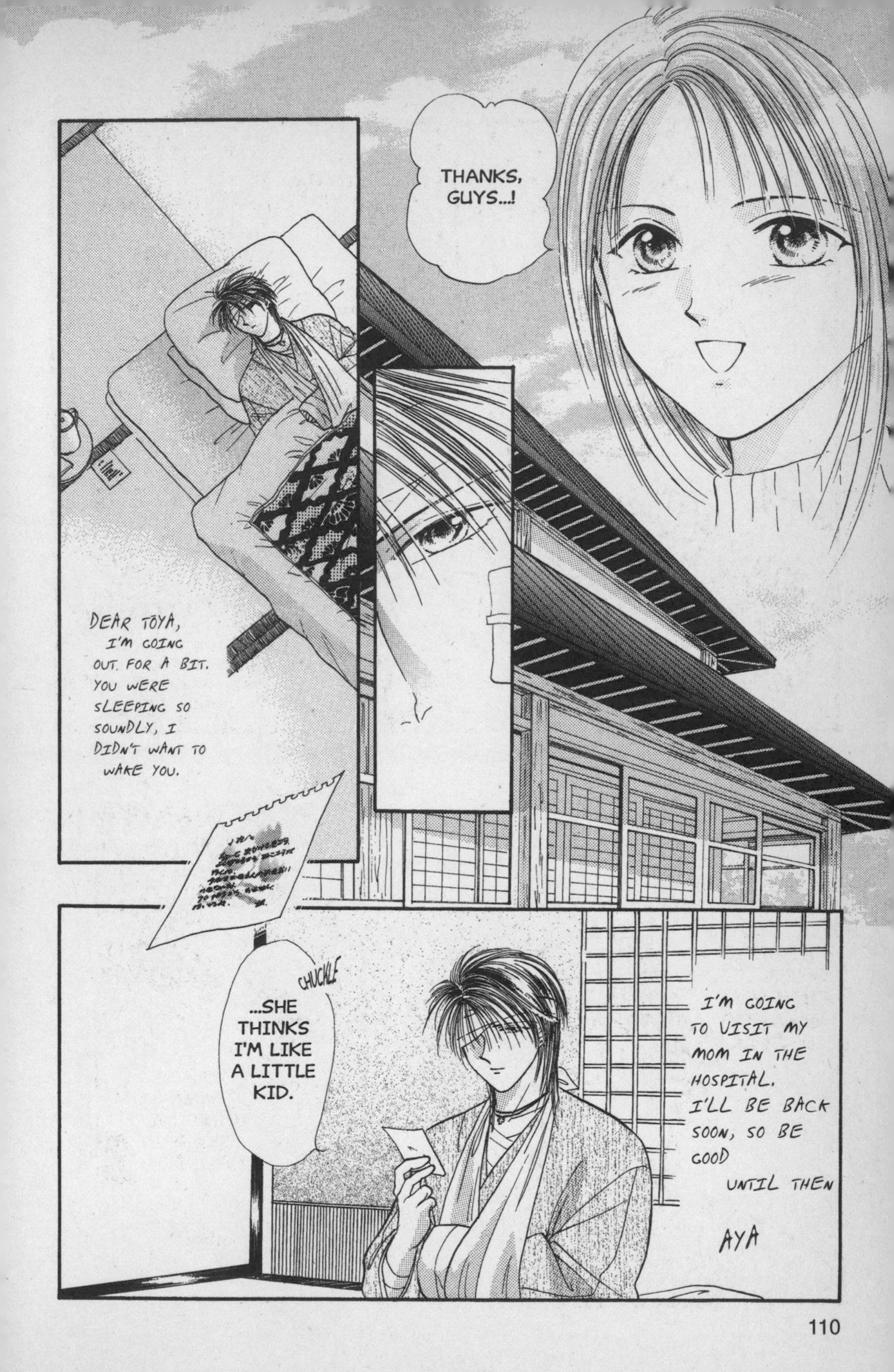
THANKS, GUYS...!
DEAR TOYA, I'M GOING OUT FOR A BIT. YOU WERE SLEEPING SO SOUNDLY, I DIDN'T WANT TO WAKE YOU.
I'M GOING TO VISIT MY MOM IN THE HOSPITAL. I'LL BE BACK SOON, SO BE GOOD UNTIL THEN
AYA
CHUCKLE
...SHE THINKS I'M LIKE A LITTLE KID.

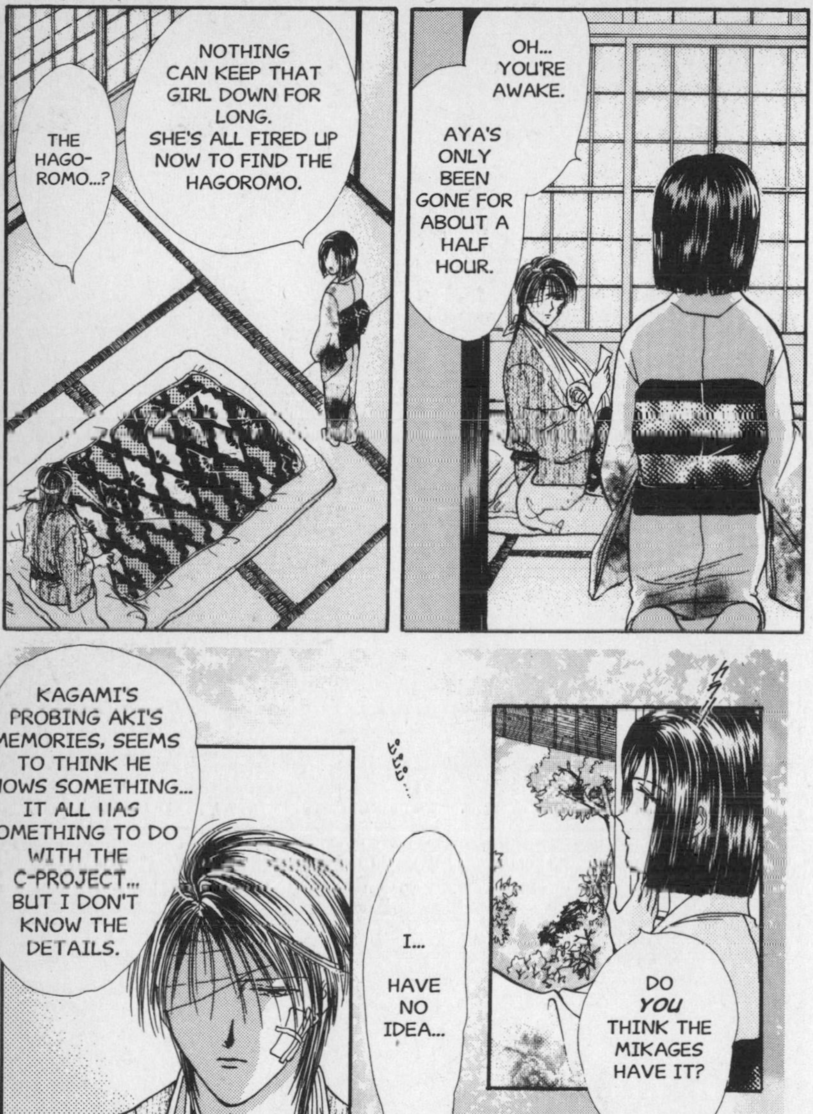
OH... YOU'RE AWAKE.
AYA'S ONLY BEEN GONE FOR ABOUT A HALF HOUR.
NOTHING CAN KEEP THAT GIRL DOWN FOR LONG. SHE'S ALL FIRED UP NOW TO FIND THE HAGOROMO.
THE HAGO-ROMO...?
DO *YOU* THINK THE MIKAGES HAVE IT?
I... HAVE NO IDEA...
KAGAMI'S PROBING AKI'S MEMORIES, SEEMS TO THINK HE KNOWS SOMETHING... IT ALL IIAS SOMETHING TO DO WITH THE C-PROJECT... BUT I DON'T KNOW THE DETAILS.

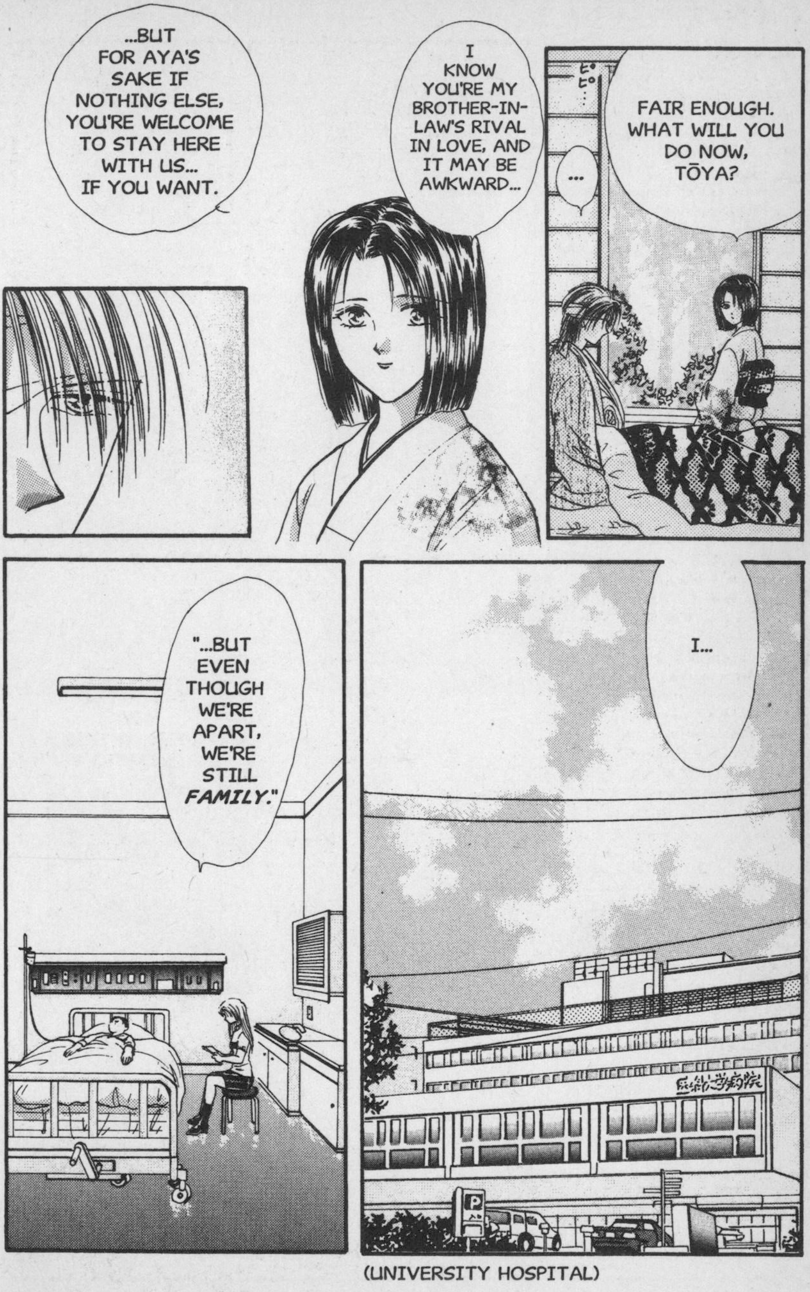
FAIR ENOUGH. WHAT WILL YOU DO NOW, TŌYA?
...
I KNOW YOU'RE MY BROTHER-IN-LAW'S RIVAL IN LOVE, AND IT MAY BE AWKWARD...
...BUT FOR AYA'S SAKE IF NOTHING ELSE, YOU'RE WELCOME TO STAY HERE WITH US... IF YOU WANT.
I...
"...BUT EVEN THOUGH WE'RE APART, WE'RE STILL *FAMILY*."
(UNIVERSITY HOSPITAL)

Now then, last time I talked about other stuff, so I couldn't write about the autograph session I had in Akita prefecture.
Thanks to everyone who came! I really appreciated it.
And thanks for the gifts, too.
The air was so fresh there, and the people were pleasant, it was very nice. I'd like to go back there again sometime. I had some "kiritanpo"—a hot-pot specialty of Akita. The autograph session was at a bookstore and I bought a couple of video games there—IQ and PaRappa the Rapper. My mom played IQ and got so good that she clear all the levels in three hours. So, I saw the ending even though I hadn't even played the game. *wait, IQ had 300 levels... huh? She actually got that far!?*
And betore that, my mom got addicted to Puyo Puyo, and she easily got up to level 99..but then she got really frustrated because she couldn't get to level 100 no matter how much she played. And now she's abducted my copy of Shanghai, and not a day has gone by without her playing it. Despite the fact that she's already finished it several times already. I can't even play FFVII because of her. I beat the merged Sephiroth in one shot even though everyone says it's really tough, but then I got killed by the single-winged Sephiroth in the last battle. I guess I shouldn't have been admiring how it looks. FFVII wasn't received very well by the people who've been playing the whole FF series... but I like the characters. I'll buy the "international" version and play it aqain with the strateqy quide. Oh, I quess I should finish Virus first... And I want to borrow Kowloon's Gate trom my assistants, and also I've asked my friend (who works at Capcom) to get me Resident Evil 2 (this is also how I got my Street Fighter II poster)... Argh, I don't have enough time. ☺ But my assistants and I are now preoccupied with Linda Cubed... ☺ I'd like to play more of it, but... Hmm, I guess even my taste in games is starting to be "dark" these days.

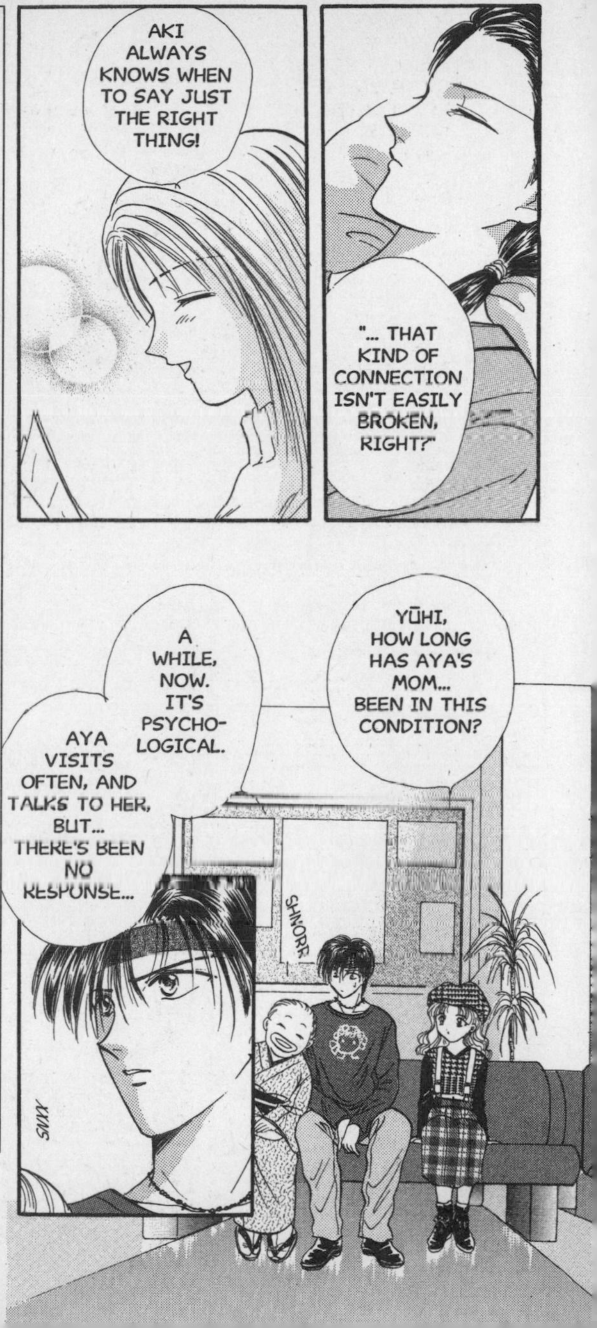
"... THAT KIND OF CONNECTION ISN'T EASILY BROKEN, RIGHT?"
AKI ALWAYS KNOWS WHEN TO SAY JUST THE RIGHT THING!
YŪHI, HOW LONG HAS AYA'S MOM... BEEN IN THIS CONDITION?
A WHILE, NOW. IT'S PSYCHOLOGICAL.
AYA VISITS OFTEN, AND TALKS TO HER, BUT... THERE'S BEEN NO RESPONSE...
SHNORR
SNXX

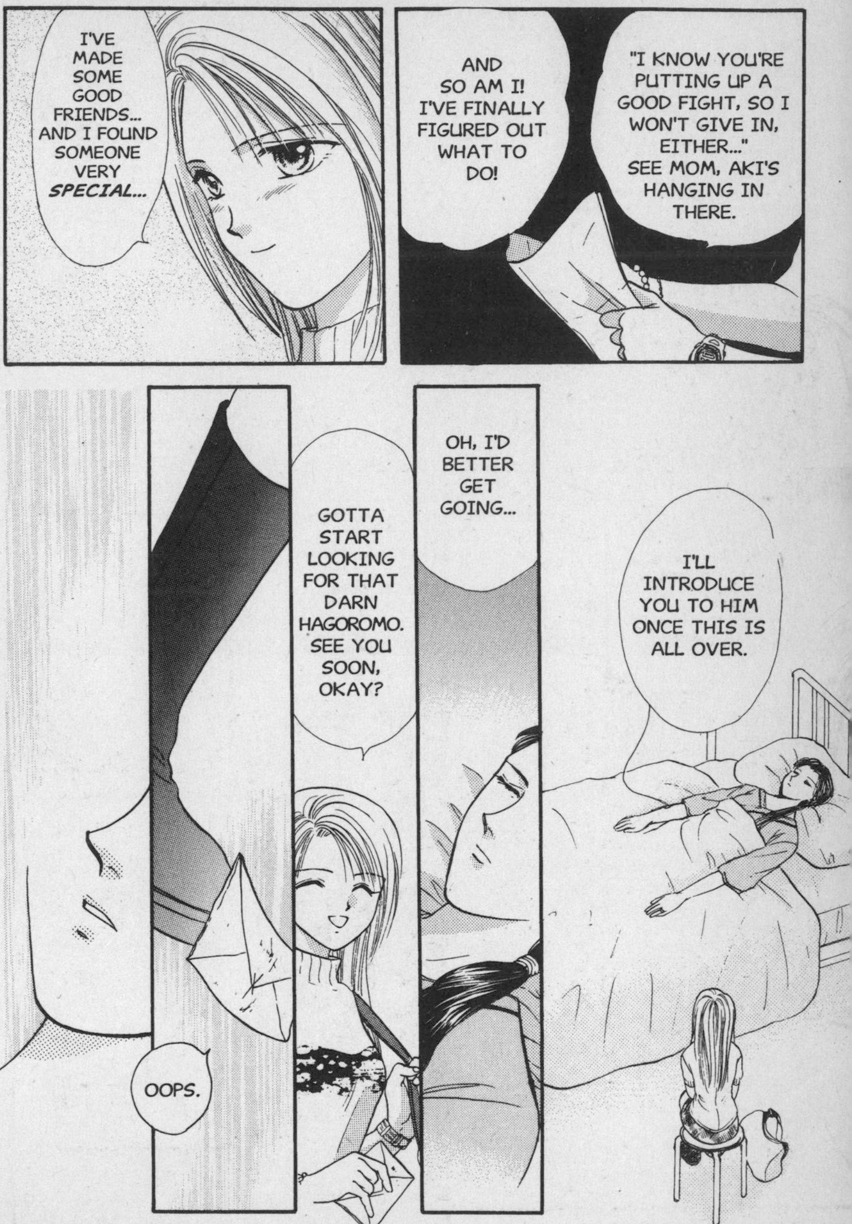
"I KNOW YOU'RE PUTTING UP A GOOD FIGHT, SO I WON'T GIVE IN, EITHER..." SEE MOM, AKI'S HANGING IN THERE.
AND SO AM I! I'VE FINALLY FIGURED OUT WHAT TO DO!
I'VE MADE SOME GOOD FRIENDS... AND I FOUND SOMEONE VERY *SPECIAL*...
I'LL INTRODUCE YOU TO HIM ONCE THIS IS ALL OVER.
OH, I'D BETTER GET GOING...
GOTTA START LOOKING FOR THAT DARN HAGOROMO. SEE YOU SOON, OKAY?
OOPS.

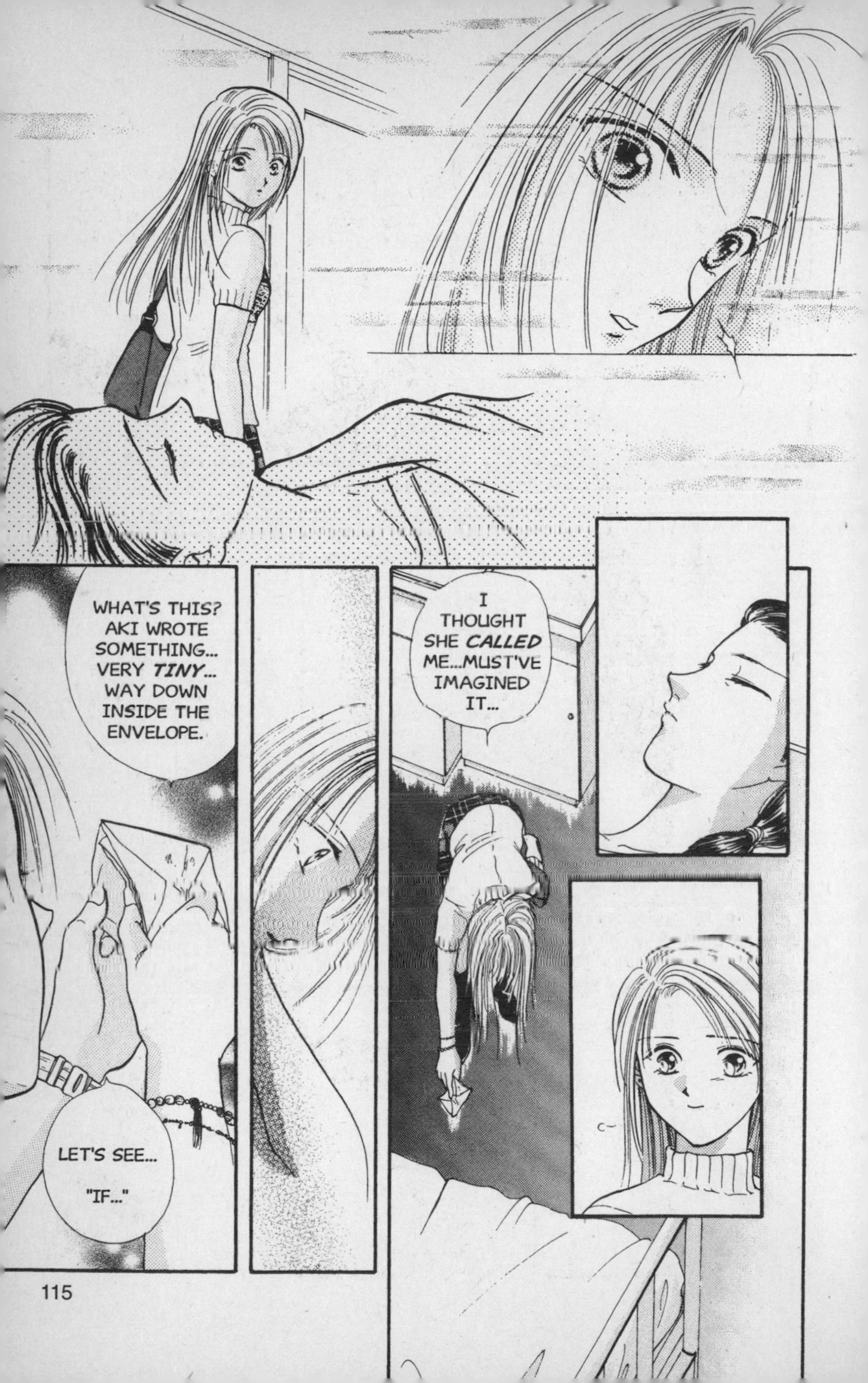
I THOUGHT SHE *CALLED* ME...MUST'VE IMAGINED IT...
WHAT'S THIS? AKI WROTE SOMETHING... VERY *TINY*... WAY DOWN INSIDE THE ENVELOPE.
LET'S SEE... "IF..."

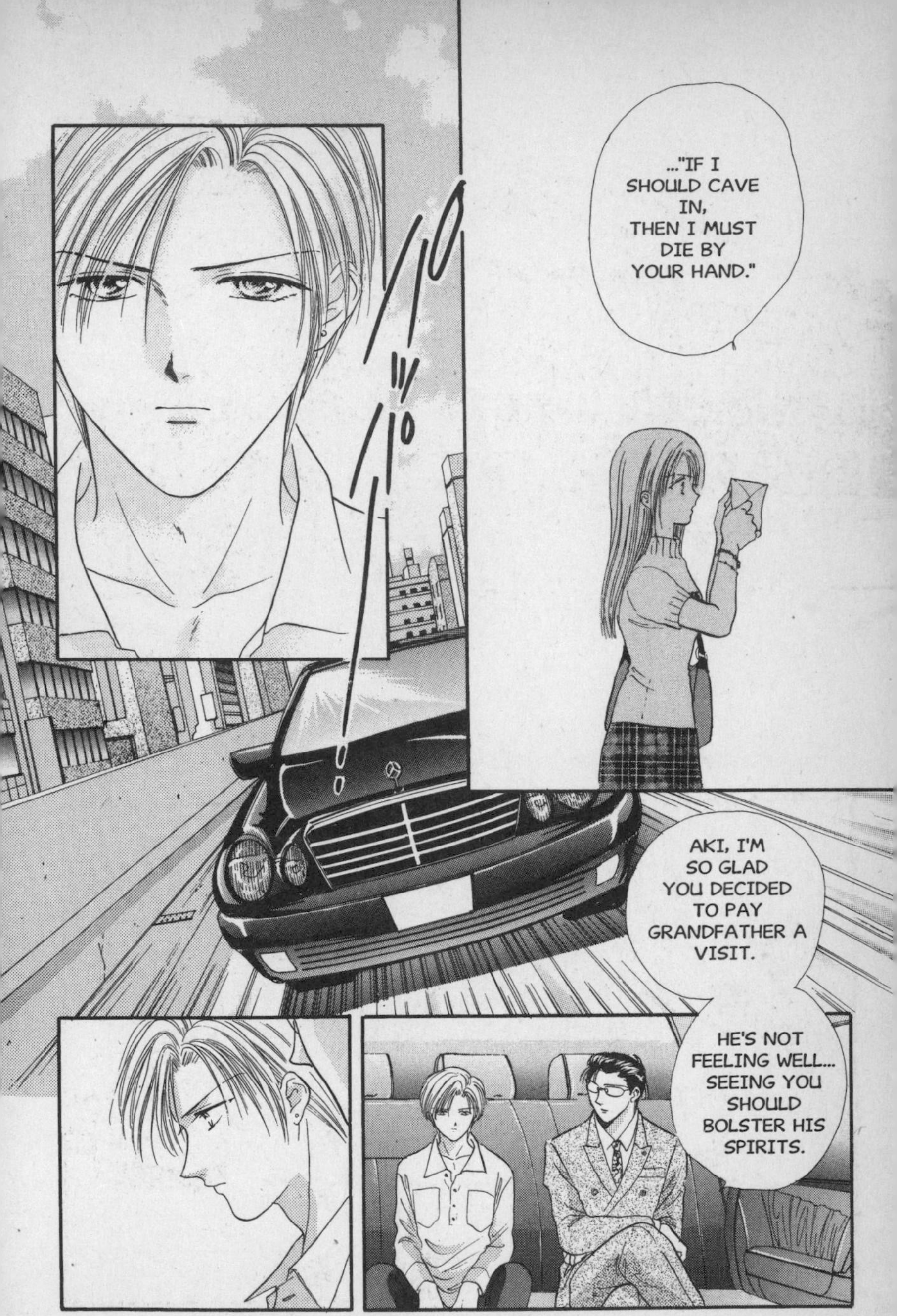
..."IF I SHOULD CAVE IN, THEN I MUST DIE BY YOUR HAND."
AKI, I'M SO GLAD YOU DECIDED TO PAY GRANDFATHER A VISIT.
HE'S NOT FEELING WELL... SEEING YOU SHOULD BOLSTER HIS SPIRITS.

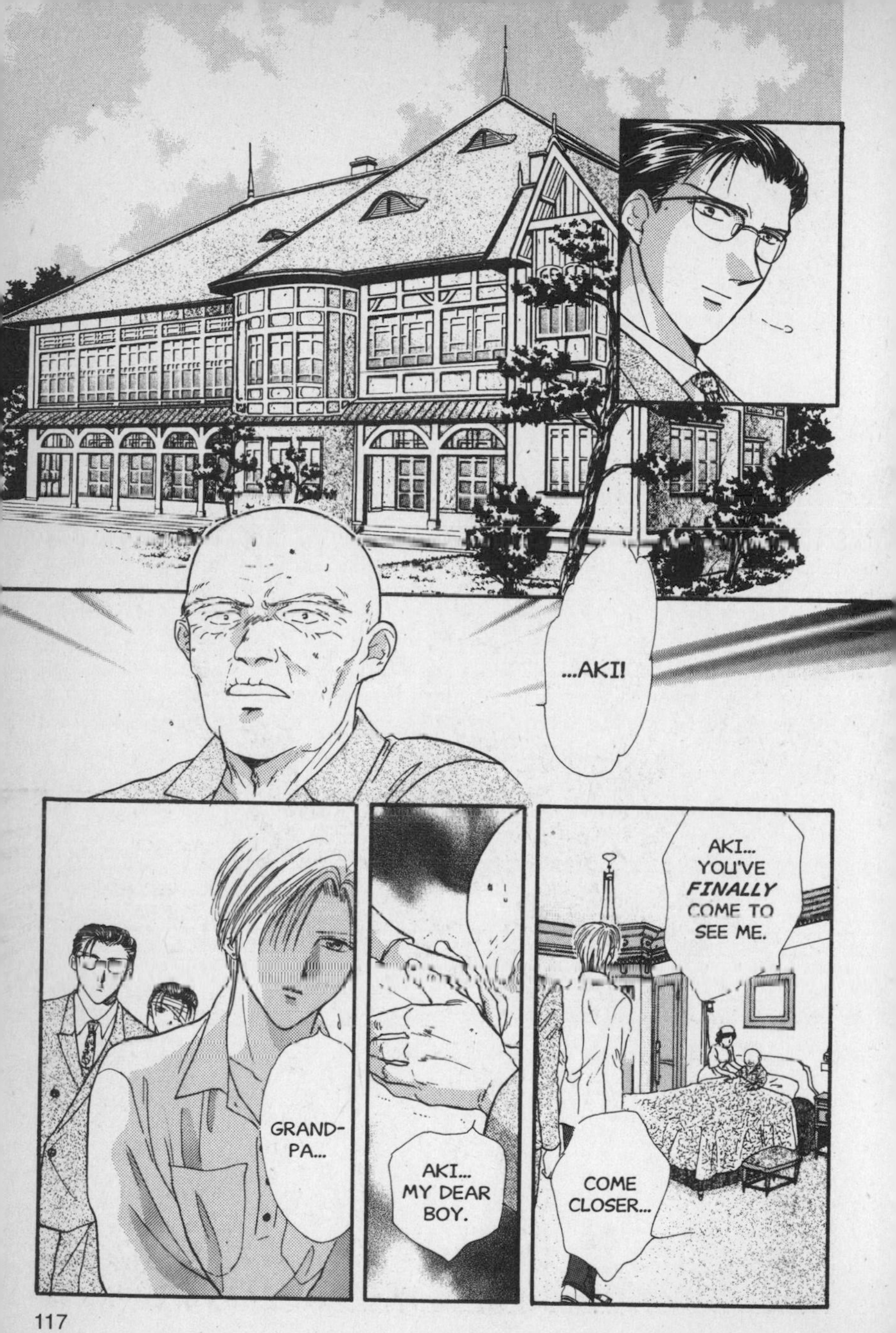
...AKI!
AKI... YOU'VE *FINALLY* COME TO SEE ME.
COME CLOSER...
AKI... MY DEAR BOY.
GRAND-PA...

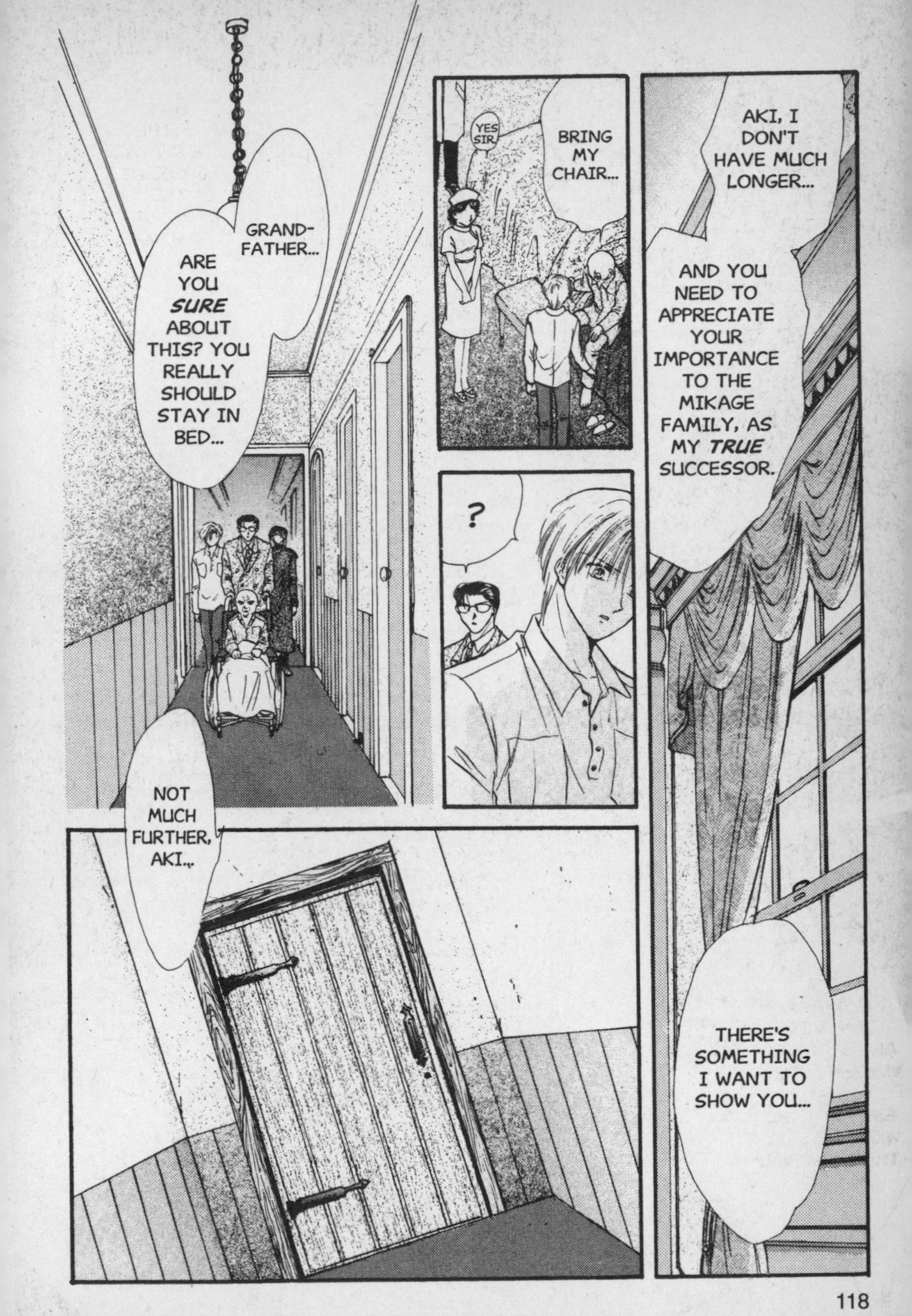
AKI, I DON'T HAVE MUCH LONGER...
AND YOU NEED TO APPRECIATE YOUR IMPORTANCE TO THE MIKAGE FAMILY, AS MY *TRUE* SUCCESSOR.
THERE'S SOMETHING I WANT TO SHOW YOU...
BRING MY CHAIR...
YES SIR.
?
GRAND-FATHER...
ARE YOU *SURE* ABOUT THIS? YOU REALLY SHOULD STAY IN BED...
NOT MUCH FURTHER, AKI...

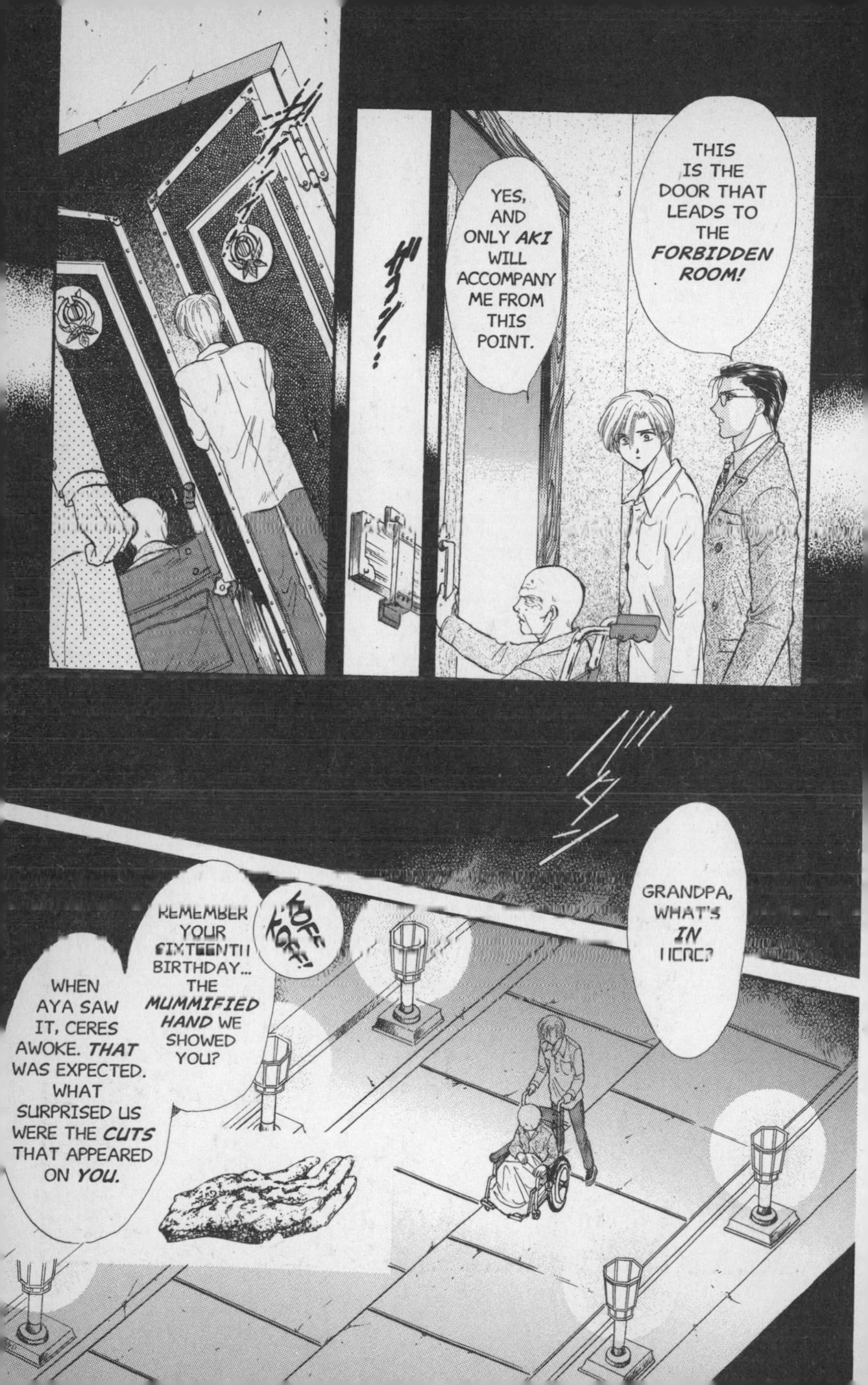
THIS IS THE DOOR THAT LEADS TO THE *FORBIDDEN ROOM!*
YES, AND ONLY *AKI* WILL ACCOMPANY ME FROM THIS POINT.
GRANDPA, WHAT'S *IN* HERE?
KOFF KOFF!
REMEMBER YOUR SIXTEENTH BIRTHDAY... THE *MUMMIFIED HAND* WE SHOWED YOU?
WHEN AYA SAW IT, CERES AWOKE. *THAT* WAS EXPECTED. WHAT SURPRISED US WERE THE *CUTS* THAT APPEARED ON *YOU.*

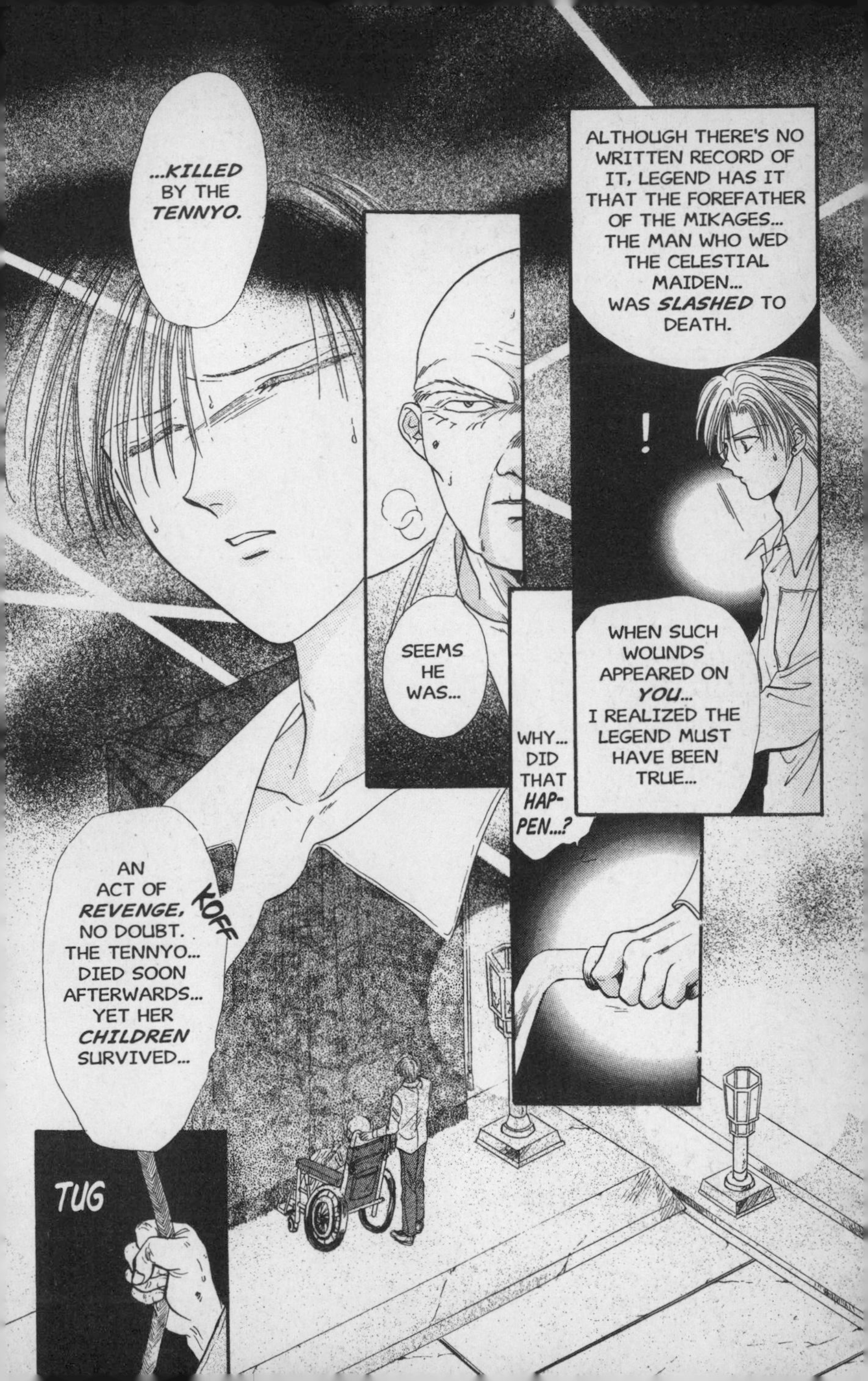
ALTHOUGH THERE'S NO WRITTEN RECORD OF IT, LEGEND HAS IT THAT THE FOREFATHER OF THE MIKAGES... THE MAN WHO WED THE CELESTIAL MAIDEN... WAS *SLASHED* TO DEATH.
!
WHEN SUCH WOUNDS APPEARED ON *YOU*... I REALIZED THE LEGEND MUST HAVE BEEN TRUE...
WHY... DID THAT *HAP-PEN...?*
SEEMS HE WAS...
...*KILLED* BY THE *TENNYO.*
KOFF
AN ACT OF *REVENGE,* NO DOUBT. THE TENNYO... DIED SOON AFTERWARDS... YET HER *CHILDREN* SURVIVED...
TUG

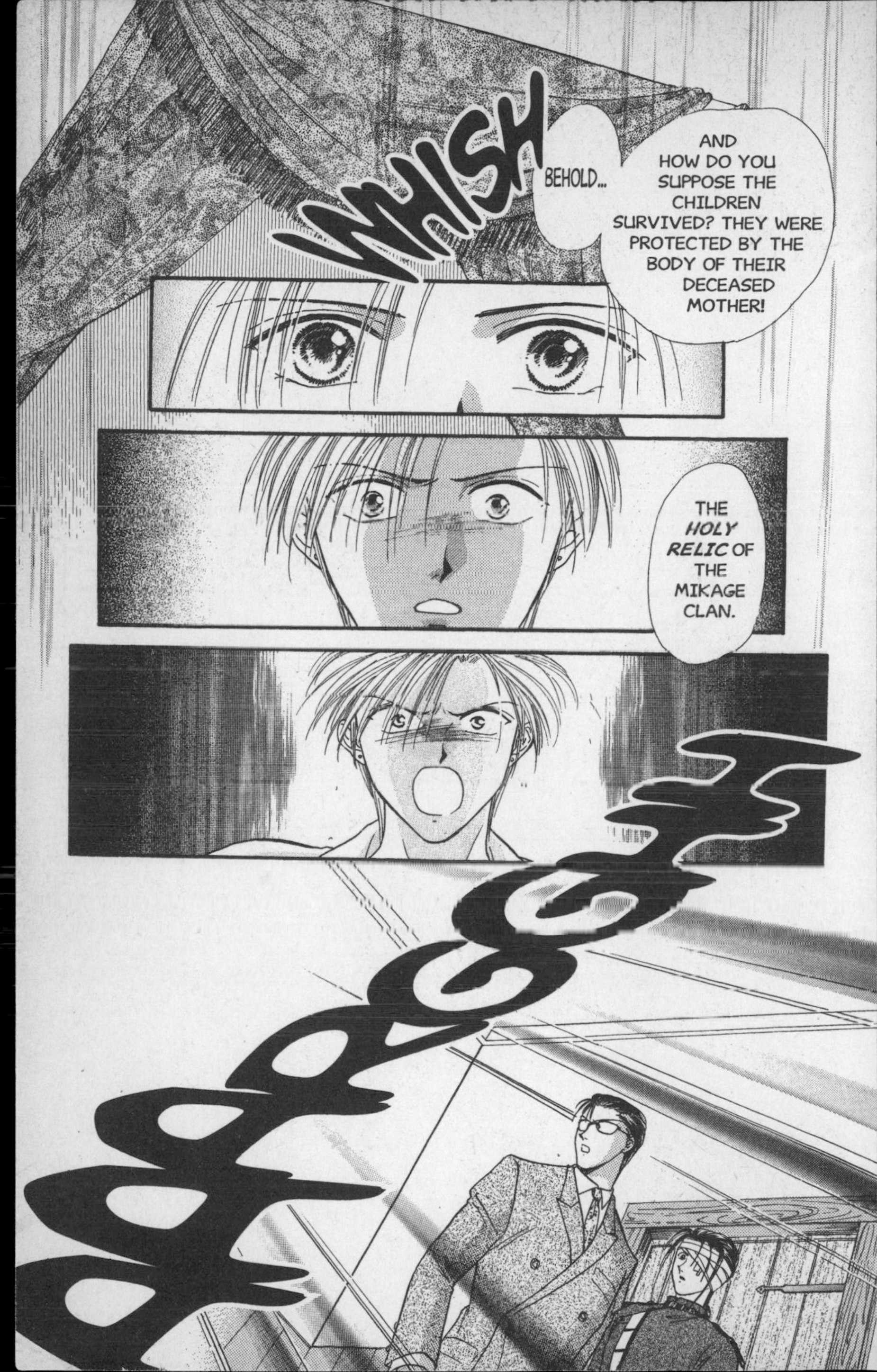
AND HOW DO YOU SUPPOSE THE CHILDREN SURVIVED? THEY WERE PROTECTED BY THE BODY OF THEIR DECEASED MOTHER!
BEHOLD...
WHISH
THE *HOLY RELIC* OF THE MIKAGE CLAN.

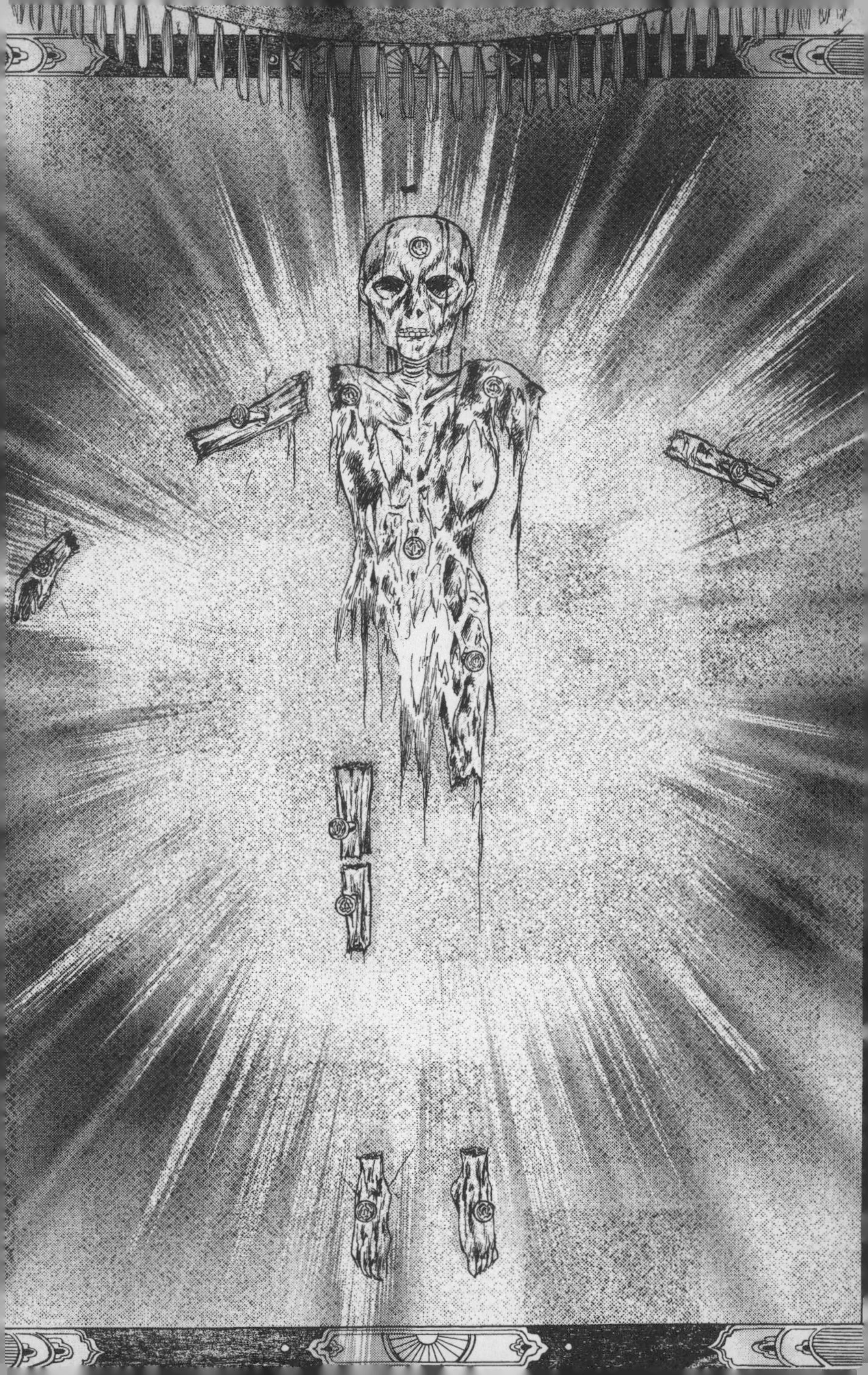

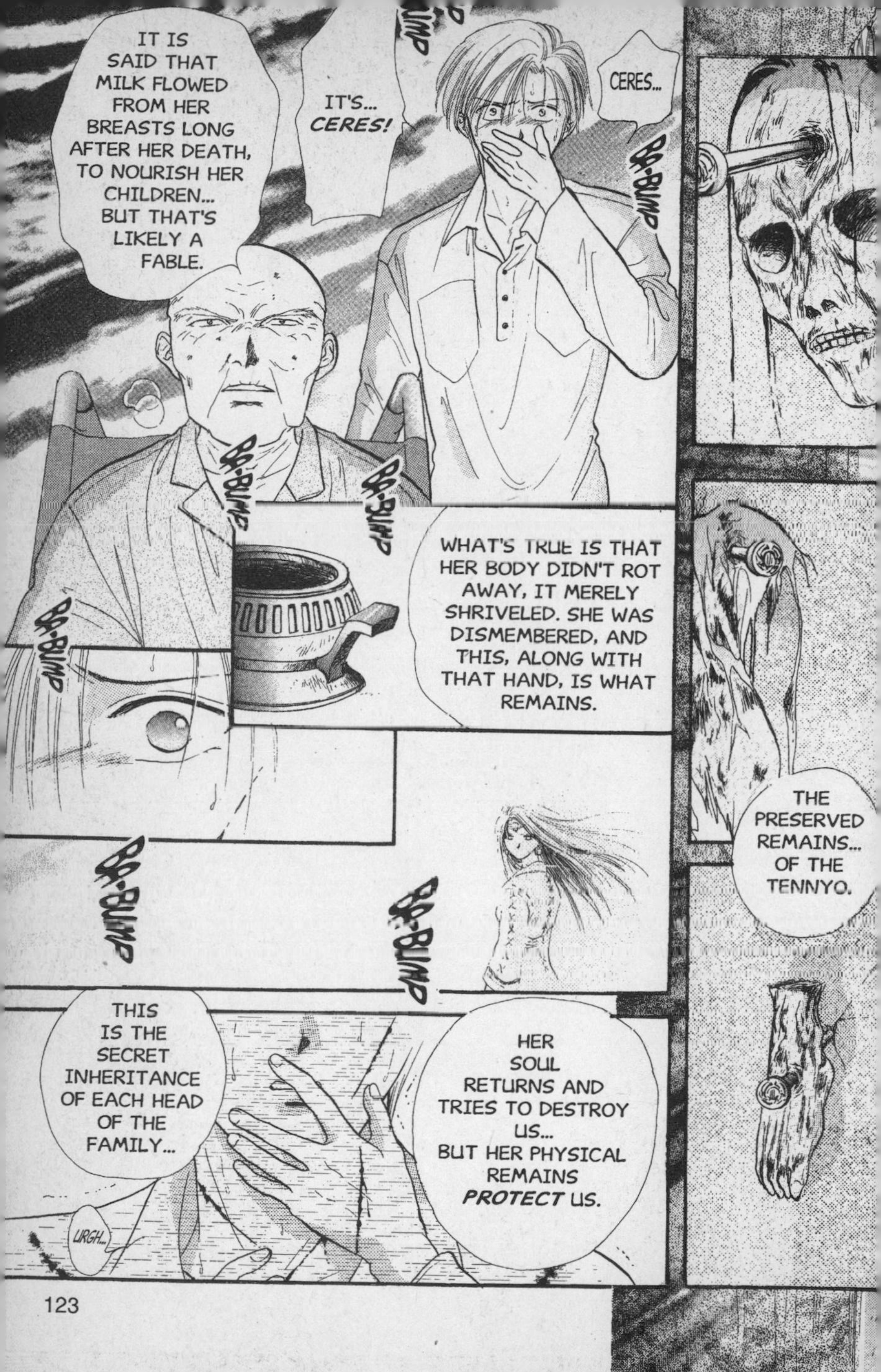
CERES...
BA-BUMP
IT'S... CERES!
IT IS SAID THAT MILK FLOWED FROM HER BREASTS LONG AFTER HER DEATH, TO NOURISH HER CHILDREN... BUT THAT'S LIKELY A FABLE.
BA-BUMP
BA-BUMP
WHAT'S TRUE IS THAT HER BODY DIDN'T ROT AWAY, IT MERELY SHRIVELED. SHE WAS DISMEMBERED, AND THIS, ALONG WITH THAT HAND, IS WHAT REMAINS.
BA-BUMP
THE PRESERVED REMAINS... OF THE TENNYO.
BA-BUMP
BA-BUMP
HER SOUL RETURNS AND TRIES TO DESTROY US... BUT HER PHYSICAL REMAINS *PROTECT* US.
THIS IS THE SECRET INHERITANCE OF EACH HEAD OF THE FAMILY...
URGH...

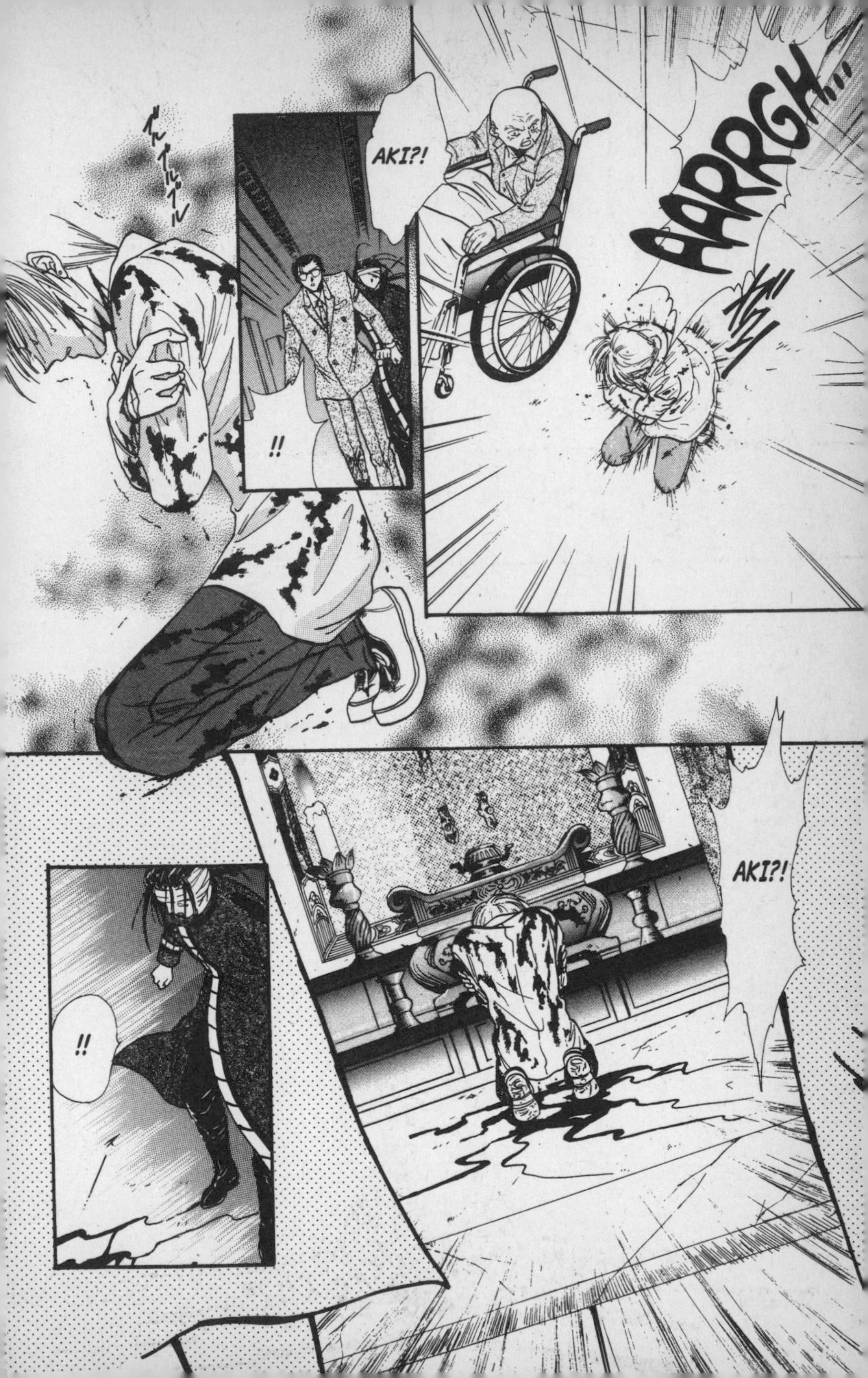
AARGH...
AKI?!
!!
AKI?!
!!

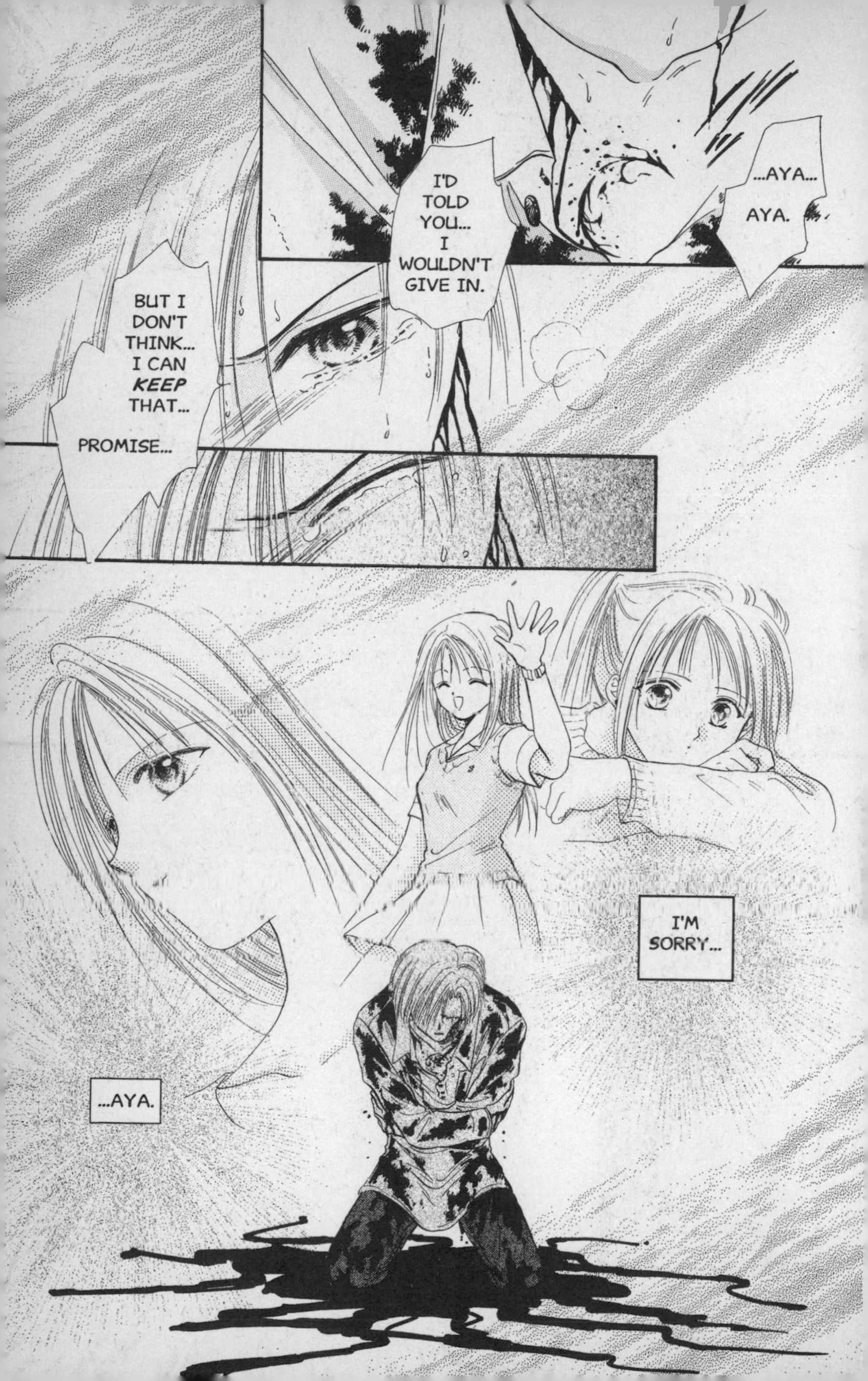
...AYA...
AYA.
I'D TOLD YOU... I WOULDN'T GIVE IN.
BUT I DON'T THINK... I CAN *KEEP* THAT...
PROMISE...
I'M SORRY...
...AYA.

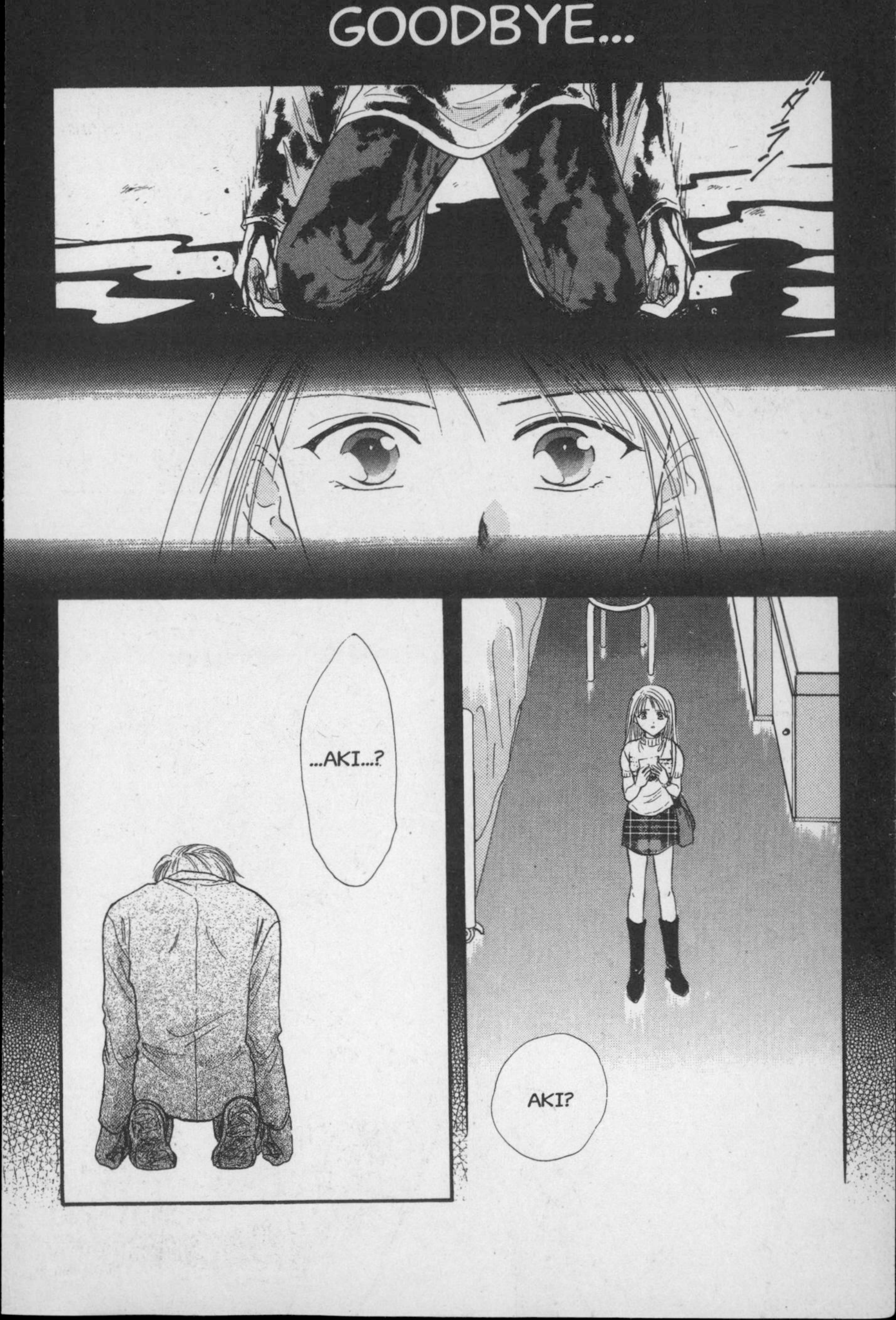
GOODBYE...
AKI?
...AKI...?

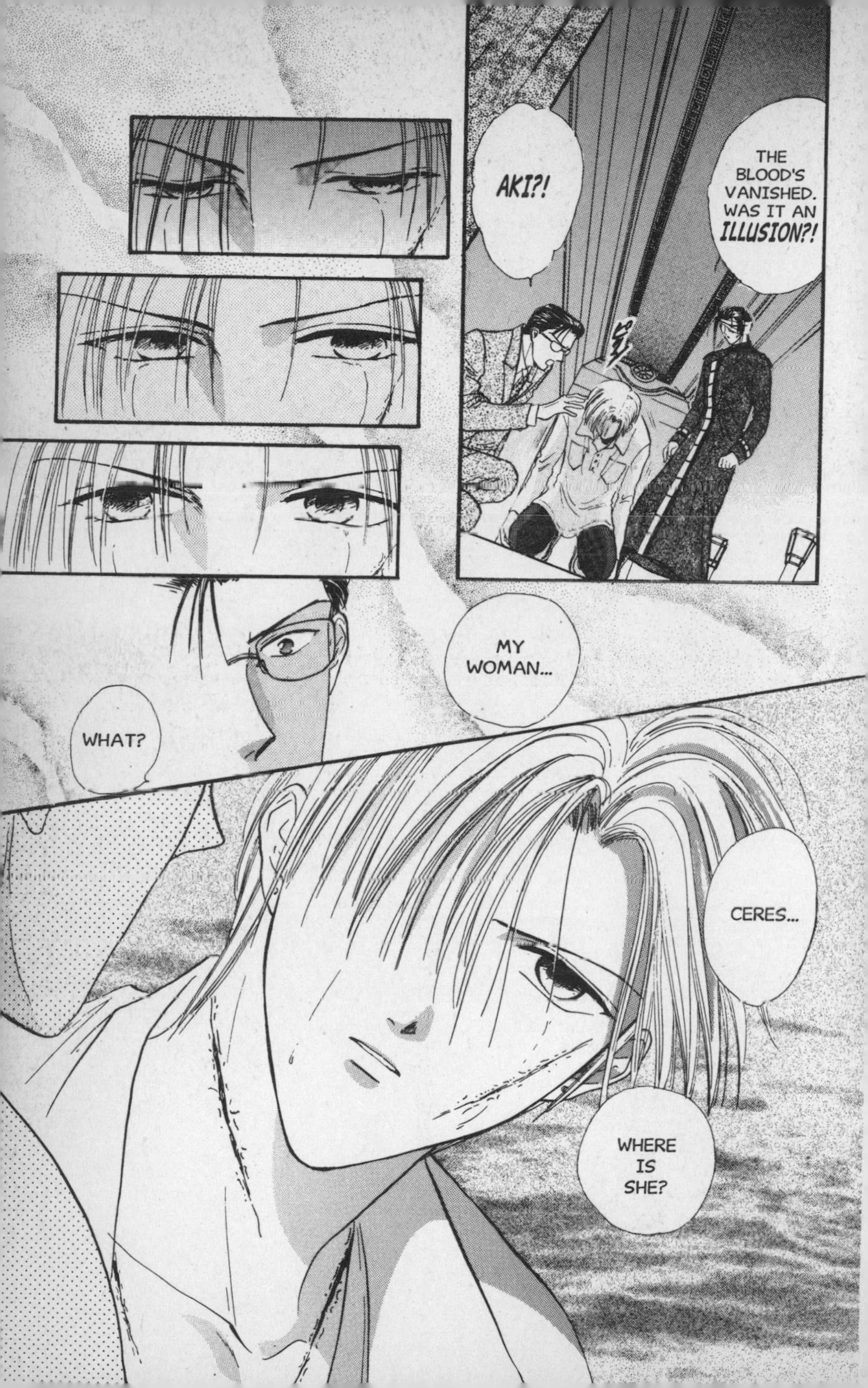
THE BLOOD'S VANISHED. WAS IT AN ILLUSION?!
AKI?!
MY WOMAN...
WHAT?
CERES...
WHERE IS SHE?

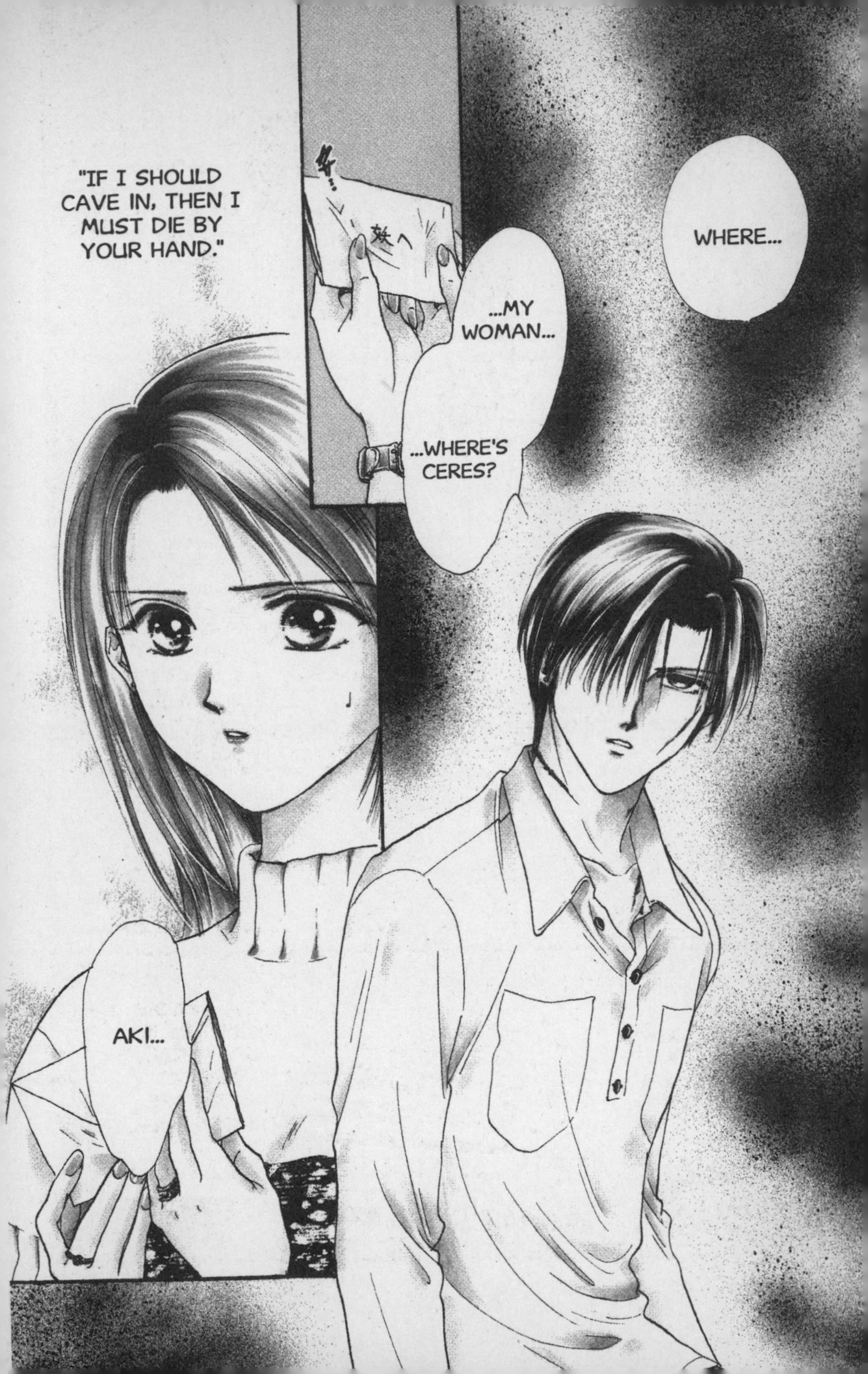
WHERE...
...MY WOMAN...
...WHERE'S CERES?
妹へ
"IF I SHOULD CAVE IN, THEN I MUST DIE BY YOUR HAND."
AKI...

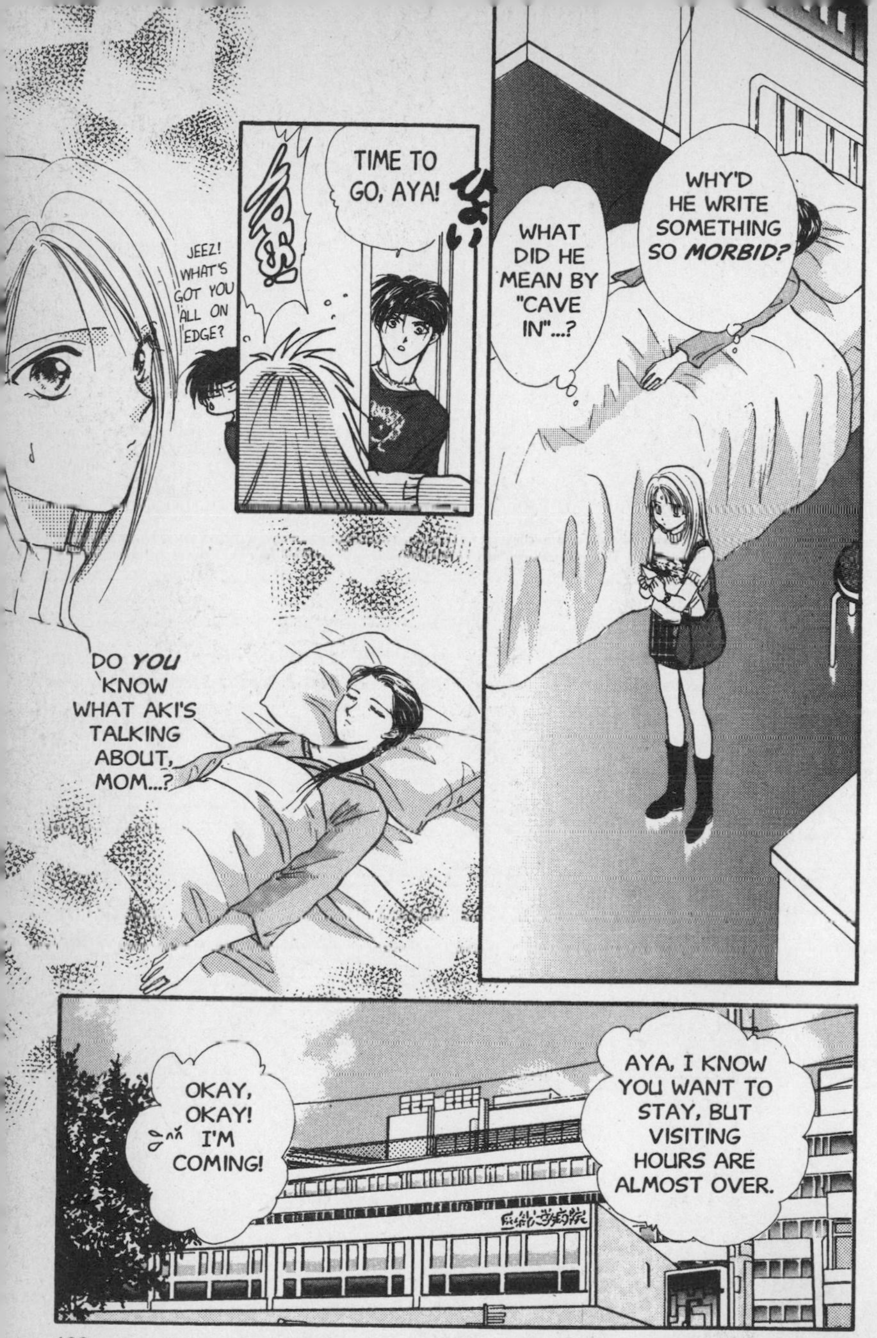
WHY'D HE WRITE SOMETHING SO *MORBID?*
WHAT DID HE MEAN BY "CAVE IN"...?
TIME TO GO, AYA!
JEEZ! WHAT'S GOT YOU ALL ON EDGE?
DO *YOU* KNOW WHAT AKI'S TALKING ABOUT, MOM...?
AYA, I KNOW YOU WANT TO STAY, BUT VISITING HOURS ARE ALMOST OVER.
OKAY, OKAY! I'M COMING!

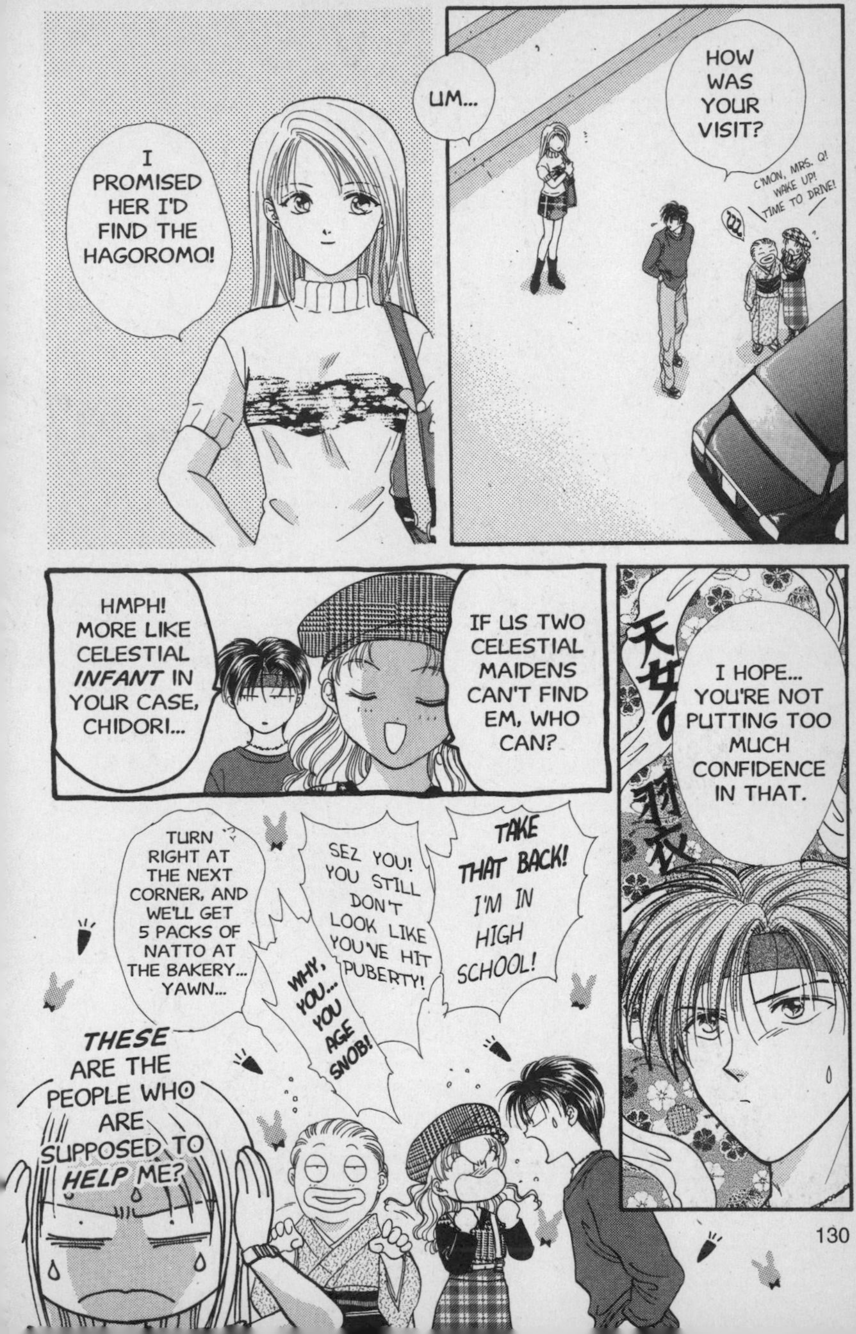
HOW WAS YOUR VISIT?
C'MON, MRS. Q! WAKE UP! TIME TO DRIVE!
UM...
I PROMISED HER I'D FIND THE HAGOROMO!
天女の羽衣
I HOPE... YOU'RE NOT PUTTING TOO MUCH CONFIDENCE IN THAT.
IF US TWO CELESTIAL MAIDENS CAN'T FIND EM, WHO CAN?
HMPH! MORE LIKE CELESTIAL *INFANT* IN YOUR CASE, CHIDORI...
TAKE THAT BACK! I'M IN HIGH SCHOOL!
SEZ YOU! YOU STILL DON'T LOOK LIKE YOU'VE HIT PUBERTY!
WHY, YOU... YOU AGE SNOB!
TURN RIGHT AT THE NEXT CORNER, AND WE'LL GET 5 PACKS OF NATTO AT THE BAKERY... YAWN...
THESE ARE THE PEOPLE WHO ARE SUPPOSED TO *HELP* ME?

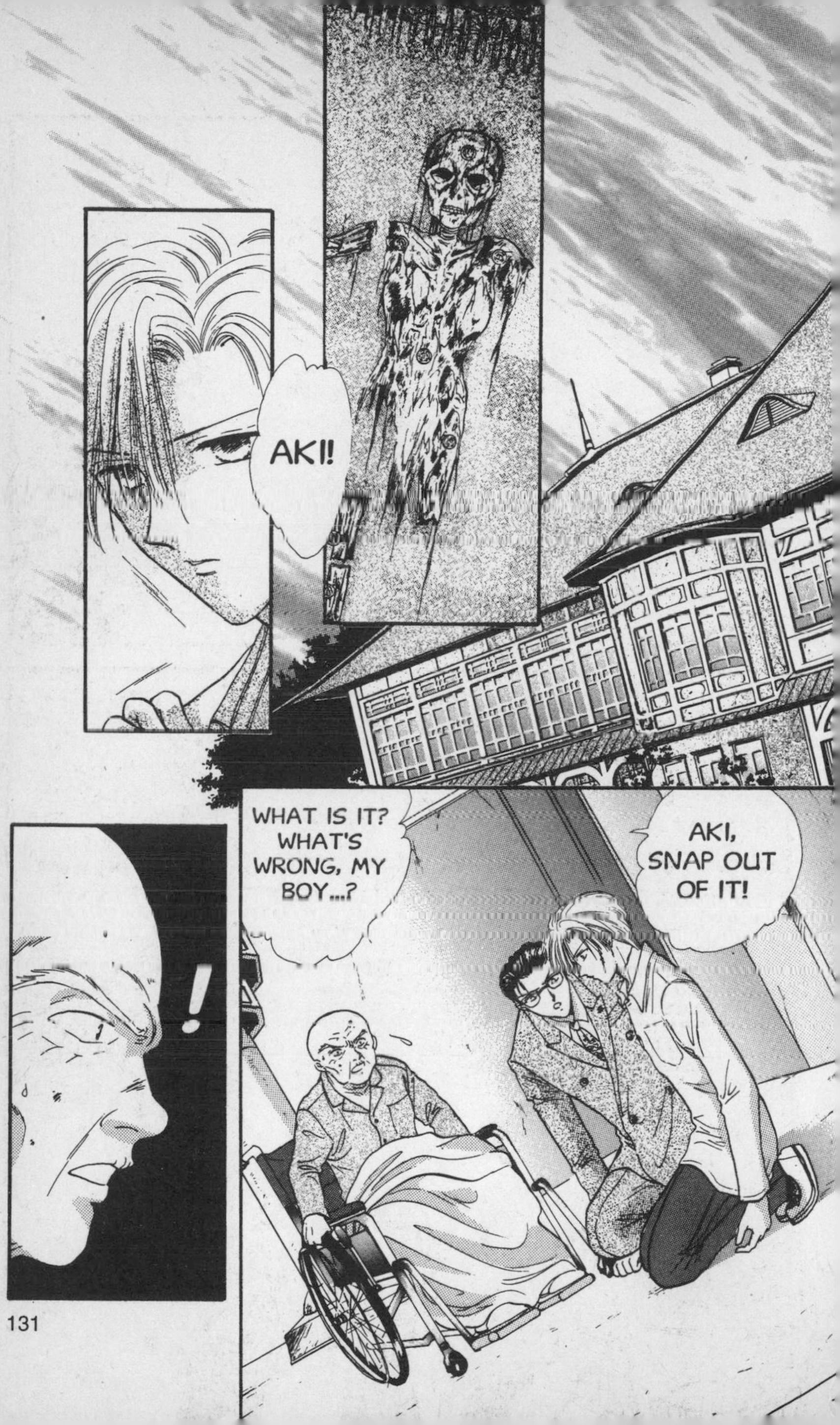
AKI!
AKI, SNAP OUT OF IT!
WHAT IS IT? WHAT'S WRONG, MY BOY...?
!

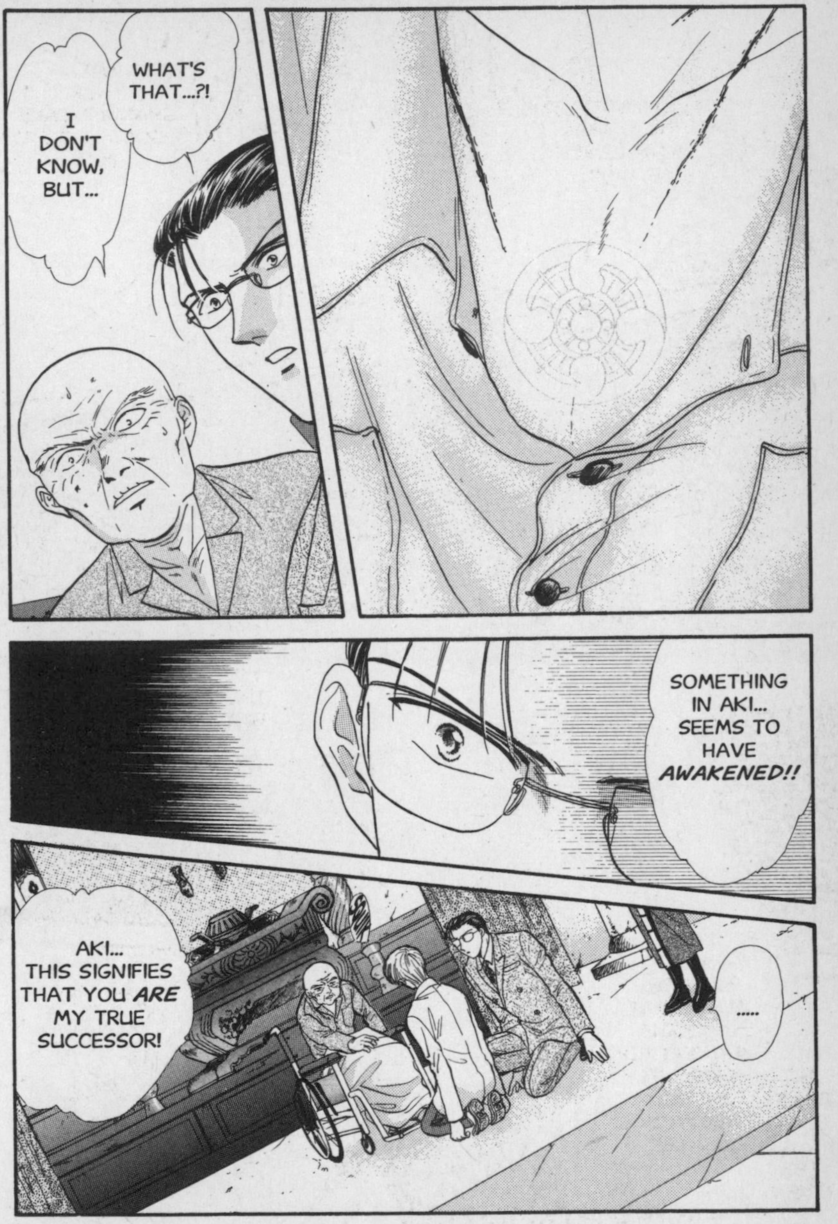
WHAT'S THAT...?!
I DON'T KNOW, BUT...
SOMETHING IN AKI... SEEMS TO HAVE AWAKENED!!
.....
AKI... THIS SIGNIFIES THAT YOU ARE MY TRUE SUCCESSOR!

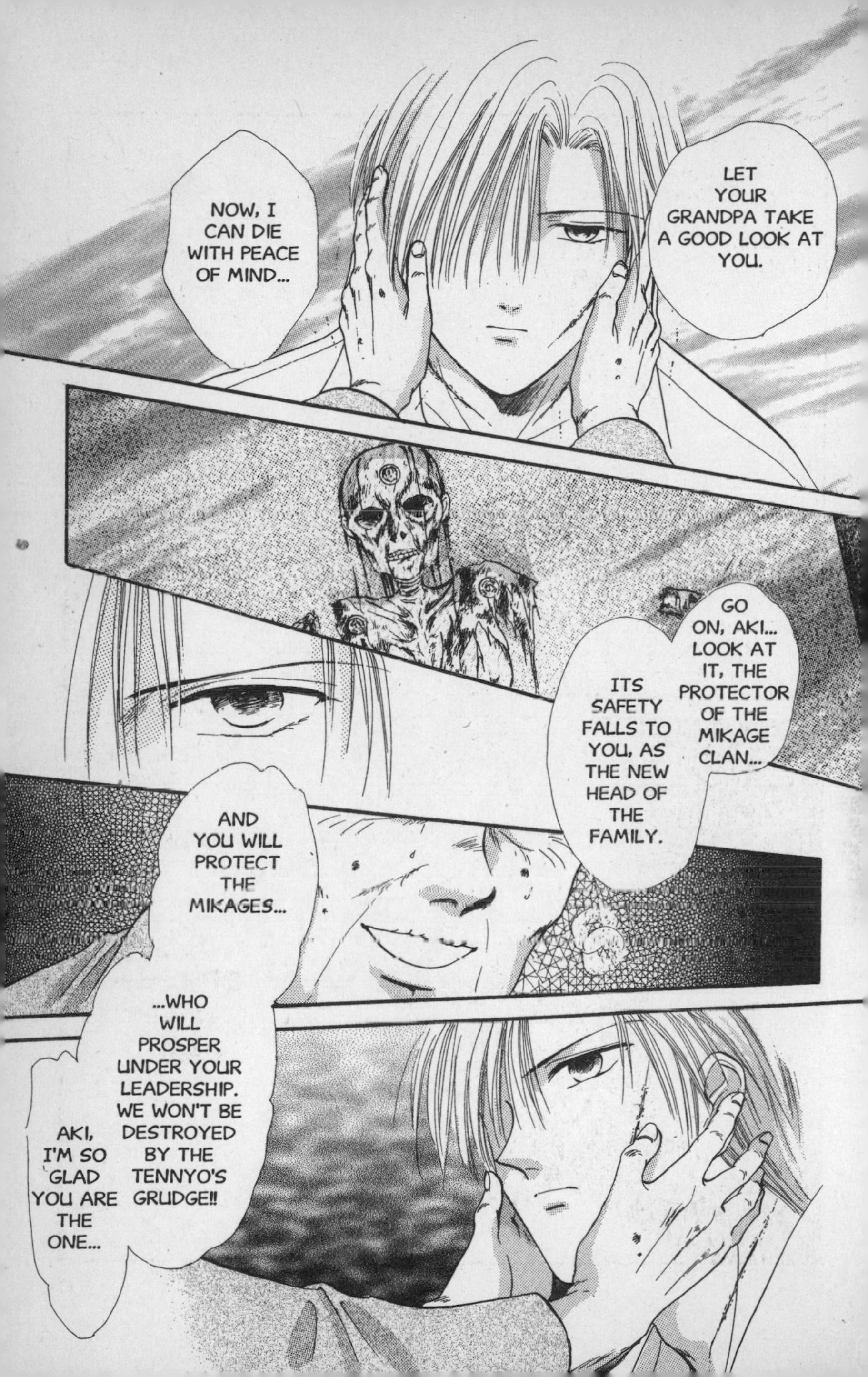
LET YOUR GRANDPA TAKE A GOOD LOOK AT YOU.
NOW, I CAN DIE WITH PEACE OF MIND...
GO ON, AKI... LOOK AT IT, THE PROTECTOR OF THE MIKAGE CLAN...
ITS SAFETY FALLS TO YOU, AS THE NEW HEAD OF THE FAMILY.
AND YOU WILL PROTECT THE MIKAGES...
...WHO WILL PROSPER UNDER YOUR LEADERSHIP. WE WON'T BE DESTROYED BY THE TENNYO'S GRUDGE!!
AKI, I'M SO GLAD YOU ARE THE ONE...

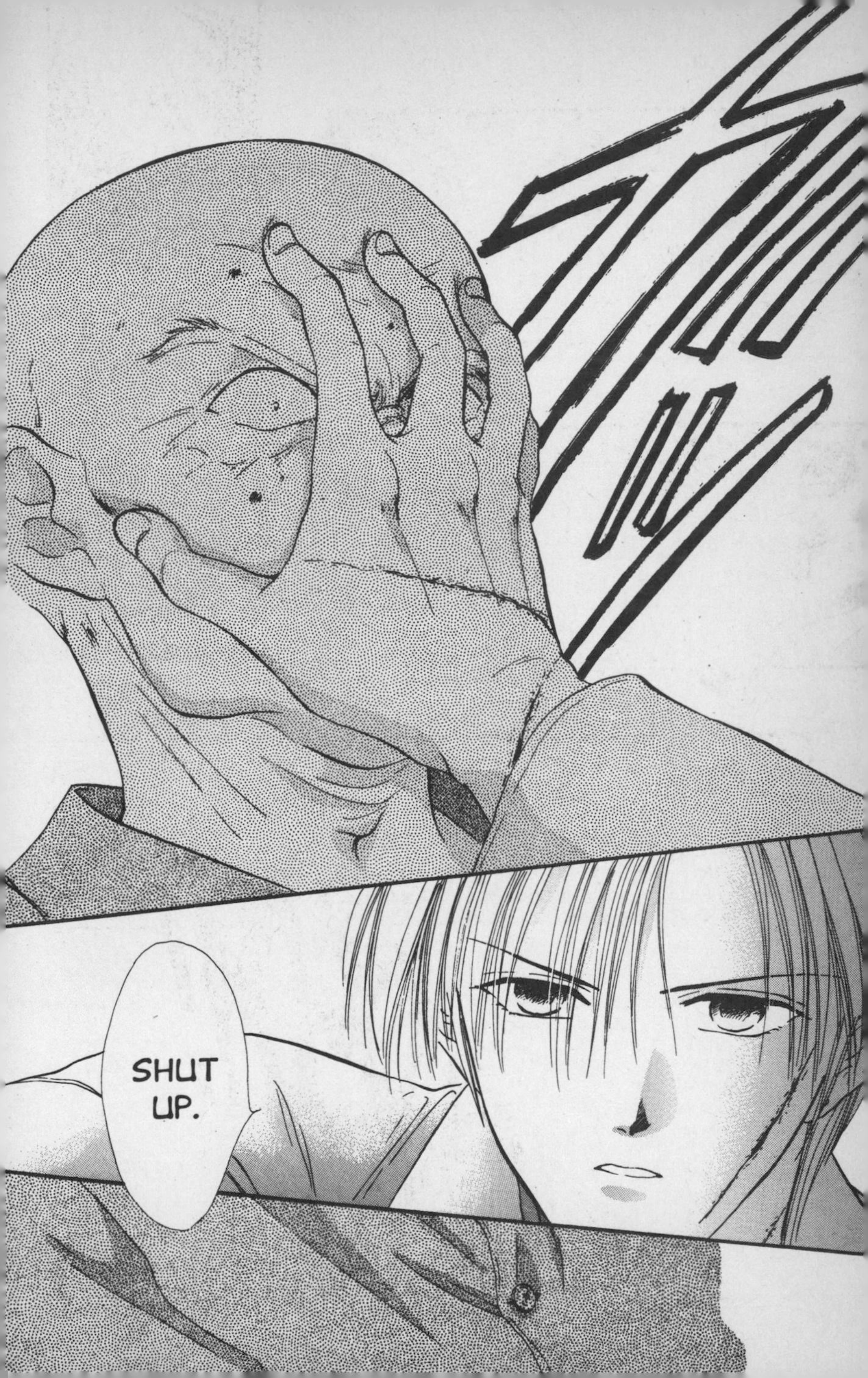
SHUT UP.

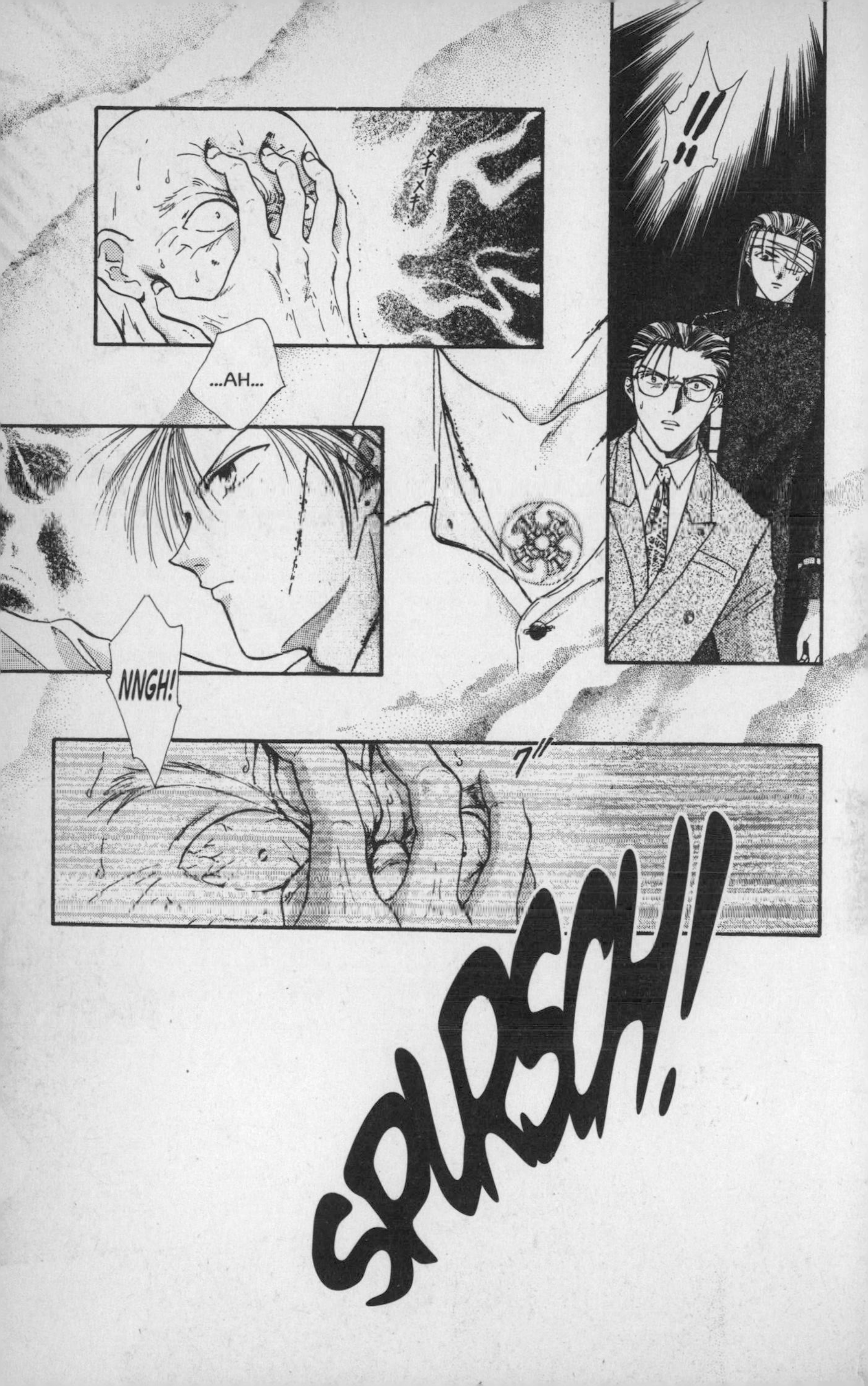
!!
メキメキ
...AH...
NNGH!
グ
SPLASCH!!

...THIS IS JUST...

...EMPTY SHELL...

...A DRY HUSK...

...NO...

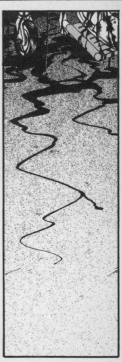

◆ Mikage ◆

Now then, it occurred to me that I haven't yet talked about my musical matching for Ceres! We have a variety of music we listen to while we work: Ghost in the Shell (soundtracks from the movie and the PSX game), Fried Dragon Fish from director Shunji Iwai, and other soundtracks like Parasite Eve and Eko Eko Azarak.

Also good is music by Ken Ishii, KURO etc. (this is mostly stuff I copied from my assistants CDs). Stuff called "trance-techno" is good! It's cool.

I listen to techno when I'm working on violent fight scenes. Cyber trance seems to fit well. Oh, I can't forget to mention the great Yoko Kanno! We're all great fans of her, here at work. She did the music for Macross Plus, Escaflowne, the Nobunaga's Ambition game, and even an NHK documentary on China! ← As well as Memories.

I listened to this a lot while I was doing FY.

I'm sure you can find them. I listen to the first two a lot. She's awesome. She can make all different types of music (and they're all good!). I'd love for her to make music for my work. I'm pretty picky about music. ◡ Sometimes a track inspires a scene that will lead to the creation of an entire episode. I'm very sensitive to whether music goes well with my work or not. The keywords for Ceres are... hmm... Dark, cool, beautiful, and mysterious... Well ◡ at least it looks that way in my head. I guess I just can't draw it that way. Sniff!

As for vocal music, I like the worldview although not necessarily the lyrics of "Mystery of Sound" by Yuko Tsuburaya. I like that type of stuff.

Upbeat is ok, but no happy songs!

Some cheerful songs might work for Aya though... Oh, Ceres's song would be Yuming's "Sand Planet." It's so her! ◡

There isn't anything specific for Yūhi but... the song "Almost Love" in the album by Rainbow Capsule...

Out of room! To be continued...

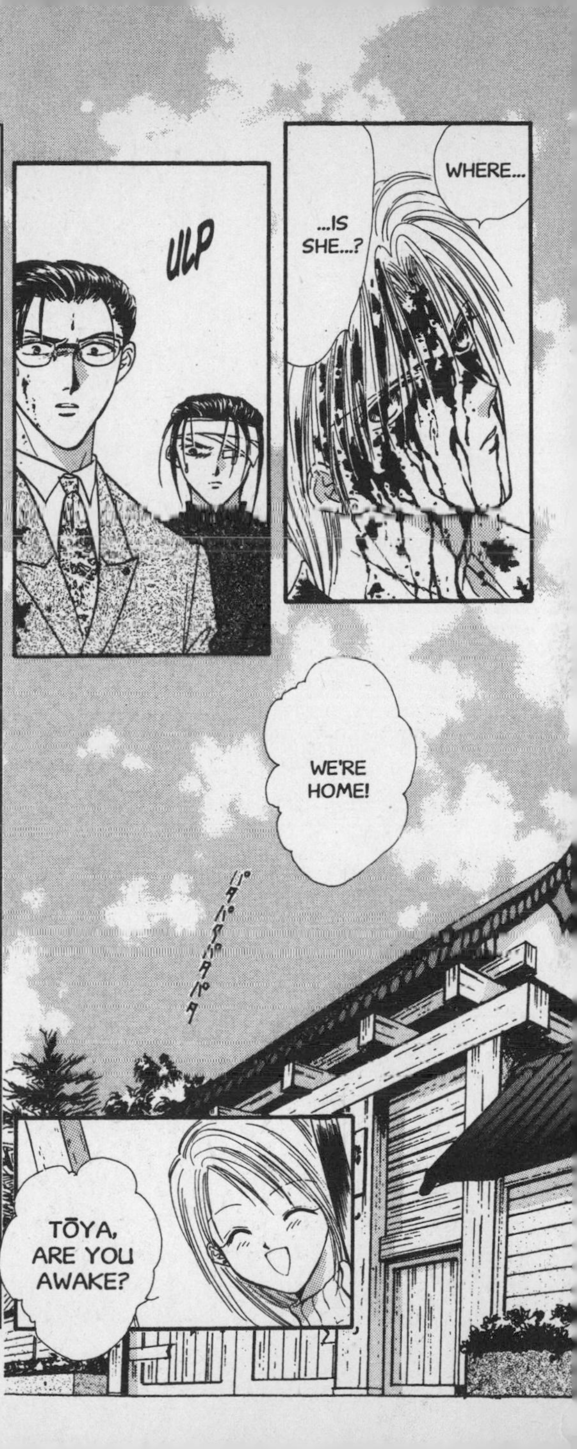
WHERE...
...IS SHE...?
ULP
WE'RE HOME!
パタパタパタ
TŌYA, ARE YOU AWAKE?

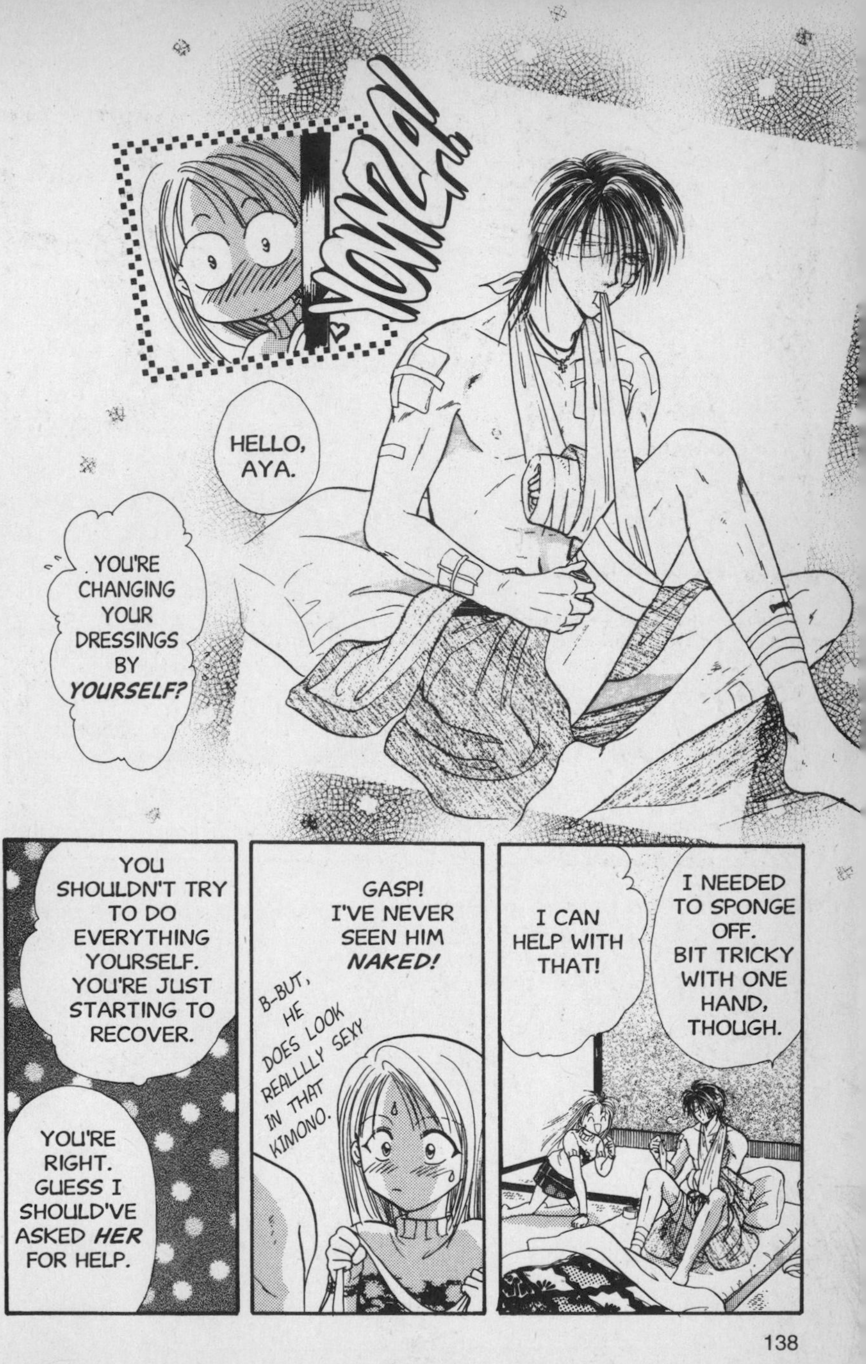
YOWZA!
HELLO, AYA.
YOU'RE CHANGING YOUR DRESSINGS BY ***YOURSELF?***
I NEEDED TO SPONGE OFF. BIT TRICKY WITH ONE HAND, THOUGH.
I CAN HELP WITH THAT!
GASP! I'VE NEVER SEEN HIM ***NAKED!***
B-BUT, HE DOES LOOK REALLLLY SEXY IN THAT KIMONO.
YOU SHOULDN'T TRY TO DO EVERYTHING YOURSELF. YOU'RE JUST STARTING TO RECOVER.
YOU'RE RIGHT. GUESS I SHOULD'VE ASKED ***HER*** FOR HELP.

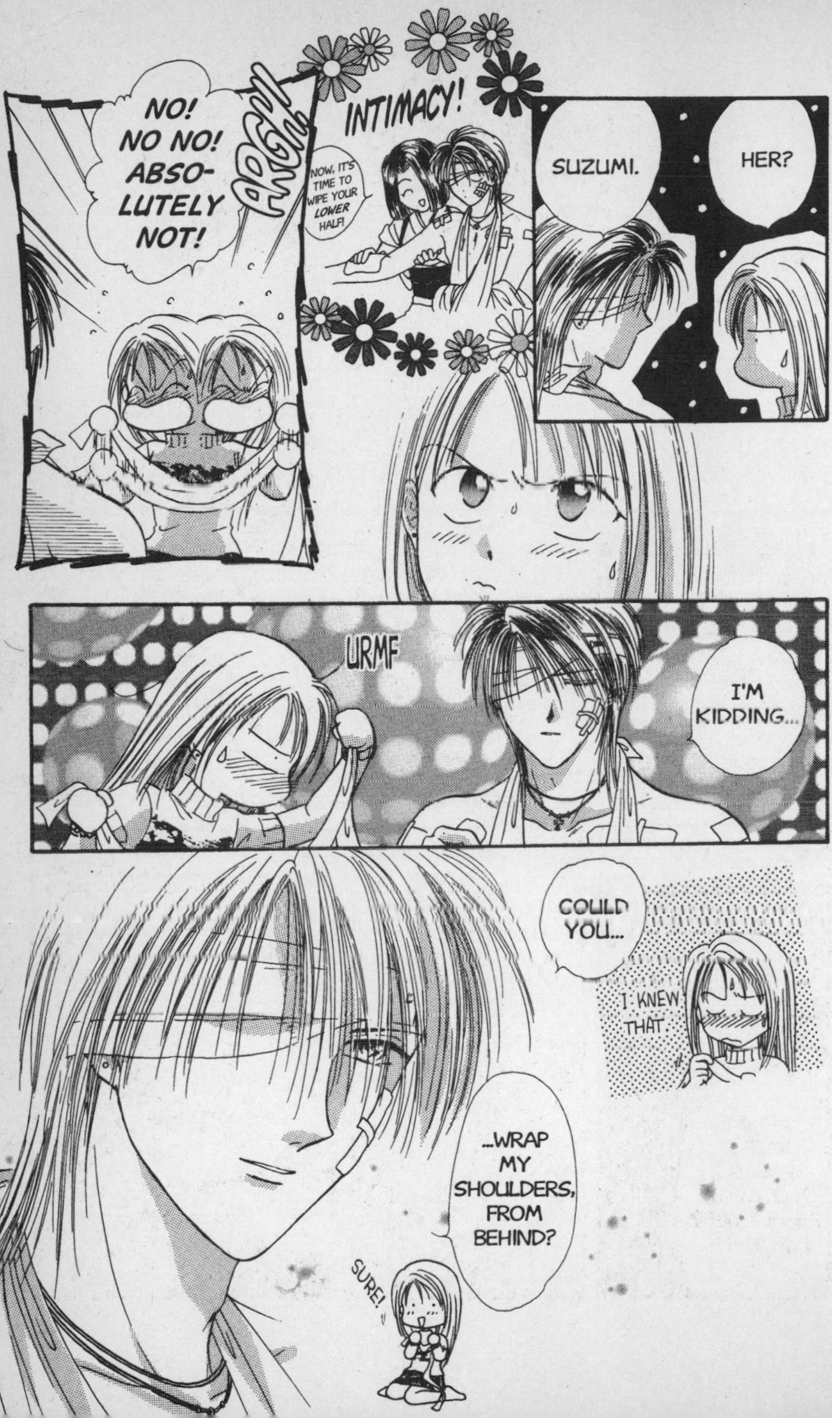
HER?
SUZUMI.
INTIMACY!
NOW, IT'S TIME TO WIPE YOUR *LOWER* HALF!
ARGH!
NO! NO NO! ABSO-LUTELY NOT!
I'M KIDDING...
URMF
COULD YOU...
I KNEW THAT.
...WRAP MY SHOULDERS, FROM BEHIND?
SURE!

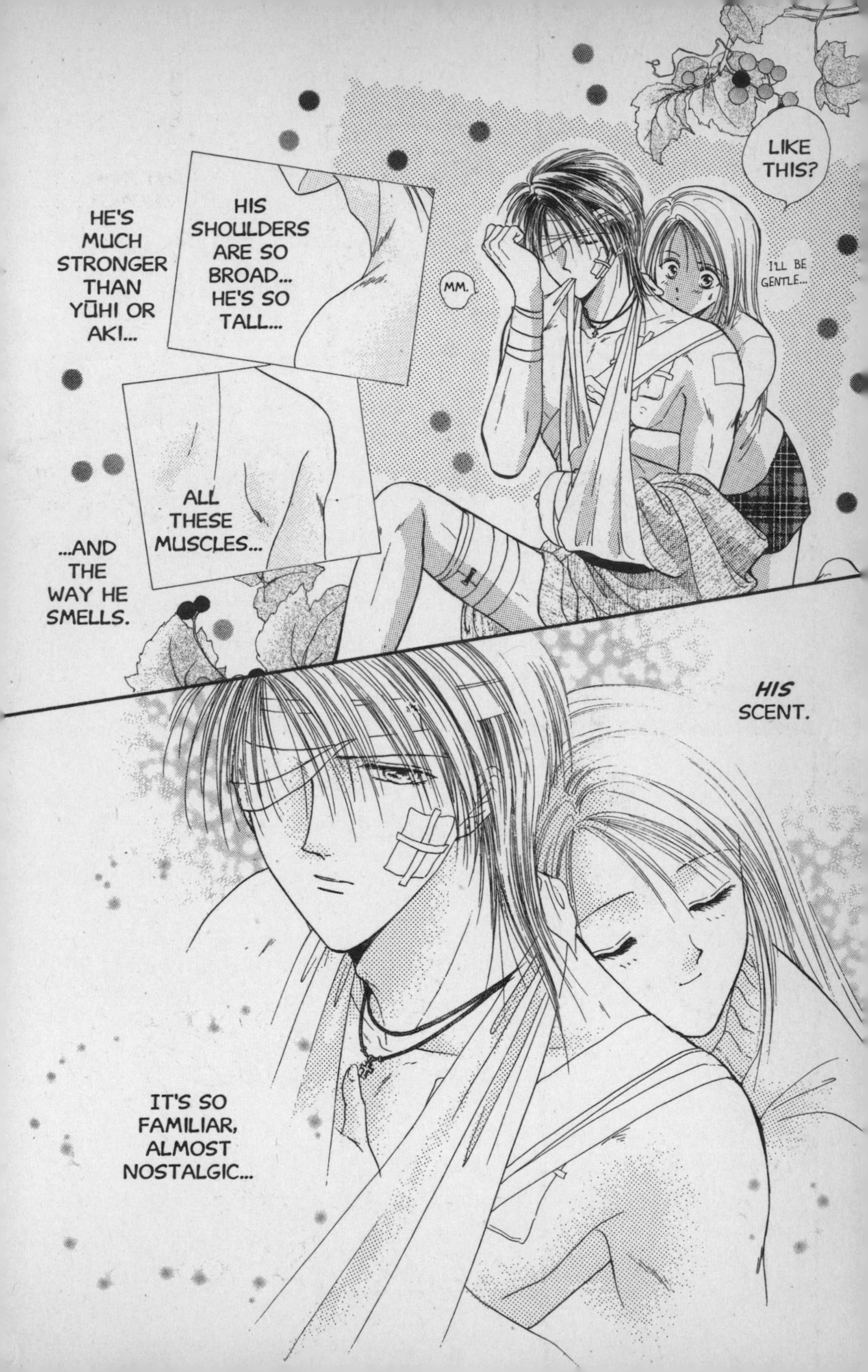
LIKE THIS?
I'LL BE GENTLE...
MM.
HIS SHOULDERS ARE SO BROAD... HE'S SO TALL...
HE'S MUCH STRONGER THAN YŪHI OR AKI...
ALL THESE MUSCLES...
...AND THE WAY HE SMELLS.
HIS SCENT.
IT'S SO FAMILIAR, ALMOST NOSTALGIC...

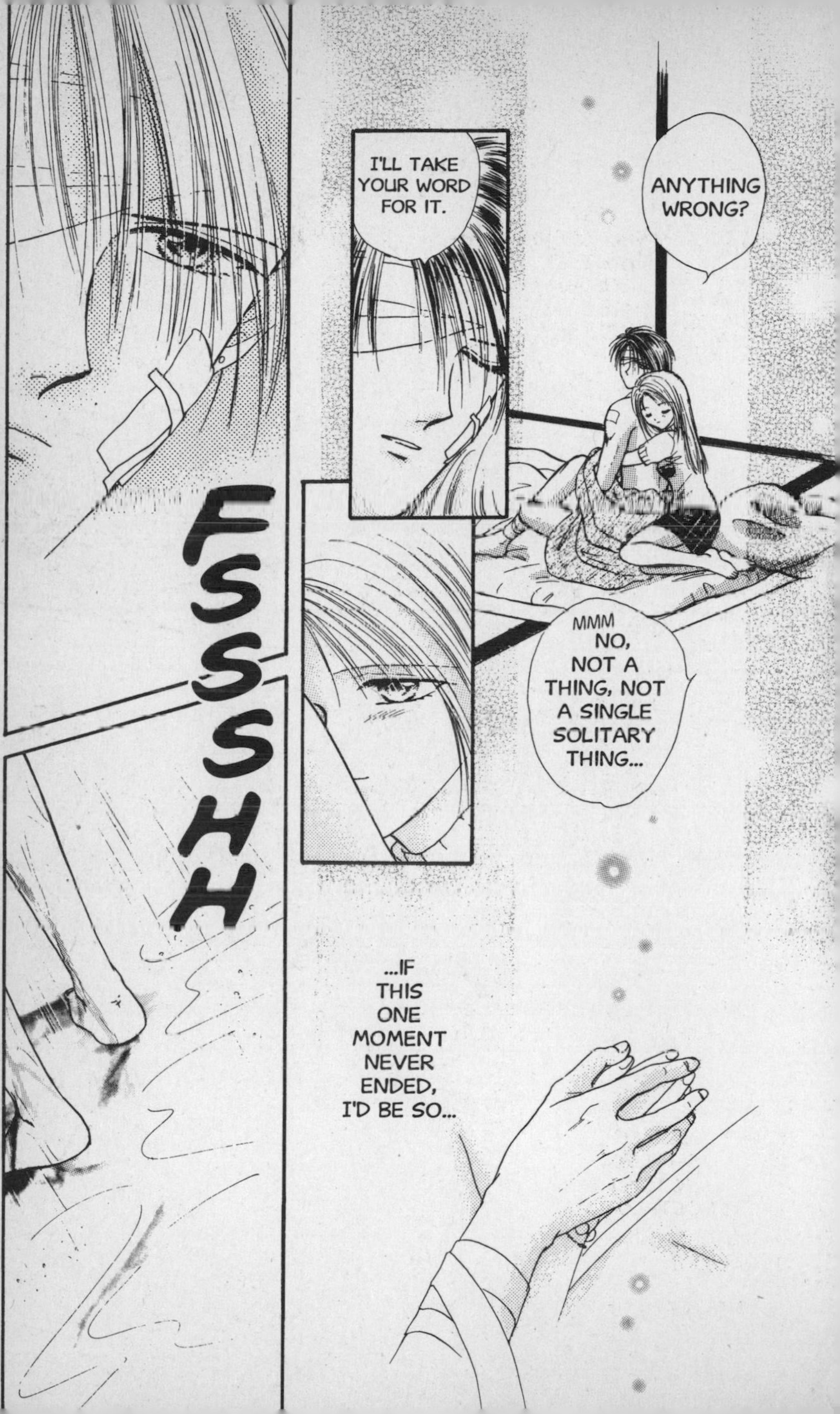
ANYTHING WRONG?
MMM NO, NOT A THING, NOT A SINGLE SOLITARY THING...
I'LL TAKE YOUR WORD FOR IT.
FSSSHH
...IF THIS ONE MOMENT NEVER ENDED, I'D BE SO...

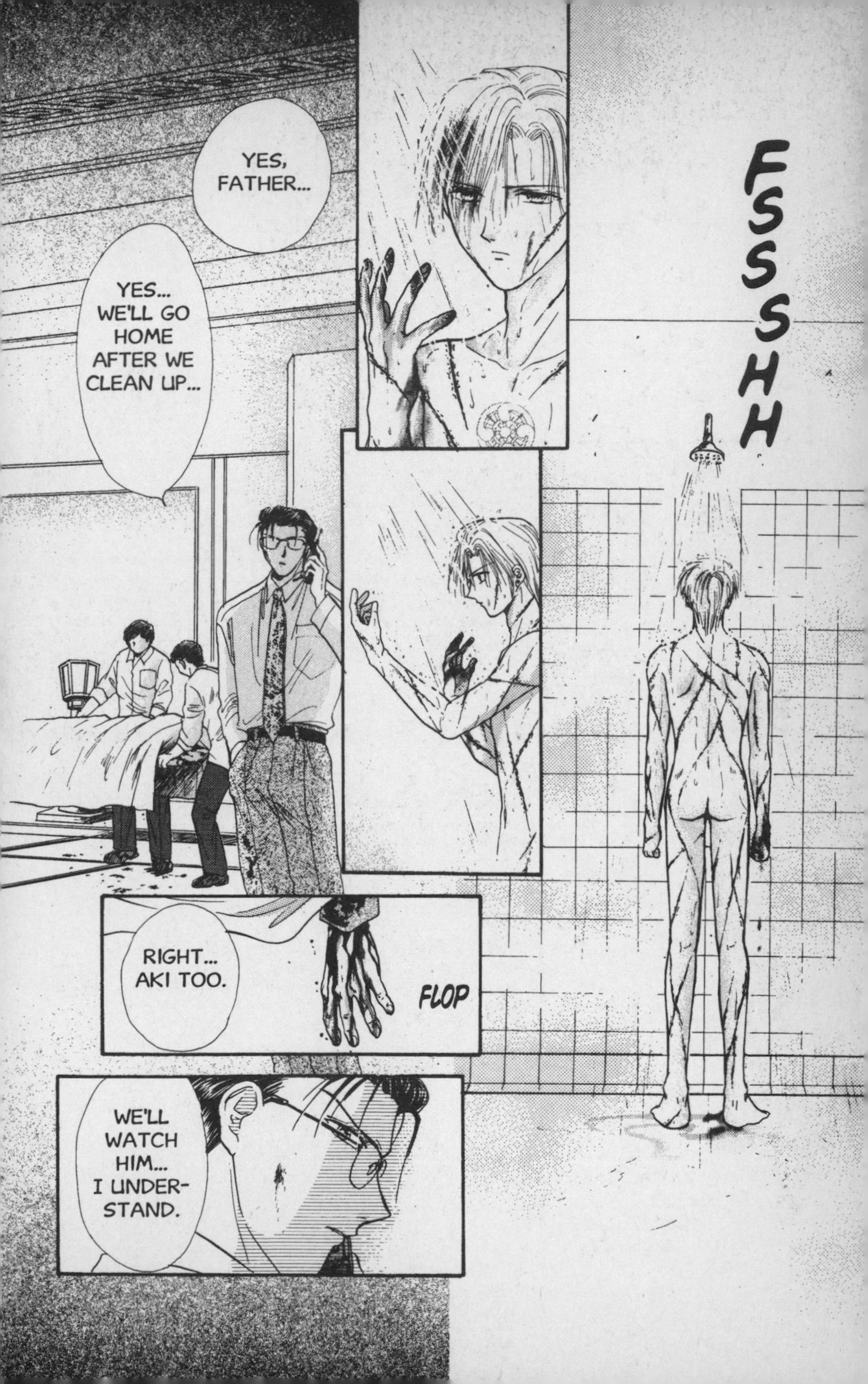
FSSSHH
YES, FATHER...
YES... WE'LL GO HOME AFTER WE CLEAN UP...
RIGHT... AKI TOO.
FLOP
WE'LL WATCH HIM... I UNDER-STAND.

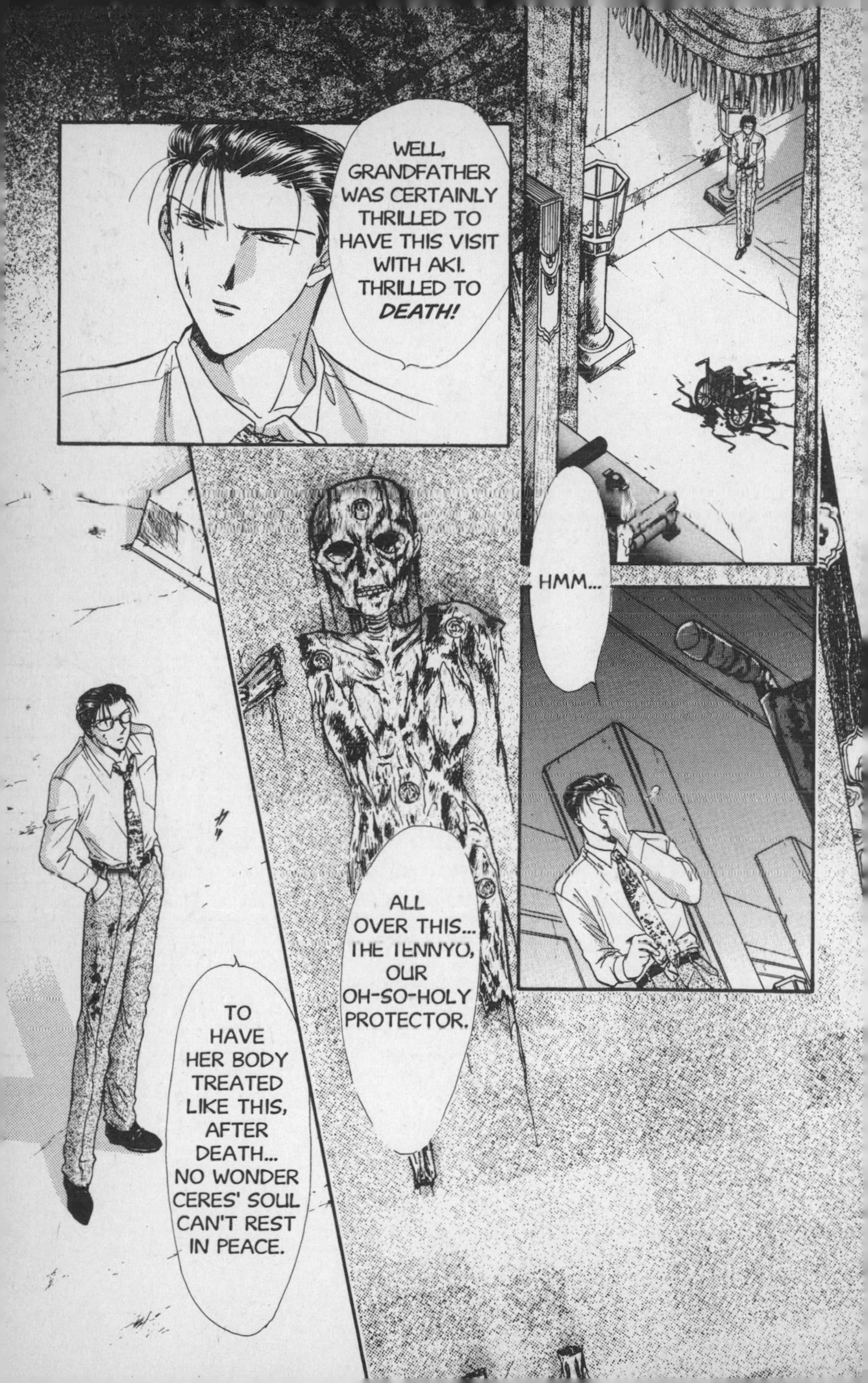
HMM...
WELL, GRANDFATHER WAS CERTAINLY THRILLED TO HAVE THIS VISIT WITH AKI. THRILLED TO *DEATH!*
ALL OVER THIS... THE TENNYO, OUR OH-SO-HOLY PROTECTOR.
TO HAVE HER BODY TREATED LIKE THIS, AFTER DEATH... NO WONDER CERES' SOUL CAN'T REST IN PEACE.

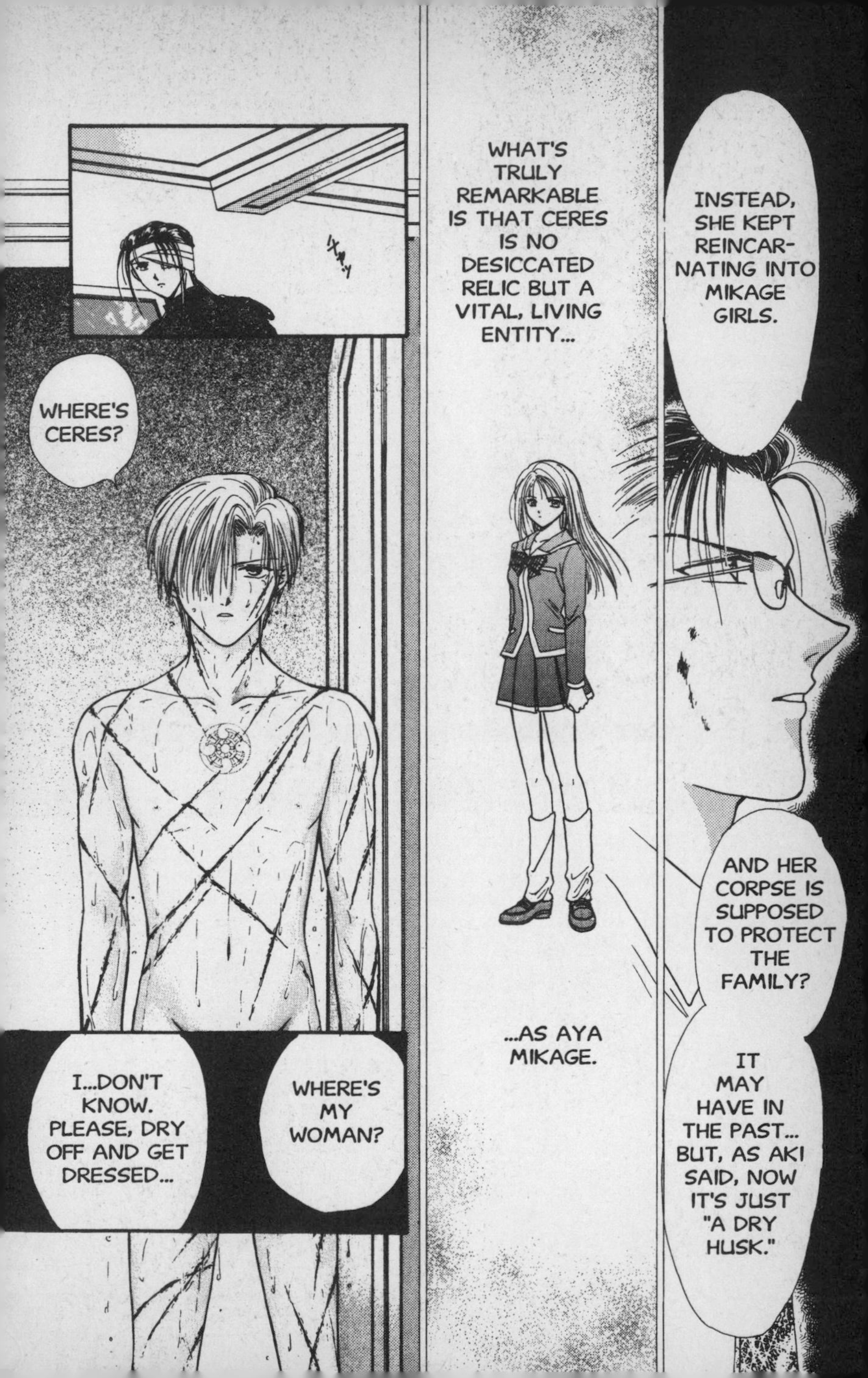
INSTEAD, SHE KEPT REINCARNATING INTO MIKAGE GIRLS.
AND HER CORPSE IS SUPPOSED TO PROTECT THE FAMILY?
IT MAY HAVE IN THE PAST... BUT, AS AKI SAID, NOW IT'S JUST "A DRY HUSK."
WHAT'S TRULY REMARKABLE IS THAT CERES IS NO DESICCATED RELIC BUT A VITAL, LIVING ENTITY...
...AS AYA MIKAGE.
WHERE'S CERES?
WHERE'S MY WOMAN?
I...DON'T KNOW. PLEASE, DRY OFF AND GET DRESSED...

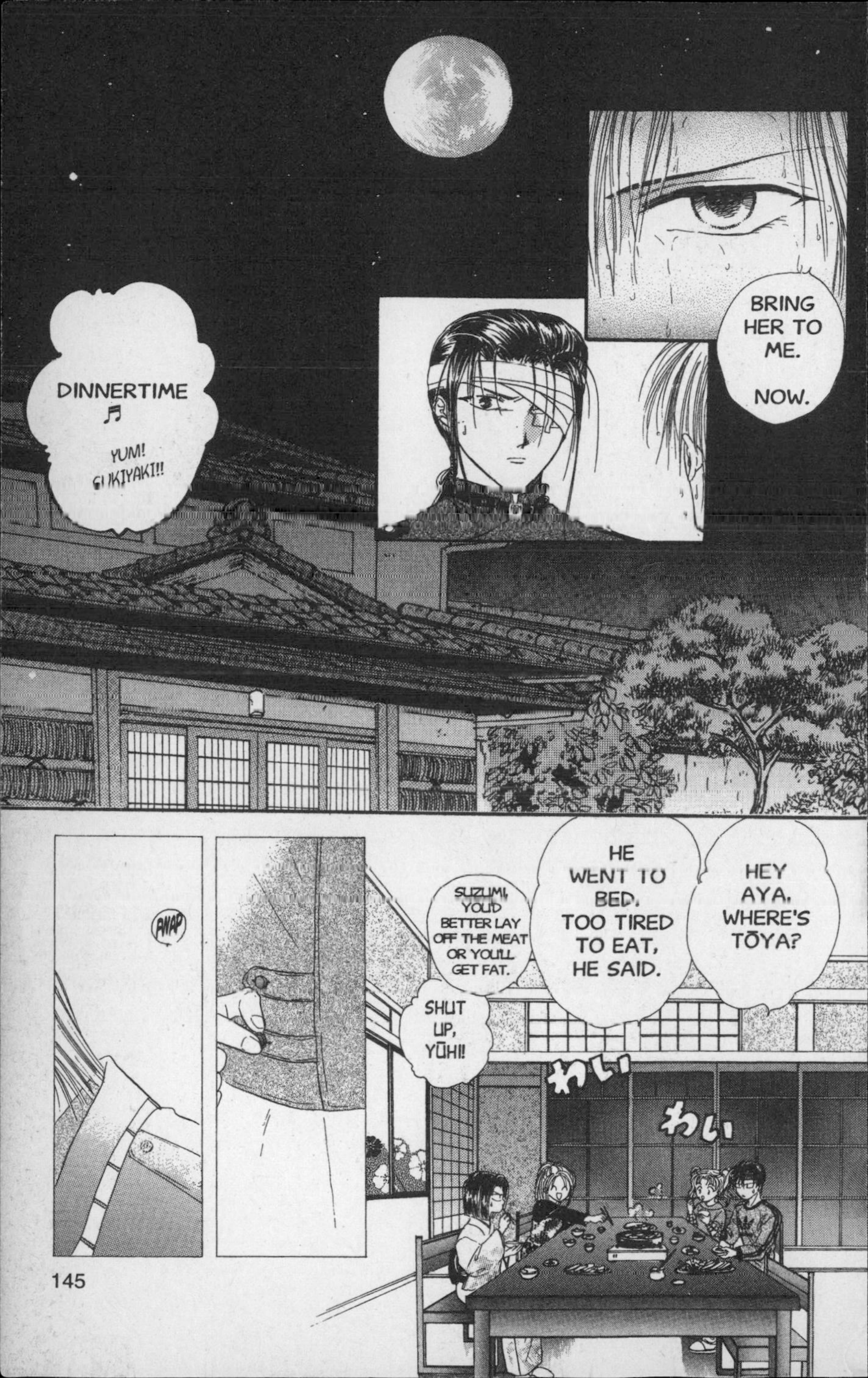
BRING HER TO ME.
NOW.
DINNERTIME ♬
YUM! SUKIYAKI!!
HEY AYA. WHERE'S TŌYA?
HE WENT TO BED. TOO TIRED TO EAT, HE SAID.
SUZUMI, YOU'D BETTER LAY OFF THE MEAT OR YOU'LL GET FAT.
SHUT UP, YŪHI!
わい
わい
AWAP

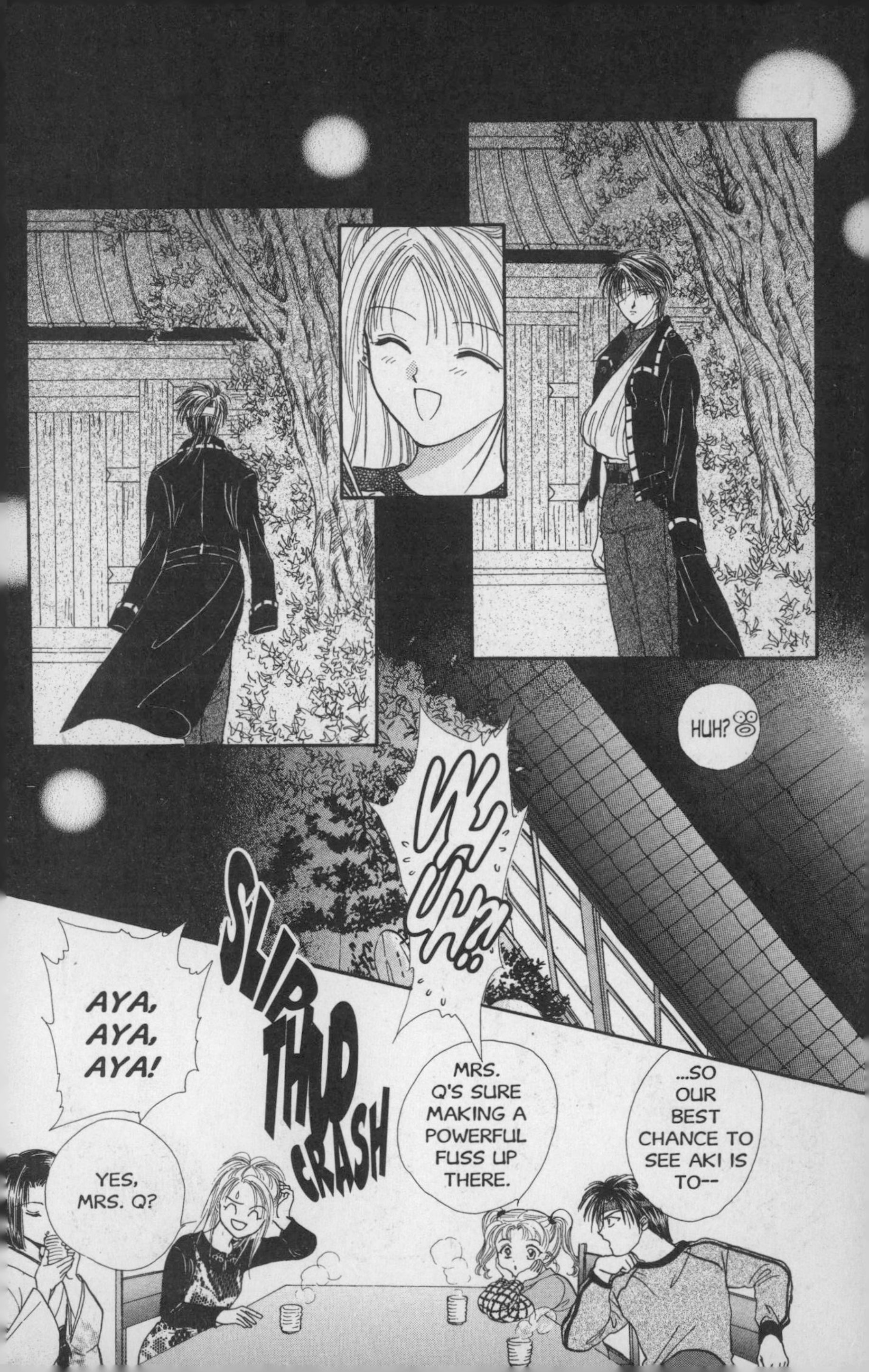
HUH?
...SO OUR BEST CHANCE TO SEE AKI IS TO--
SLIP THUD CRASH
MRS. Q'S SURE MAKING A POWERFUL FUSS UP THERE.
AYA, AYA, AYA!
YES, MRS. Q?

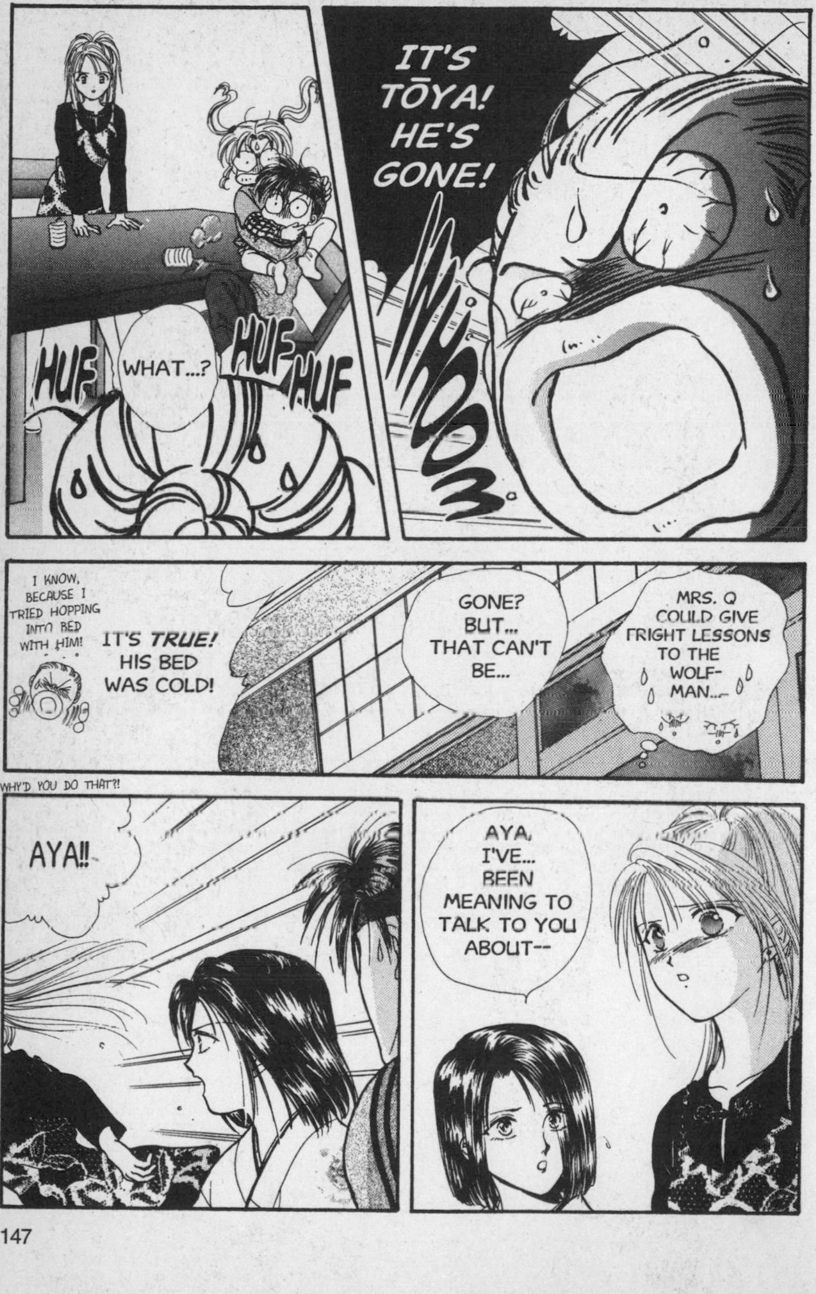
IT'S TŌYA! HE'S GONE!
WHOOM
HUF
WHAT...?
HUF HUF
MRS. Q COULD GIVE FRIGHT LESSONS TO THE WOLF-MAN...
GONE? BUT... THAT CAN'T BE...
IT'S *TRUE!* HIS BED WAS COLD!
I KNOW, BECAUSE I TRIED HOPPING INTO BED WITH HIM!
WHY'D YOU DO THAT?!
AYA, I'VE... BEEN MEANING TO TALK TO YOU ABOUT--
AYA!!

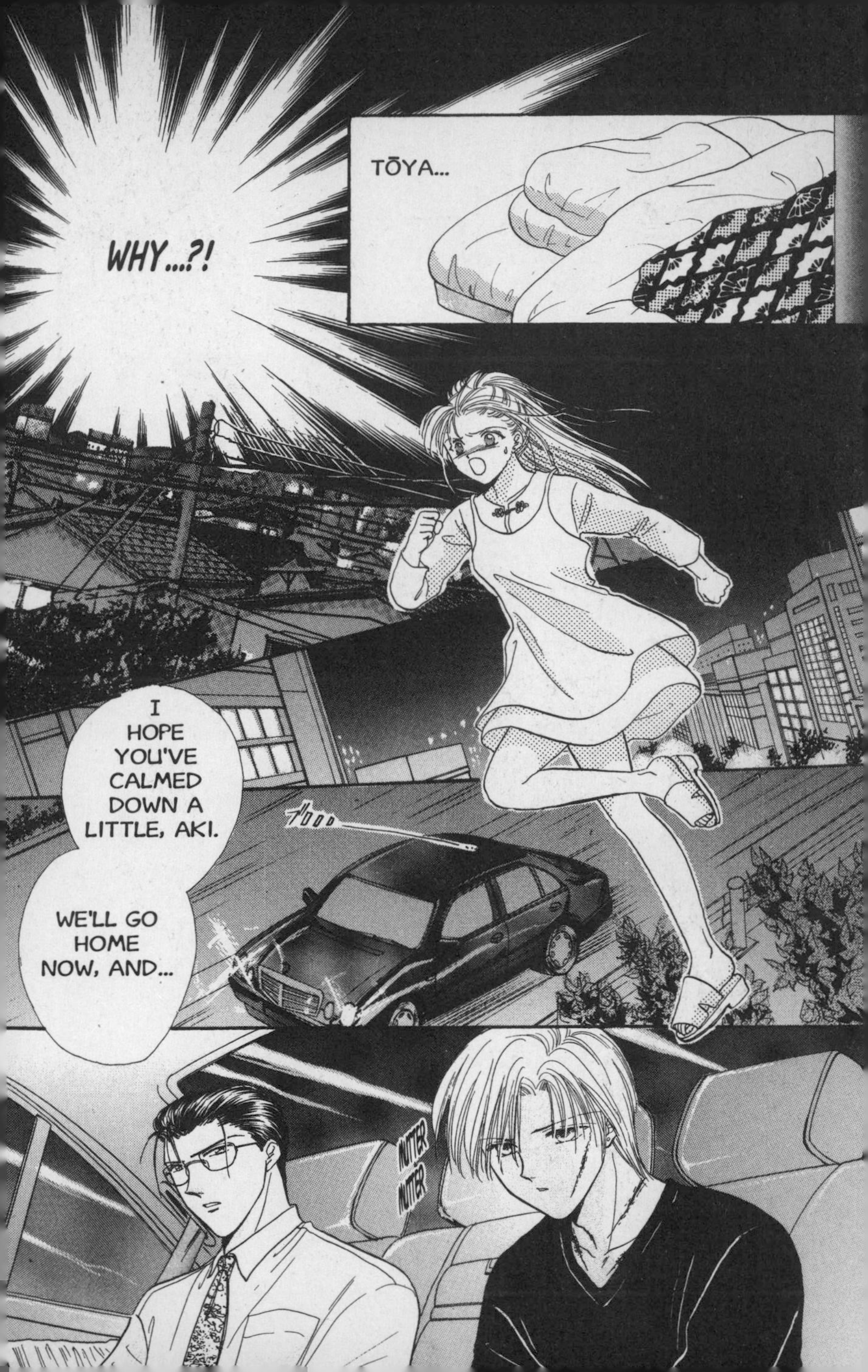
TŌYA...
WHY...?!
I HOPE YOU'VE CALMED DOWN A LITTLE, AKI.
WE'LL GO HOME NOW, AND...
MUTTER MUTTER

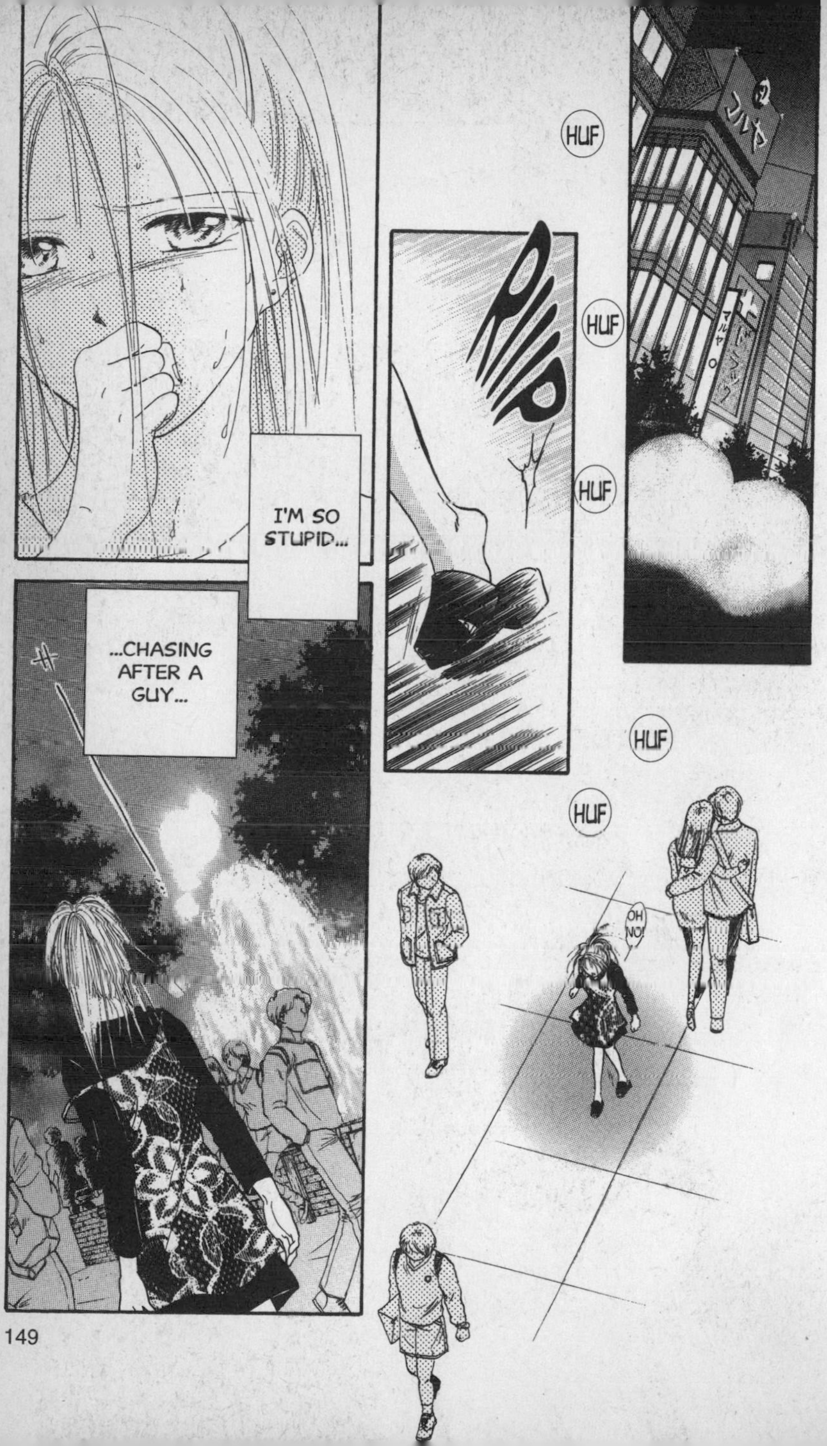

HUF
HUF
RIIP
HUF
I'M SO STUPID...
HUF
HUF
OH NO!
...CHASING AFTER A GUY...

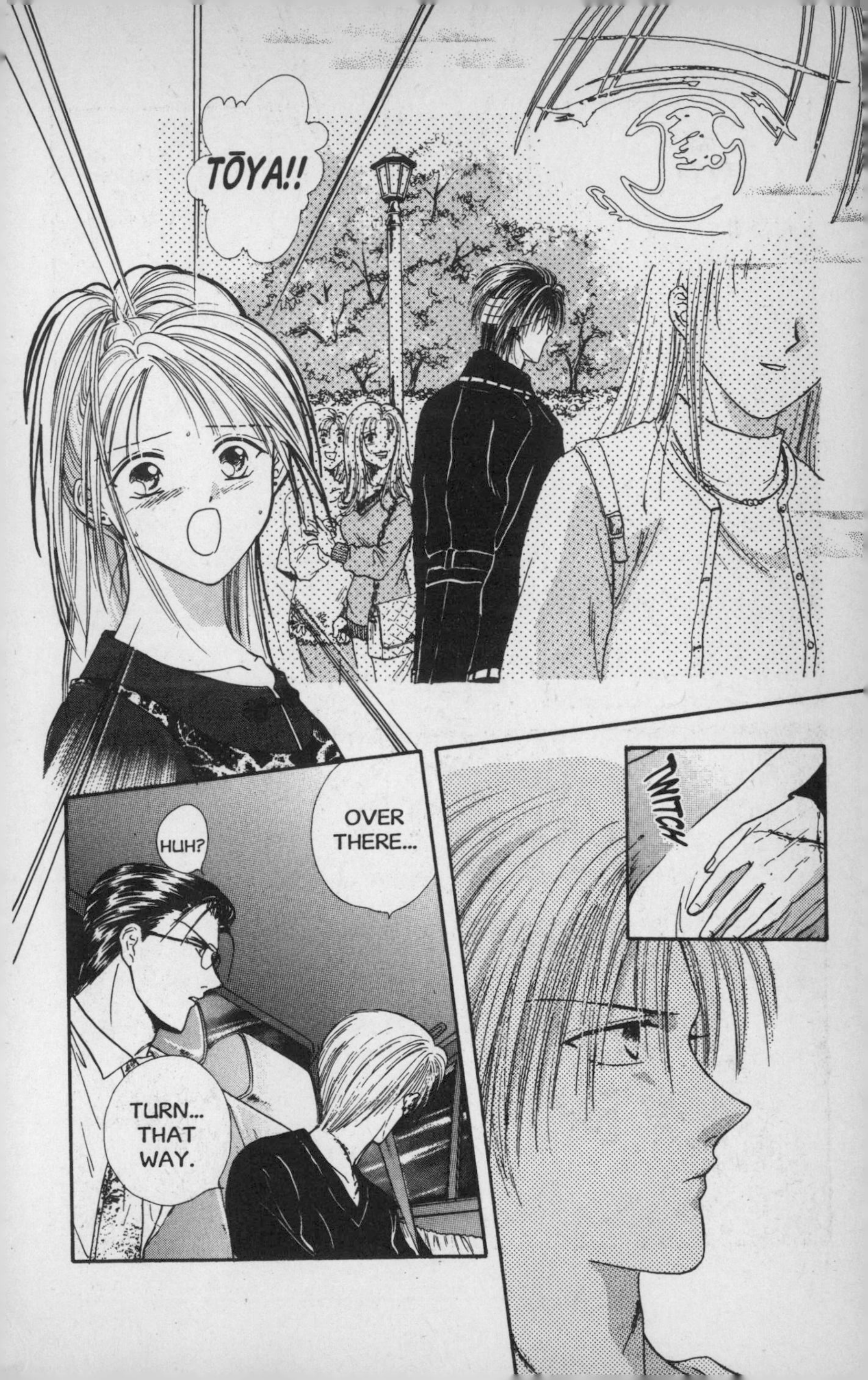
TŌYA!!
TWITCH
OVER THERE...
HUH?
TURN... THAT WAY.

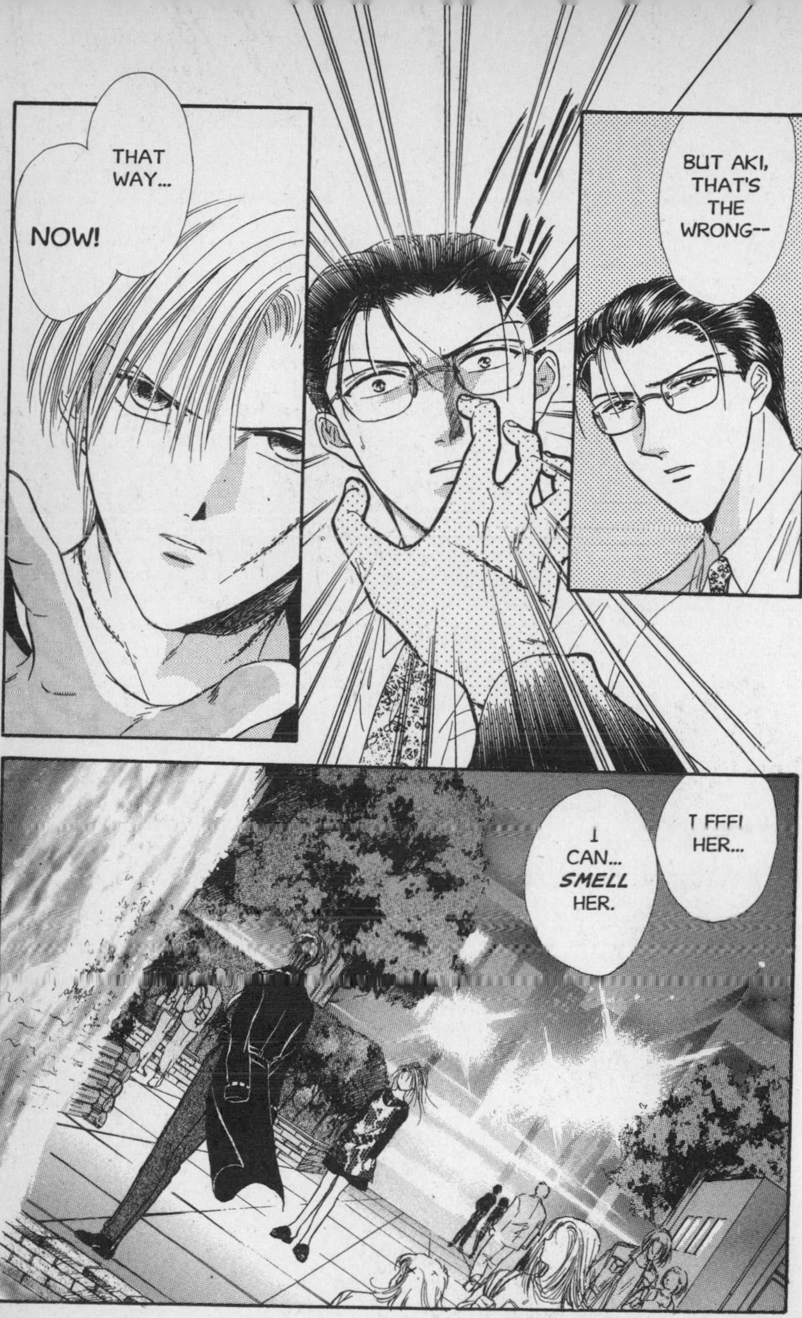
BUT AKI, THAT'S THE WRONG--
THAT WAY...
NOW!
I FEEL HER...
I CAN... *SMELL* HER.

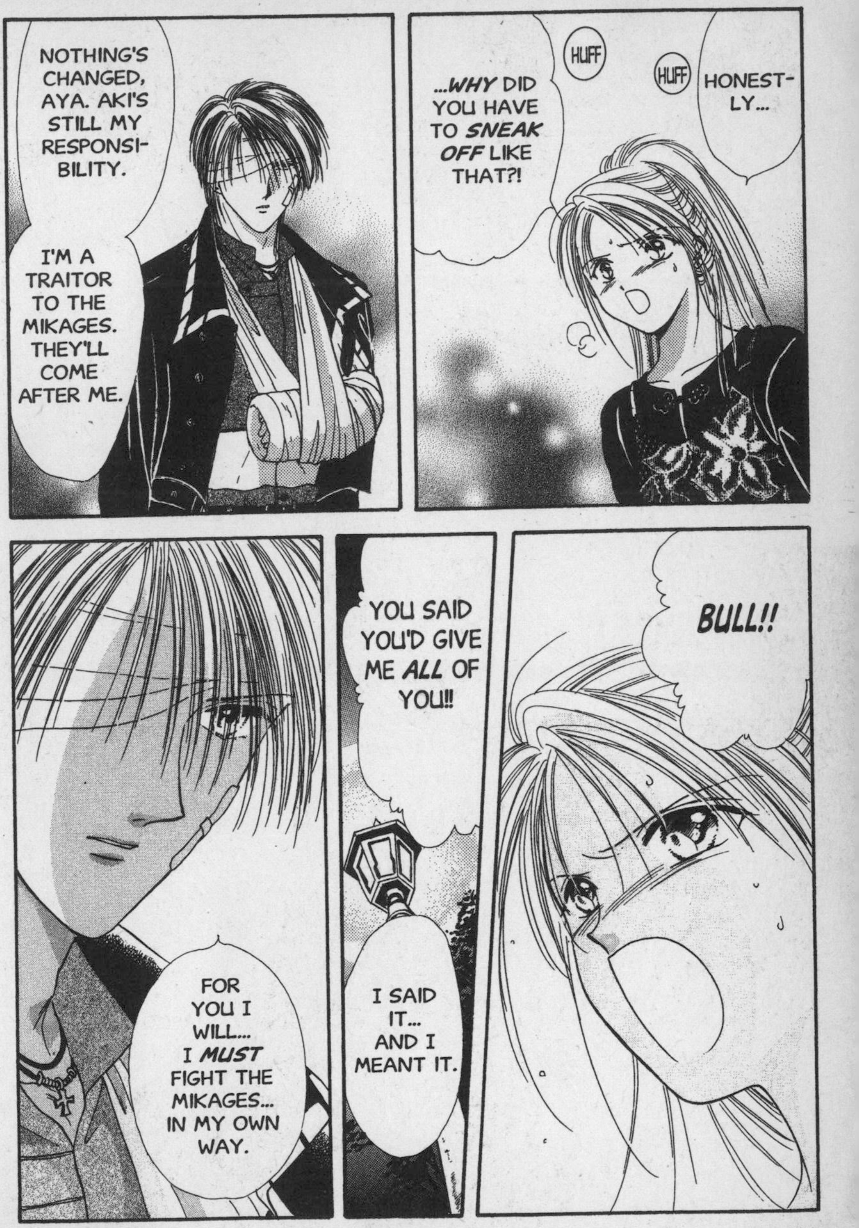
HONESTLY...
HUFF
HUFF
...WHY DID YOU HAVE TO SNEAK OFF LIKE THAT?!
NOTHING'S CHANGED, AYA. AKI'S STILL MY RESPONSIBILITY.
I'M A TRAITOR TO THE MIKAGES. THEY'LL COME AFTER ME.
BULL!!
YOU SAID YOU'D GIVE ME ALL OF YOU!!
I SAID IT... AND I MEANT IT.
FOR YOU I WILL... I MUST FIGHT THE MIKAGES... IN MY OWN WAY.

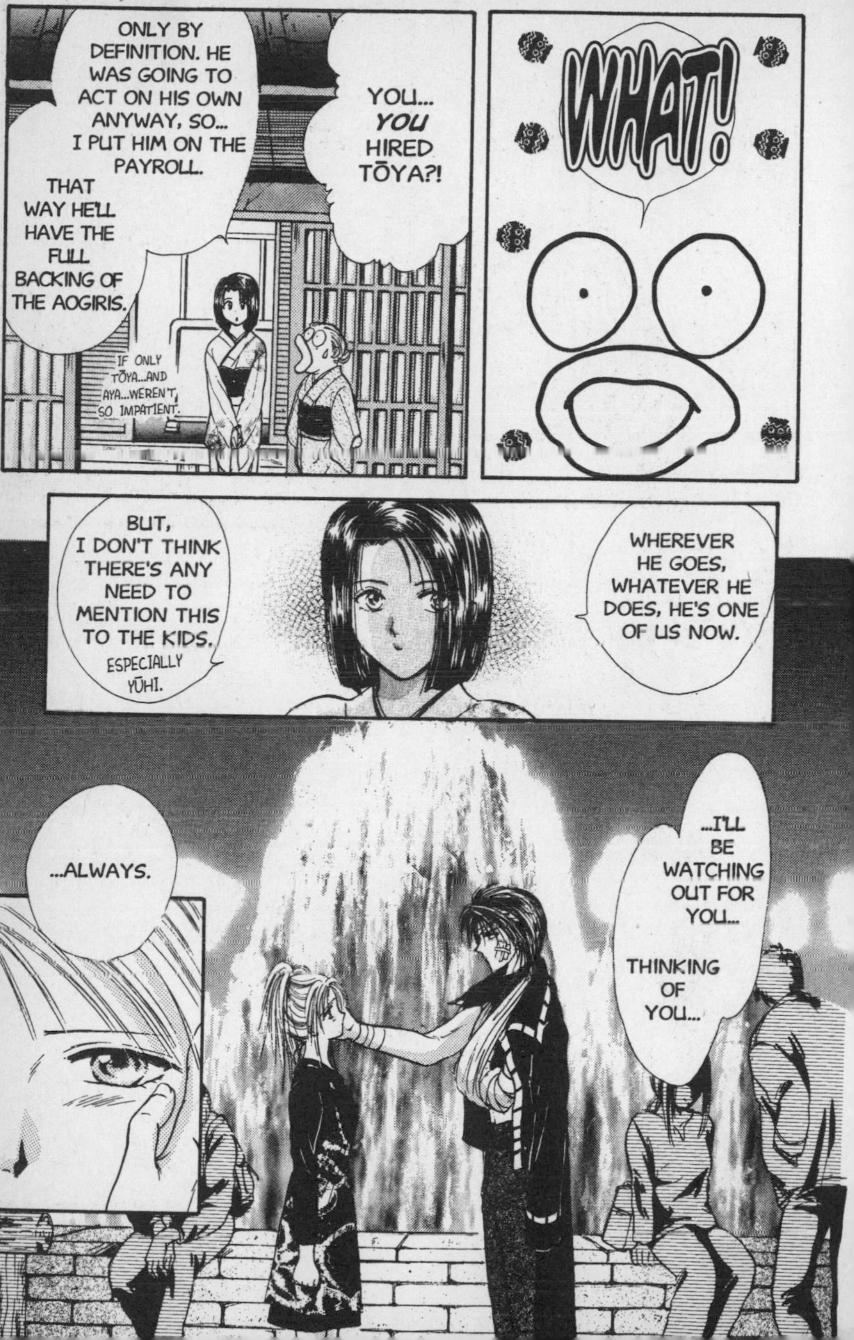
WHAT!
YOU... YOU HIRED TŌYA?!
ONLY BY DEFINITION. HE WAS GOING TO ACT ON HIS OWN ANYWAY, SO... I PUT HIM ON THE PAYROLL.
THAT WAY HE'LL HAVE THE FULL BACKING OF THE AOGIRIS.
IF ONLY TŌYA...AND AYA...WEREN'T SO IMPATIENT.
WHEREVER HE GOES, WHATEVER HE DOES, HE'S ONE OF US NOW.
BUT, I DON'T THINK THERE'S ANY NEED TO MENTION THIS TO THE KIDS.
ESPECIALLY YŪHI.
...I'LL BE WATCHING OUT FOR YOU...
THINKING OF YOU...
...ALWAYS.

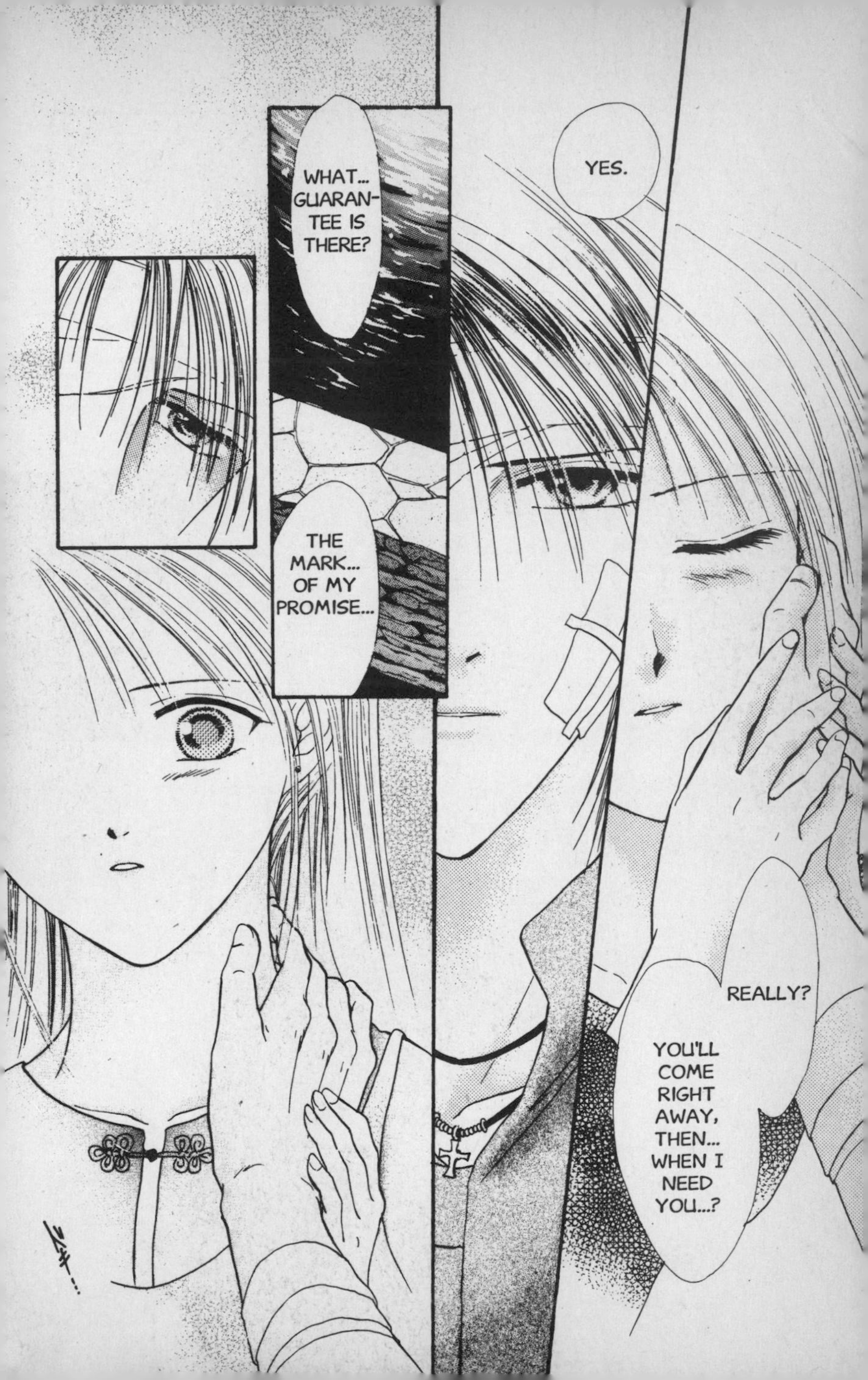
REALLY?
YOU'LL COME RIGHT AWAY, THEN... WHEN I NEED YOU...?
YES.
WHAT... GUARAN-TEE IS THERE?
THE MARK... OF MY PROMISE...

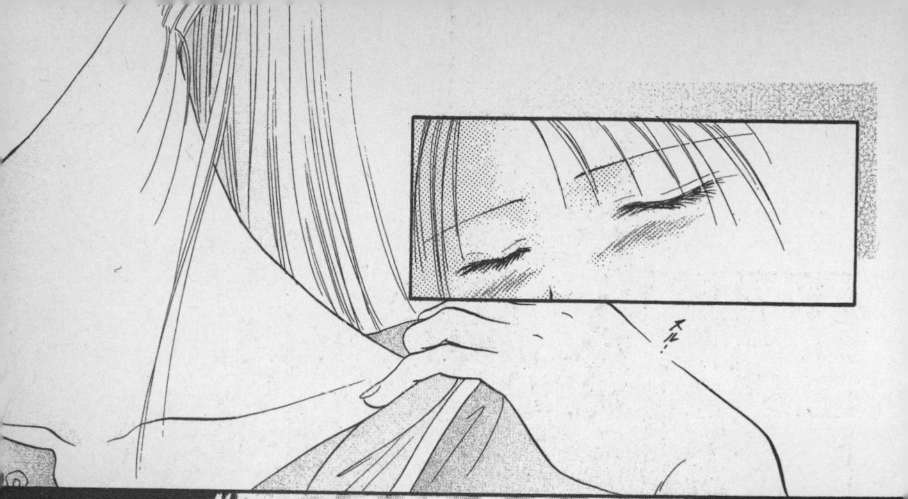
スル…
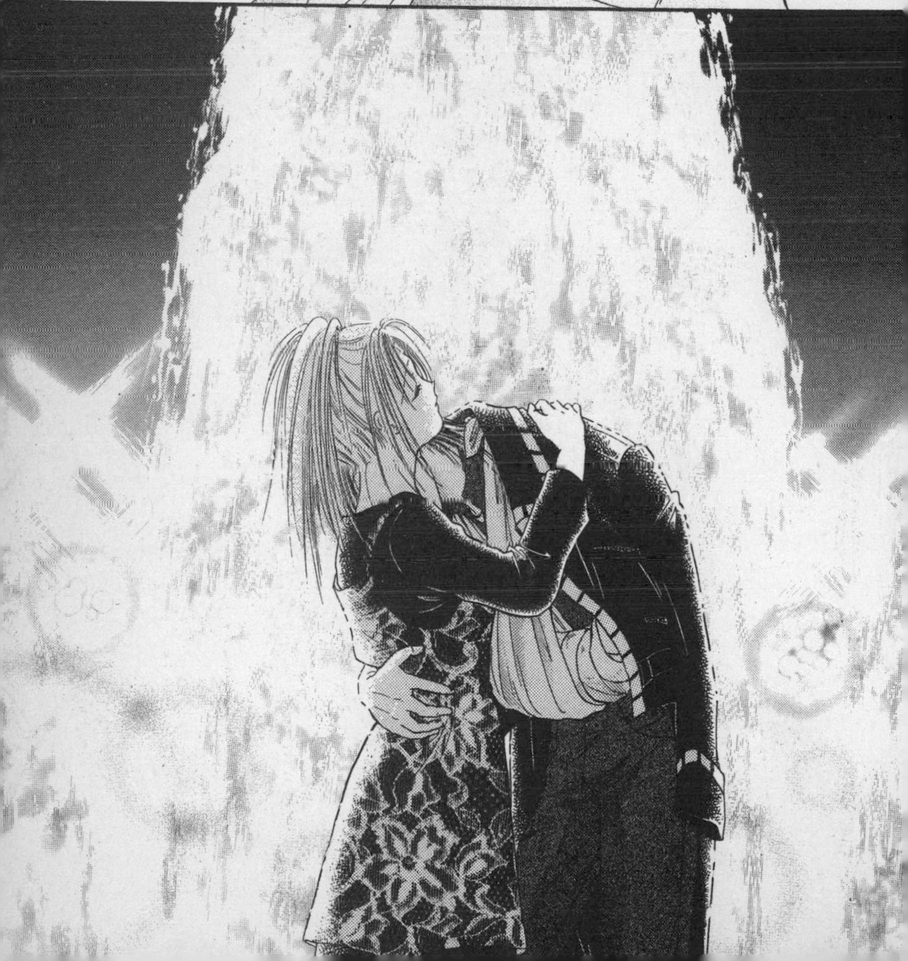

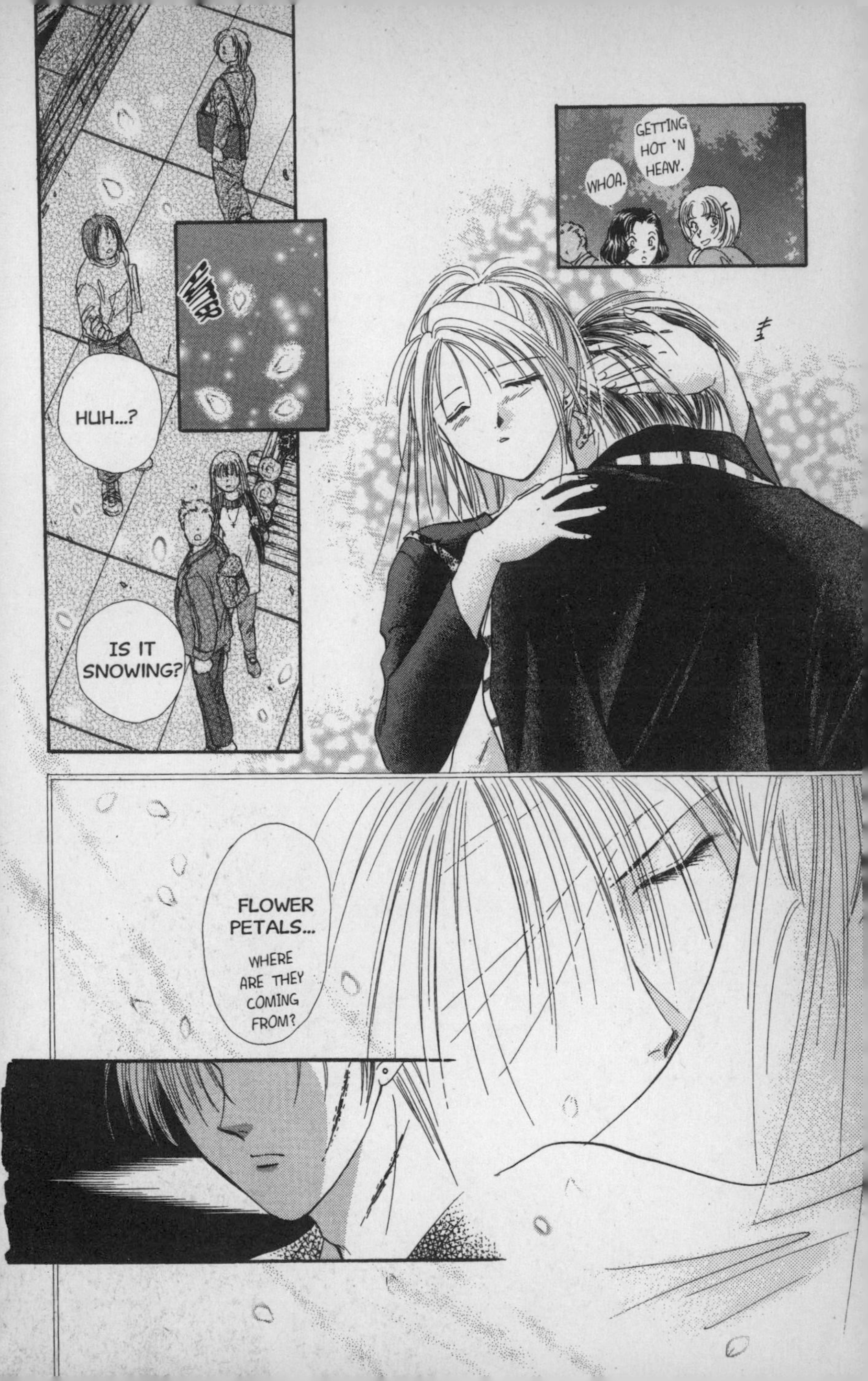
GETTING HOT 'N HEAVY.
WHOA.
GLITTER
HUH...?
IS IT SNOWING?
FLOWER PETALS...
WHERE ARE THEY COMING FROM?

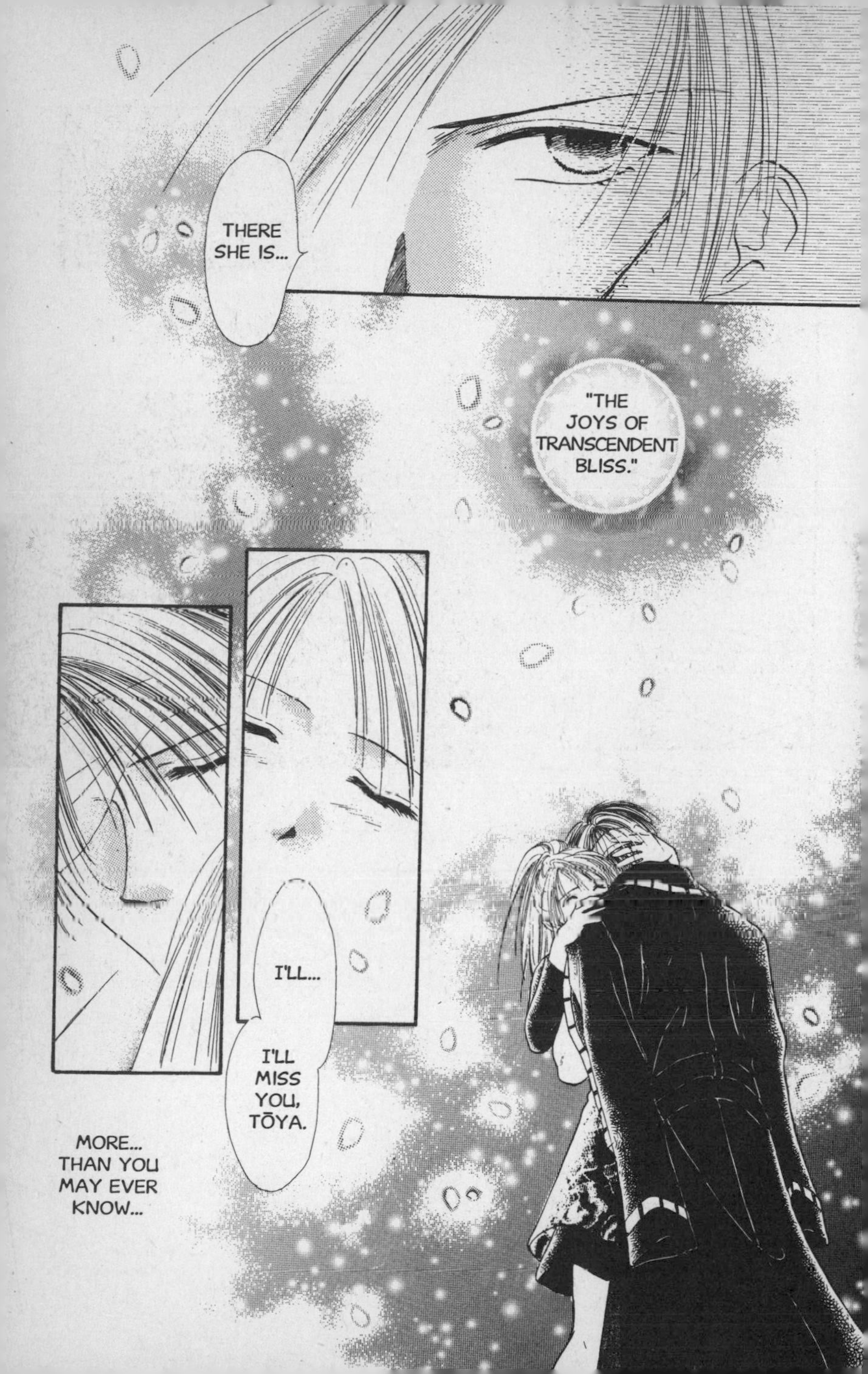
THERE SHE IS...
"THE JOYS OF TRANSCENDENT BLISS."
I'LL...
I'LL MISS YOU, TŌYA.
MORE... THAN YOU MAY EVER KNOW...

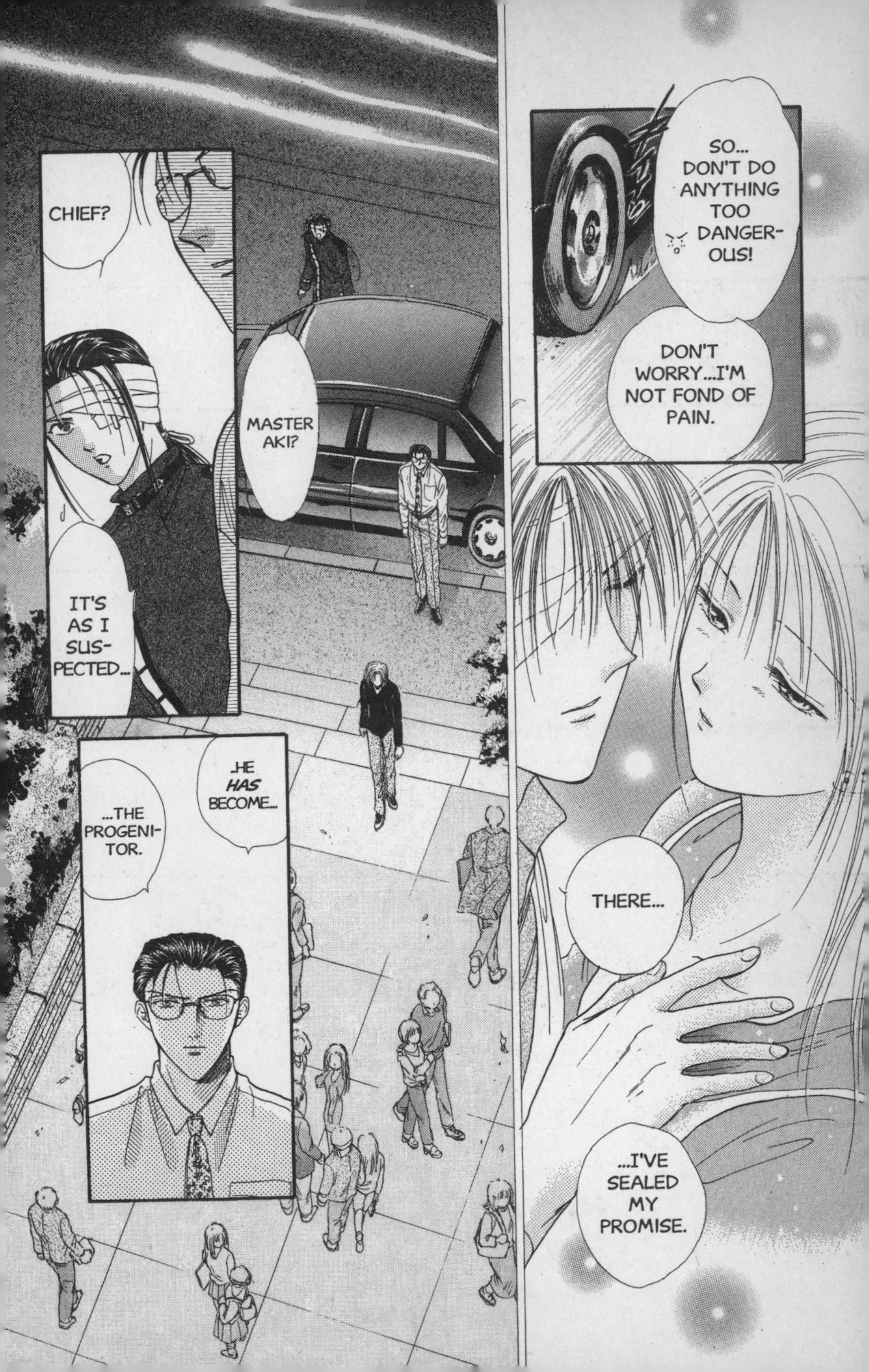
SO... DON'T DO ANYTHING TOO DANGER-OUS!
DON'T WORRY...I'M NOT FOND OF PAIN.
THERE...
...I'VE SEALED MY PROMISE.
CHIEF?
MASTER AKI?
IT'S AS I SUS-PECTED...
.HE *HAS* BECOME...
...THE PROGENI-TOR.

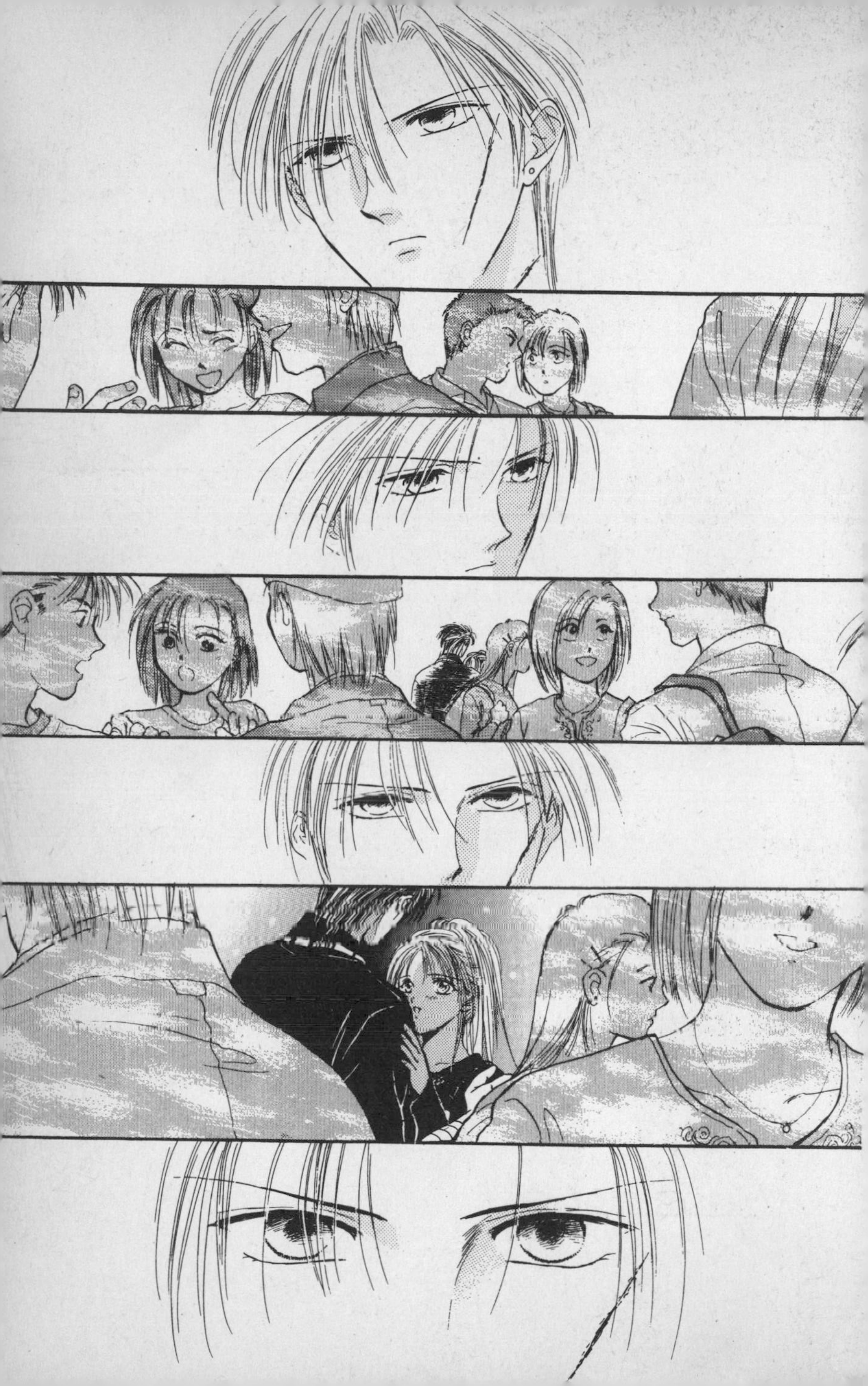

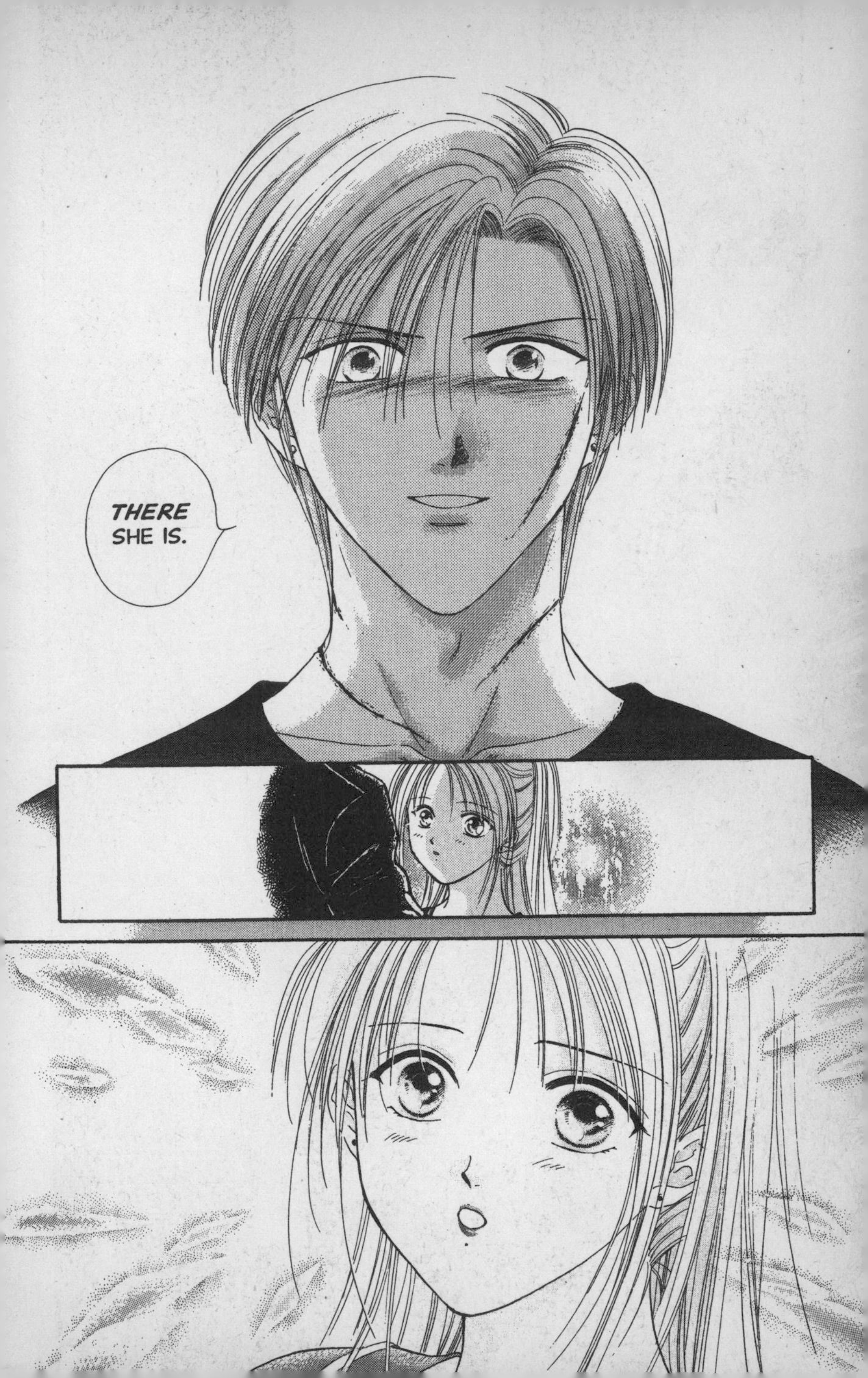
THERE SHE IS.

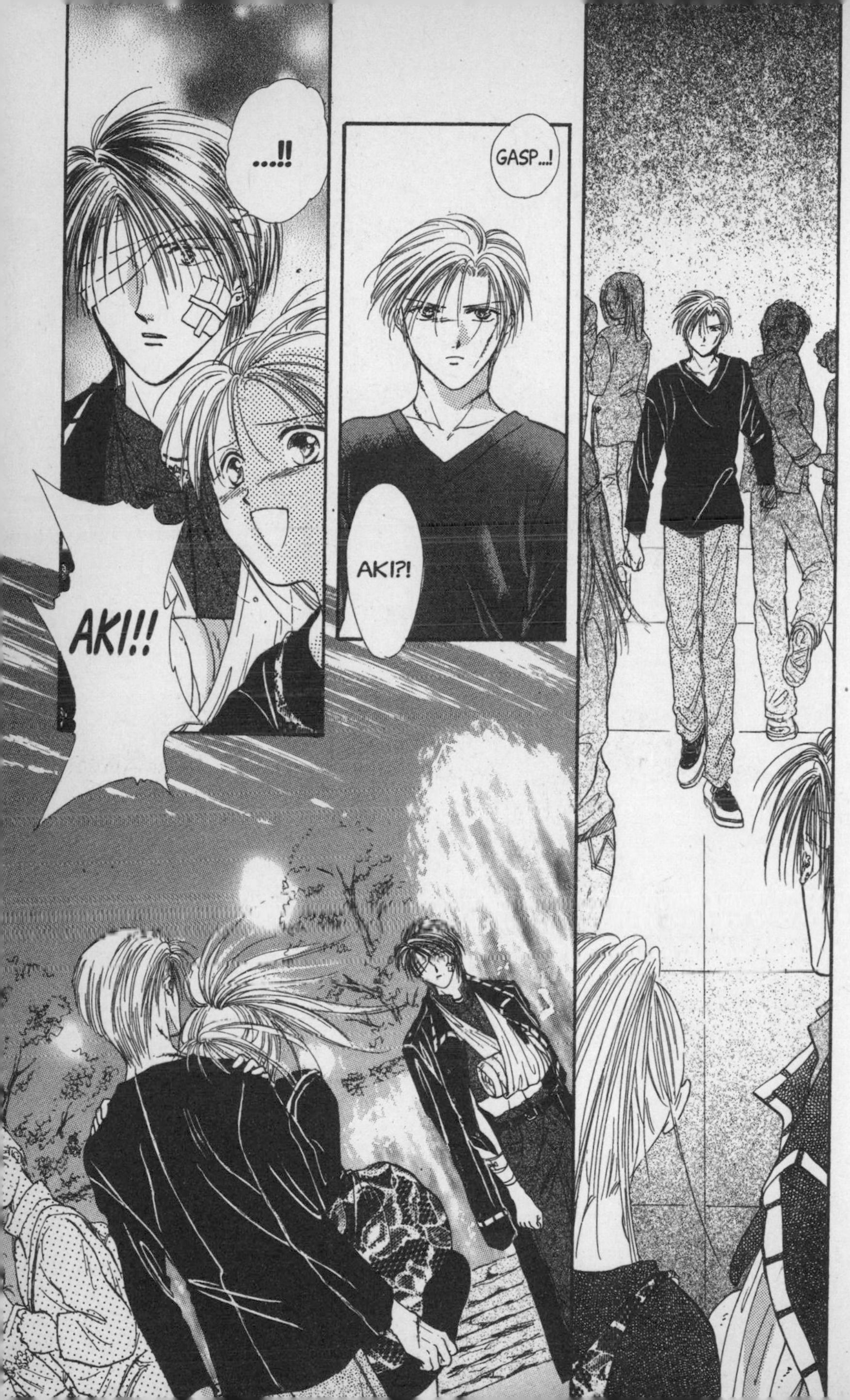
GASP...!
AKI?!
...!!
AKI!!

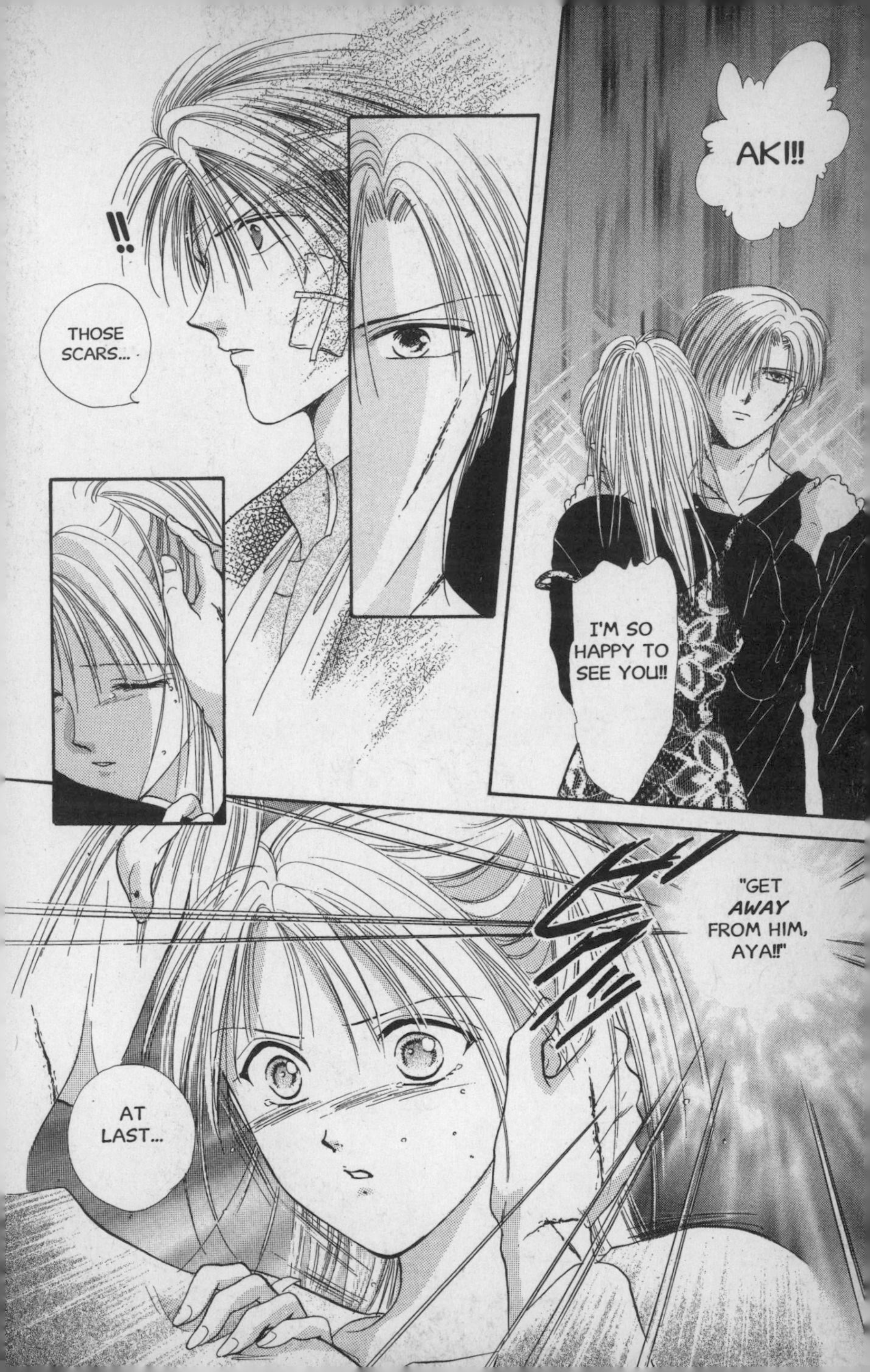
AKI!!
I'M SO HAPPY TO SEE YOU!!
!!
THOSE SCARS...
"GET *AWAY* FROM HIM, AYA!!"
AT LAST...

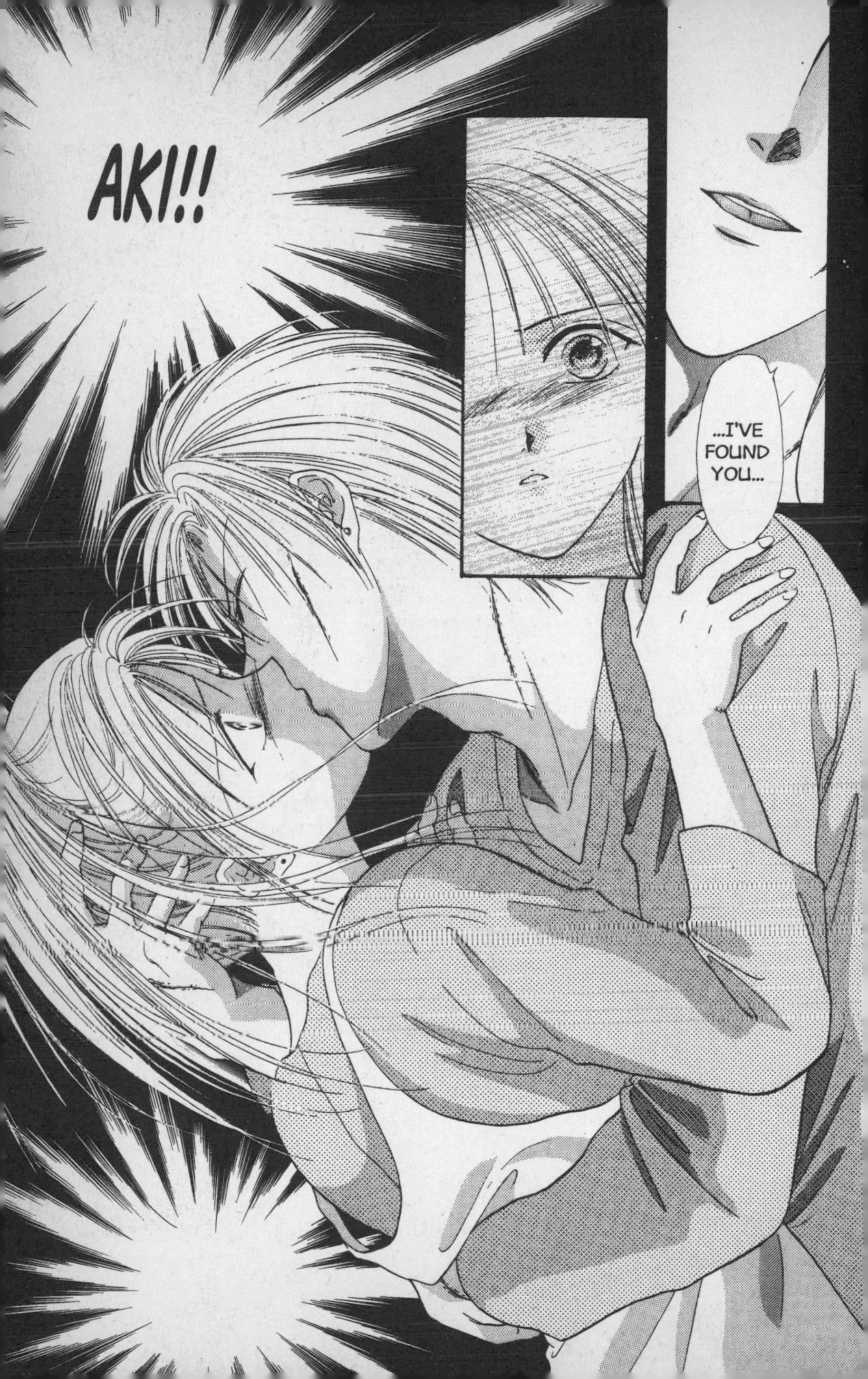
...I'VE
FOUND
YOU...
AKI!!

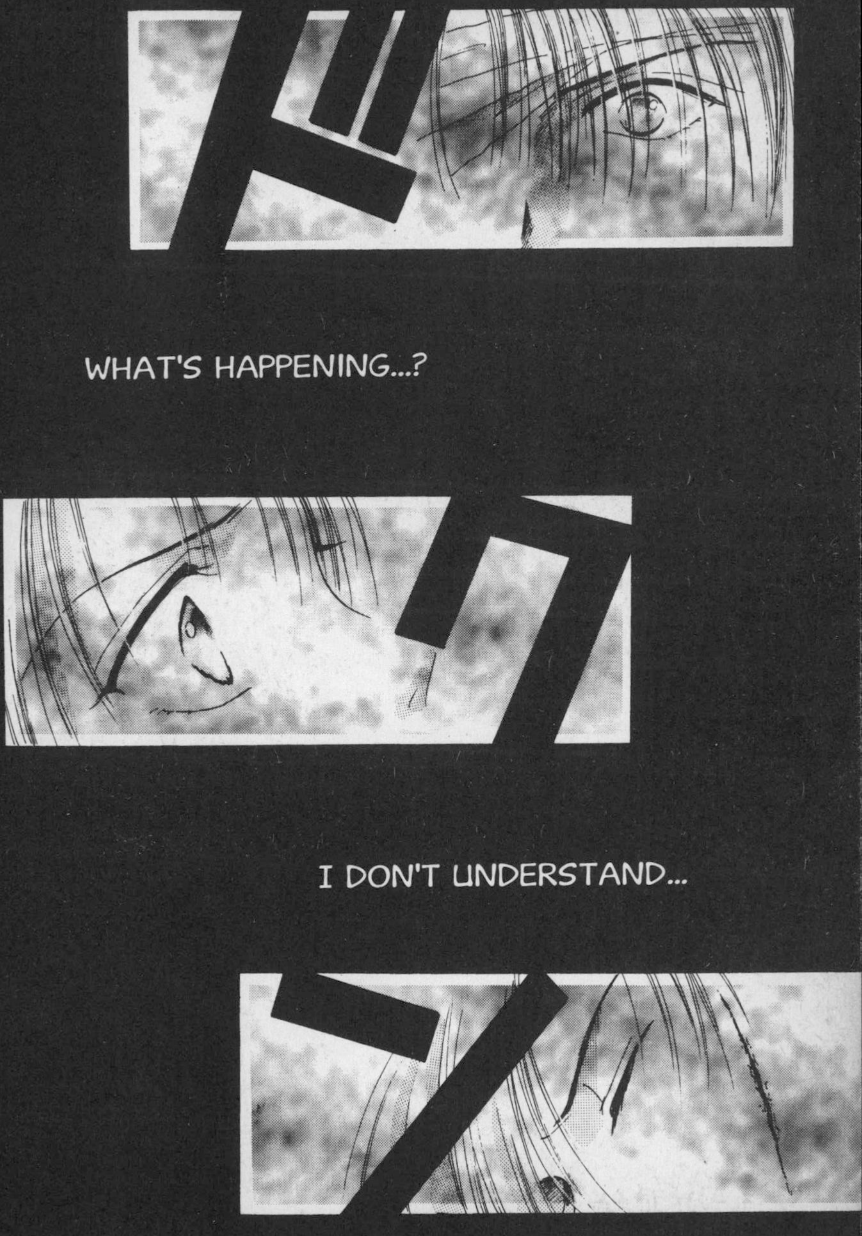
ド
WHAT'S HAPPENING...?
ク
I DON'T UNDERSTAND...
ン

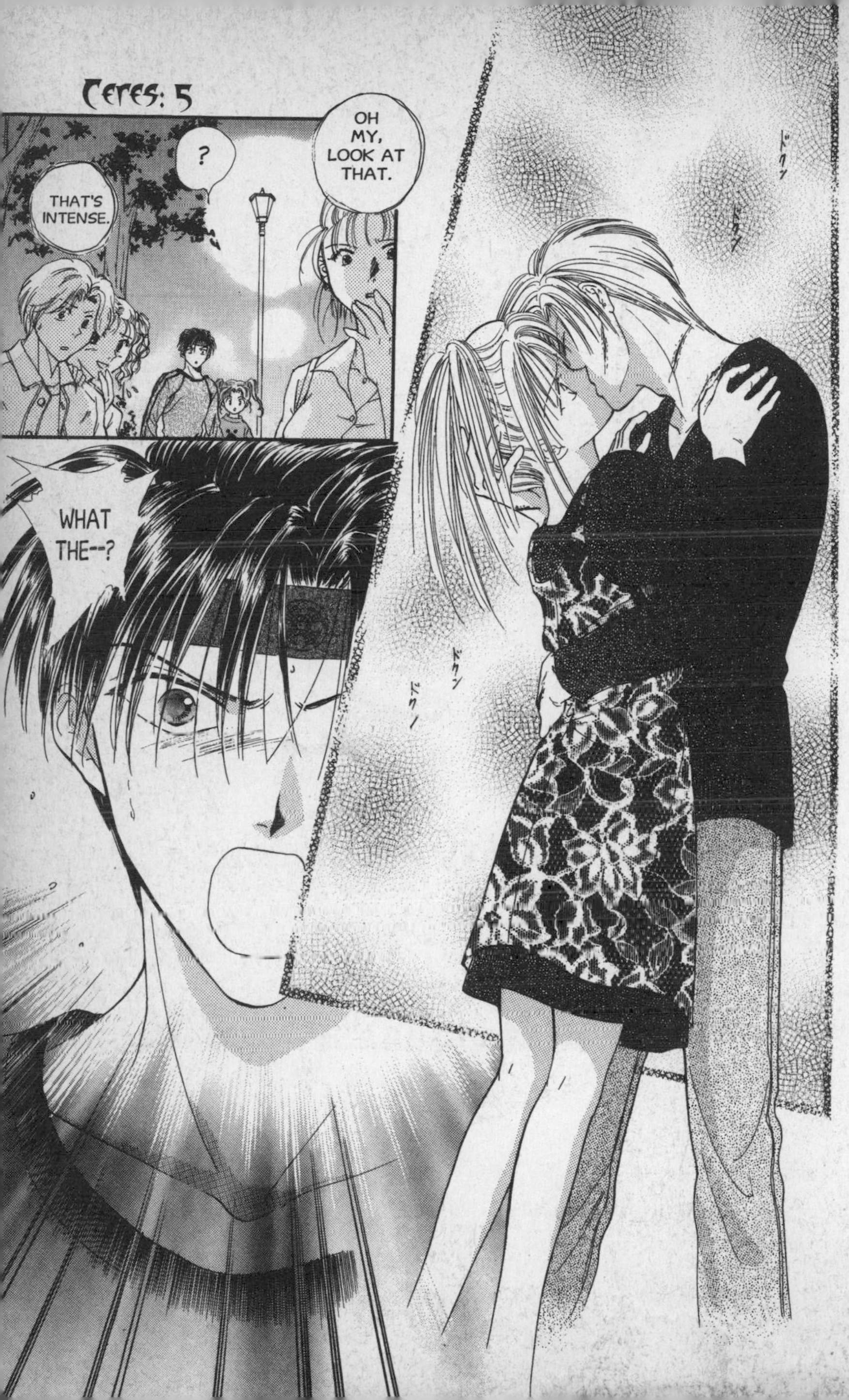
ドクン
ドクン
ドクン
ドクン
OH MY, LOOK AT THAT.
?
THAT'S INTENSE.
WHAT THE--?

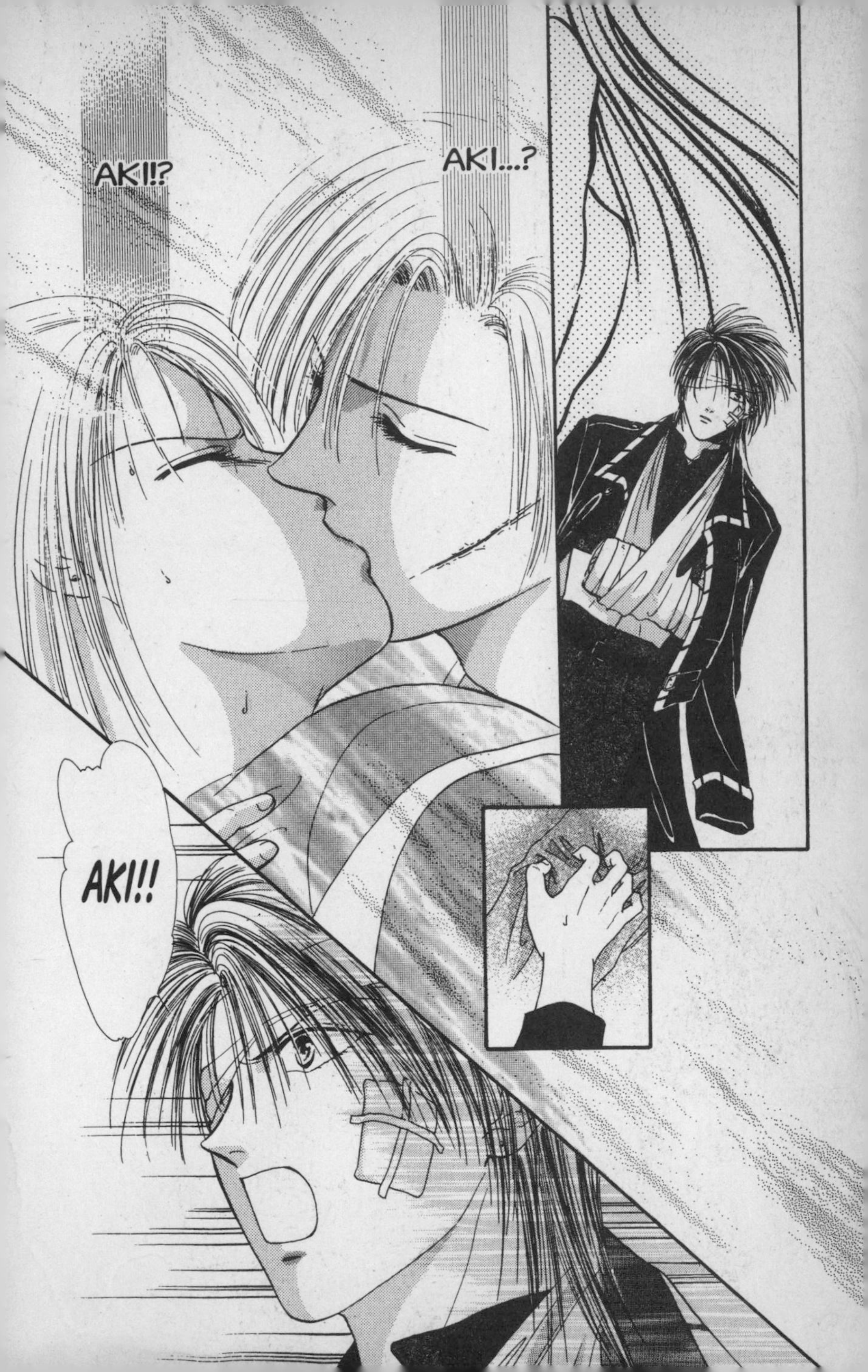
AKI...?
AKI!?
AKI!!

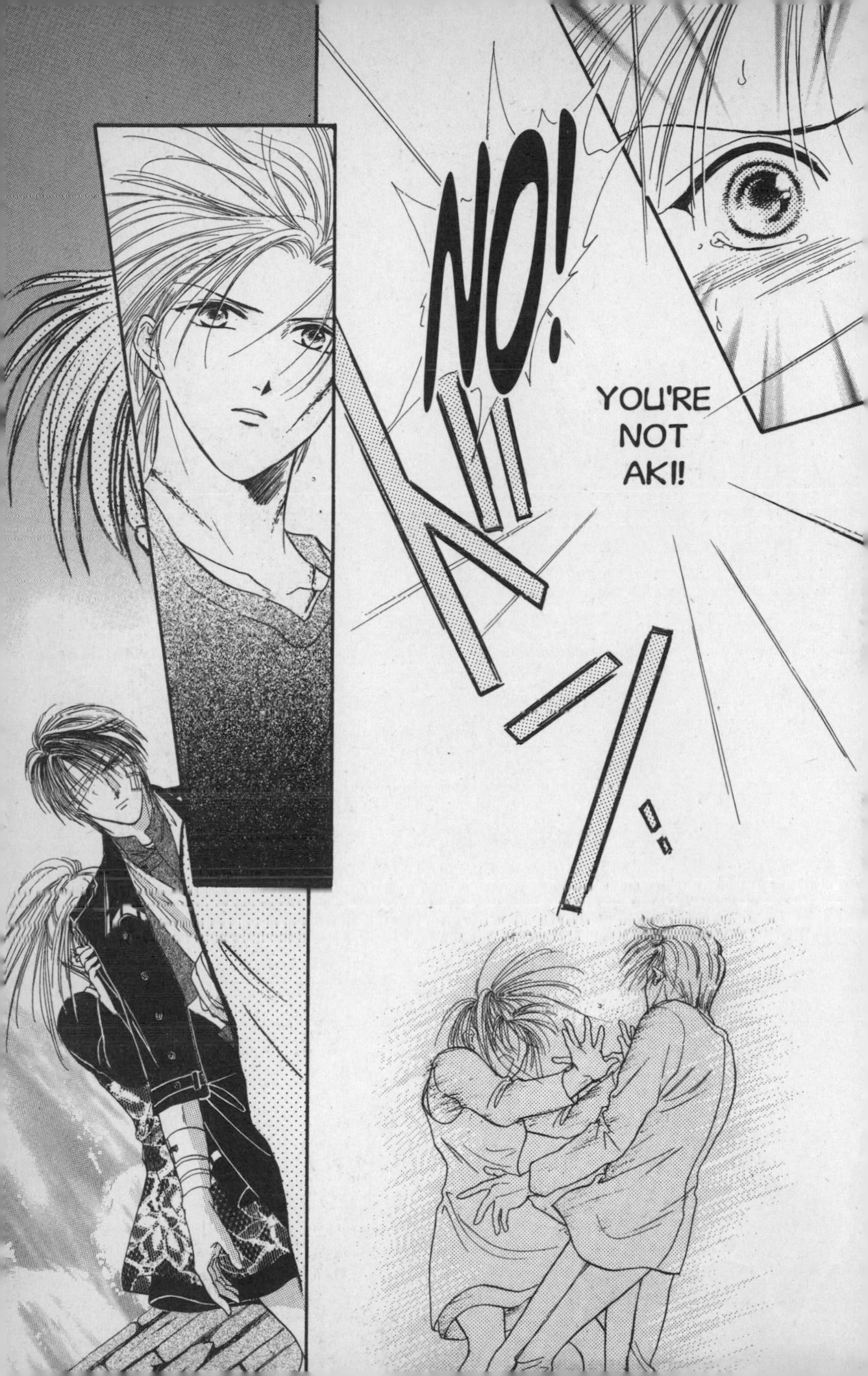
NO!
YOU'RE NOT AKI!

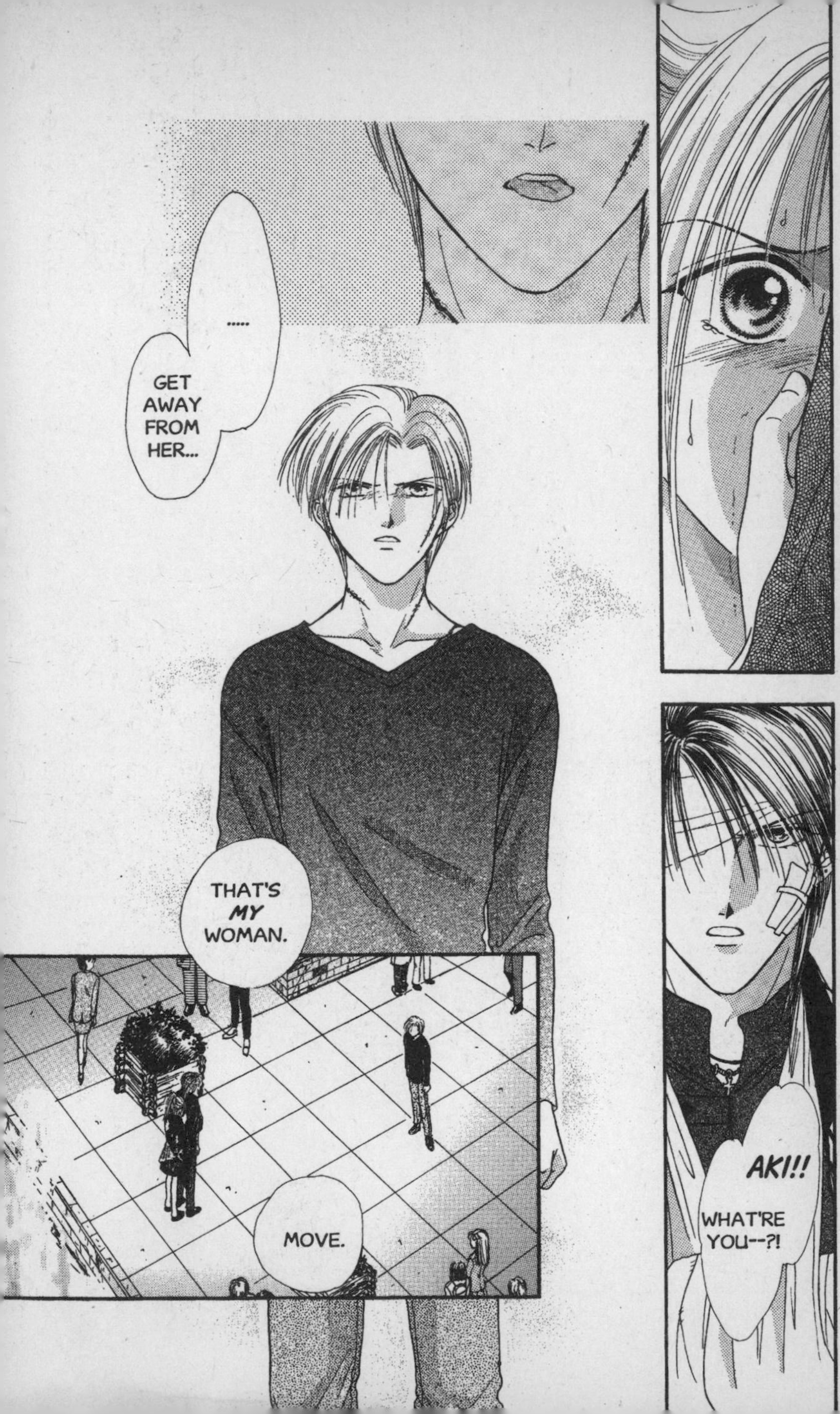
.....
GET AWAY FROM HER...
THAT'S *MY* WOMAN.
AKI!!
WHAT'RE YOU--?!
MOVE.

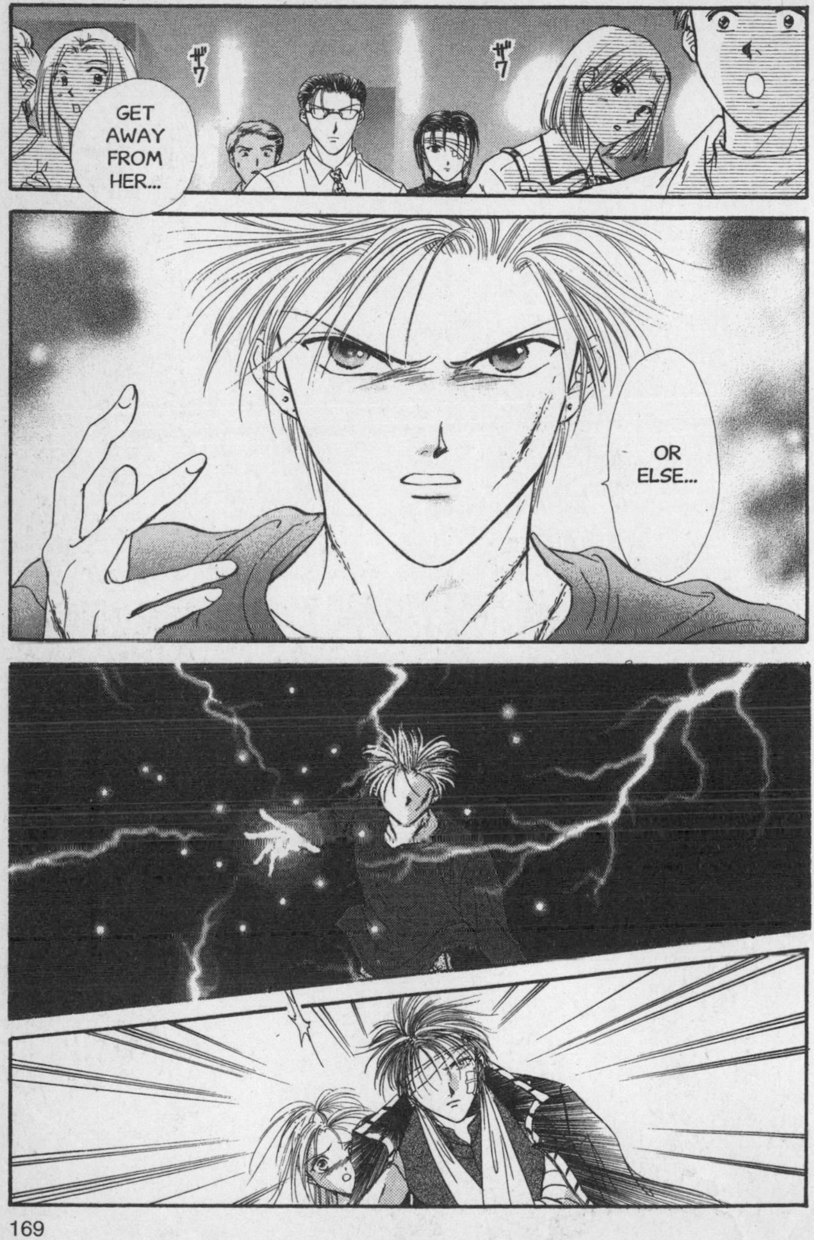
ザワ
ザワ
GET AWAY FROM HER...
OR ELSE...

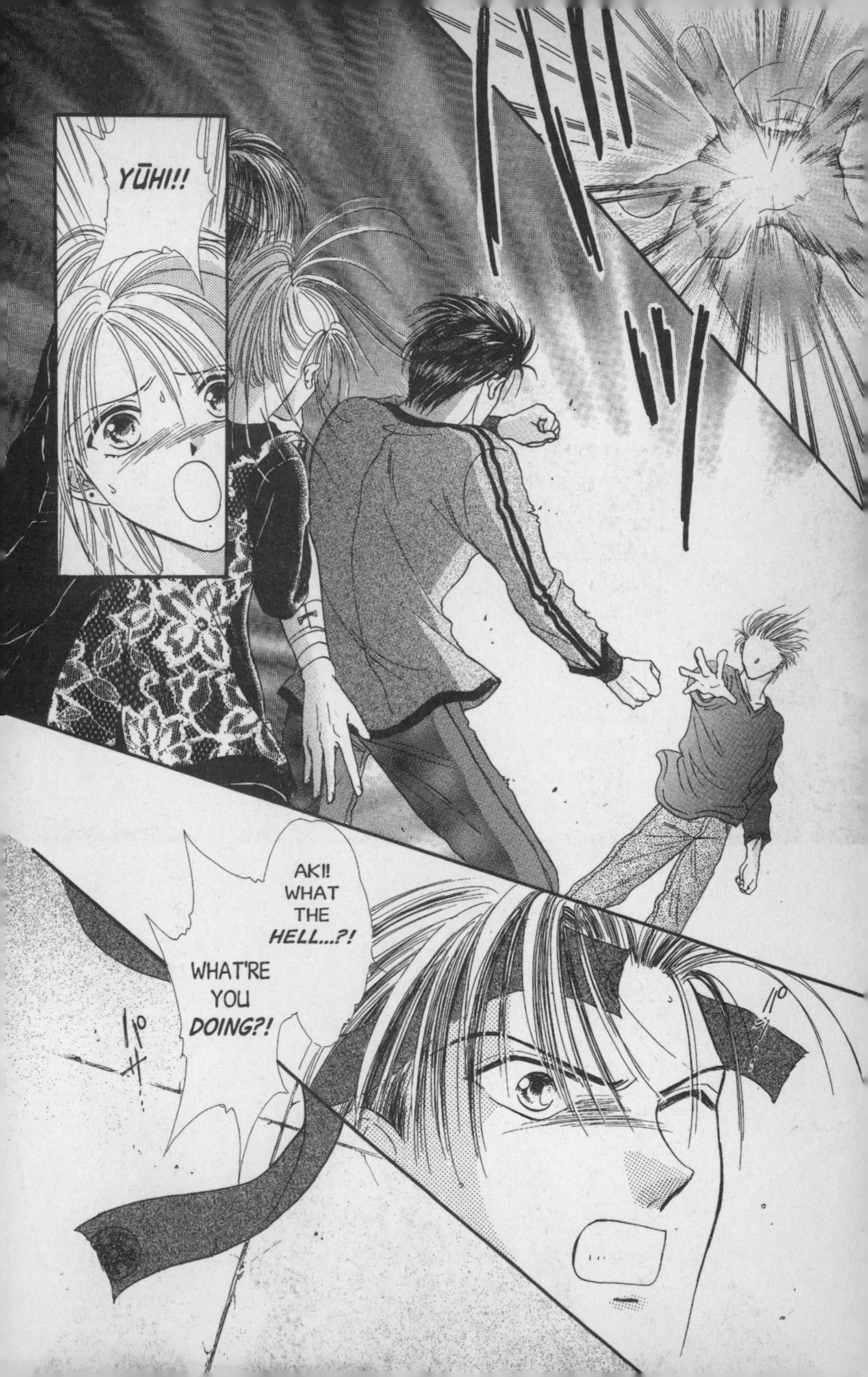
YŪHI!!
AKI! WHAT THE HELL...?!
WHAT'RE YOU DOING?!
...

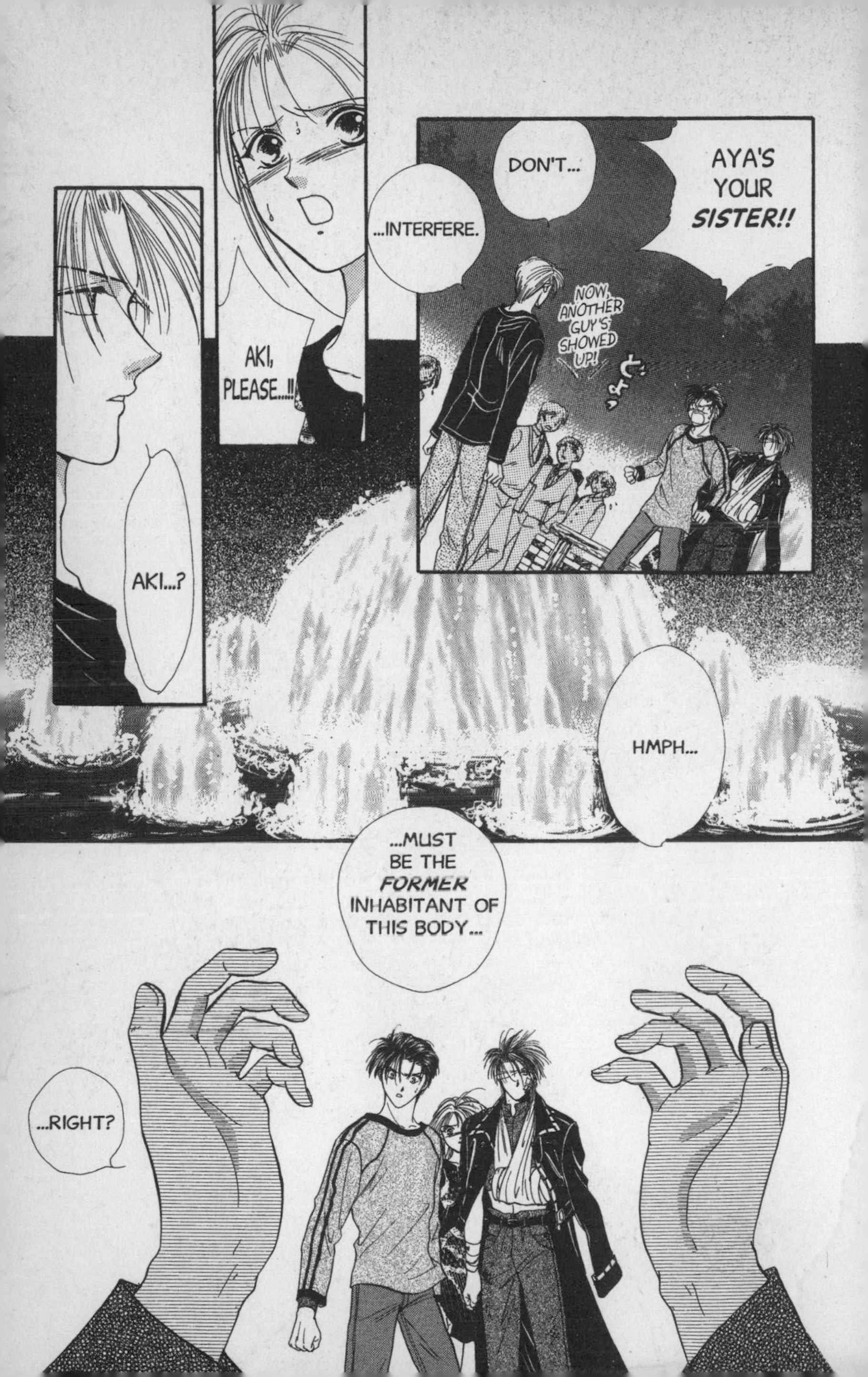
AYA'S YOUR SISTER!!
DON'T...
...INTERFERE.
NOW, ANOTHER GUY'S SHOWED UP!
AKI, PLEASE...!!
AKI...?
HMPH...
...MUST BE THE FORMER INHABITANT OF THIS BODY...
...RIGHT?

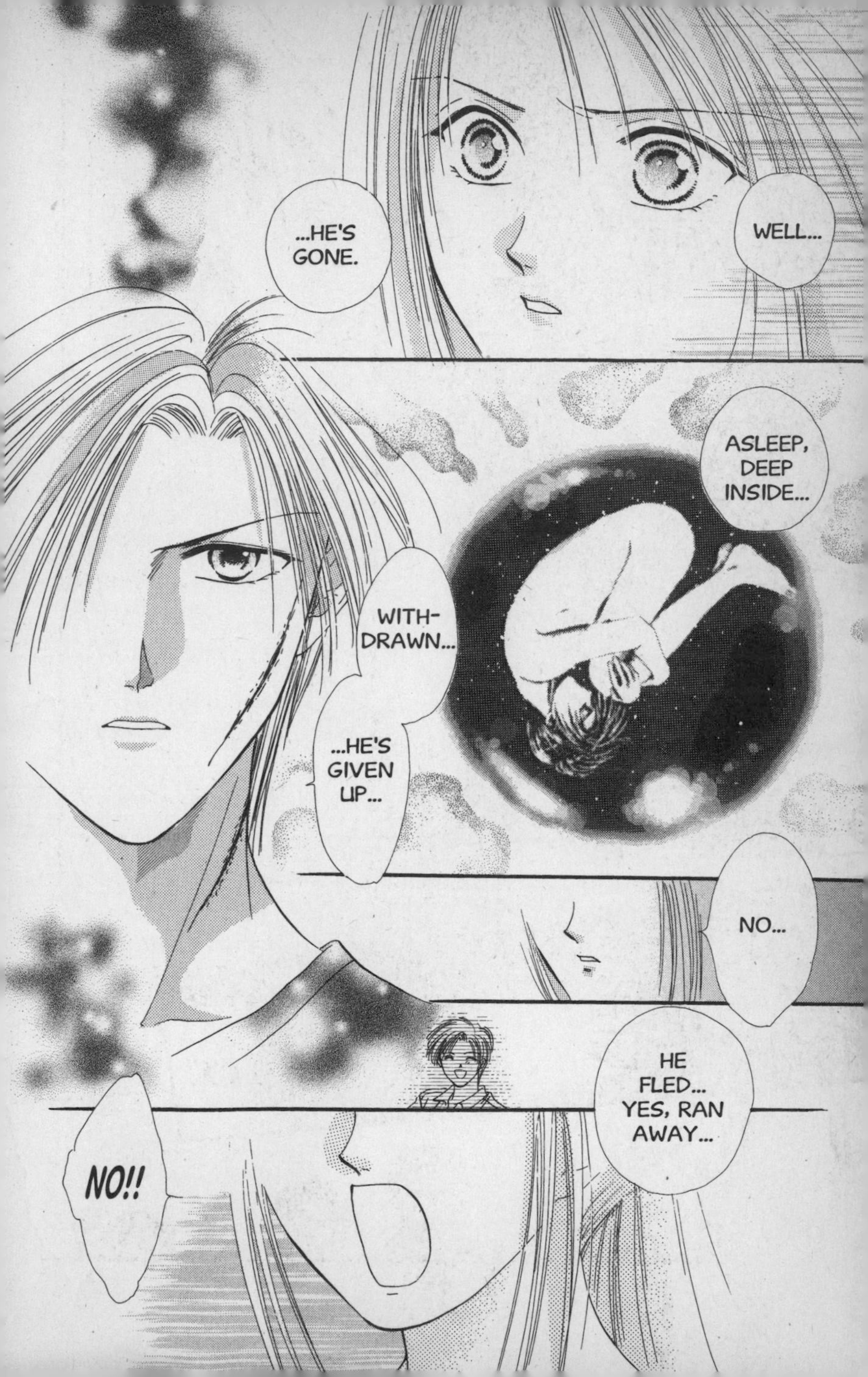
WELL...
...HE'S GONE.
ASLEEP, DEEP INSIDE...
WITH-DRAWN...
...HE'S GIVEN UP...
NO...
HE FLED... YES, RAN AWAY...
NO!!

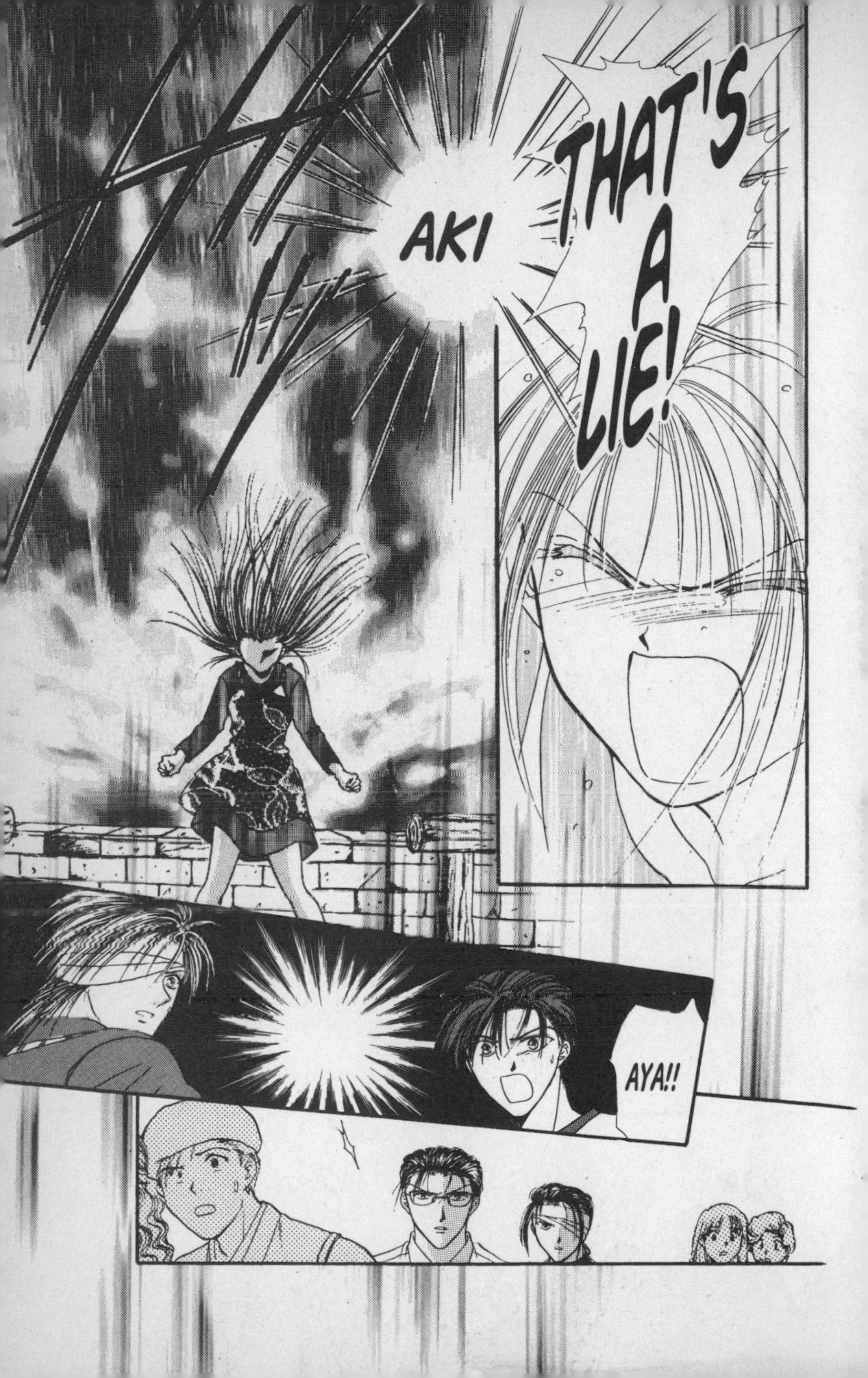

AKI
THAT'S A LIE!
AYA!!

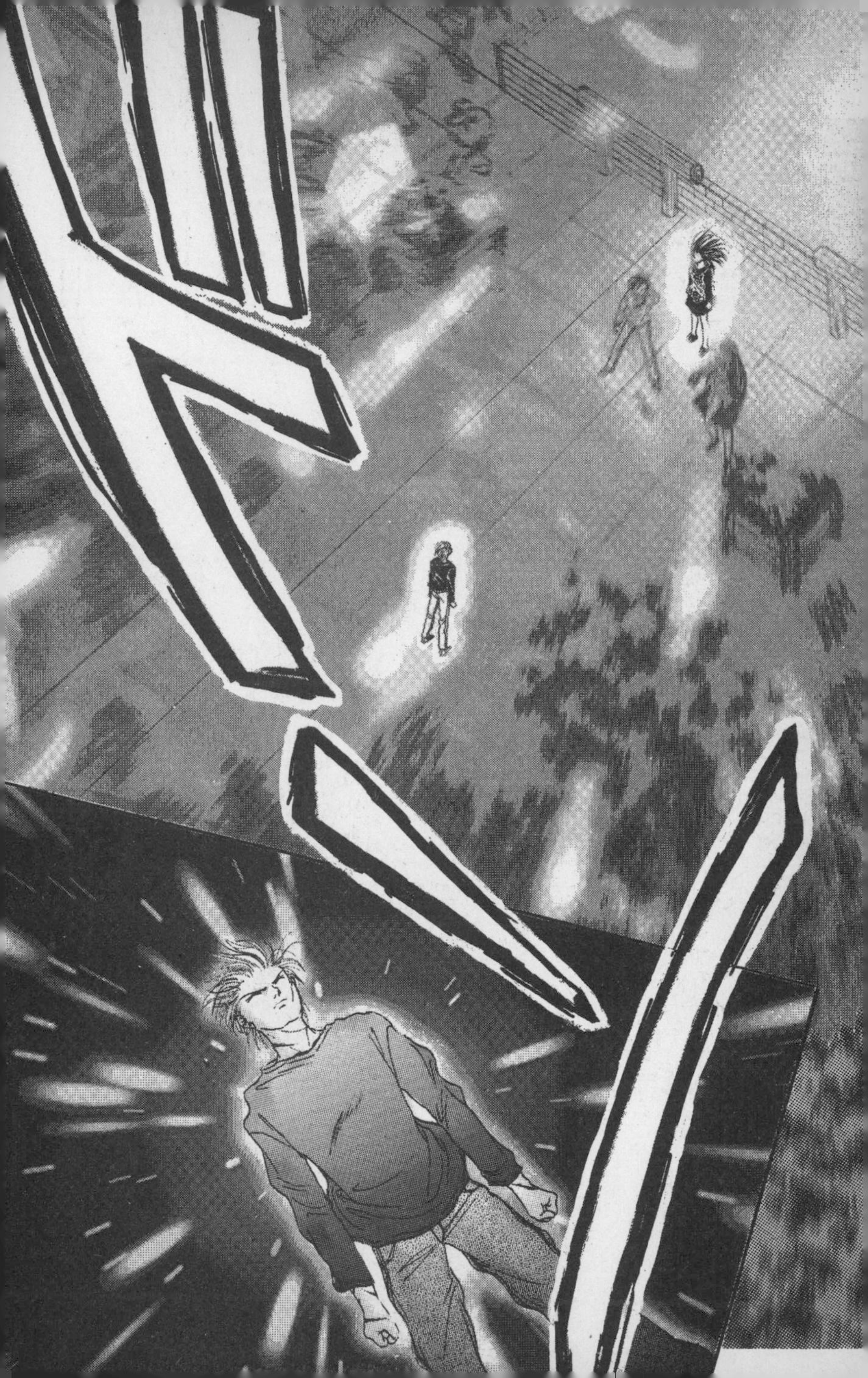

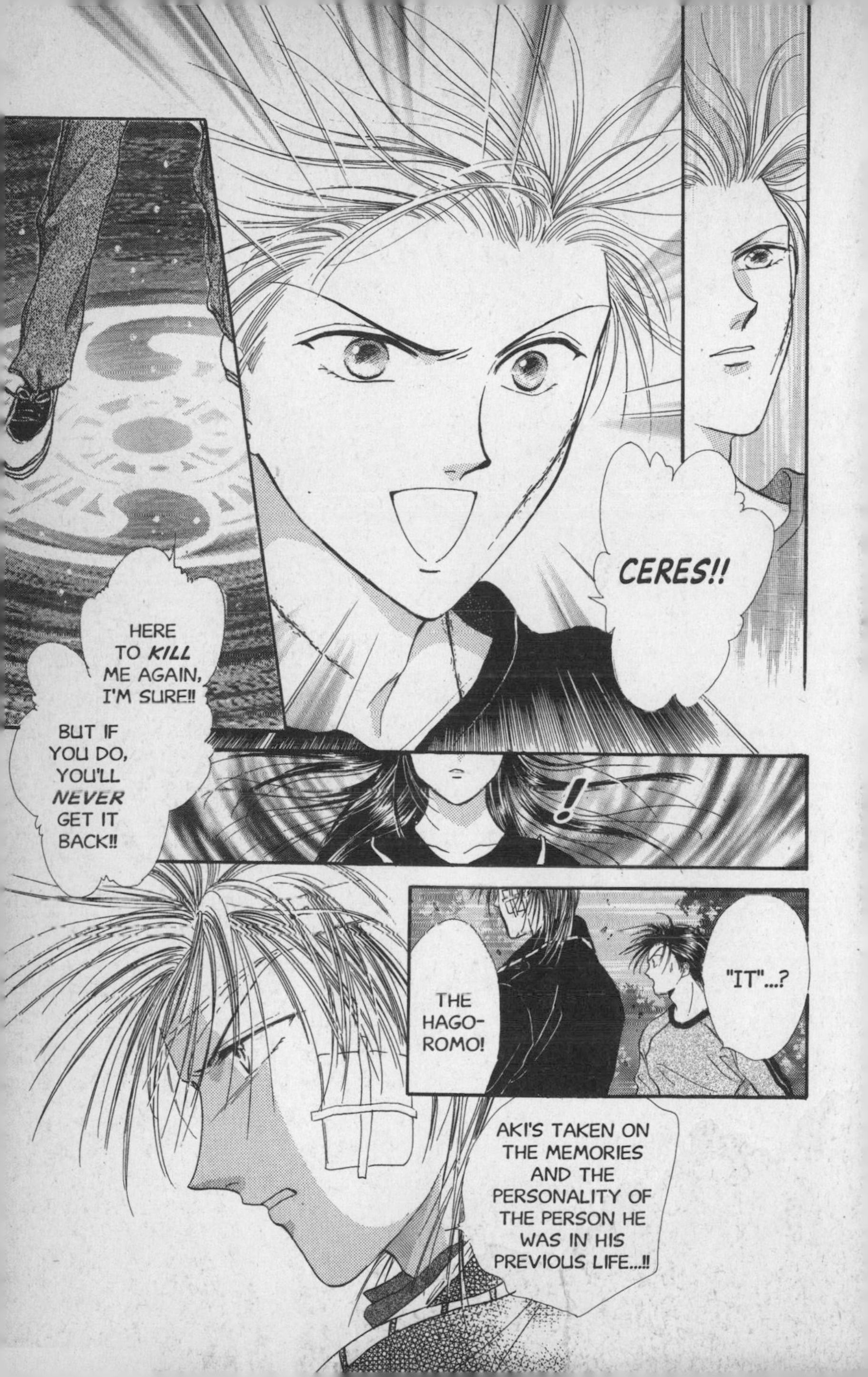
CERES!!
HERE TO KILL ME AGAIN, I'M SURE!!
BUT IF YOU DO, YOU'LL NEVER GET IT BACK!!
!
"IT"...?
THE HAGO-ROMO!
AKI'S TAKEN ON THE MEMORIES AND THE PERSONALITY OF THE PERSON HE WAS IN HIS PREVIOUS LIFE...!!

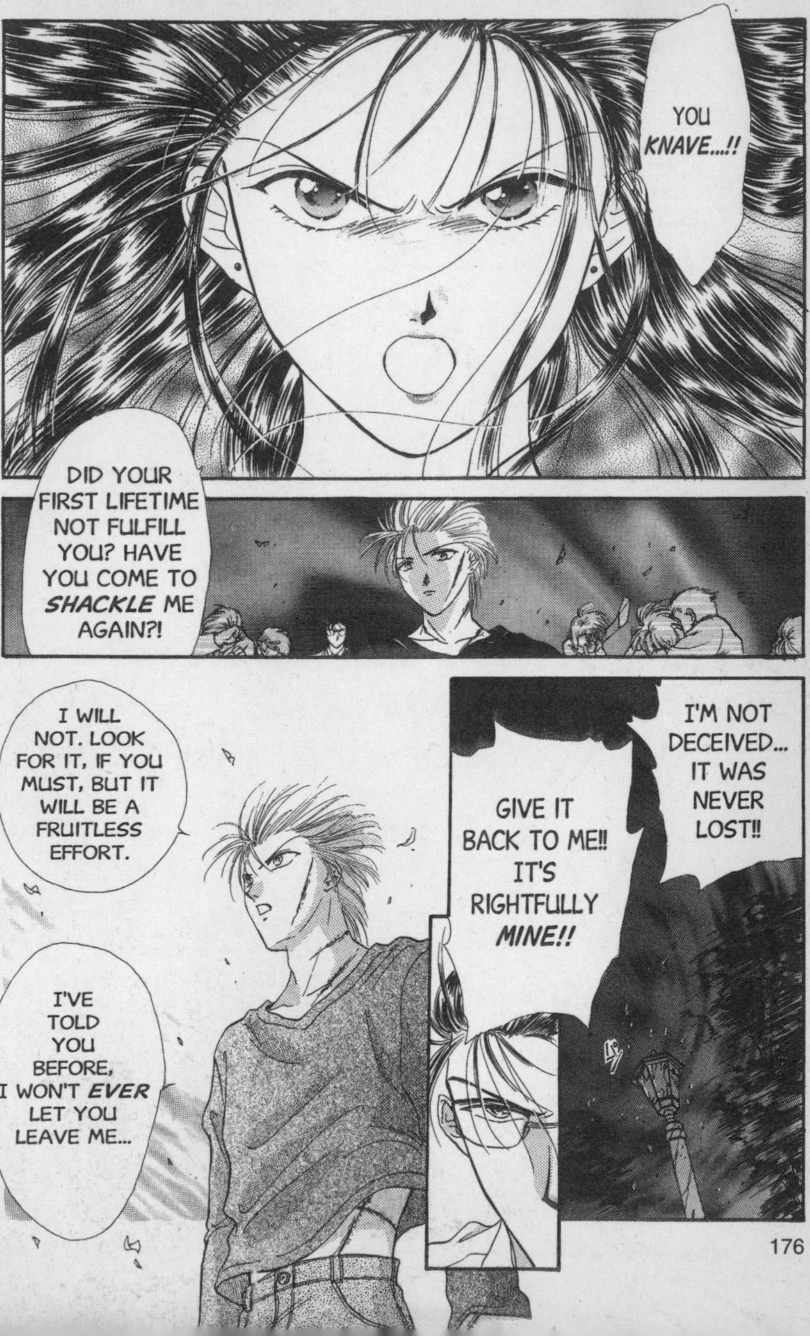
YOU *KNAVE...!!*
DID YOUR FIRST LIFETIME NOT FULFILL YOU? HAVE YOU COME TO ***SHACKLE*** ME AGAIN?!
I'M NOT DECEIVED... IT WAS NEVER LOST!!
GIVE IT BACK TO ME!! IT'S RIGHTFULLY ***MINE!!***
I WILL NOT. LOOK FOR IT, IF YOU MUST, BUT IT WILL BE A FRUITLESS EFFORT.
I'VE TOLD YOU BEFORE, I WON'T ***EVER*** LET YOU LEAVE ME...

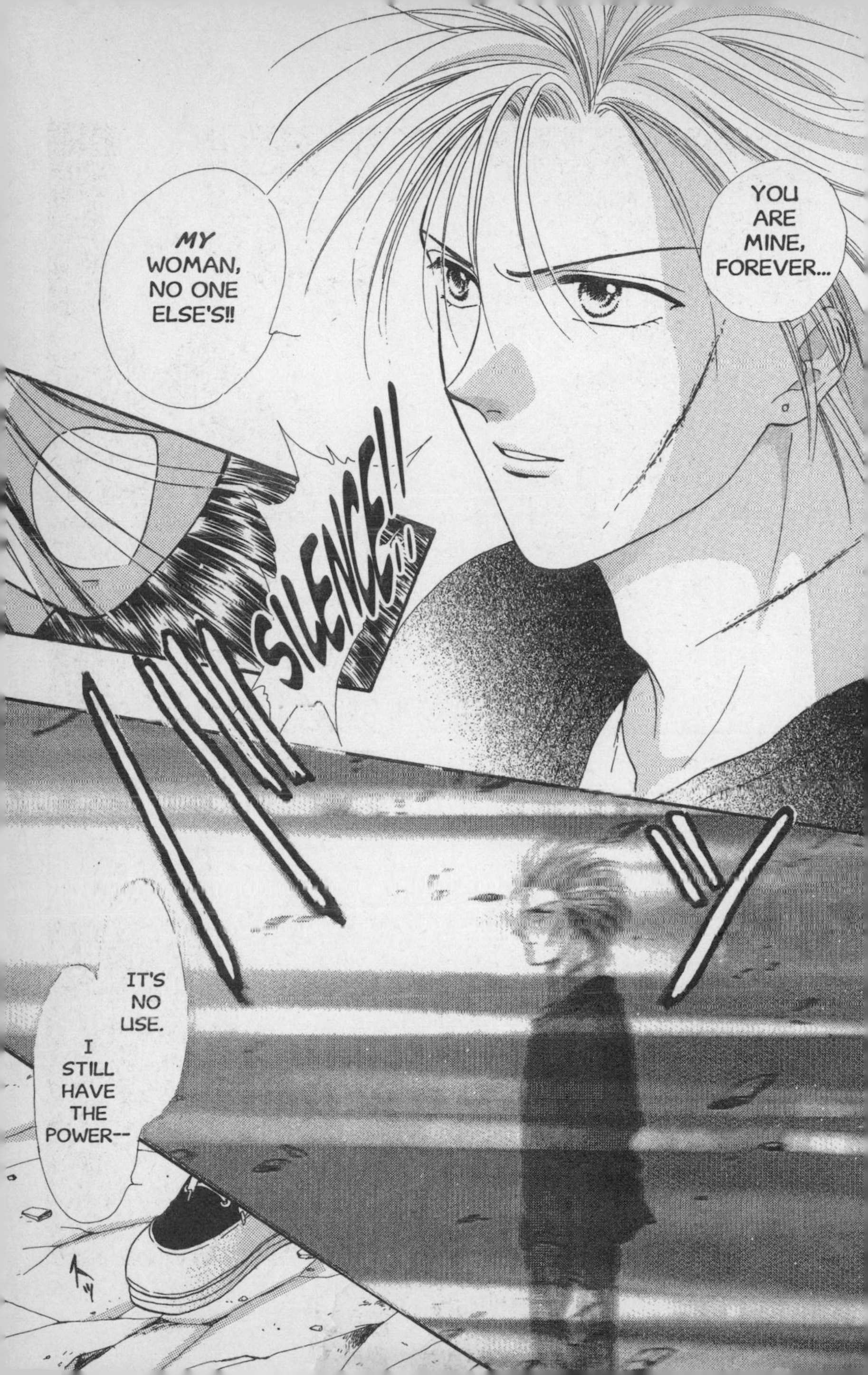
YOU ARE MINE, FOREVER...
MY WOMAN, NO ONE ELSE'S!!
SILENCE!!
IT'S NO USE. I STILL HAVE THE POWER--

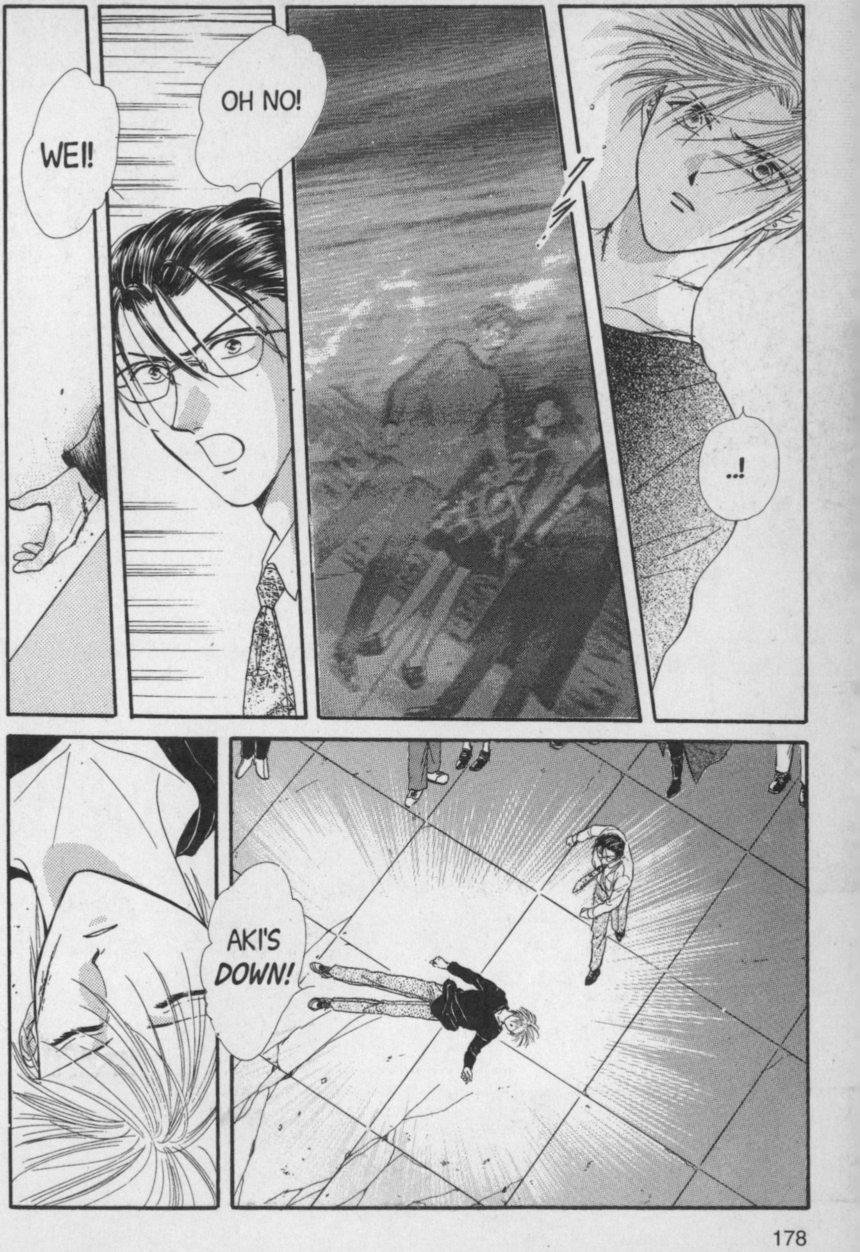
..!
OH NO!
WEI!
AKI'S DOWN!

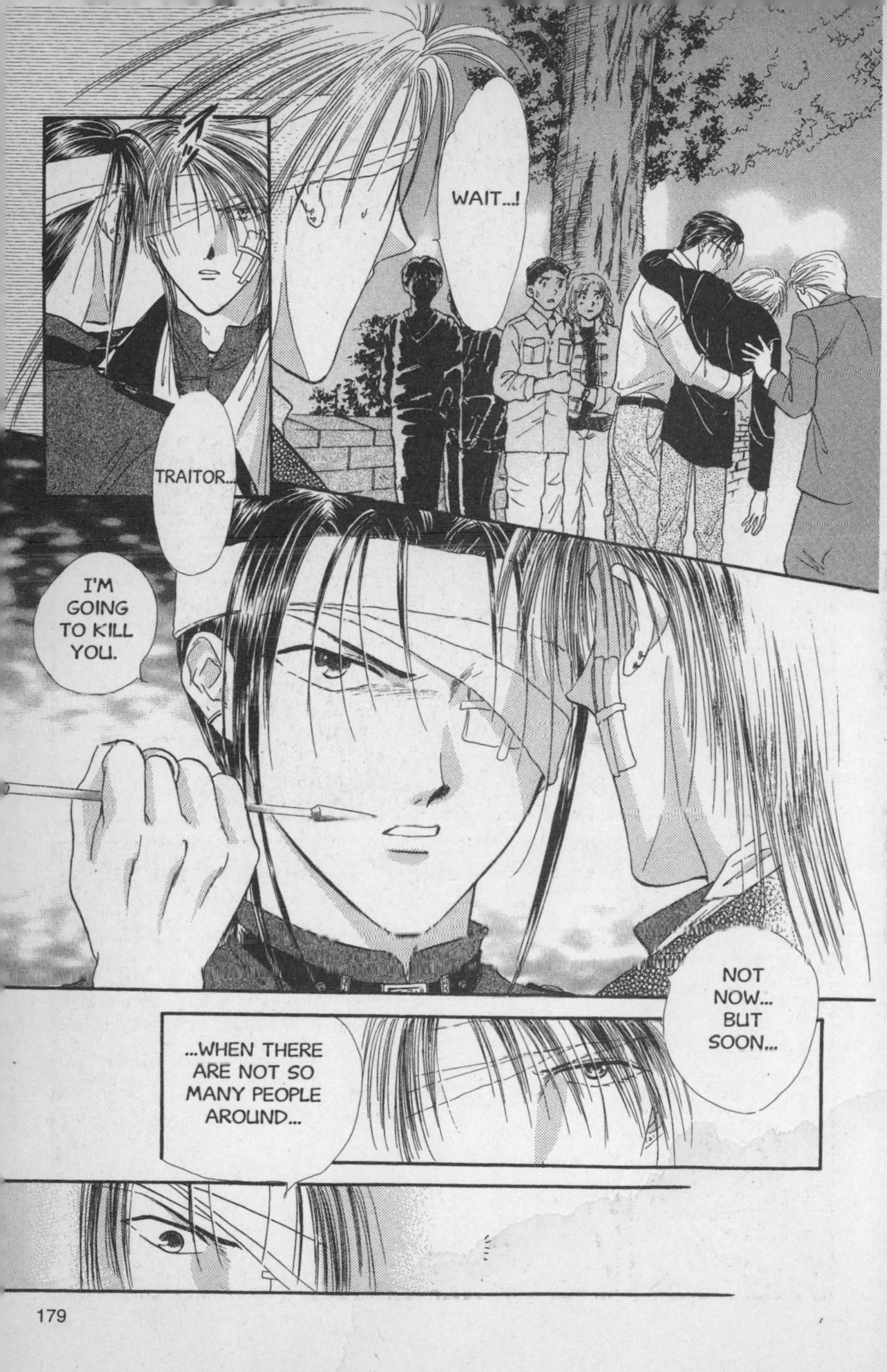
WAIT...!
TRAITOR...
I'M GOING TO KILL YOU.
NOT NOW... BUT SOON...
...WHEN THERE ARE NOT SO MANY PEOPLE AROUND...

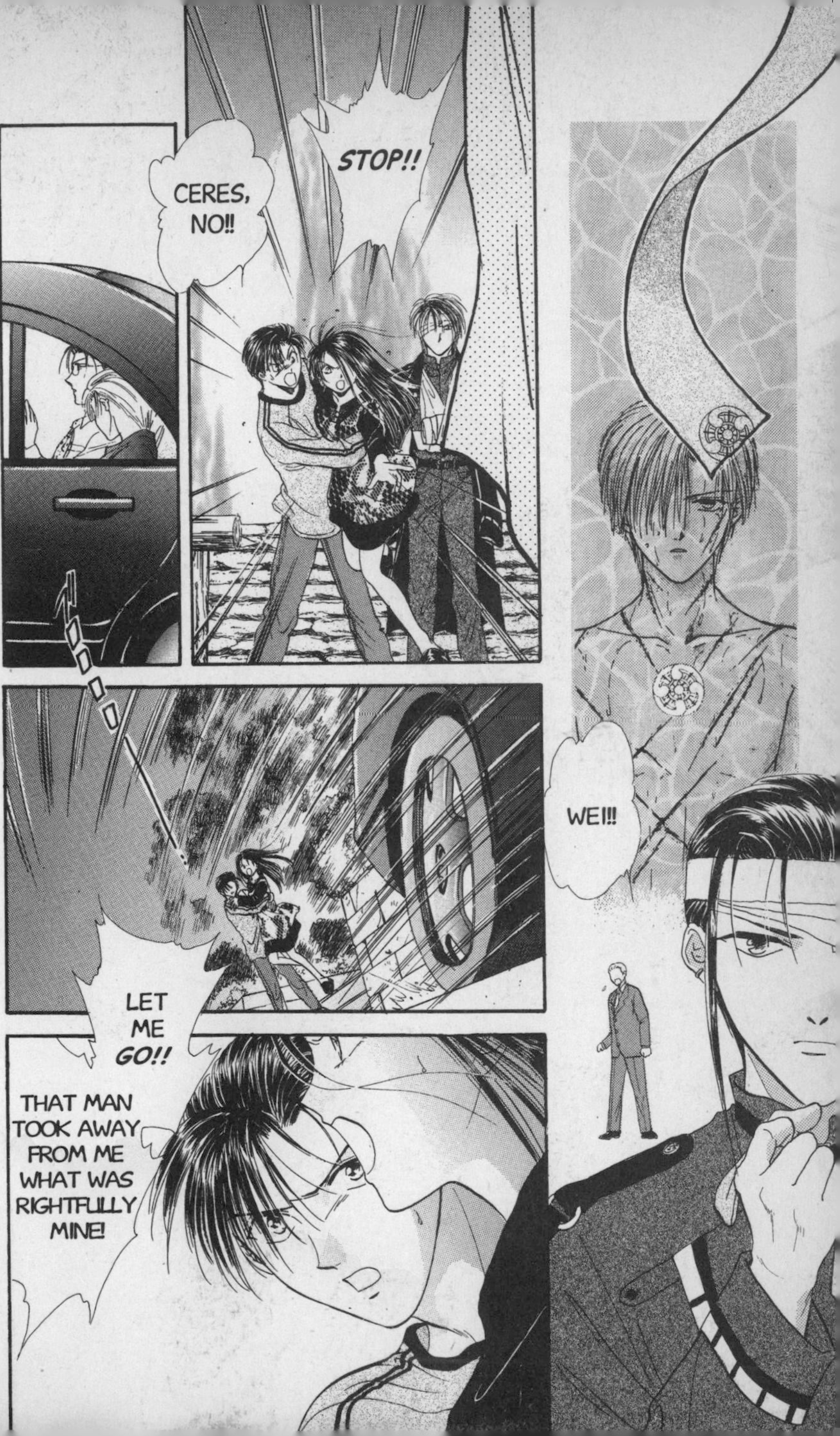
STOP!!
CERES, NO!!
WEI!!
LET ME GO!!
THAT MAN TOOK AWAY FROM ME WHAT WAS RIGHTFULLY MINE!

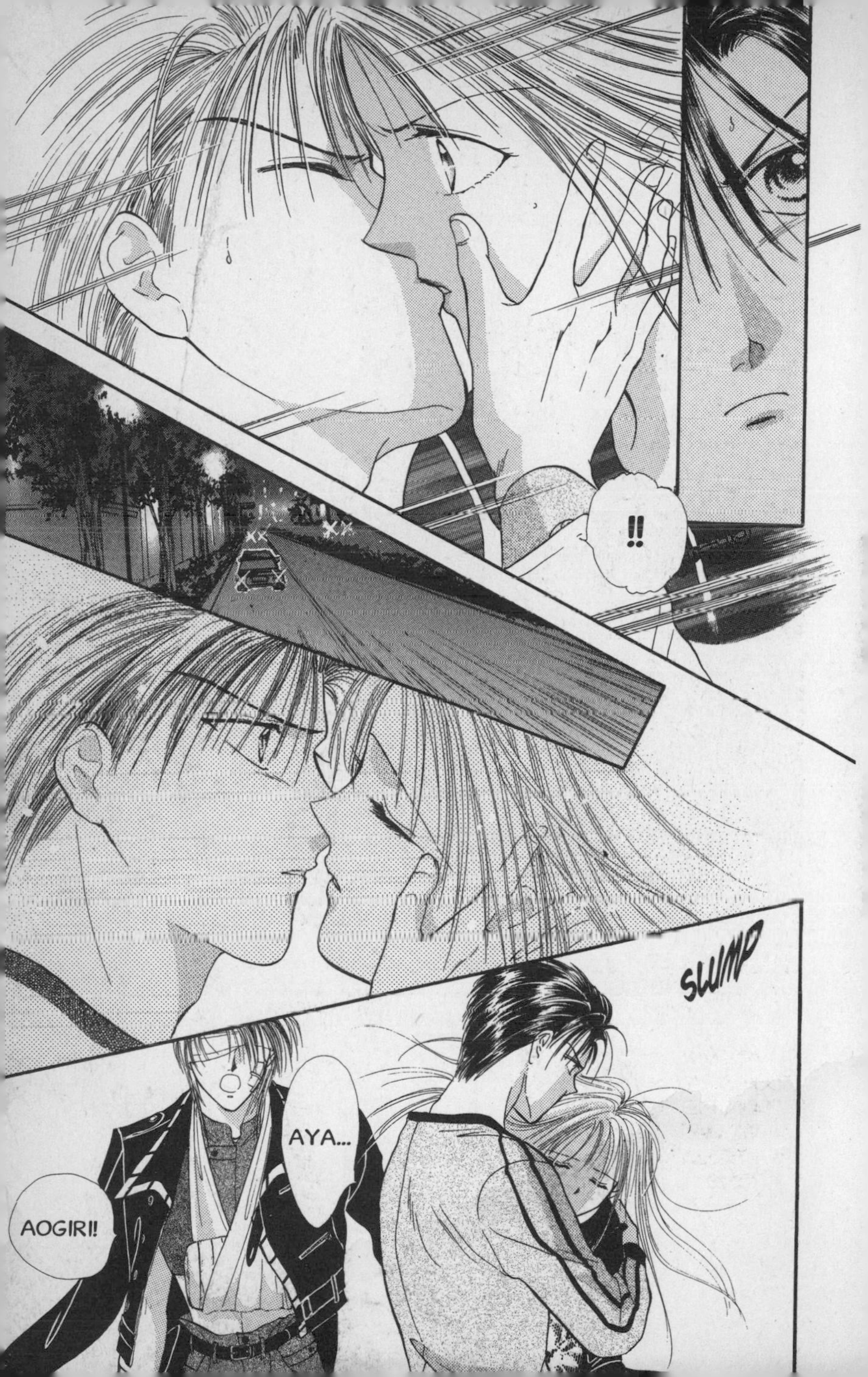
!!
SLUMP
AYA...
AOGIRI!!

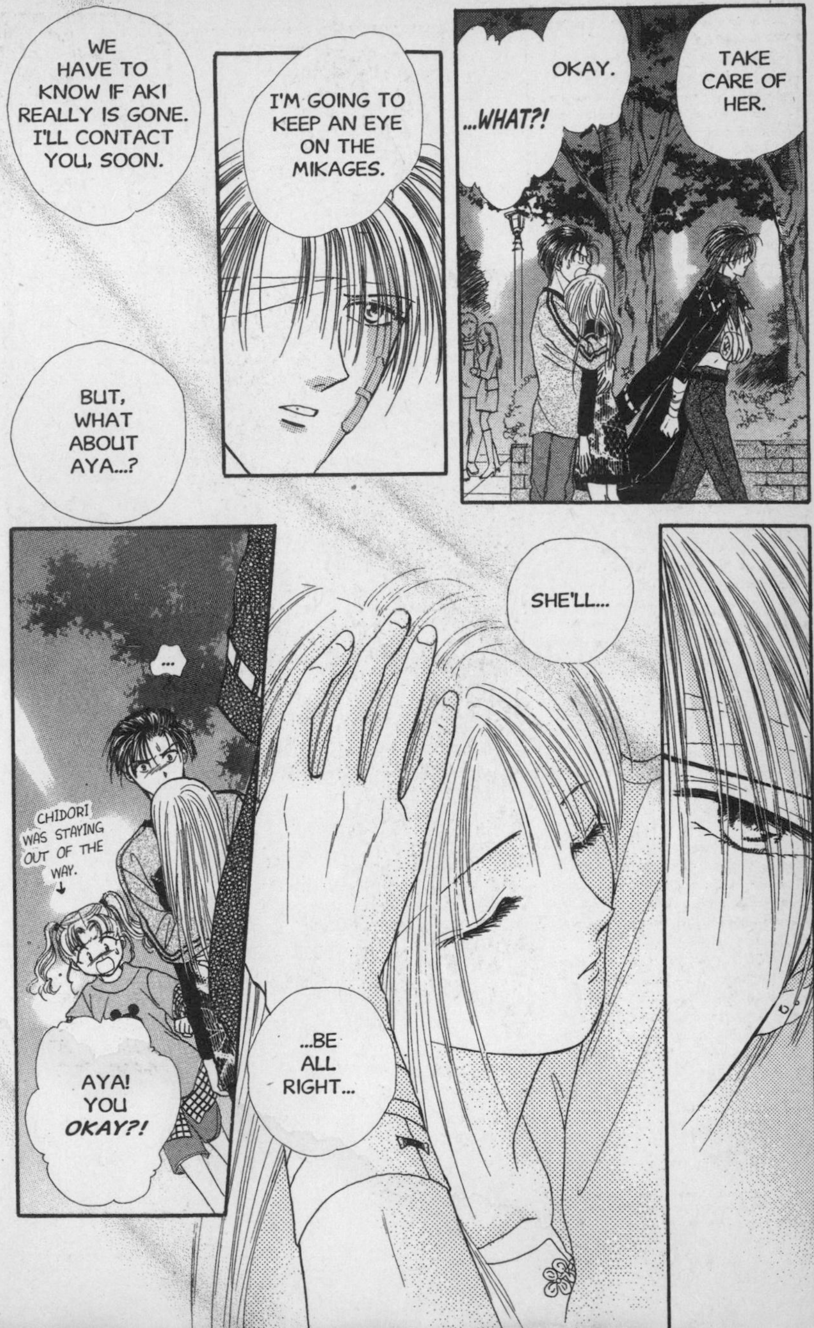
TAKE CARE OF HER.
OKAY.
...WHAT?!
I'M GOING TO KEEP AN EYE ON THE MIKAGES.
WE HAVE TO KNOW IF AKI REALLY IS GONE. I'LL CONTACT YOU, SOON.
BUT, WHAT ABOUT AYA...?
SHE'LL...
...BE ALL RIGHT...
...
CHIDORI WAS STAYING OUT OF THE WAY.
AYA! YOU OKAY?!

Ceres: 5

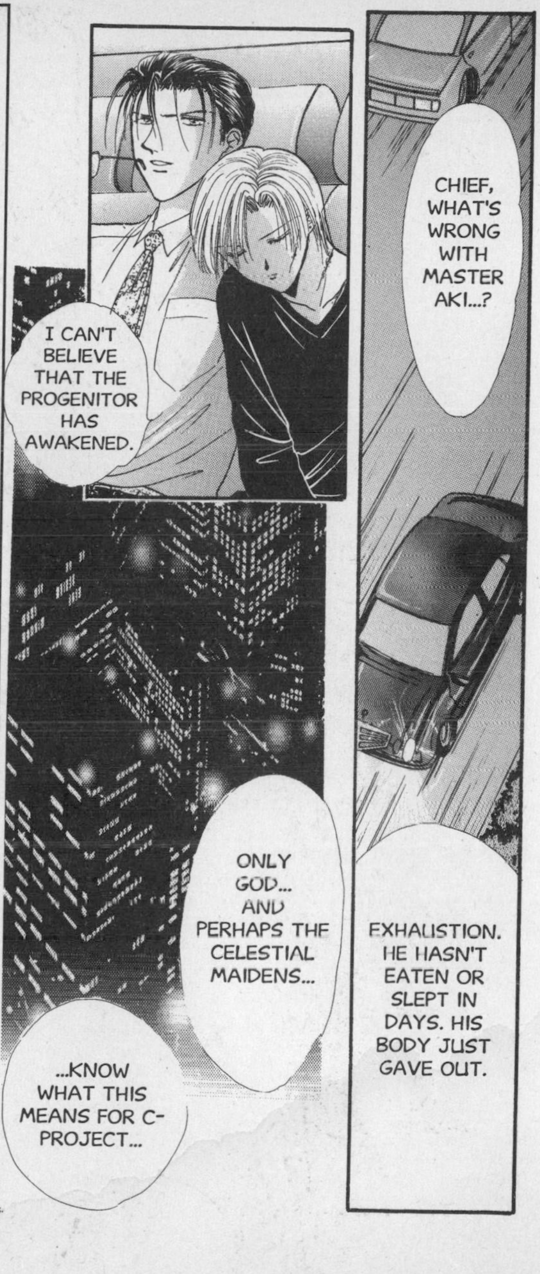

CHIEF, WHAT'S WRONG WITH MASTER AKI...?
EXHAUSTION. HE HASN'T EATEN OR SLEPT IN DAYS. HIS BODY JUST GAVE OUT.
I CAN'T BELIEVE THAT THE PROGENITOR HAS AWAKENED.
ONLY GOD... AND PERHAPS THE CELESTIAL MAIDENS...
...KNOW WHAT THIS MEANS FOR C-PROJECT...

...by Jungle Smile fits well for Aya and Yūhi in volumes 3 and 4. For Tōya...something with synthesizer and piano, and the melody would be beautiful and melancholy. If I were to pick a song...hmm, one band we often (?) listen to is Luna Sea...maybe "Providence"? "Eden" is good song, too.
It's got to be a visual band!
As for Aki, as you've now seen in volume 5, there's 2 sides to Aki. I like wacked out lyrics for "the new and improved Aki." :) Maybe a visual band, too...? Or, maybe a mysterious track like the theme song from Ghost in the Shell would be good—Japanese taiko drums, and a raw sound.
The juxtaposition would be excellent!
The Mikages have an image that suits classical music.
Something solemn and serious. These days, I'm into choral music. I love the created terminology. And also, I'm into Bulgarian music—like in the soundtrack for the British gangster thriller, Face. You might think this kind of music wouldn't fit with powerful scenes of destruction, but actually the juxtaposition work's frighteningly well. The holier the voices, the better. I also recommend Adiemus I & II. ...Hmm, these genres are all so different. But the image I have for Ceres is pretty well established. If you listen to all this music, you'll get a pretty good idea of its mood. :)
I'm always looking for dark and beautiful music. :)
Background music is very important.
There's one less chat column in this volume because of all the retouching I did. There are so many pages that there's no room for the extra art at the end of the book! Sorry.
Ooh, FYI! A Fushigi Yugi novel is finally coming out next year ('98), or is it?! But I didn't actually write it. (I didn't have enough time...) But, I created the story and the characters. It's an outside story about Tasuki's past! It should be coming out from Palette Bunko. The OAVs are also on sale now! And I hear that the FY TV series is going to be shown on the internet? I'll give details next time!
I wonder what Aki fans thought of this volume.
The "new and improved Aki" is popular with us, though. He's gonna get even scarier! (just kidding) :)

10/28/97 Written while listening to The End of Evangelion soundtrack. I happened to get ill while watching this movie.

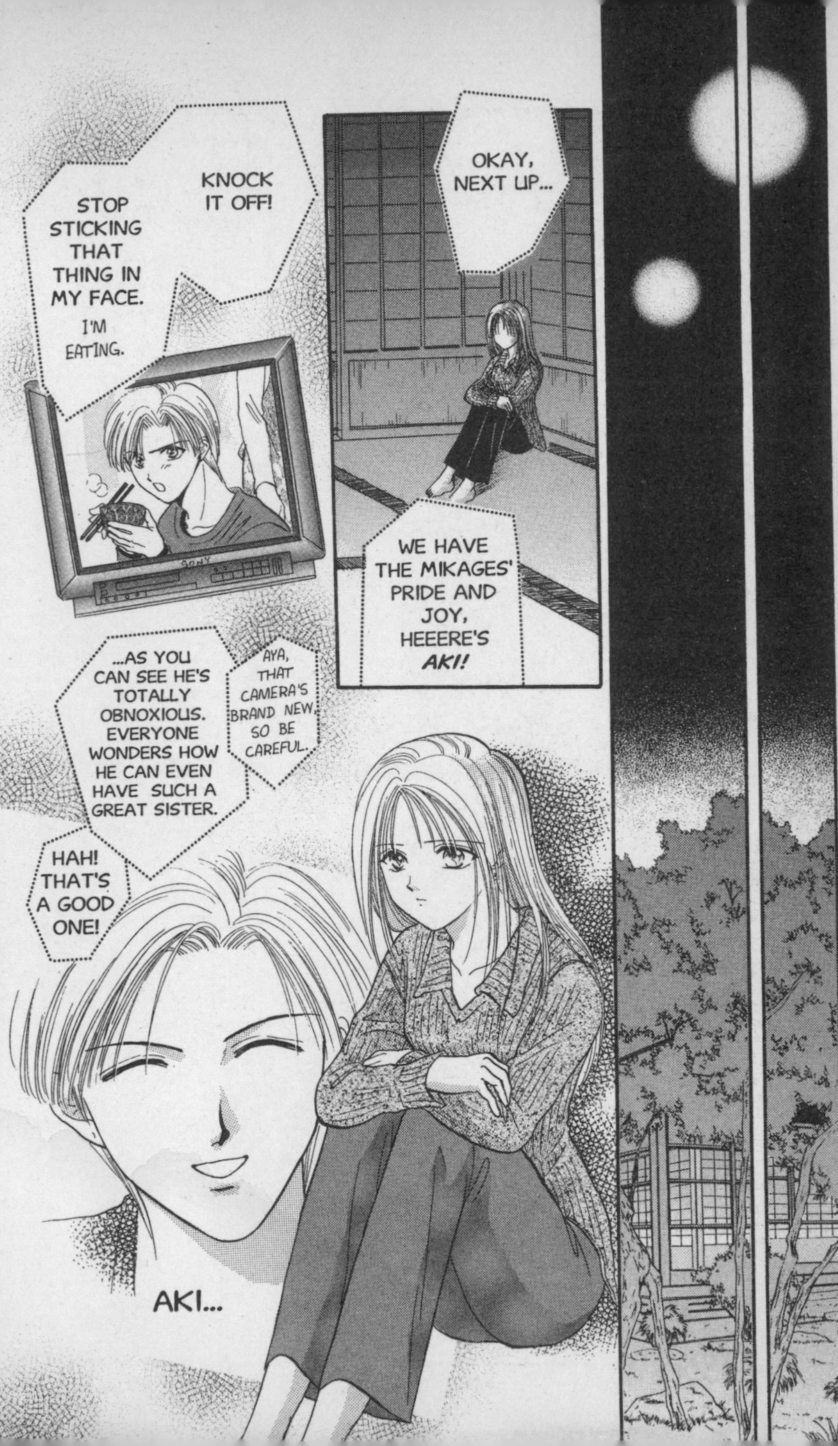
OKAY, NEXT UP...
WE HAVE THE MIKAGES' PRIDE AND JOY, HEEERE'S *AKI!*
KNOCK IT OFF!
STOP STICKING THAT THING IN MY FACE.
I'M EATING.
AYA, THAT CAMERA'S BRAND NEW, SO BE CAREFUL.
...AS YOU CAN SEE HE'S TOTALLY OBNOXIOUS. EVERYONE WONDERS HOW HE CAN EVEN HAVE SUCH A GREAT SISTER.
HAH! THAT'S A GOOD ONE!
AKI...

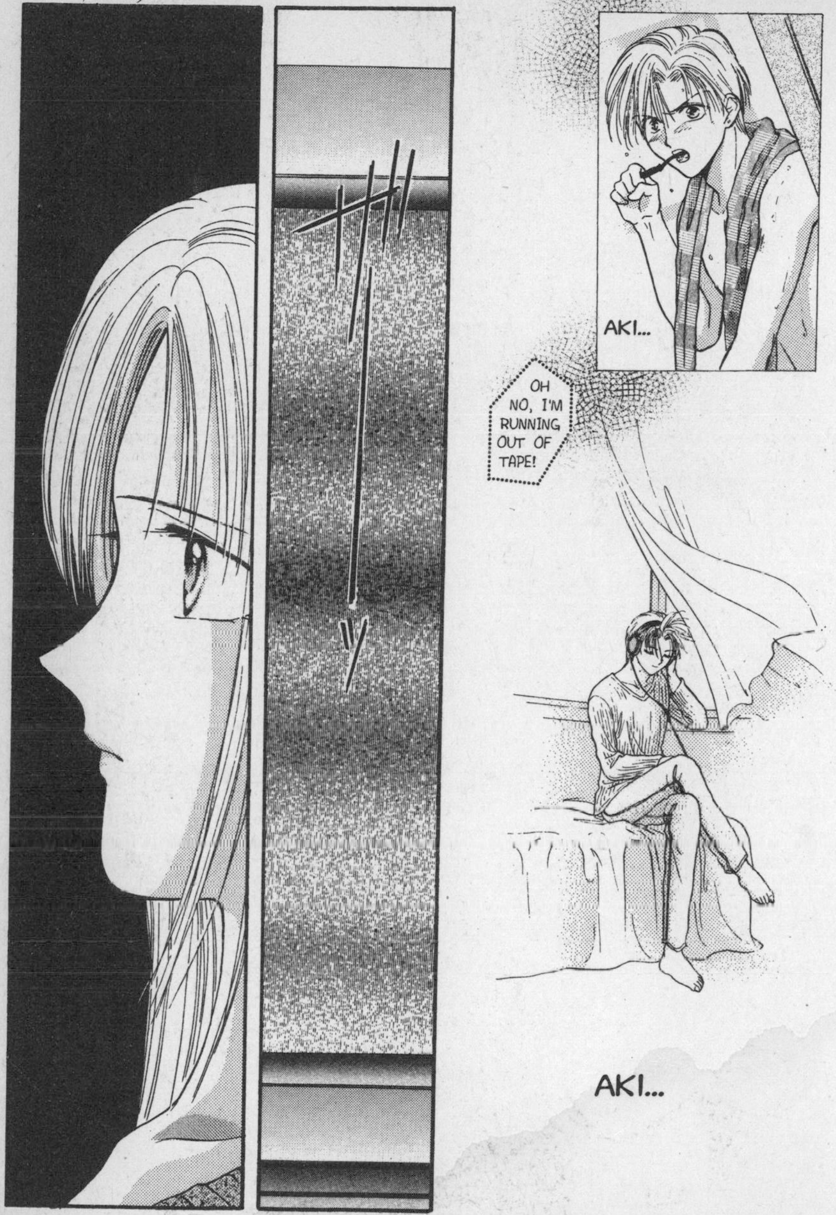
AKI...
OH NO, I'M RUNNING OUT OF TAPE!
AKI...

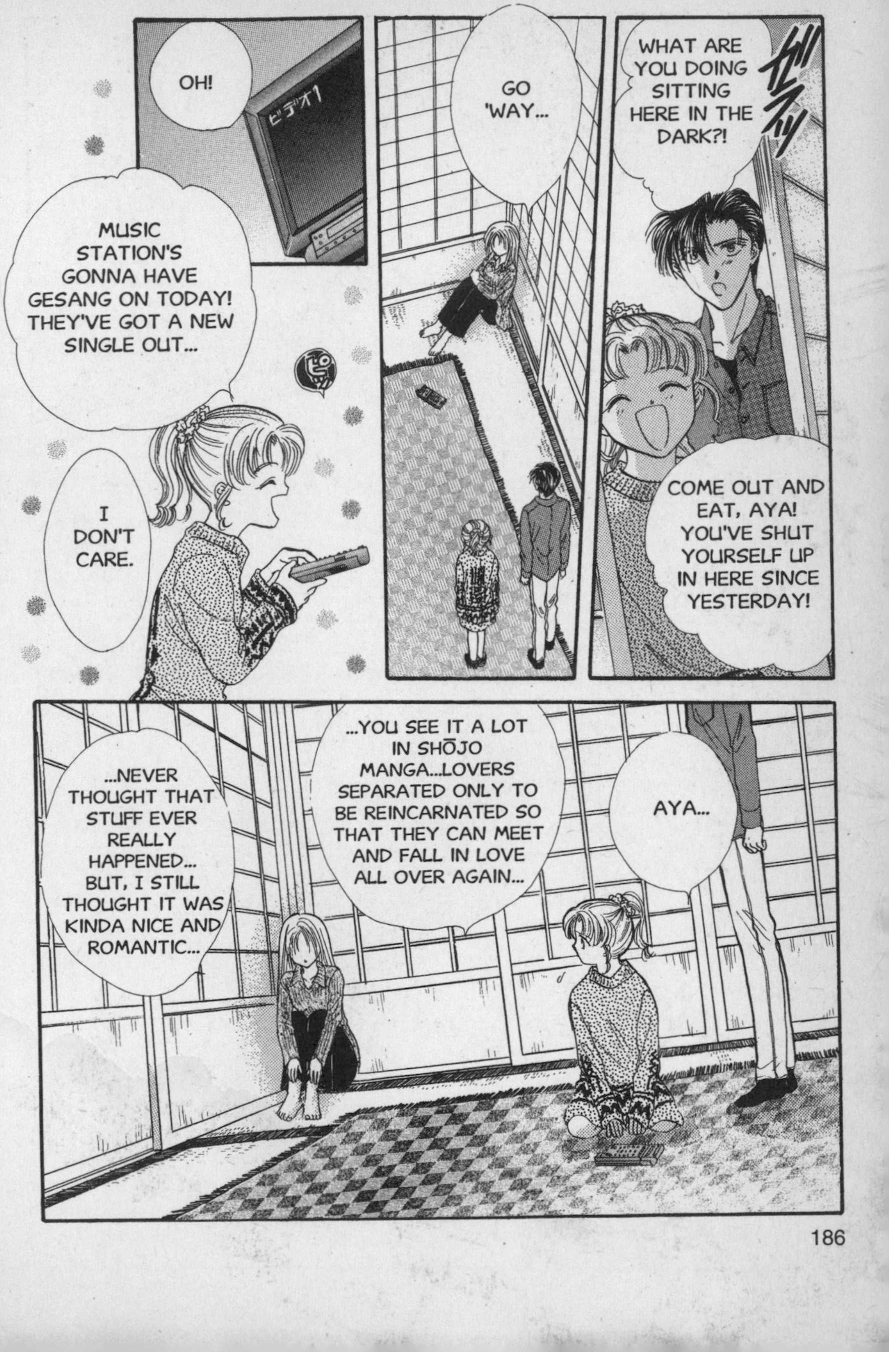
WHAT ARE YOU DOING SITTING HERE IN THE DARK?!
COME OUT AND EAT, AYA! YOU'VE SHUT YOURSELF UP IN HERE SINCE YESTERDAY!
GO 'WAY...
OH!
ビデオ1
MUSIC STATION'S GONNA HAVE GESANG ON TODAY! THEY'VE GOT A NEW SINGLE OUT...
I DON'T CARE.
AYA...
...YOU SEE IT A LOT IN SHŌJO MANGA...LOVERS SEPARATED ONLY TO BE REINCARNATED SO THAT THEY CAN MEET AND FALL IN LOVE ALL OVER AGAIN...
...NEVER THOUGHT THAT STUFF EVER REALLY HAPPENED... BUT, I STILL THOUGHT IT WAS KINDA NICE AND ROMANTIC...

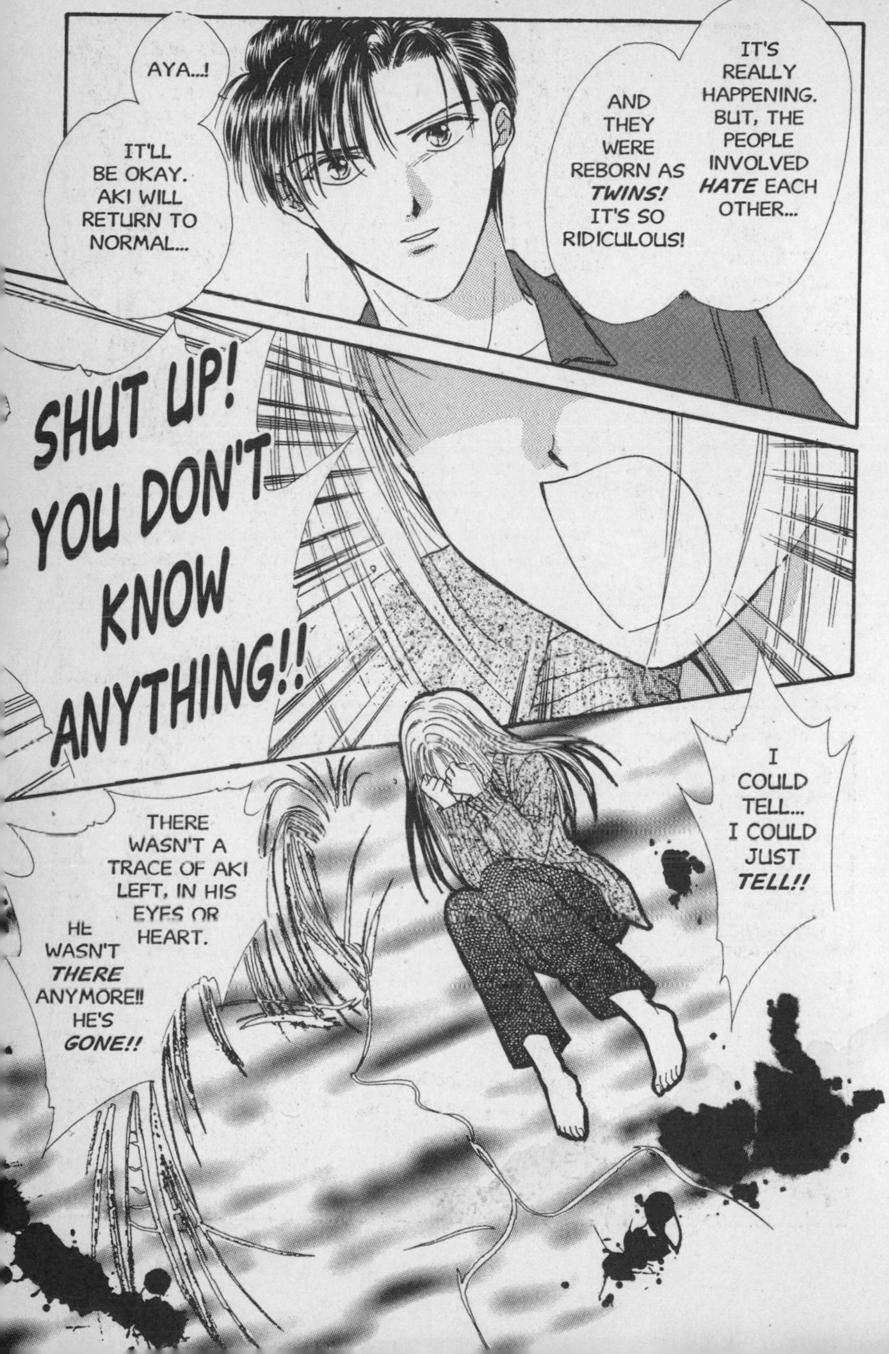
IT'S REALLY HAPPENING. BUT, THE PEOPLE INVOLVED *HATE* EACH OTHER...
AND THEY WERE REBORN AS *TWINS!* IT'S SO RIDICULOUS!
AYA...!
IT'LL BE OKAY. AKI WILL RETURN TO NORMAL...
SHUT UP! YOU DON'T KNOW ANYTHING!!
I COULD TELL... I COULD JUST *TELL!!*
THERE WASN'T A TRACE OF AKI LEFT, IN HIS EYES OR HEART.
HE WASN'T *THERE* ANYMORE!! HE'S *GONE!!*

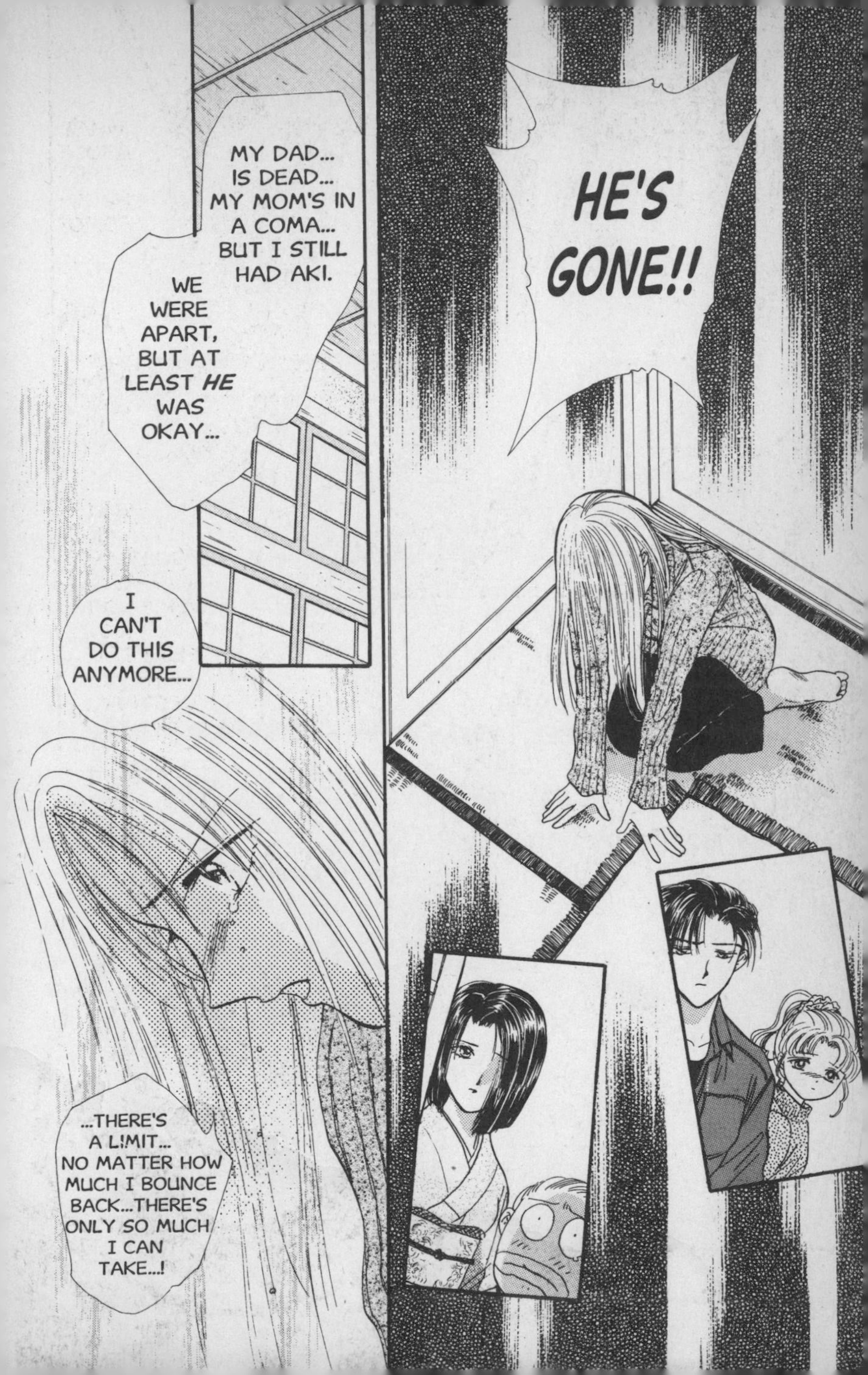
HE'S GONE!!
MY DAD... IS DEAD... MY MOM'S IN A COMA... BUT I STILL HAD AKI.
WE WERE APART, BUT AT LEAST *HE* WAS OKAY...
I CAN'T DO THIS ANYMORE...
...THERE'S A LIMIT... NO MATTER HOW MUCH I BOUNCE BACK...THERE'S ONLY SO MUCH I CAN TAKE...!

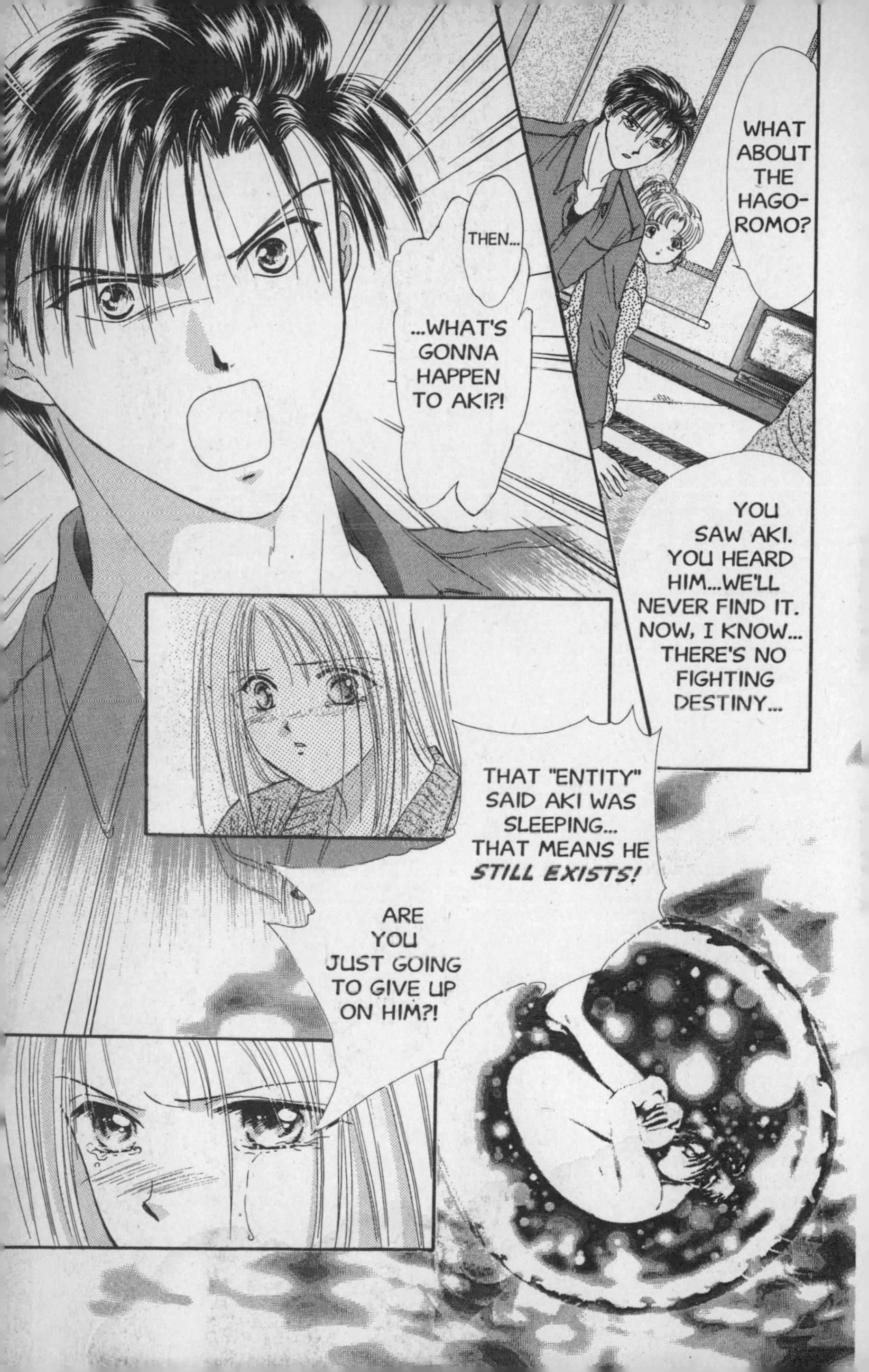
WHAT ABOUT THE HAGO-ROMO?
YOU SAW AKI. YOU HEARD HIM...WE'LL NEVER FIND IT. NOW, I KNOW... THERE'S NO FIGHTING DESTINY...
THEN...
...WHAT'S GONNA HAPPEN TO AKI?!
THAT "ENTITY" SAID AKI WAS SLEEPING... THAT MEANS HE STILL EXISTS!
ARE YOU JUST GOING TO GIVE UP ON HIM?!

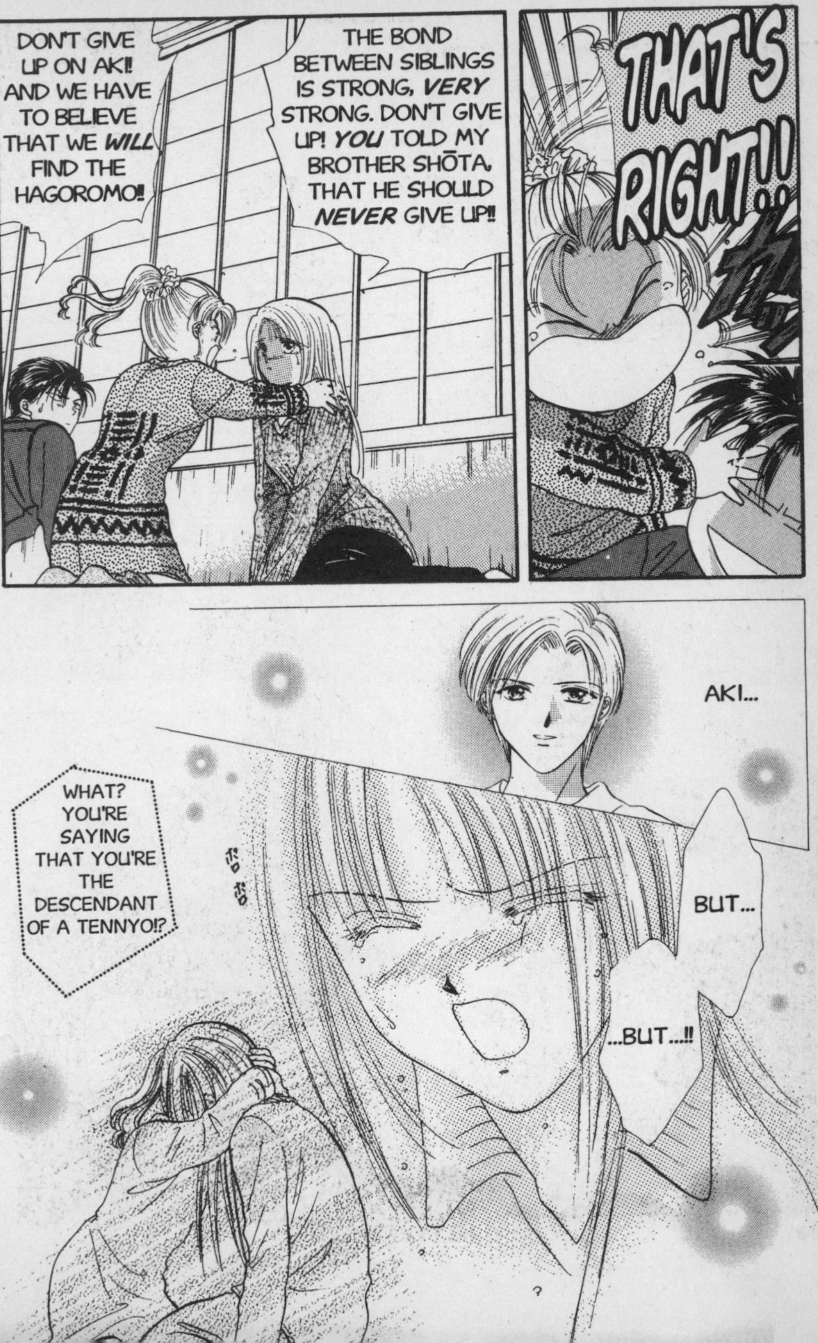
THAT'S RIGHT!!
THE BOND BETWEEN SIBLINGS IS STRONG, VERY STRONG. DON'T GIVE UP! YOU TOLD MY BROTHER SHŌTA, THAT HE SHOULD NEVER GIVE UP!!
DON'T GIVE UP ON AKI!! AND WE HAVE TO BELIEVE THAT WE WILL FIND THE HAGOROMO!!
AKI...
BUT...
...BUT...!!
WHAT? YOU'RE SAYING THAT YOU'RE THE DESCENDANT OF A TENNYO!?

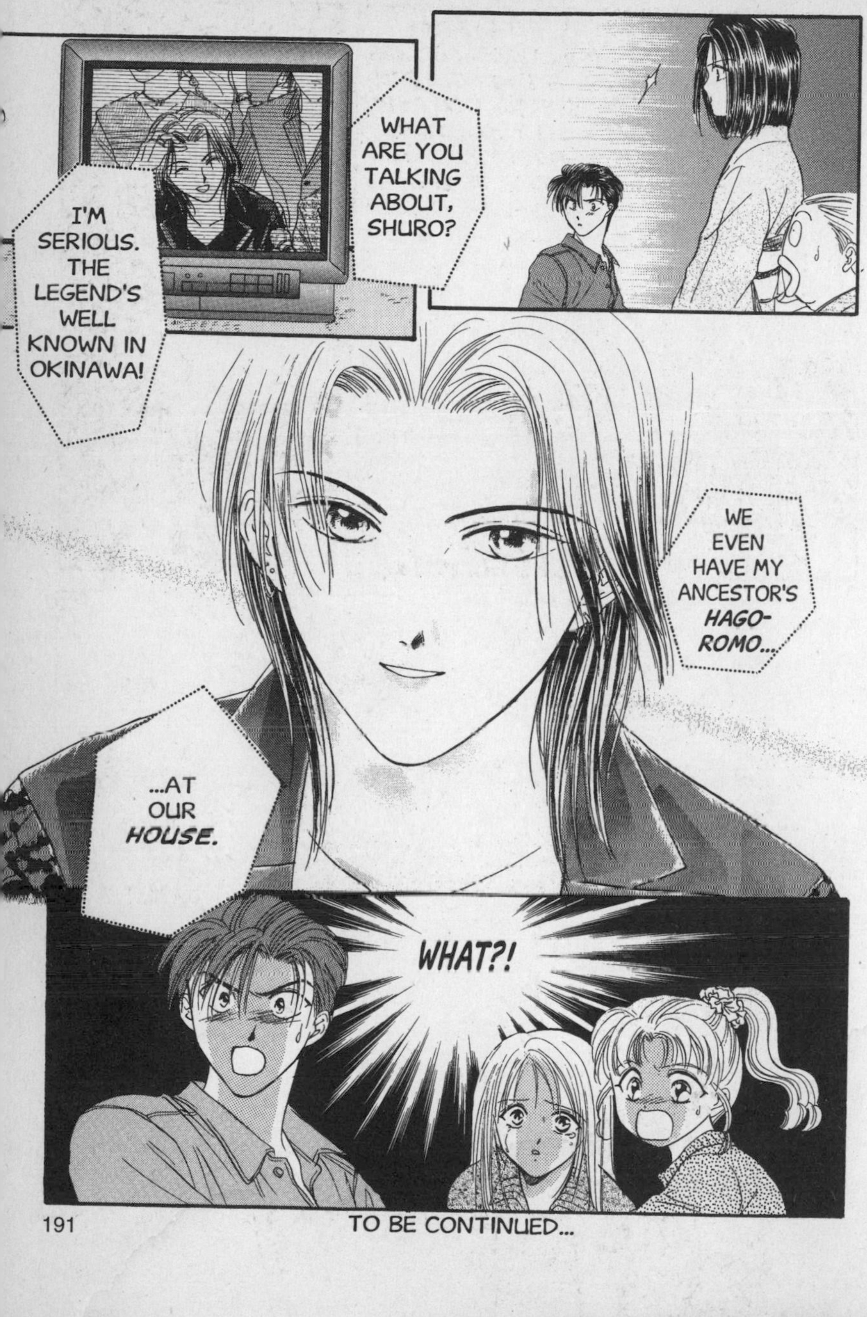
WHAT ARE YOU TALKING ABOUT, SHURO?
I'M SERIOUS. THE LEGEND'S WELL KNOWN IN OKINAWA!
WE EVEN HAVE MY ANCESTOR'S *HAGO-ROMO*...
...AT OUR *HOUSE.*
WHAT?!

TO BE CONTINUED...

IF YOU LIKE *CERES*
HERE ARE SOME OTHER MANGA
YOU MIGHT BE INTERESTED IN:

©1986 Saki Hiwatari

PLEASE SAVE MY EARTH

Reincarnation, adventure, and romance in a science fiction and fantasy *shōjo* setting—If you enjoyed these plot elements in *CERES*, then you won't want to miss Saki Hiwatari's classic about Alice, a girl who dreams of the moon.... Could she have actually lived a "former" life up there?

©1997 Kazuo Umezu/Shogakukan

OROCHI BLOOD

If you enjoy the dark and creepy elements in *CERES* and you're looking for something even creepier, then give manga master of horror Kazuo Umezu's *OROCHI BLOOD* a try. But be forewarned, it's not for the faint of heart and it's strictly for mature readers!

©1984 Rumiko Takahashi/Shogakukan

MAISON IKKOKU

A classic in the romantic love comedy genre, Rumiko Takahashi's *MAISON IKKOKU* is as heartwarming as it is hilariously wacky. Follow the exploits of chronically wishy-washy Yusaku Godai as he tries to win over his beautiful apartment manager, Kyoko Otanashi. All the while, the bizarre and nosey cast of characters that are the other residents of the building are there to chastise Godai as well as cheer him on.

Glossary of Sound Effects, Signs, and other Miscellaneous Notes

Each entry includes: the location, indicated by page number and panel number (so 3.1 means page 3, panel number 1); the phonetic romanization of the original Japanese; and our English "translation"—we offer as close an English equivalent as we can.

8.3——FX: kari kari kari (scribble)

8.5——FX: kari kari (scribble)

8.6——FX: piku (!)

9.1——FX: kin (headache)

9.5——FX: gatan (thunk)

10.4——FX: bikun (!)

13.4——FX: pachi pachi (clap clap)

16.2——FX: buho (pbbt)

16.3——FX: boko (bonk)

16.4——FX: kyaa (eek)

19.4——FX: kin (headache)

20.3——FX: dadada (tumptumptump)

22.2——FX: dokin dokin dokin (ba-bump ba-bump)

26.3——FX: pinpon (ding dong)

26.5——FX: gakon (klang)

28.3——FX: ka (step)

29.4——FX: kotsu (step)

29.5——FX: kotsu kotsu

30.3——FX: ka (flash)

30.5——FX: dou (boom)

31.1——FX: pishi (crack)

32.2——FX: jara (clatter)

37.1——FX: papaa paa (car horns)

38.3——FX: don (crash)

38.4——FX: bashu (zap)

38.5——FX: don (boom)

39.6——FX: kacha kacha (clacketa clacketa)

40.4——FX: ba (leap)

41.1——FX: zaza (shkshhh)

41.2——FX: don (boom)

41.3——FX: wii (whirr)

41.4——FX: ba (slice)

41.5——FX: gashaan (klang)

42.5—FX: pi (zap)

43.4—FX: don (boom)

45.1—FX: kin (fwoosh)

45.5—FX: za (slash)

46.1—FX: chi chi chi (tic toc tic toc)

47.2—FX: doka (wham)

47.4—FX: gacha (chk)

48.3—FX: ha (!)

48.4—FX: ga (whock)

49.1—FX: kashin (klang)

49.4—FX: jaki (chk)

49.6—FX: fu (fft)

49.6—FX: fu (fft)

51.4—FX: ban (blam)

51.5—FX: dokun (ba-bump)

53.2—FX: dosu (bonk)

53.4—FX: dashu (dash)

54.1—FX: paa papaa (beep beeeep)

55.2—FX: ban (pop)

55.4—FX: don (shove)

55.6—FX: ba... (b...)

56.1—FX: ...n (...am)

56.2—FX: dan (thud)

—FX: gashan (klang)

56.5—FX: ka (step)

57.2—FX: kashin (klink)

58.2—FX: gugu (stabbing further)

59.3—FX: gachan (clink)

60.4—FX: ta (step)

—FX: gaa (whirr)

60.5—FX: zuki (throb)

62.1—FX: gashan (klang)

63.4—FX: gu (tug)

65.1—FX: don (tump)

68.2—FX: zuru (slump)

72.3—FX: zuru (drag)

72.5—FX: zuru (drag)

73.2—FX: zuru (feeling unsteady)

73.3—FX: zuru (feeling unsteady)

74.3—FX: za (shk)

75.3—FX: ba (close-up)

75.4—FX: zuru (slump)

107.2—FX: ta (dash)

109.4—FX: pin (plink)

110.4—FX: karari (rattle)

111.3—FX: karari (rattle)

111.4—FX: pipipi (chirp)

112.1—FX: pipi (chirp)

114.6—FX: pasa (fwap)

116.2—FX: pappaa (beeep- cars)

119.2—FX: gakon (klang)

119.3—FX: gii (creak)

119.4—FX: batan (slam)

124.1—FX: gakun (slump)

124.3—FX: buru buru (tremble)

124.5—FX: suu (fft)

125.1—FX: ba (spurt)

126.2—FX: daran (limp)

127.1—FX: pikun (twitch)

128.2—FX: kasa (rustle)

129.2—FX: hyoi (pop)

134.1—FX: ga (glomp)

135.2—FX: meki meki (crack)

79.3—FX: karari (rattle)

80.2—FX: pashin (slam)

80.4—FX: pashin (door closing)

—FX: pata pata (running in slippers)

80.6—FX: niko (heh)

81.1—FX: fuu fuu (puff puff)

85.1—FX: piku (!)

85.3—FX: bashi (whap)

85.5—FX: biku (!)

86.2—FX: ban (slam)

86.3—FX: za (whoosh)

86.4—FX: zaa (fsshh- shower)

90.5—FX: fluster

92.2—FX: su (lift)

92.3—FX: zu (slurp)

96.4—FX: hyoi (pop)

103.2—FX: ban (slam)

105.1—FX: bishi (snap)

106.1—FX: za (splash)

106.2—FX: saa (shower)

106.5—FX: karari (rattle)

170.1 —FX: ba (power)

170.4 —FX: para (slip)

170.5 —FX: pasa (fwap)

171.1 —FX: doyo (whoa!)

173.2 —FX: za (water)

174.1 —FX: don (boom)

175.4 —FX: piku (!)

176.3 —FX: pan (pop)

177.3 —FX: ba (whoosh)

———FX: su (step)

178.1 —FX: kura (stagger)

179.2 —FX: su (stepping in front)

180.4 —FX: buroroo (vroom)

185.3 —FX: zaa (snow)

186.1 —FX: gara (rattle)

186.4 —FX: pi (blip)

190.1 —FX: ga (shove)

190.4 —FX: poro poro (tears falling)

135.5 —FX: gu (squ)

137.2 —FX: biku (!)

137.3 —FX: pata pata pata (running in slippers)

143.5 —FX: ka (step)

144.3 —FX: cha (chk)

145.4 —FX: wai wai (chatter)

148.4 —FX: buroro (vroom)

149.3 —FX: ga (rip)

149.5 —FX: saa (fountain)

151.2 —FX: ba (fwah)

152.1 —FX: huff huff

154.5 —FX: doki (ba-bump)

155.2 —FX: suru (slip)

156.2 —FX: kyu (squeeze)

158.1 —FX: kii (screech)

162.5 —FX: biku (!)

164.1-3—FX: dokun (heartbeat)

165.1 —FX: dokun dokun dokun (heart beats)

167.2 —FX: do (shove)

169.1 —FX: zawa zawa (murmur)

Hell Hath No Fury Like a Heavenly Maiden

When an angel named Ceres is reincarnated in 16-year-old Aya Mikage, Aya becomes a liability to her family's survival. Not only does Ceres want revenge against the Mikage family for past wrongs, but her power is also about to manifest itself. Can Aya control Ceres' hold on her, or will her family mark her for death?

From Yû Watase, creator of ALICE 19TH, FUSHIGI YÛGI, and IMADOKI!— complete your collection today!

CERES
Celestial Legend

Complete anime series on two DVD box sets— 12 episodes per volume

only $49.98 each!

shôjo

COMPLETE OUR SURVEY AND LET US KNOW WHAT YOU THINK!

☐ Please do NOT send me information about VIZ products, news and events, special offers, or other information.

☐ Please do NOT send me information from VIZ's trusted business partners.

Name: _____

Address: _____

City: _____ **State:** _____ **Zip:** _____

E-mail: _____

☐ Male ☐ Female **Date of Birth** (mm/dd/yyyy): ___ / ___ / _____ (Under 13? Parental consent required)

What race/ethnicity do you consider yourself? (please check one)

☐ Asian/Pacific Islander ☐ Black/African American ☐ Hispanic/Latino

☐ Native American/Alaskan Native ☐ White/Caucasian ☐ Other: _____

What VIZ product did you purc_____ **tle purchased)**

☐ DVD/VHS _____

☐ Graphic Novel_____

☐ Magazines ____

☐ Merchandise ____

Reason for purch

☐ Special offer

☐ Recommendatio

Where did you make your

☐ Comic store ☐ Mass/Grocery Store

☐ Newsstand ☐ Video/Video Game Store ☐ Other: _____

☐ Online (site: _____)

What other VIZ properties have you purchased/own? _____

_____

How many anime and/or manga titles have you purchased in the last year? How many were VIZ titles? **(please check one from each column)**

ANIME	MANGA	VIZ
☐ None	☐ None	☐ None
☐ 1-4	☐ 1-4	☐ 1-4
☐ 5-10	☐ 5-10	☐ 5-10
☐ 11+	☐ 11+	☐ 11+

I find the pricing of VIZ products to be: **(please check one)**

☐ Cheap ☐ Reasonable ☐ Expensive

What genre of manga and anime would you like to see from VIZ? **(please check two)**

☐ Adventure ☐ Comic Strip ☐ Science Fiction ☐ Fighting

☐ Horror ☐ Romance ☐ Fantasy ☐ Sports

What do you think of VIZ's new look?

☐ Love It ☐ It's OK ☐ Hate It ☐ Didn't Notice ☐ No Opinion

Which do you prefer? **(please check one)**

☐ Reading right-to-left

☐ Reading left-to-right

Which do you prefer? **(please check one)**

☐ Sound effects in English

☐ Sound effects in Japanese with English captions

☐ Sound effects in Japanese only with a glossary at the back

THANK YOU! Please send the completed form to:

NJW Research
42 Catharine St.
Poughkeepsie, NY 12601

All information provided will be used for internal purposes only. We promise not to sell or otherwise divulge your information.